Praise for

THE ISLAND OF
EXTRAORDINARY CAPTIVES

WINNER OF THE WINGATE PRIZE

"In Simon Parkin's riveting account, a shameful chapter in British history is also a testament to creativity and hope. . . . A truly shocking story of what officials are wont to term 'national misjudgment,' is electrifyingly told by the journalist and historian Simon Parkin, whose breadth and depth of original research has produced an account of cinematic vividness. . . . Parkin skillfully draws the reader into the serendipitously rich environment in which Fleischmann, along with a constellation of some of the most brilliant artistic, philosophical, and scientific minds of the day, suddenly found themselves."

—*The New York Times Book Review*

"Extraordinary yet previously untold true story . . . meticulously researched . . . it's also taut, compelling, and impossible to put down."

—*Daily Express*

"Parkin [has an] inimitable capacity to find the human pulse in the underbelly of Britain's war. . . . *The Island of Extraordinary Captives* is multi-layered . . . a reminder that conflict has always been a convenient mask behind which thuggery and xenophobia thrive. Yet, despite the stark injustice it describes, it is a curiously exhilarating read: an example of how individuals can find joy and meaning in the absurd and mundane."

—*The Spectator*

of thousands of men and women because of their German or Austrian ancestry. . . . A vivid recounting of a shameful event that still resonates."

—*Kirkus Reviews*

"Meticulously researched."

—*Literary Review*

"The story of how art and intellect triumphed in Britain's bleak internment camps for 'enemy aliens' on the Isle of Man . . . Excellent . . . Parkin has told his story with energy and flair. . . . A powerful tribute to the wartime internees, and a timely reminder of how much Britain gained from their presence."

—*The Guardian*

"Parkin's rich and vivid account makes clear just how much the displaced artists did suffer, and the remarkable resilience and creativity with which they respond."

—*The Observer*

"A brisk, vivid narrative."

—*Times Literary Supplement*

"Clear-eyed and compelling . . . Parkin recreates the texture of camp life with marvelous specificity. . . . Indeed, Parkin's account glitters with strange incidents—and even stranger personalities. . . . Parkin doesn't pull his punches when examining the ghastly saga of internment. As his afterword notes, the same corrosive paranoia and xenophobia flickers through today's debates."

—*The Critic*

"Parkin deserve[s] praise for shining such revealing light on that forgotten history."

—*Irish Times*

ALSO BY SIMON PARKIN

Death by Video Game: Danger, Pleasure, and Obsession on the Virtual Frontline

A Game of Birds and Wolves: The Ingenious Young Women Whose Secret Board Game Helped Win World War II

THE ISLAND OF EXTRAORDINARY CAPTIVES

A PAINTER, A POET, AN HEIRESS, AND A SPY
IN A WORLD WAR II BRITISH INTERNMENT CAMP

SIMON PARKIN

SCRIBNER
New York   London   Toronto   Sydney   New Delhi

For Klaus Hinrichsen:
Historian of Art,
who made art history

Scribner

An Imprint of Simon & Schuster, Inc.

1230 Avenue of the Americas

New York, NY 10020

First Scribner trade paperback edition October 2023

SCRIBNER and design are registered trademarks of The Gale Group, Inc., used under license by Simon & Schuster, Inc., the publisher of this work.

For information about special discounts for bulk purchases, please contact Simon & Schuster Special Sales at 1-866-506-1949 or business@simonandschuster.com.

The Simon & Schuster Speakers Bureau can bring authors to your live event. For more information or to book an event, contact the Simon & Schuster Speakers Bureau at 1-866-248-3049 or visit our website at www.simonspeakers.com.

Interior design by Wendy Blum

Manufactured in the United States of America

1 3 5 7 9 10 8 6 4 2

Library of Congress Control Number: 2021056257

ISBN 978-1-9821-7852-9
ISBN 978-1-9821-7853-6 (pbk)
ISBN 978-1-9821-7854-3 (ebook)

CONTENTS

PART THREE

In a pool

so small I could step over it,

I saw reflected all of the sky.

And I said to myself:

How best can I measure this bit of water?

By the earth that holds it?

Or by the heavens inside?

Kurt Schwitters, "Short Hills,"

Hutchinson camp, 1940

Map of Hutchinson Camp, 1940-45

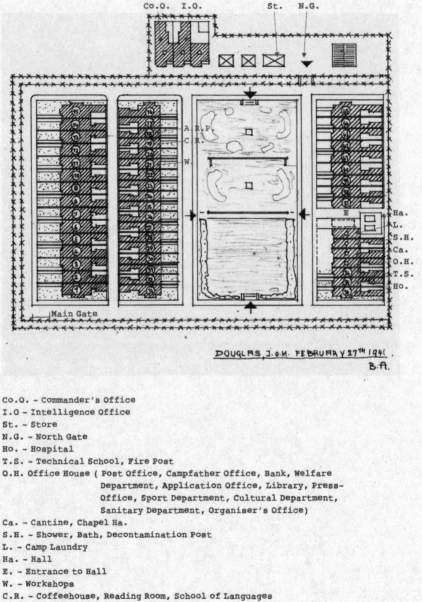

DOUGLAS J.O.M. FEBRUARY 27TH 1941.
B.A.

Co.O. - Commander's Office
I.O - Intelligence Office
St. - Store
N.G. - North Gate
Ho. - Hospital
T.S. - Technical School, Fire Post
O.H. Office House (Post Office, Campfather Office, Bank, Welfare
                   Department, Application Office, Library, Press-
                   Office, Sport Department, Cultural Department,
                   Sanitary Department, Organiser's Office)
Ca. - Cantine, Chapel Ha.
S.H. - Shower, Bath, Decontamination Post
L. - Camp Laundry
Ha. - Hall
E. - Entrance to Hall
W. - Workshops
C.R. - Coffeehouse, Reading Room, School of Languages
A.R.P. - A.R.P., First Aid

AUTHOR'S NOTE

The Island of Extraordinary Captives is a work of historical narrative non-fiction. The events described in this book are not fabricated or embellished, but drawn from diaries, letters, memoirs, oral histories, newspaper reports, and other primary source material according to the best recollections of the various players and protagonists. Quotations and dialogue recalled by any speaker or witness years after the event in question should be taken as impressionistic rather than verbatim. Where there are discrepancies in dialogue between sources, the version closest to the date of the event described has been used. A full list of references and sources can be found at the end of the text.

I

BARBED-WIRE MATINEE

THE ISLAND
SEPTEMBER 7, 1940

AS THE DAY BEGAN TO gather itself in, Peter Fleischmann watched the musician clamber onto the rostrum in the middle of the lawned square and settle himself at the grand piano. Before Peter fled Berlin, the eighteen-year-old orphan had buried pieces of silverware on the outskirts of the city; his collection of rare stamps had been taken from him by a Nazi inspector on the train that brisked him out of Germany. His only valuable was a silver dragonfly brooch, once owned by the mother he never knew. Peter was destitute. He could not normally have afforded a ticket to a performance by a renowned pianist, a favorite of kings and presidents.

Clear warm air, immense blue skies: the day had been one of the fairest of the century, a shimmering Saturday that evoked the languishing summers of childhood. So fine, in fact, that this was the day Germany chose to send their planes to bomb London for the first time, a blitz that would continue for the next eight months. Still, here on the misted Isle of Man, hundreds of miles from England's capital city, the audience would have turned out whatever the weather. There was little else to do here in the middle of the Irish Sea.

Behind the pianist Peter saw a backdrop of neat Edwardian boardinghouses. The buildings appeared unremarkable: hotels for middle-class holidaymakers who wanted the frisson of overseas tourism without the effort and expense. Closer inspection revealed unlikely details. Each window was covered in dark film. The polymer material, used as a makeshift solution after a German U-boat had sunk the ship carrying blackout supplies to the island, peeled away when sliced with a razor blade. A fashion for silhouette carvings had spread through the camp: zoo animals, unicorns, characters from Greek myth adorned the ground-floor windows. At night, and viewed from street side, the pictures glowed with the light of the air-raid-safe, brothel-red light-bulbs from inside, a novel backdrop for the celebrated pianist.

In front of the piano, on a crescent of wooden chairs, sat a line of British army officers laughing and smoking next to their wives. Beyond them, beneath the darting midges, sat hundreds of men, mostly refugees, arranged in untidy rows on the grass. From the open windows of the surrounding houses, their bedrooms full of dusk, other men perched and leaned, the glow of their cigarette ends fireflies in the dying light. Peter could turn to see Douglas harbor behind him, where boats pottered and chugged, trailing their wakes on the tinseled sea. A few hundred yards away, somewhere above the frequency of conversation, the waves frothed on the shingle, like a broom sweeping glass from a shattered shop window.

A palisade of barbed wire separated and barred the men from the harbor, a perimeter that marked the boundary of what was officially known as "P" camp, or, to the men, simply, "Hutchinson." Outside the wire fence, a group of locals had gathered. They peered in, hoping to glimpse and understand what was happening, the only obvious clue that tonight's was a captive audience.

EIGHT WEEKS EARLIER, ON SATURDAY, July 13, 1940, Captain Hubert Daniel, a kindly, keen-drinking forty-eight-year-old army officer, had declared the camp open. Hutchinson was the seventh of ten internment camps to open on the Isle of Man, an island positioned sufficiently far from the neighboring coasts to be ideally suited for imprisonment.* The island's boat-owning residents had been instructed to stow the oars and remove the spark plugs from their vessels' engines at night. Even if an escapee were to board a suitable craft, the journey to the mainland was perilous. If you were here, you were here for good.

Hutchinson was currently home to around twelve hundred prisoners, predominantly refugees from Nazi Germany who had been living peacefully in Britain at the time of their arrest. In recent months rumors abounded that a fifth column—a neologism to Britain, now universally understood to refer to traitors living within their country of asylum—had assisted the Nazi occupation of the Netherlands. Newspapers had stoked national paranoia with claims that a similar network of spies lurked in Britain.

Even before the outbreak of war, Scotland Yard, working in conjunction with MI5, the British domestic intelligence service, had been deluged with tip-offs about suspicious refugees and foreigners. The police detained one man when investigators found an entry in his diary that read: "Exchange British Queen for Italian Queen." The detective assumed he had exposed a fascist plot against the crown. In fact, the man was a beekeeper, planning to overthrow only the tiny monarch that ruled his hive.

The police were first alerted to one of Hutchinson camp's internees, the young art historian Dr. Klaus Hinrichsen, and his fiancée, Gretel, when a neighbor reported hearing the young couple's lovemaking. The distrustful neighbor suspected the rhythmic knocking of the bed might contain a coded message. It was difficult, Klaus pointed out, to prove that one did not understand Morse code.

The recent German occupation of France meant an invasion attempt seemed not only plausible but imminent. Days after he became prime minister, Winston Churchill authorized the arrest of thousands of so-called "enemy aliens." In the chaotic roundups that followed,

* The others were: Mooragh, Peveril, Onchan, Central, Palace, Metropole, Granville, and Sefton for male internees, and Rushen for women internees and, later, married couples.

thousands of Jews who had fled Nazi Germany—including some teenagers like Peter who came via the feted *Kindertransport* trains—were imprisoned by the same people in whom they had staked their trust, a nightmarish betrayal. The refugees that comprised the majority of tonight's audience had experienced a collective trauma: to be imprisoned by one's liberator is to endure an injustice of chronology.

Status and class, those twin, usually indefatigable armaments of privilege, had provided no protection. Oxbridge dons, surgeons, dentists, lawyers, and scores of celebrated artists were taken. The police arrested Emil Goldmann, a sixty-seven-year-old professor from the University of Vienna, on the grounds of Eton College, Britain's most elite school. At Cambridge University dozens of staff and students were detained in the Guildhall, including Friedrich Hohenzollern, also known as Prince Frederick of Prussia, a grandson of Queen Victoria. That year's law finals were almost canceled because one of the interned professors had the exam papers locked in his desk and had no time to pass someone the key.

The police came for Peter in the early hours of the morning, without prior warning, a manner of detention that had reminded him of the Gestapo's moonlit roundups and the muggy world of fear and distrust from which he had just fled.

In the weeks that followed its opening, Hutchinson had bristled with a creative energy, its inhabitants organizing events, much like this evening's, that drew upon the unlikely inmates' considerable talents. Still, no man could quite escape the demoralizing fact that the terms "internee" and "internment camp"—even "concentration camp," as Hutchinson and the other island camps were sometimes referred to at the time*—were euphemistic: Peter and every other man there were, in every way that mattered, captives, arrested without charge or trial, confined without sentence to a prison camp, and forbidden to leave.

---

* The terms "internment camp" and "concentration camp" are, strictly, interchangeable. Modern readers associate the latter with atrocity, but neither the *Oxford English Dictionary* nor the Holocaust Museum draw any distinction in their respective definitions.

Regardless of their age or station, geopolitical history, blunt and undiscerning, had visited each man's life.

Still, Peter was thrilled to be among this crowd. As the men had been imprisoned because of where they were from and not for who they were or what they had done, Hutchinson contained a dazzling cross section of society. It was happenstance, however, that brought so many brilliant achievers to this camp. Together they made up one of history's unlikeliest and most extraordinary prison populations. While there were no tuxedos or ball gowns, no champagne flutes or chandeliers for tonight's show, Peter sat among a constellation of brilliant individuals, luminaries from the worlds of art, fashion, media, and academia; an exceptional audience, even discounting the circumstances.

From an early age Peter had aspired to be numbered among the great artists. Events both international and domestic had at first conspired against his ambition, his dream to become an artist exploded by exile. Then the currents of history had carried him into the orbit of his heroes; he shared the camp with a raft of eminent artists, including Kurt Schwitters, the fifty-three-year-old pioneering Dadaist in front of whose "degenerate" work the failed painter Adolf Hitler had sarcastically posed. The artists, in turn, took this skinny, bespectacled outsider into their care.

Since he had arrived at Hutchinson, tonight's performer Marjan Rawicz had been hounded by depression. Internment had interrupted his packed summer schedule. On May 3, 1940, he and his musical partner, Walter Landauer, played a benefit concert at the London Palladium to raise money for variety artists. Ironically, considering the duo was soon to be arrested on suspicion of being Nazi spies, their performance was broadcast on a radio channel dedicated to the British Armed Forces. Three weeks later, on May 23, at half past three in the afternoon, the pair gave a live demonstration of a Welmar grand piano on the second floor of the consummate British luxury department store Harrods. The police arrested the musicians a few weeks later, in Blackpool, where they had just begun a run of sellout performances.

While his world collapsed, habit held. Rawicz was a performer, and performers must perform. His only stipulation had been that tonight's show would be a solo concert, that the program would be entirely his choice, and that he could use a grand piano—actually, a Steinway. Captain Daniel had pointed out to the musician that the inventory of houses listed eleven pianos already inside the camp.

"Can't you use one of them?" the commandant asked, adding that it might prove difficult to secure official sign-off for a hired grand, considering, well, everything.

Reluctantly, Rawicz agreed. A small crowd trailed the musician as he toured the houses, testing each instrument for its suitability. Rawicz, not one to disregard an audience, had amused his trail of followers with sarcastic quips and condemnations.

"Even a deaf man would feel pain from this one," Rawicz joked as he tested one neglected example. When one hanger-on expressed surprise at the shortness of his fingers, Rawicz shot back: "My friend, I am a pianist, not a gynecologist."

Under the impact of Rawicz's forceful playing, one piano collapsed. Onlookers soon dismantled the instrument and removed its keys, planks, and tangles of wire. A wood-carver, Ernst Müller-Blensdorf, took the mahogany sides. The animal trapper Johann "Brick" Neunzer, a lion tamer at Burnt Stub Zoo—later known as Chessington Zoo—pocketed the ivories, hoping to carve them into dentures, while the engineers among the internees collected the wire to make electric fires.

Rawicz had made his point. Captain Daniel relented. The camp's maintenance department wheeled a hired Steinway onto a sturdy rostrum built for the occasion. A date was set, and the commandant, eager to demonstrate the superiority of his camp, issued invitations to his rival officers on the island.

THERE WAS NO SCORE TO flutter away on the wind when the audience's applause stilled to intermittent coughs and rustles as Rawicz began to play. The pianist had prepared a wide-ranging program from waltzes to rhapsodies, from the "Radetzky March" to Bach, from show tunes like "Smoke Gets in Your Eyes" to a composition of his own, "Spinning Wheel," each one played from memory. The crowd greeted each piece with enthusiastic applause; transported to the prewar concert halls of Berlin, Vienna, and Prague—a distraction from the precariousness of the situation, the risk of deportation or of imminent Nazi invasion. The evening's performance was, as one audience member put it, "unforgettable."

For the finale, Rawicz had selected two pieces designed to draw a veil of ironic dissonance across the scene. Ignoring classics from the European composers, he opted instead for the sixteenth-century folk tune "Greensleeves"—a quintessentially English melody—before he segued into a rendition of the British national anthem. Peter and the other internees stood to their feet and sang.

> May he defend our laws,
> And ever give us cause,
> To sing with heart and voice,
> God save the king.

The square resounded with the chorus, sung in various degrees of accented English, a tribute to the country that had offered each man refuge only to turn against him. Rawicz's pointed choices highlighted the tortuous absurdity of the situation. Here were hundreds of refugees from Nazi oppression, pledging loyalty to the country and allegiance to the king, under whose authority they had been imprisoned, without charge or trial, on suspicion of being Nazi spies. Still, swept up in the moment, few checked to see if any among them had chosen to remain silent.

PART ONE

Quocunque Jeceris Stabit

"Whithersoever you throw him, he will stand."

The Isle of Man motto

II

FIVE SHOTS

PARIS
TWO YEARS EARLIER

SHORTLY AFTER THE SUN ROSE, the shadows shrunk, and the day began to unspool, Madame Carpe cranked open the iron shutters of her Parisian shop.

"I want to buy a gun," she heard a voice call out behind her.

The woman turned to see a rakish boy with doleful eyes wearing a wide-lapelled suit, tie, and baggy overcoat. She called to her husband, Léopold, who appeared in the doorway. It was 8:35 on the morning of November 7, 1938. À la Fine Lame (At the Cutting Edge) was not yet open, but, eager to commence the day's business, the shopkeeper beckoned his first customer of the day inside.

"Why do you need a gun?" he asked the boy, who was eyeing the heavy-laden displays lining the walls. The boy opened his wallet to display a sheaf of bills and explained that, as he was often called upon by his father to deliver large sums of money, he needed something for protection.

The explanation was both sufficient and superfluous. According to French law, a gun shop owner could only refuse a sale to a customer if he or she judged the person to be of unsound mind. The boy was fractious and exhausted. He had barely slept the previous night, having been three times shaken awake by nightmares, his heart pounding so fast that he had to place a hand on his chest to calm himself. But if his customer showed any signs of exhaustion, Carpe was not moved to ask further questions. The boy seemed intense, but not disturbed.

The shopkeeper clunked a selection of weapons onto the counter. His customer looked blankly from one to the next. Monsieur Carpe recognized the hesitancy of a novice, but, for now, resisted the urge to instruct. Finally, the boy asked if Carpe had a .45 pistol in stock, the caliber of pistol he knew from American films.

Alas, the shopkeeper explained, this would be a poor choice for the task: too heavy, too bulky. Better to choose a 6.35-millimeter revolver, a gun small enough to be carried as a concealed weapon, light enough to be quickly drawn, yet suitably menacing to frighten a thief.

Carpe demonstrated how to load, fire, and unload the weapon. The boy watched the smooth, well-practiced movements of the salesman's hands. Finally, the shopkeeper placed a box of twenty-five cartridges on the counter and explained that, before he could sell the weapon, he needed to see some proof of identity. The young man slid his passport across the counter. Carpe saw a foreign name on the document: Herschel Grynszpan.

It was while wandering the streets the previous night that Herschel first noticed À la Fine Lame. The seventeen-year-old was aimless and stewing in the residual agitation that follows a major argument. Earlier, he had stormed from the home where he lived with his uncle and aunt. Ostensibly the row was about money, but it had been heightened by resentments and frustrations both unspoken and unnamed, and by circumstances outside the control of any participant.

Herschel was an undocumented immigrant. Two years earlier he had come to France, leaving his immediate family in his hometown of Hanover, and had moved in with his relatives. Herschel's father successfully smuggled three thousand francs out of Germany to fund his son's care. Now the boy wanted this money to be returned to his family, who he believed were in mortal danger.

His parents owned a small tailor's shop in Hanover. Since Adolf

Hitler came to power five years earlier, they had endured tremendous economic hardship. The hope that anti-Semitism was limited to a minority of crackpot, die-hard party supporters was dispelled when a local police officer handed them extradition papers: they, along with some twelve thousand other Polish Jews living in Germany, were to be forcibly expelled from the country they called home. On the bleak journey to the station, where they were to embark on the train that would carry them to the Polish border, the streets were black with people shouting: *"Juden raus!"*—Jews out!

The deportation was chaotic and cruel. Having disembarked at Zbąszyń on the Polish border, Herschel's family was hounded across the German frontier, then turned back by the Polish guards. The exiled men and women trudged back to German territory, just to be repelled there, too. It was only when the Nazis set dogs on the crowd that the Polish border guards relented, allowing the haggard group into no-man's-land, where they spent the night sleeping in barns and pig sties. Earlier that week Herschel received a postcard from his older sister, Esther, who explained the situation, ending with a declaration of the family's newfound destitution: "We don't have a pfennig."

Uncle Abraham—who, like his brother, worked as a tailor—knew that events were unfolding quickly. It would be irresponsible to send money into a scene of chaos, Abraham reasoned to his nephew. Wiser to await further developments. Herschel, who was prone to surges of fury that crested with threats of suicide, took his uncle's procrastination as evidence that nobody else cared about his parents' predicament. The accusation wounded Abraham.

"I've already done just about everything I can for you," he told his nephew. "If you're not satisfied, you are free to go."

Herschel tugged his coat free from his aunt's grip, who sobbed as she tried to hold him back from the door.

"I am leaving," said Herschel. "Goodbye."

Abraham pressed two hundred francs into the boy's hand before he left.

Herschel spent the remainder of the day in a sulk, resisting efforts

by his friend Naftali Kauffman—or Nathan, as he was better known—
to cheer him. Nathan had witnessed the fight and, as he followed his
friend out the front door, assured Herschel's aunt and uncle that he
would return their nephew to them unharmed.

After whiling away the rest of the afternoon with friends, in the
early evening the two young men discussed the day's events by the
light leaking from the windows of city hall. Nathan gently urged his
friend to return to the apartment. Herschel's rage reignited.

"I'd rather die like a dog than go back on my decision," he said.

Herschel explained his plan for the night: to eat dinner at his favorite café, then check into a cheap hotel. The pair parted. Herschel
walked down the rue du Faubourg Saint-Denis and there spied the gun
shop window.

THE WEAPON AND BULLETS CAME to 245 francs. Herschel paid with
the two hundred-franc notes from his uncle and made up the difference with change from his own pocket. Without removing the price
tag, which hung from a piece of red string tied to the trigger guard, the
shopkeeper wrapped the weapon and the cartridges in brown paper
and tied up the package.

Herschel was required by law to register his purchase with the authorities. As he left the shop, he made as if going to the nearest police
station. The boy continued walking until he was sure that he was out
of sight. Then he turned off the main road and circled back toward the
Tout Va Bien café where, the previous evening, he had told his friend
that he planned to eat.

At 8:55, Herschel faced the mirror in the café's bathroom. He un-
tied the package and slid the gun from its bag, feeling in his hand the
cold weight of the morning's choices, and those yet to come. He loaded
five rounds into the chamber and placed the weapon in the left interior
pocket of his suit jacket. Ten minutes later, he descended the steps into
the Strasbourg–Saint-Denis Métro station.

If during the journey Herschel harbored any residual doubt or hesitation about his plan—a plan that would, in history's tumbling, circuitous way, change the lives of millions—his mind was fixed by the time he emerged into the Paris sunlight. Just after half past nine, Herschel arrived at his destination, close to the banks of the Seine River: the German embassy, at 78 rue de Lille.

Anxious and unprepared, Herschel approached one of the on-duty police officers outside the building and asked which doorway he should use.

"What is the purpose of your visit?" asked the gendarme, François Autret.

Concentrating to keep his voice from betraying his nerves, Herschel informed the officer that he needed a German visa.

You need the consulate, not the embassy, Autret explained. The policeman waved Herschel toward the public doorway to the embassy, before turning his back on the teenager and the first bothersome inquiry of the day.

Two hours earlier, in Herschel's rented room at the Hôtel de Suez, he had written a postcard in reply to his sister after a night spent wrestling with nightmarish visions of the mistreatment of his parents.

"God must forgive me," read his message, written in a mixture of Hebrew and German. "My heart bleeds when I think of our tragedy and that of the 12,000 Jews. I have to protest in a way that the whole world hears, and this I intend to do. I beg your forgiveness."

Herschel had meant to post the message on his way to the gun shop. Preoccupied with his mission, he had neglected to do so. What was intended as a private plea for forgiveness was now a carried confession of premeditation. Herschel had come to the embassy intending to shoot and kill a senior staff member to protest the Nazi treatment of his parents and, more generally, the Jewish people. As Herschel opened the door, a distinguished sixty-year-old man strode out. Unbeknownst to Herschel, the man was Count Johnannes von Welczeck, German ambassador to France, off to take his daily walk around the neighborhood. No target was better suited to attract the attention of the world's press than Welczeck, the highest-ranking German diplomat in Paris that day. The man and the assassin passed one another in silence. In doing so, each crossed an invisible threshold between countries and fates.

INSIDE THE BUILDING HERSCHEL MET Madame Mathis, wife of the Frenchman who served as concierge at the embassy. Having just repaired the furnace in the basement, her husband was away from the front desk, changing his clothes.

"I need to see a gentleman from the embassy," Herschel said in French. "I wish to submit some important papers to him."

The lie was well chosen. The German embassy was, as one journalist wrote at the time, a hotbed of espionage-themed intrigue: "One only had to be announced as an intelligence agent to be received without difficulty." Herschel's claim that he held secret documents of national importance was the surest way to gain an audience with a senior member of the embassy staff. Such matters were significantly above Madame Mathis's pay grade. She directed Herschel to the staircase where, on the first floor, she said the boy would find the on-duty receptionist.

Emboldened by his progress, upstairs Herschel told the receptionist, Wilhelm Nagorka, that he was in possession of "a confidential and very important document." Nagorka offered to pass the document along. No, insisted Herschel: the matter was too important; he must hand the document to "someone with knowledge of secrets" in person. Nagorka relented. It was early and the embassy was quiet. Besides, if this teenager actually had important information to share, Nagorka didn't want to be the one to hinder its progress. He invited Herschel to take a seat in the waiting room.

A few minutes later, Nagorka returned and escorted the boy to the office of a twenty-nine-year-old diplomat with a reputation among his colleagues for being willing to deal with callers of this sort. At 9:45 a.m., Herschel stepped into the office of the diplomat Ernst Eduard Adolf Max vom Rath. Rath sat behind his desk gazing out the window, his back to the door. He swiveled his chair a quarter turn to the left to face Herschel.

"So," said Rath, thin-lipped but statuesquely handsome. "Let me see the document."

Herschel pulled the revolver from the inside left pocket of his suit jacket and aimed the barrel at Rath. The price tag dangled by its red string.

"You're a *sale boche*,"* he said. "And in the name of twelve thousand persecuted Jews, here is your document."

Herschel fired five shots. Despite the proximity of the two men, three missed their target. One lodged in the coat closet. Another struck the wall. Both left holes about three feet from the ground. Two shots hit their target, entering Rath's body from the left side. One passed through his thoracic cavity and lodged in his right shoulder. The other ruptured Rath's spleen, perforated his stomach and, most troublingly for the cadre of doctors and surgeons who would soon attend to the victim, damaged his pancreas.

"*Deckiges Judenvolk*"—dirty Jew—screamed Rath, who, despite his injuries, managed to punch his attacker in the jaw. The diplomat then staggered forward and heaved open his wooden office door. "Help!" he shouted into the corridor.

Nagorka ran to the commotion from his desk, about thirty feet away.

"I am wounded," said Rath needlessly.

Herschel took a seat in the office. The gun, which the teenager had indignantly hurled at Rath after being punched in the face, lay on the floor. Herschel would later claim that his actions that morning had been conducted in a trance state. The unsent postcard in his wallet addressed to his sister suggested otherwise.

IN THE EARLY HOURS OF November 8, Hitler's personal physician, Dr. Karl Brandt, and the director of the Surgical Clinic of the University of Munich, Dr. Georg Magnus, arrived in Paris via train. The men had been

---

* Colloquial French for "dirty Kraut." The sole source of this dialogue, which exudes a cheap thriller quality, is Herschel, the only surviving witness from the scene, who freely offered the account to the authorities, albeit with minor variations between each telling.

dispatched for reasons both practical and symbolic. Most obviously they were there to provide expert care to Rath, who was, by now, recovering from surgery and a blood transfusion. They were also to provide the German government with a reliable source of updates as to Rath's condition. Their swift dispatch was also intended to demonstrate to a watching world the care with which the Nazi regime took of its officials and to underscore, even exaggerate, the significance of the incident.

At around 10:30 a.m., Brandt and Magnus examined the condition of the young diplomat. As they left the hospital, they described the surgical treatment Rath had received as "excellent," but nevertheless declared the patient's condition as "extremely serious."

In Germany, Adolf Hitler remained uncharacteristically silent. He made no speech or statement about the shots fired in Paris. While the Propaganda Ministry advised the Nazi-sanctioned press to give the assassination attempt "the greatest attention," the official line was merely portentous, not instructive: the act, the ministry pointed out, "was certain to have the most serious consequences for Jews in Germany."

The next day, Rath's condition worsened. Shortly after 3:00 in the afternoon on November 9, 1938, he fell into a coma. Ninety minutes later, the diplomat was dead.

That evening Hitler sat in a smoke-filled hall in Munich, surrounded by an aromatic gaggle of his staunchest and longest-serving supporters, the Sturmabteilung—storm troopers, also known as the Brownshirts. The men jostled and cheered in celebration of what had come to be regarded as the most significant date in the party's history, the anniversary of the so-called Beer Hall Putsch of 1923.

On that day fifteen years earlier, Hitler and around six hundred of his paramilitary fighters had attempted to seize control of the government. The coup failed. Hitler's army of thugs and embittered veterans was easily repelled by a hundred or so armed police officers, although there were a few casualties. Sixteen Nazis and three police officers were killed in the clash. Hitler was duly arrested, tried, convicted, and sent to prison, a term during which he composed his infamous screed, *Mein Kampf*.

Hitler's propagandists soon twisted the defeat into a story of honor and triumph. The anniversary acquired the patina of myth for the Nazi Party, which had declared November 9 a national holiday known as *Tag der Bewegung*—Day of the Movement. Each year there was a reenactment of the march, when wreaths were laid in memory of the sixteen fallen. Afterward, Hitler would spend the evening with five hundred or so of the highest-ranking members of the party at the traditional "Old Fighters" dinner held at the Altes Rathaus, the Old Town Hall. This alcohol-fueled evening would culminate at midnight with a boisterous ceremony at which new recruits to the SS, the party's military branch, would swear "obedience unto death."

At around nine o'clock that evening, a messenger entered the hall, where the festivities were in mid-swing, and whispered into Hitler's ear. The Führer turned to Joseph Goebbels, his minister of propaganda, and the two men were seen to engage in intense, hushed conversation. One reveler reported hearing the phrase "The Brownshirts should be allowed to have their fling."

Hitler left the assembly immediately. Normally he would address his troops with a rousing speech, but tonight Goebbels spoke in his place.

"Ernst vom Rath was a good German, a loyal servant of the Reich, working for the good of our people in our embassy in Paris," he began as the crowd simmered to a hush. "Shall I tell you what happened to him? He was shot down! In the course of his duty, he went, unarmed and unsuspecting, to speak to a visitor at the embassy, and had two bullets pumped into him. He is now dead."

With the facts declared, Goebbels now turned to the subject of blame and reprisal.

"Do I need to tell you the race of the dirty swine who perpetrated this foul deed?" he asked, echoing the epithet used by Rath during the attack. "A Jew!"

The hall erupted in boozy jeers.

"Tonight, he lies in jail in Paris, claiming that he acted on his own, that he had no instigators of this awful deed behind him. But we know better, don't we? Comrades, we cannot allow this attack by international Jewry to go unchallenged."

And so, with the precisely calibrated rhetoric for which he would become known, Goebbels extrapolated blame for the attack from the individual to the community. The inference was clear: shared culpability meant shared consequence. Retribution could be indiscriminate. If reprisals were to spontaneously erupt, Goebbels clarified, "they were not to be hampered."

There would be, finally, a climax to the crescendo of force that had been building against the Jews since the Nazi Party came to power in 1933. In Paris, Herschel Grynszpan awaited trial for murder. The sentence would be delivered long before any jury made its final judgment. This much was clear as, in the room, the heckling grew to a battle roar.

Hitler's exit was significant and followed a pattern of behavior that had become well established in recent years: in private the party's leader would issue or sign off orders for violence against Jewish communities; in public he would remain stoically silent or, as in tonight's case, conspicuously absent, thereby ensuring that his name could not be linked to any brutality. In his diary, Goebbels laid out the truth of the situation. "The Führer decides: let the demonstrations continue. Withdraw the police. The Jews are to experience the rage of the people."

The pretext for a state-sponsored orgy of violence had been supplied by a teenager, the starter's gun for which a tensed regime had been long awaiting. So began a night of violence that would visit shops and homes, synagogues and cemeteries, artists and orphans, a chapter that would end, not only with the imprisonment of innocents across Germany, but also with the imprisonment of innocents across Britain.

III

FIRE AND CRYSTAL

To the other children of Berlin's Auerbach orphanage, it appeared that Peter Fleischmann never won a fight. Not that he started any, either. The short boy with the wavy hair and oval glasses was, in the ruthless universe of the playground, the archetypal target. Staff members would wade through the crescent of onlookers to heave the boys apart, and Peter would invariably limp off in defeat. The truth, however, was more complicated. In the midst of the kerfuffle, the clenched teeth and headlocks, the dusty tussling, Peter would always be sure to land at least one sharp blow. He may lose the fight, but so long as he caused some furtive pain, the other boy would be sure, thereafter, to keep away.

Every orphan is a survivor. One summer, a few weeks, months, or possibly years after he was born—nobody was ever entirely straight with him—Peter's parents, together with his aunt and uncle, were out driving near the Wannsee lake in Berlin when the car developed a steering fault. The driver lost control and crashed into the water. By the time passersby discovered the vehicle, all the passengers had drowned. There were no eyewitnesses.

Like Herschel Grynszpan, who was nine months his senior, Peter blamed the Nazis for his misfortune. His father, Moritz, had worked as a reporter for *Die Freie Meinung*—The Free Opinion!—a publication founded in January 1919 by Peter's uncle Hugo. From their offices in Breslau the Fleischmann brothers documented city life in all its grim fullness. Hugo, the editor who wrote under the pseudonym Hans Hanteda-Fleischmann, believed with all the zeal of a fundamentalist preacher in a journalist's moral obligation to hold power to account. He also needed to sell newspapers, and in 1920s Breslau, nothing sold like gossip. *Die Freie Meinung*'s coverage provided a salacious record of dingy, local sins. (A regular column ran with the title *Aus den düstersten Winkeln Breslaus*—From the Murkiest Corners of Breslau.) The Fleischmanns soon made enemies in positions of power. In one 1922 article published in a rival newspaper, the city councillor, Max Gruschwitz, maligned Hugo as a "common slanderer" and, with an anti-Semitic flourish, a "well-poisoner."

The police reported the deaths of the Fleischmanns as the result of a freak car accident. Regular readers of *Die Freie Meinung* suspected otherwise. While murder remained unproven, the foundational story offered to Peter as an explanation for the chasmic void in his life was that his family had been assassinated, probably by Nazi sympathizers. Whatever the precise circumstances of his parents' disappearance, the fact remained: by the time he was three years old, Peter Fleischmann was an orphan.

PETER'S GRANDFATHER, A RETIRED BANKER named Dr. Alfred Deutsch, provided stability and income. Peter moved into his palatial apartment, which boasted two bathrooms and eleven bedrooms—far too many for Alfred and his live-in housekeeper, Elizabeth Altenhain—on the well-to-do Aschaffenburger Strasse. Alfred cared for Peter as if he were the boy's father, and Elizabeth as if she were his mother—a curious, if welcome couple. Nonetheless, the boy needed an education and so, when Peter was five, Alfred sent him to the Auerbach orphanage, where he stayed during the week, returning home to his unconventional family on Sundays.

Fate was not quite finished heaping trouble upon the surviving Fleischmann. In October 1929 the US stock market crash knocked the financial supports from beneath the postwar Weimar economy. Lenders refused to issue new loans and called in existing ones. Peter's grandfather, like millions of other Germans, lost his money. Alfred kept the apartment, but on the weekends, he and Peter were forced to walk the streets of Berlin, eating in soup kitchens, and collecting and drying out horse manure to use in place of fire logs.

Alfred's lament was but one voice in a chorus of misery. In the twelve months between September 1929 and September 1930, unemployment in Germany more than doubled to three million. Peter and his grandfather were privileged: they had a house and its associated securities, but Alfred did not survive his precipitous decline into hardship. He died within the year. The housekeeper moved out to begin a new life in a farmhouse in Dahlewitz, just south of Berlin. At the age of twelve, Peter had no remaining family, or at least none that he was aware of. The illusion that is human stability had shattered; the boy became a full-time resident at the Auerbach orphanage, where he learned to scuffle.

Echoes of Peter's old life of relative wealth and privilege returned during the school holidays. Before Alfred lost his money, he would take his grandson to the city's most famous restaurant, Kempinski's at 27 Kurfürstendamm, one of a high-class and profitable chain of shops and restaurants that had spread across the city since the late nineteenth century. The vast restaurant was magnificently outfitted: wine-red carpets, mahogany furniture, glinting cutlery, white napery. The ground floor housed a delicatessen store where saleswomen in black uniforms with white-frilled aprons and headbands served crystallized pineapple from silver trays using silver tongs.

During visits Peter would wander off and explore the hotel building, areas that were typically closed off to members of the public. During one of these sojourns, Peter met the owner of the wine-importing business that supplied the restaurant. To Peter the man seemed kindly and good-humored, playing hide-and-seek among the pillars and racks. It would be some time before Peter found out that his unlikely playmate was Joachim von Ribbentrop, the future Nazi foreign minister.

It was here at the restaurant that Peter first met Elisabeth Kohsen, heiress to the Kempinski empire, a vivacious socialite with two children of her own, just a little younger than Peter. Echen, as she was known to her friends, had remained, despite the exceptionally favorable circumstances of her birth, empathetic and compassionate. She donated money to support the work of the Auerbach orphanage. After Alfred's death, Echen invited Peter to stay with her family during the holidays, paying for him to accompany the family skiing in Switzerland one winter. Once, when Peter fell ill, she paid for him to recuperate in the countryside, away from the other orphans.

Echen became like family to Peter. When he visited her vast and luxurious third-floor apartment in the fashionable Berlin district of Charlottenburg, she invited him to call her "aunt" and ordered her two daughters to call him "cousin." His visits assumed a dreamlike quality. Before dinner he would watch Echen take live lobsters out of a low sink and drop them with a haunting hiss into a pot of boiling water, where their black carapaces turned a bright red. In the dining room a pink Venetian glass chandelier hung above an enormous light green and crimson carpet. Through the window, Peter and the sisters would sometimes watch parades of young Nazi Brownshirts march past or would drop coins down to a local organ-grinder and his performing monkey. For a few weeks, here and there, Peter experienced brief sojourns into the vanished life he had once enjoyed with his grandfather, before he had to return to the chores and routine of the orphanage.

PLAYGROUND FIGHTS ASIDE, AUERBACH WAS a place of relative peace and plenty. The orphanage was not like the workhouses of Dickens, with their bowls of thin gruel and ruthless governesses. The campus was old and substantial. While the dormitories resembled hospital wards, with white metallic beds and identical blankets, they were comfortably furnished. The playground was tree-lined and the grounds meticulously kept by a caretaker, Mr. Gross. Peter lived with around eighty other Jewish children, both boys and girls, ranging from nursery to school-leaving age.

Not all of the residents were "full orphans," as those who had lost both parents were bluntly known. Single parents also sent their children to Auerbach as weekly boarders. All families paid what they could afford. A gymnasium equipped with parallel bars, vaulting horses, and rings connected the boys' and girls' dormitories and, after finishing their homework each day, the students would meet in the courtyard to brush hands and steal kisses. Toys were plentiful: radio and chess sets, ping-pong tables, playing cards, little wooden kitchens, and an outdoor sandpit as wide and deep as a swimming pool, where the younger children could build castles and protective moats.

There were daily chores—shoe-shining, step-scrubbing, banister-polishing—and a few seasonal hardships: in winter the taps in the coach house at the bottom of the garden would occasionally freeze over, and the children would have to chip the ice from the basins before they could wash. Life was, however, comfortable for the students, who benefited from the donations of wealthy benefactors such as the banker and philanthropist Eugen Landau, a bust of whom watched over the dining room. On Saturday mornings Peter and the others received a slice of cake in celebration of Shabbat alongside their spoonful of cod liver oil. Every Hanukkah each boy was given a new suit.

Jonas Plaut, a jovial, broad-chested man in his mid-forties, and his wife, Selma, ten years his junior, had run the orphanage since 1922. The couple hired progressive interns as guardians for the children, young people who were primarily concerned with furthering their charges' growth. One of the governesses would frequently give the students money out of her own pocket to go to movies or visit the bakery next door. While Selma Plaut was prone to a favoritism that rankled and excluded those who did not fall under the beam of her attention, the couple succeeded in fostering an experience that most looked back on with fondness.

In accordance with the wishes of the orphanage's founder, Baruch Auerbach, the Plauts wanted their institution to meet not only the physical and spiritual needs of its orphans, but also their intellectual and cultural longings. So the orphans staged classic plays, performing in full costume. One night each week was set aside for classical music, while the tutors read to the younger children in their beds until lights-out. Visiting teachers gave piano lessons or taught woodwork or bookbinding.

Auerbach's founder had emphasized the importance of caring for a child's mental well-being as much as their physical needs. "To fulfil its true purpose," Auerbach once wrote, an orphanage "must become a family home." There was discipline, but children were never beaten. Nonviolence was encouraged in implicit ways, too. The students used gun stocks left over from the Great War for hockey sticks, while a statue of Friedrich III, Germany's distinctively pacifist emperor, surveyed the courtyard in the center of the campus. Auerbach was a haven of sanctuary, if not—with sixteen children to each dormitory—much privacy.

Outside the building's sturdy gates, which had stood at 162 Schönhauser Allee since the turn of the century, a depression-gripped Berlin swilled with homelessness and hunger, strikes and street fights. The British novelist Christopher Isherwood, a resident in Berlin, described young men waking up to "another workless, empty day" in a dreary city, to spend their hours variously "selling boot-laces," "hanging about urinals," and sharing stumps of cigarette ends stolen from the gutter. As the grip of Nazi oppression tightened, the orphanage, home to a small, liberal synagogue, gained a whispered reputation for being one of the most secure places for young Jewish children. Here was an oasis of refuge, in a rising tide of muck. Like many sanctuaries situated in a place of great need, the Auerbach orphanage was destined to become contested ground.

AT ELEVEN O'CLOCK THAT EVENING of November 9, a few hours after the doctors declared Rath dead in Paris, Hugo Moses, a forty-four-year-old employee of the Oppenheimer bank, stepped out of a meeting in the center of the small German town in which he and his family lived, into an empty street. The local bars still rumbled with Nazi revelers, but Hugo's walk home to his apartment, where his wife and children were already in bed, was tranquil. Soon he, too, was asleep, until the insistent ringing of the doorbell jerked him awake.

Moses walked to the window and pulled back the curtain to see that the streetlights had been extinguished. Against the near-black of the sky, he made out the menacing silhouette of a transport vehicle and the shapes of men, either disembarking or already huddled at his front door.

"Don't be afraid," he called to his wife in the bedroom. "They are party men; stay calm."

Still in his pajamas, Moses opened the front door. He smelled his attackers before he saw them: a wave of alcohol, followed by a firm shove to the chest as the first of the men, emboldened by drink and the electric promise of violence, pushed past and yanked the telephone from the wall. The leader, an SS man, stood in front of Hugo, his face tinged green and ominous in the darkness. He made a showy display of cocking his revolver.

"Do you know why we've come here?" he asked, raising the weapon to press the tip of the cold barrel against Moses's forehead.

"No," Moses replied.

"Because of the outrageous act committed in Paris, for which you are also to blame. If you even try to move, I'll shoot you like a pig."

Moses did not reply, but stood with his hands behind his back, pressed against the wall. November air blustered through the open door and into the hallway, blowing the cold present into the past, the unthinkable into reality. Moses listened while the men clattered through the apartment in heavy boots. He heard the whip and rustle of his desk being emptied, the tiny smashes of glass of framed photographs knocked to the floor, the domestic manifestation of an assault on identity.

"What do you want with my children?" he heard his wife scream from the next room. "You'll touch my children over my dead body."

Then suddenly, the man pressing the revolver to Hugo's head blew sharply on a whistle. The ransackers trampled through the corridor and filed out into the street. When the last of the men passed, their leader took the muzzle from Hugo's forehead, pointed the gun at the ceiling, and fired two shots. Believing his eardrums to have burst, Moses stood motionless. Then the officer struck Moses on the side of his head with the stick he had used to smash pictures.

"There you are, you Jewish pig," he shouted as the parked van outside spluttered awake. "Have fun."

Similar scenes of ritualistic intimidation, degradation, humiliation, and assault were, at that moment, occurring across many of Germany's towns and cities. A few hours after Goebbels made his speech calling for violent remonstrations against Jews, Reinhard Heydrich, director of the Gestapo, composed a telegram to every police station and intelligence office in the country.

"Following the attempt on the life of Secretary of the Legation vom Rath in Paris, demonstrations against the Jews are to be expected in all parts of the Reich in the course of the coming night," Heydrich wrote. He outlined a series of bullet-point instructions for precisely how the state police were to moderate the incoming surge of violence, a set of restraints intended to minimize collateral damage and ensure the violence was precise, discriminate.

Any synagogue could be torched, Heydrich instructed, "only where there is no danger of fire in neighbouring buildings." Jewish shops and homes "may be destroyed," but "not looted." Even if they are Jewish, foreign citizens are "not to be molested"—an instruction that implied what should be done to German Jews. Heydrich's telegram closely mirrored instructions telephoned by the storm trooper chiefs gathered in Munich to their various regional sections a few hours earlier. A prearranged plan, it seemed, had been prepared in anticipation of Rath's death.

In Wittlich, a small town in the western part of Germany, Nazi supporters threw furniture through the intricate lead-crystal window above the main door to the synagogue, showering the pavement with shards of bright-colored glass. One man climbed onto the roof.

"Wipe your asses with it, Jews," he screamed as he threw scrolls of the Torah into the air so that they unraveled like ribbons of confetti.

In Germany's capital city the violence was deferred until two o'clock in the morning, as specially trained squads cut telephone lines to Jewish buildings and switched off electricity and heating. The police diverted traffic from the areas of Berlin that would be most affected, a degree of calculation that resisted any claims that the night's attacks were the result of spontaneous civilian outbursts.

The major synagogues were the first targets of the razzia. Goebbels specifically ordered the largest of these, the Fasanenstrasse, to be destroyed. Situated close to the Berlin Zoo, Kaiser Wilhelm II had attended the synagogue's opening on August 26, 1912. Twenty-four years later, in 1936, the Nazis forced its closure. The building was still maintained, however, by Magnus Davidsohn, its cantor. Davidsohn was a neighbor of the assassinated Rath's parents. Before the diplomat died in Paris from his wounds, Davidsohn had visited the couple to express the sympathy of the Jewish community.

"My dear Reverend," Rath's father had told Davidsohn. "Neither you nor any other Jew is responsible for this."

Now, as the flames rose retributively inside the synagogue, Davidsohn implored the fire chief to extinguish the fire.

"I can't help," said the captain. "We've come to protect the neighboring buildings."

The synagogue's porter emerged into the courtyard, his nightclothes stained with blood. When he had refused to surrender the keys to the sanctuary, storm troopers had forced open the doors, heaved the seventy-eight-stop organ over the balcony, then ripped up and thrown holy texts, garments, and prayer books into the Wittenbergplatz square outside. The men then drenched the wooden benches in petrol, accelerating the speed and intensity of the blaze.

Davidsohn and the porter watched as the group piled the synagogue's artifacts and documents into a pyre, set it alight, then danced around the flames. At the Auerbach orphanage some of the older boys climbed onto the building's roof and, from their vantage point, saw the glow of the distant fire color the sky. Meanwhile, the attackers climbed into one of the thirty taxis hired to carry them to the city's Jewish hospitals, to its old people's homes, to its orphanages.

FOLLOWING THE NAZI PARTY'S RISE to power in 1933, it did not take long for the Auerbach children to begin to notice the world shift. Less than eight weeks after the Nazis came to power, German state schools were ordered to limit the number of Jewish pupils to less than 5 percent of their total intake. Teachers began to seat non-Aryan pupils separate from their fellow students and refer to them by racial epithets such as "Jew-boy." Some schoolteachers would lift the shorts of Jewish students who talked during class or offered an incorrect answer when called upon and beat them on the thighs with a stick, a punishment never aimed at their classmates.

At the age of ten, each child at the orphanage enrolled in one of a number of secondary schools, according to their individual talents and predilections. Children who excelled in languages, mathematics, or science attended the Königstädtische Oberrealschule, a college famed for the tall tower that stood within its grounds, topped with a powerful telescope. Those who showed an aptitude for humanities-based subjects were sent to the Heinrich-Schliemann-Gymnasium.

Peter was an average student. He found it difficult to spell and struggled with languages. He ping-ponged between classes as his teachers tried to find a subject in which he might, if not excel, then flourish. Art was Peter's salvation. He was a natural draftsman who spent lessons endlessly sketching and doodling, playing with shape, color, and typography. Rather than direct Peter toward core subjects, the teachers at the Auerbach encouraged their student's passion and secured him a place at the Königliche Kunstschule zu Berlin—the Royal School of Art in Berlin. Having found his place, Peter excelled, learning to paint, etch, and engrave, and showing sufficient talent to secure freelance contracts to design travel and film posters. The teachers' encouragement had a profound effect.

"There and then I decided I would become an artist," he said.

While the Auerbach staff attentively guided their charges in directions that supported their students' talents and interests, they were unable to protect them from the escalating cruelties of the outside world. Older children like Peter left the orphanage together around 7:30 in the morning, before breaking off into smaller groups according to their final destination. For most, school was at least a forty-minute walk, a journey on which, as the months passed, the children were increasingly the targets of harassment.

One day a group of Auerbach students spied a gang of Hitler Youths who appeared to be lying in wait for them along the route.

"Stay together," said one as the group approached the uniformed boys. "Don't do anything to irritate them."

The ploy was unsuccessful. The older boys began to hurl stones at the children. One missile struck an Auerbach student in the head, opening a gushing wound.

"Look at the Jewish blood!" exclaimed a member of the gang.

Soon, harassment became a daily part of schooling. Even after Jewish children were finally expelled from state schools, and the Auerbach staff began teaching classes on the Rosenstrasse, a thirty-minute walk from the orphanage, the orphans were routinely attacked with belts and buckles by members of the Hitler Youth.

The attacks were orchestrated by older party members as a way to desensitize young Hitler supporters to committing acts of violence on Jews. And it was these young supporters who, in the early hours of November 10, 1938, arrived at the Auerbach orphanage midway through their lusty tour of destruction, rapped on the front gate, and demanded to be allowed in.

The signs that fate was, once again, coming for Peter had become clear in the months leading up to the assassination of the German diplomat Rath in Paris. On July 27, a number of Berlin streets bearing the names of Jews were renamed. On September 27, Jewish lawyers were banned from practicing. On October 5, the passports of all Jews were withdrawn and reissued with a red-stamped *J*. Then, shortly before the mob arrived at the Auerbach, a plainclothes police officer knocked on the front gate.

"The Gestapo are on the way," he said. "They are coming for Peter Fleischmann."

The secret police, it seemed, had finally tracked down the "leftovers" of the Fleischmann clan, which had been otherwise wiped out.

"Have you somewhere to go?" Jonas Plaut asked Peter.

Six weeks shy of his seventeenth birthday—the time at which he would have to bid goodbye to Auerbach, the institution that had provided stability in the tumult of his young life—Peter Fleischmann knew how to survive: inconspicuously. There were two people to whom Peter thought to flee: his "aunt," Echen Kohsen, heiress to the Kempinski fortune, and his grandfather's housekeeper, Elizabeth Altenhain. While neither woman was a relative, he had a close bond with both. Peter settled on the housekeeper, whose modest farmhouse was situated in the suburb of Dahlewitz, away from the city.

Peter packed up his belongings—a few clothes, a violin, and an art folder filled with his drawings—and said his goodbyes. So it was that, on the night the German diplomat Rath died, when the mob of Nazi support-ers arrived at the gates of the Auerbach orphanage, Peter Fleischmann was hiding in the cellar of the farmhouse that belonged to his late grandfather's housekeeper, sixteen miles south of his empty orphanage bed.

AUERBACH'S DIRECTOR, JONAS PLAUT, CREAKED open the gate to a crowd of young men, some in uniform, others wearing plain clothes. He had known the mob was on its way; the plainclothes policeman had warned him earlier that night to take the children somewhere else. But where to hide eighty young people without notice? It seemed safer to stay put and pray the looters would pass them by—an understandable miscalculation.

Jonas Plaut feared that the young men had come for the children. In fact, they had come for the building. In 1923, a local seminary teacher, Hermann Falkenberg, had built a liberal synagogue on the orphanage grounds. This place of worship, known as the North Synagogue, was where the children would celebrate Jewish holidays, led by the resident cantor, Kurt Jakubowski, who would also train the boys in preparation for their bar mitzvah ceremonies. The Auerbach synagogue was well known to the secret police, whose members would sometimes attend ceremonies on the premises. Auerbach's synagogue was, it seemed, on the list of the night's targets.

"You need to leave now," said one of the attackers. "We want to set fire to the building."

Walter Frankenstein, a quick-thinking fourteen-year-old orphan and apprentice bricklayer, pointed out that any fire would likely spread to other buildings on the street.

Perhaps recalling Heydrich's warning to burn only those synagogues where there was no danger that the fire could spread to neighboring buildings, the storm troopers heeded the boy's warning and changed their plans.

"*Beeilt euch*," said one of the men, who seemed barely older than some of the children. "Hurry up . . . Everyone into the synagogue."

The storm troopers shepherded Auerbach's residents into the hall, where they squeezed among the pews in front of the curtained altar. The children heard the door being locked from the outside, then one of the orphans began to cough.

Natural gas had been odorized in Germany since the 1880s, a mercaptan liquid added to ensure that leaks could be detected by smell. As Walter noticed the deepening odor in the room, he realized one of the attackers had, on his way out, blown out the eternal flame and opened the gas tap in front of the *Aron Kodesh*, the ornamental closet in the synagogue where the Torah scrolls were kept. The room was filling with fumes.

Frankenstein scrabbled to locate the tap and closed off the valve. The scent of gas hung heavy in the room. While some of the younger children wept, others made suggestions for how they might force their way out. An older boy reasoned that the attackers might be waiting outside the door, ready to shoot anyone who escaped.

The children heard the rumble of a truck's engine, its pitch rise and volume fall as the vehicle pulled away. There was an abrupt crash as an older boy hurled a chair through one of the synagogue's stained glass windows to allow a life-saving transfer of air.

While Peter and the other orphans had, in their respective ways, survived the night, the sun rose on a changed city. Wreckage both material and emblematic littered Berlin's shattered streets. Glass made the pavements crunch underfoot, the debris from which the atrocity subsequently took its name: *Kristallnacht*—the Night of Broken Glass.

Any residual hope that the Nazi regime's escalating persecution of German Jews might still be reversed had evaporated with the rising of the sun. While Peter Fleischmann had evaded disaster, a threshold had been passed. None of the orphans knew it yet, but their survival was now dependent on their escape.

IV

THE RESCUERS

As THE GRAY DAWN ROSE on a changed and smoldering Berlin and the first reports of the night's violence began to wend their way to Britain, Bertha Bracey was in her London office picking at a pile of paperwork. Positioned opposite Euston station on one of London's busiest roads, Drayton House had become as hectic as the railway terminal it faced, the nerve center of a chaotic but diligent operation dedicated to bringing individuals and families—mostly lapsed Jews—from Nazi Germany to Britain. In 1933, the operation's first year, Bertha and her part-time assistant dealt with just eighteen cases. Now, five years later, the Germany Emergency Committee employed a staff of fifty-nine—mostly women, mostly Quakers—and the caseload numbered more than fourteen thousand.

Short, prim, and plain-looking, Bertha's diminutive stature belied her inexhaustible energy. In order to help with her petitions, she had begun a number of correspondences with the offices of various high-ranking Nazi officials, including Reinhard Heydrich, architect of the previous night's violence, the officer whom Hitler famously referred to as "the man with the iron heart." She had written letters to Hermann Göring, Joachim von Ribbentrop—the wine seller with whom Peter Fleischmann once played in the Kempinski cellars, now the Nazi foreign minister—and even Hitler himself in order to request the release of a German social worker imprisoned by the Nazis.

The work was rewarding, but overwhelming. Documentation spilled from her office into the building's cramped corridors, where scores of penniless and terrified men, women, and children now sat and patiently awaited meetings. There was need everywhere: for emigration papers, for lodging, for language training, for employment. Together with Otto Schiff, her counterpart at the Jewish Refugees Committee, Bertha had become a central figure in a network working to forestall complications in refugee applications and avoid delays that, considering the previous night's events, could prove fatal.

It wasn't easy to rescue a person from Germany. Writing in the *New Statesman*, Bertha's friend and collaborator, the politician Eleanor Rathbone, likened the work to scraping away at prison bars with tiny files before finally dragging tortured men, women, and children through the gaps, one by one. An escapee faced a series of monumental barriers: the Nazis' desire to steal their money before they left; the difficulty of finding a country willing to take a person unable to contribute to the cost of resettlement; the obstinacy of a British government concerned that, by welcoming refugees, it might enflame anti-Semitism and the jealousy of the unemployed, or, as Rathbone tersely put it, "encourage other nations to unload their Jews on us."

Trade union opposition to immigration had allowed the government to adopt a more restrictive policy, as had the countrywide fear that an influx of refugees could threaten both national stability and identity. Most problematic for Jews attempting to flee Germany, the British government viewed the "Jewish problem" as a side issue within Nazi policy. British officials simply did not believe that Hitler would or could devote so much effort and expense to the extermination of the Jewish race across Europe. Accordingly, the scale of response did not match the scale of threat; even the best-connected individual needed help to plan and execute her life-changing journey.

For many, Drayton House and, when the operation outgrew the premises, its successor Bloomsbury House, represented a person's best hope of securing emigration papers for their loved ones in Germany. Bertha knew that she was often a person's only hope—the benevolent, unseen force for which all humans long in moments of profound crisis—especially for someone in Peter Fleischmann's position, hiding from the Gestapo in a cellar, with few connections and no family to petition on his behalf.

FEW WERE BETTER EQUIPPED FOR this difficult work. Bertha spent much of her twenties living in Austria and Germany and spoke fluent German. She had worked on providing aid to families impoverished by the First World War, and witnessed firsthand the rise of Fascism. Her mission was driven by her Quaker faith, a small but welcoming Christian denomination more committed to social justice than dogma, which Bertha adopted when she was a teenager living next to the cocoa-chuffing chimneys of the Cadbury chocolate factory, where her father worked as a carpenter.

After graduating from Birmingham University, Bertha had accepted a post as a teacher at Luton High School for Girls. She spent her first summer holiday volunteering in Austria in 1922, collecting and distributing aid to families in need, and promptly resigned from teaching to continue her work. She soon came to understand the impact that she could have on people's lives if she summoned the courage to knock on the right doors. Through the work she systematically built a formidable network of friends and colleagues across Austria and Germany, all equally committed to welfare and, as time went on, rescue.

From her vantage point among the suffering proletariat, Bertha witnessed attitudes change and tensions rise in Germany. During a two-year stay living in Nuremberg in the mid-1920s, she watched in disbelief as men previously seen as extremist cranks rose to positions of power. Julius Streicher, the ferocious racist who founded *Der Stürmer*, the weekly tabloid newspaper that printed what she called "appalling anti-Semitic statements and horrifying Jewish caricatures," served on the city council. Bertha watched as others looked away, hoping these objectionable figures would, after a spell of responsibility, retreat. "The poison, however, was spreading."

After she had returned to England in April 1934, Bertha addressed the Religious Society of Friends at Swarthmoor Hall, where she warned her audience of how postwar bitterness and resentment in Germany were curdling into poisonous ideology.

"What we see now," she told the assembled crowd, "is an overgrown, hot-headed, big-headed form of Nationalism which is afraid of internationalism." It is the duty of English people, she said, "to resist the oncoming tide of Fascism and dictatorship and all its forms," before pointing out to any audience members who might be feeling an air of moral superiority that these tyrannies were also "certainly growing here in our land."

In truth, attitudes in Britain toward Jews were, in fact, dispiritingly close to those in Germany. Home Intelligence, a department of the government's Ministry of Information, gathered statements made by members of the public regarding Jewish people. Their comments made for grim reading. Jews, one stated, "seem to have all the money nowadays." Another claimed Jews "can always get out of anything," while one interviewee pointed at "low business morals." One of the Home Intelligence officers concluded: "[M]any have the sneaking feeling that Hitler, and those of like thought throughout the ages, were right."

Anti-Semitism, in all its various and complex forms, did not arrive in Britain with the influx of Jewish exiles from Nazi oppression. As in Europe, there was a centuries-old belief that Jews, as a group, had opposed Christ—overlooking the muddling factor that Jesus was a Jew who practiced in the rabbinical tradition. While in Britain Jewish people were not forced to live in ghettos or wear marks of racial identification on their clothing, Jews were the subject of a diverse range of prejudices, from working-class xenophobia and concern about unemployment, to fears of cultural contamination from within the intelligentsia.

In Britain, anti-Semitism did not find its primary expression in physical violence, but in reflexive attitudes and jokes. The diplomat Sir

Harold Nicolson articulated a widespread attitude among the British literary class when he said: "Although I loathe anti-Semitism, I do dislike Jews."

On the morning of Thursday, November 10, 1938, as the first reports of the events of *Kristallnacht* arrived in Britain, Bertha's prescience was vindicated, and Britain's old and enduring islander mentality—that the country does not have the capacity to absorb foreigners, whatever their need—sharply challenged. Here was the undeniable proof that anti-Semitic violence had always been foundational to the Nazi regime's aims. It was not in Bertha's character to gloat. Nor was there time. A quickening crescendo of events would demand from Bertha, her team, and the Jewish aid organizations with whom they collaborated an entirely new category of ambition.

THE DAWN LIGHT HAD NOT cooled the night's violence. The British government's man-in-Berlin, George Ogilvie-Forbes, left home early and stepped into the debris-strewn morning. He began with a tour of Friedrichstrasse, the city's major shopping district. Around him, the looting and destruction continued. Grinning crowds tailed looters, gawking and sometimes surreptitiously pocketing valuables that spilled onto the pavement. Police officers, Ogilvie-Forbes wrote in a telegram sent to his superiors in Whitehall later that day, took no notice.

Foreign journalists based in Berlin corroborated the account. A reporter from the *News Chronicle* saw Jews "chased through the streets by young Nazis, pummelled and knocked down." Another foreign reporter noted that "the average German looked on either apathetic or astonished." While many were appalled by the events of the night, others eagerly joined in with, if not the violence, then the theft; one Berlin jewelry store, Margraf, reported losses of 1.7 million marks.

At five o'clock in the afternoon, Joseph Goebbels, initiator of the pogrom, issued the order to end the violence: "The natural and fully justified outrage felt by the German people at the brutal assassination in Paris has been expressed this evening in reprisals against Jewish shops and businesses," he stated in his message, relayed via radio stations across the country. "I now appeal to the entire population to desist at once from any further demonstrations or action against the Jews. The last word on the Paris assassination will be spoken in legislation."

By November 1938, German Jews had been banned from using radio sets; Goebbels's message would have gone unheard by the community it was, ostensibly, supposed to protect. Even among the attackers, the order did not have an immediate effect. "Not even the proclamation of Dr. Goebbels, the propaganda minister—broadcast this afternoon and again tonight—ordering the stoppage of pogroms could curb the madness of the mobs," wrote one journalist. "The only thing that could finally slow then stop the violence," the reporter observed, was a "lack of further damage to be done."

In the final tally, 7,500 Jewish homes and businesses had been looted, 267 synagogues and congregational buildings razed, including thirty in the city of Berlin and at least ninety-one Jews murdered across the country. In the coming days, forty thousand Jews would be taken to the prison camps—Dachau, Buchenwald, or Sachsenhausen—where men were forced to stand for hours at a stretch or to perform exercises while repeating the words, painted on a board: "We killed Secretary vom Rath."

THE NEWS OF WANTON DESTRUCTION was not unexpected in Whitehall. In the hours between Rath's shooting and his death, Germany's Jewish leaders had sent a desperate plea asking the British government to select "some prominent non-Jewish Englishman to go to Berlin immediately" to dispel the looming threat of violence. Officials had decided, however, that to intervene at this point would be to meddle in "a wasp's nest." There was no intercession.

News of the murders, lootings, and arrests was met with condemnation from all sections of the British government, public, and press.

Reports of what had happened across Germany "went through Britain like a sort of electric current," recalled one observer. "Every little town, every village in England said, 'We must save the children.'"

In a letter to the London *Times* published on November 12, the archbishop of Canterbury, Cosmo Gordon Lang, who had long advocated friendship between Britain and Hitler's Germany, wrote: "Whatever provocation may have been given by the deplorable act of a single Jewish youth, reprisals on such a scale, so fierce, cruel and vindictive, cannot possibly be justified." These "excesses of hatred and malice," Lang wrote, "put upon the friendship we are ready to offer an almost intolerable strain."

The focus of Lang's letter on *Kristallnacht's* deleterious effects on international relations, rather than on the victims, was telling. The archbishop did, however, conclude with a request that congregations pray for the victims of persecution "whose future seems to be so dark and hopeless."

It fell, then, to others to take a more pragmatic approach. Shortly after *Kristallnacht*, Wilfrid Israel, a Jewish businessman and owner of Israel's Department Store, one of the largest in Berlin, wrote to Bertha Bracey. Israel, a descendant of the first chief rabbi of Britain, Hermann Adler, was well connected—his friend Albert Einstein later said of Israel: "Never in my life have I come in contact with a being so noble, so strong and as selfless . . . a living work of art."

Israel had already begun work to secure the release of Jews who had been arrested during the pogrom. He invited the commandant of Sachsenhausen, the concentration camp where Jewish men were being forced to accept the blame for Rath's murder, to do his Christmas shopping at the store for free in exchange for the release of captives.

Now Israel wanted to organize the rescue of Jewish children up to the age of seventeen and find a way to send them to Britain. Israel knew that he needed the assistance of regional committees to quickly establish the machinery to realize such a plan, but British Jews were forbidden to visit Berlin. He had remained in contact with Bertha ever since they met in Nuremberg. Bertha was at her Euston office when she received the invitation from her old friend to visit him in Berlin.

The Quakers, a group that numbered just twenty-three thousand in Britain at the time, were permitted to travel freely to and from Nazi Germany. This generous attitude was the result of the group's humanitarian work after the First World War, the so-called *Quakerspeisung*— Quaker feeding—a program that provided five million German children with food in the aftermath of the war and recession.

Many children who benefited from this philanthropic work grew up to become senior Nazi officers; the memory of the group's benevolence remained clear across the nation and political divides. In 1936 a Nazi dictionary for children provided just three entries for church denominations: *Protestanten*, *Katholische*, and *Quäker*. The definition for *Quäker* identified the group as having "sacrificially cared for destitute children in Germany after the Great War." As a result, the Nazi regime allowed the Quakers to continue their philanthropic work relatively unimpeded.

In the days after *Kristallnacht*, Bertha traveled to Berlin with a delegation of five colleagues to confer with Wilfrid Israel as to how they might, with the utmost urgency, evacuate children to Britain. When she arrived, Bertha attempted to keep her presence in the city secret, fearing that German Quakers living in the city might experience reprisals were the group's plans exposed. These plans, first suggested by the German Jewish social worker and refugee activist Solomon Adler-Rudel and devised in collaboration with the Jewish Refugees Committee, were a masterpiece of collaboration and international organization.

Vulnerable German children up to the age of seventeen would take a train from Germany to the Netherlands, which, the day after *Kristallnacht*, had agreed to allow temporary residence to an unlimited number of German and Austrian children. From Holland, they would take the ferry to Britain, to be accepted into the home of a willing family. There would be unimaginable pain as children were parted from their parents, not knowing when or if they would again meet, but the plan seemed preferable to any alternative. As she returned to Britain, Bertha knew that without the backing of the British government— which would need to issue the immigration permits—it would come to naught.

Prime Minister Neville Chamberlain was torn on how his government should respond to current events. As news from Germany spread, the prevailing tide of public opinion had shifted; national anxieties about asylum seekers were, it seemed, matched and even surpassed by the urge to demonstrate compassion on the international stage. Outrage had finally grown to the monstrous proportions necessary for action.

Chamberlain told the House of Commons that his government would consider "any possible way by which we can help these people." An "open doors" policy was out of the question, however, not least because of fears that refugees might compete for jobs at a time of high unemployment. Even prominent Jewish representatives appeared to oppose the large-scale admission of Jews, seemingly afraid of agitating anti-Semitism in Britain.

Four days after the attacks, a meeting of the Cabinet Committee on Foreign Policy discussed possible responses. The home secretary, Sir Samuel Hoare, who was from a Quaker family, suggested that part of the British annual quota of sixty thousand immigrants—of which only about a quarter had currently been used—might be earmarked for German Jews suffering from Nazi oppression. The previous September, Winston Churchill had written an open letter in the *Evening Standard* imploring Hitler to cease his persecution of Jews; now he suggested settling refugees in a colony such as British Guiana. The discussion ended without resolution.

On the morning of November 21, eleven days after the violence of *Kristallnacht*, Bertha Bracey met the home secretary, accompanied by five other humanitarian representatives. Among them was Ben Greene, who had returned from a trip to Germany only that morning. The members of this interfaith group, called the Movement for the Care of Children from Germany, outlined a plan that, Hoare soon realized, might represent precisely the kind of grand gesture that the British public required.

At first, Hoare expressed some doubt that any parents would willingly send their child alone to a foreign country, to live with strangers.

Greene explained that, while he was in Berlin, he had put the same question to Jewish families in person.

"They were," Greene told the politician, "almost unanimously in favor of parting with their children." Better to assume the risks of their children going to a foreign country, most parents had told him, than keep them to face the capricious dangers at home.

Moved by Bertha's tragic descriptions of Berlin, challenged by her display of Quaker faith in action, and no doubt inspired by what seemed like a public relations coup, Hoare at last committed to a course of action. Provided they had a guarantor to offer food, shelter, and the cost of a ticket home, "transmigrant" children, as they were to be known, would be welcome in Britain. Visas and alien cards would be waived in place of a new permit bearing the child's name and those of his or her parents.

That evening Hoare made good on his promise. In a debate in the House of Commons he pledged that, while the refugee issue was "an international problem" that "no single country can hope to solve," Britain was "prepared to play [its] full part.

"I believe that we could find homes in this country for a very large number [of children] without any harm to our own population," he continued. We shall, Hoare promised, "put no obstacle in the way of children coming here."

There was much to be done. In addition to the logistical challenges involved in bringing unaccompanied minors across Europe, there was the issue of locating and vetting British families who could provide safe lodging. Ideally these individuals would be equipped to ease the children's psychological turmoil at having been separated from their parents. Regional committees needed to be set up to enlist foster parents and organize accommodations.

Then there was the question of how—considering that the need vastly outstripped the provision—places would be allocated. Priority would be given to middle-class candidates, perceived to be likely to adapt most quickly to a new country, and—in a grim paralleling of the Nazi preference for Aryan-looking children—blond girls were favored, as potential British foster parents and guarantors were more inclined to choose them from photographs.

Dennis Cohen, chair of the Jewish Refugees Committee's emigration department, and his wife left for Berlin on November 28, 1938, to finalize arrangements with the German government and consult with the welfare organizations responsible for making selections—the Reichsvertretung in Germany, and the Kultusgemeinde in Austria—from more than six hundred applications that had already arrived.

The children were to be brought out of Germany by various means, mainly train, but also by plane in some cases. The proposal was dubbed by the German Railway Authority as simply *Kindertransport*—the Children's Transport.

The Nazis cooperated with the plan: so long as no money or valuables were removed from Germany, and the emigration was handled discreetly and with no cost to the state, the party voiced no objection to sending Jewish children to Britain. The SS organized extra carriages for the refugees to be attached to regular trains. The refugees would be accompanied by a minimum number of adult supervisors, around one adult per twenty-five children in the first instance. The British act of benevolence was also conditional: all young people accepted into the country were expected to have left Britain for a new country of asylum within two years, preferably one.

Spaces for the first delegation of children to England were reserved for the most vulnerable: those without families and, therefore, the most obvious candidates for fostering. The orphans of Auerbach fitted the profile. They would be joined by evacuees from three other Berlin institutions: the Fehrbelliner Strasse children's home, the Reichenheim orphanage, and the Ahawah orphanage, which would later become the building where the Gestapo administered the sending of Jews to death camps. The first *Kindertransport* would depart Berlin on November 30, 1938, carrying children from other German cities, including Hanover and Leipzig. The Berlin children were allocated the second train, which would depart from the city the following day, December 1.

* * *

THREE WEEKS SHY OF HIS seventeenth birthday, Peter Fleischmann received word that, despite being close to the upper age limit for rescue, his name was on the list. Peter would need a passport photograph and a medical certificate to show, among other things, that he was "free of vermin." Otherwise, all that remained to do was to pack a single suitcase, the allowance for each child leaving Berlin, then return to the orphanage on Wednesday, November 30, the night before the planned trip.

When the morning came, Peter stood in the orphanage courtyard, with its wintery trees and forsaken sandpit. In one hand he held a bag in which he had hidden what few family treasures remained in his possession—some silver knives and forks, a dragonfly brooch with tiny diamonds on the wings once owned by his mother, and his treasured stamp collection—and, under the other arm, an unwieldy art folder filled with his posters and paintings.

Accompanied by Rafael and Max Plaut, brother and nephew of Auerbach's director, Jonas Plaut, Peter and the other children boarded a bus outside the orphanage that had been a place of refuge and stability in his turbulent life since the age of five. It was a twenty-minute drive to the Anhalter Bahnhof, one of Berlin's busiest railway terminals. There the Auerbach children joined the other Berliners with whom they would make their train journey to the German border and into Holland, where the boat that would take them to Britain awaited. For Peter, opportunity had, at least for now, followed disaster.

V

SUNSET TRAIN

WITH THEIR BULGING SATCHELS AND coats, the orphans looked like schoolchildren excited to embark on a day trip. At five feet five inches, Peter was short for his age, but he still towered over the younger evacuees who made up the majority of the group standing in the grand surroundings of the Anhalter Bahnhof. The Gestapo officers who had come to watch the children, with their unpatriotic dark hair and brown eyes, make their pioneering journey out of the city, might have mistaken the older boy in the tan raincoat for a chaperone.

In coming weeks and months, Berlin's stations would provide a backdrop to scenes of unthinkable distress as parents parted from their children, not knowing when or if they would see one another again. Some parents would place their hands gently on their child's head to give the Jewish blessing. Others would wail in anguish. One father had a last-minute change of mind and hauled his daughter by her wrists through the window as the train tugged from the station. Moments before the doors closed, another mother, who either did not have the necessary documentation for her children or who had been unable to secure them a place on a train, slid a laundry basket into the carriage; inside, beneath the blanket covering, lay twin baby girls.

So chaotic and harrowing were the goodbyes that, later, parents were forbidden from standing on the platform in most stations to conceal the scenes of distress from the paying passengers. Temperament and, often, the reaction of the adults around them guided each child's response to their journey.

"I remember crying bitterly, and saying: 'Please, Mummy, don't send me away,'" recalled one evacuee as an adult. Another had the opposite response: "My mother insisted on kissing me over and over again, and I got impatient with her demonstrativeness, not realizing of course that this was to be the final parting." Some regarded it to be a great adventure. Others, who had been told that their parents would soon be joining them in England, were confused as to why there was so much crying. Many of the children carried no photographs of their family or other pieces of memorabilia, their parents careful to not include anything that might suggest the parting was final.

Some were fearfully conscious of onlookers, urging their parents to contain their grief lest they draw attention. Others sat in quiet contemplation, aware that they were about to experience a monumental change in their life, but unable to fathom the true shape of its significance. The suddenness of the parting meant that, whatever their immediate reaction, this event would be a lifelong, defining trauma.

ON DECEMBER 1, 1938, THERE were few adults around to wave off the pioneering orphans. The atmosphere on the platform—one of six at the Anhalter Bahnhof, which sent and received trains to and from cities such as Paris and Moscow—was, as one of the children described it, "strangely quiet." There had not been enough spaces in this, the first *Kindertransport* for Berliners, to accommodate every child from the city's threatened orphanages. Accordingly, the Auerbach's directors, Jonas and Selma Plaut, had picked the "full orphans" for the delegation, those children like Peter who had the fewest reasons to remain in Berlin. While this station and others across Germany would, in the coming months, provide a backdrop to scenes of unbearable pain, Peter had learned to submit to the yanks and shoves of providence that had so far defined his life. Forced exile was not a routine occurrence, but neither did it feel contrary to the pattern of his existence.

Beneath the station's vaulted roof, supported by paired bowstring trusses made from slender steel, the train eased to a standstill and let out a pneumatic sigh. In subsequent evacuations, some parents of *Kindertransport*ees would take a taxi from station to station, waving from each concourse, an act of love that, depending on the child, could either be received as a welcome declaration of devotion or a protracted irritation. For these first children, nobody raced to extend the goodbye.

At the Osnabrück station, on the German side, the Berlin orphans were joined by the other evacuees who had made their way across various cities toward Holland. From there, the train continued to Bad Bentheim, the last stop in Germany, where it arrived just before four o'clock in the afternoon. It was the tensest moment of the journey, as SS officers boarded to inspect the passengers' belongings. Aware that this might be the last time the children would feel the stamp of Nazi authority, the officers seemed intent on making an impression. In later journeys, some children would be cruelly removed from the train here, a few short miles from freedom.

Peter had hidden valuables among his clothes to circumvent the financial limit of ten reichsmarks imposed on every *Kindertransport* child. In England, he would be able to sell the silver knives and forks hidden in his laundry if the need arose. Likewise, his stamp album could also be used to raise funds, since it contained a set of the first German stamps, including a One kreuzer black, the German equivalent of the Penny Black. Peter hoped to keep the collection intact, though, if possible.

Johnny Eichwald, a schoolboy from Kappelin four years Peter's junior, had also brought his stamp collection. The inspector roughly rifled through Johnny's bag, then drew the album out and laid it on the seat beside the boy. As the man began to search another child's belongings, Johnny surreptitiously slid his stamp album toward himself, then sat on it. The inspector caught sight of the movement, turned, and slapped the boy across the face.

"You can start another collection when you're in England," he said.

Neither did Peter's stamp collection escape the search. When the inspector saw his collection, with its tidy phalanxes of rare stamps, he said, bluntly: "I'll have that." The silver dragonfly brooch, which Peter had wrapped in clothing, remained hidden.

Even after the train pulled from the station, the children and their chaperones could not relax. A squeal of brakes brought Peter's carriage to a standstill at the border. From the window the passengers watched German soldiers' marching drills. After what seemed like an age, the train finally began to move again; the children imperceptibly crossed the border.

LIFE UNDER A REGIME THAT wants you and your family impoverished, invisible, or dead exerts an oppressive, bewildering psychological pressure on the human mind, the feeling that reality itself is somehow working against your existence. As the train moved from one country to the next, the psychic burden under which the children had been living lifted. Their conversations became lighter, the result of an overwhelming shift in prospects.

The emerging tableaux outside heightened the elation of escape. From his position in a carriage at the rear, Peter watched the canals light up with the red glow of the setting sun. The train tilted into a bend and tugged into freedom.

"The grey smoke at the front, that sunset, the orange and reds, just appearing as night fell . . ." Peter later recalled of this numinous moment. The sight raised in him a feeling of almost uncontainable joy. "The image has never left me . . . Leaving the German frontier, the Gestapo, the sunset over Holland. You could see for miles."

An oppressor can delay and derail a dream but, while the oppressed lives the dream survives. As the winter colors streaked past the window, Peter Fleischmann renewed his private pledge that he would become an artist no matter where he landed, so that, when faced with moments of equivalent splendor, he might put onto canvas that which he could not put into words.

The juxtaposition of the children's somber departure from Bentheim with their arrival at the Dutch town of Oldenzaal, the train's first stop in Holland, was dizzying. A crowd greeted the passengers like heroes, a gaggle of press photographers ready to capture the moment of safe passage, a scene with the rare quality of presenting a refugee story that was universally sympathetic and palatable to the watching world.

Women had set up tables on the platform laden with pots of vegetables and kosher meat. Adults helped the children move their watches back an hour, to Dutch time, and pressed rag dolls into the hands of the younger ones. Well-wishers thronged to present the evacuees with sparkling water and lemonade, bars of chocolate and baskets filled with bread rolls and apples.

At the Dutch port of the Hook of Holland, Peter and the other 195 children who had been gathered on the journey across Germany detrained and approached the ship that would carry them on the final leg of their journey.

Since its launch in November 1929, the TSS *Prague* had worked as the nightly ferry service on the Hook of Holland–Harwich route. Three hundred fifty feet long and twin-funneled, the boat cut a handsome silhouette. As they boarded, the children dropped their luggage onto the accumulating tower of bags ready to be stowed. For Rafael and Max Plaut and the other six adults accompanying the evacuees to England, it would be a fleeting taste of freedom. Once the ship reached the port of Harwich, the adults would be obliged to immediately return to Germany. Failure to do so would jeopardize any future transports of children.[*]

For most of the passengers it was their first sea crossing. They were ushered to their bunks, two to a cabin. There were not enough rooms for everyone, so Peter and around fifty of the older children spent the voyage huddled in one of the ship's saloons, which had been improvised into a dormitory. At eleven o'clock on the night of December 1,

---

[*] In nine months and hundreds of *Kindertransport* journeys, only one chaperone was known to defect.

the TSS *Prague* headed into the night and toward the British coast, its only passengers the children and their eight carers.

The sea was rough, whipped into a white-frothed fury by the North Sea gale, and the effects of the pitching and rolling on the children were immediate. Many became violently seasick, calling mournfully for their loved ones or trying to comfort their younger siblings. For any child who could stomach food and drink, there were two unfamiliar English delicacies available: sliced white bread and milky tea.

In the packed saloon, however, there was an atmosphere of giddy freedom.

"We did not need to look over our shoulders or lower our voices," recalled one of the children. "The realization that we could say what we liked with impunity engendered an atmosphere of enormous gaiety."

At 5:30 IN THE MORNING on December 2, 1938, two hours before sunrise, the ship cleaved the mist hanging over the water and docked at Parkeston Quay, Harwich, on the Essex coastline. Peter and the other children dozily gathered their belongings, then filed into the ship's lounge, which had been turned into a temporary office by Major Geoffrey Langdon, a former officer of the British army turned businessman, whom the Jewish Refugees Committee had placed in charge of receiving the evacuees and ensuring that their permits were in order.

As Langdon called out the names on his list, each child stepped forward in turn, removing their hat to allow a helper to tie an identification tag around their neck. Processing close to two hundred individuals in this manner took more than four hours. By the time the children emerged on deck, name tags dangled from their coats like they were human luggage destined for some new frontier. As they filed along the gangplank, the sun rose behind the clouds, casting the dock in the thin milk light of an English winter.

Photographers, journalists, and a film crew from Pathé News greeted the children, who were now accustomed to being the subject of media fascination. For the assembled media, it was an appealing scene.

The sight of unaccompanied evacuees, many tearful, humanized the reports of the treatment of Jewish people that had dominated newspaper headlines throughout November. Cherubic orphans presented the ideal image of a refugee to inspire compassion, even to salve the collective guilt of a country still reckoning with its government's failed attempt at Nazi appeasement. Neither did the child refugee threaten British workers. In his long coat and bookish glasses, Peter appeared much older than his sixteen years, but he benefited from being part of a nonthreatening group.

Many journalists reported the story in a mode of high pathos.

"Out of the North Sea mist they came . . . as tragic a freight as ever set forth across the sea to a strange new land," wrote a reporter for the *Gloucester Citizen*. "Germany is a grim memory: many of the children are fatherless and motherless, and came with vivid memories still lurking, of the orphanage where they were sheltered in Berlin, fired above their heads, and of their dash for life."

Another described the crowd as being "sad-eyed" and "pursued by the shadows of unseen grief." They "sighed," he wrote, "as they trod on English soil." Numerous reporters noted the boy of nine, from Breslau, who stood clutching a violin in a battered case and told one journalist: "I am glad they let me bring this. Perhaps I will make the music in our camp?"

Onshore a customs official searched each child. The tragic sight of children, who had been stripped of their valuables by the Nazi regime, now presenting their meager worldly belongings to the British authorities was not lost on the reporters.

"As the officers patted them trying to put the children at ease with smiles and words of broken German, some of them timorously emptied their pockets," wrote one journalist who witnessed the scene. "There was laid out on the long tables an odd assortment of fountain pens, propelling pencils, cheap flash lamps and schoolboy odds and ends—their only possessions apart from the clothes they wore, and the few garments stuffed in the rucksacks."

Cleared for entry to England, Peter finally walked across the railway tracks to board the double-decker bus that would carry him to the holiday camp that, for the coming days, would become home.

AS WELL AS THE RELIEF at having safely arrived in England, Peter was grateful that the weather in Britain seemed mild compared to the bitter cold of Berlin. From the bus window, he was astounded to see young girls wearing what appeared to be summer dresses in December. More astonishing still was the unthinkable sight of a teenage girl smoking not one but two cigarettes simultaneously, a brazen act of decadence and rebellion. Not everyone on the bus was so beguiled. One of Peter's fellow passengers spied a copy of *Mein Kampf* in a passing bookshop window.

"My God," she wondered. "What have I come to?"

The bus pulled into the Dovercourt Bay holiday camp, a ten-minute drive from Harwich. During the summer months, holidaymakers could rent huts here at a rate of £2 a week. The holiday camp was comprised of dinky chalets with pebble-dashed frontages and mock-Tudor porches, a flimsy facsimile of wealth and well-to-do-ness designed to disguise what was otherwise rudimentary living space. There was no heating or surface drainage—unnecessary luxuries during the summer months when the camp was usually occupied. Until heating stoves could be installed, the refugee children would have to make do with woolen socks and sweaters worn over their pajamas at night.

AFTER ENDURING THE LENGTHY IMMIGRATION process, the children were relieved to eat their first meal in England, a breakfast served at long tables draped with white cloths and decorated with vases of flowers. They ate porridge, kippers, bread, butter, and jam on white china, and drank tea or cocoa from mugs. Some penned letters and postcards to their loved ones in Germany, copying down the *Unsere Adresse*—the camp's return address—from a blackboard. Midway through their first breakfast, a group of about a dozen evacuees surprised the staff by

emerging with towels and bathing costumes before running and jump-
ing into the freezing water of the camp's open-air swimming pool.

That morning, the children were introduced to Anna Essinger, the
tall and imposing camp commandant who, at short notice, had been
chosen to oversee the operation. Essinger, a Jew who had converted to
Quakerism, was a friend of Bertha Bracey and the former headmistress
of Landschulheim Herrlingen, a nondenominational boarding school
in southern Germany. In April 1933, she had become the subject of a
Nazi investigation. On the day the Nazi regime ordered all German
public institutions to fly the swastika flag, Essinger took the entire
school on a field trip; the flag flew over an empty building in protest.
When the Nazis threatened to install an inspector inside the school,
Essinger hatched an ambitious plan: to transpose the school and its
pupils from Germany to England.

She appealed to British Quakers for help to raise funds for the relocation. These funds enabled Anna to rent and later purchase Bunce
Court, a sixteenth-century manor house in Kent, to which she brought
sixty-five of her pupils. Her knowledge of both the German and English
school systems made Essinger the ideal person to run Dovercourt Bay.

She was nevertheless frustrated by the speed at which arrangements had to be made. "None of us will ever forget those heart-
breaking days," she later recalled. "Thousands of children were saved,
but these were necessarily hurried arrangements; perhaps it was only
natural that serious mistakes could not be avoided."

The children's stay had, by definition, a purgatorial quality: it was a
temporary arrangement until each boy or girl could be processed and
placed, either with a foster family who had responded to one of the
advertisements placed in various newspapers, or to one of the various
Quaker or Jewish schools or hostels offering food and accommodation. Still, many embraced their holiday-like surroundings.

Two days after their arrival, a representative from the *Jewish
Chronicle* visited the camp and described scenes of calm recreation:
table tennis, darts, piano playing. To a casual onlooker the camp's population seemed composed of contented schoolchildren. Still, the writer

made note of subtle tells of an ordeal, the "three little girls seated quite silently in a corner," or the "boy rubbing his eyes furtively."

As media reports of the children's arrival spread, the camp became inundated with pledges of help. To onlookers what had, to date, felt like a distant tragedy had assumed human form and character. Empathy no longer required a leap of the imagination. Offers to foster children were redirected to the relevant administrative committee in London, but other gifts were accepted on-site.

One man drove forty miles to bring more than a hundred pounds of sweets for the children. A local dentist turned up offering to check teeth, and, after the weekend, volunteers arranged a series of classes to teach English language and British customs. The younger children, many of whom struggled to correctly pronounce "Harwich" as "Ha'rich," learned songs like "Daisy Bell," and "The Chestnut Tree." For Peter, the messages broadcast through a speaker system and the schedule of lessons gently foreshadowed all that was to come.

At sixteen Peter was an undesirable candidate for most foster parents, who wanted a young, malleable child who could fit around existing domestic rhythm and routine. Despite this, a couple from Bournemouth responded to an advertisement and agreed to take the sixteen-year-old on. Peter packed his bags and, with a small group of other children, was driven two hundred miles from Harwich to the rotary club in Swanage, a few miles south of Bournemouth on the south coast of England.

Now, just prior to his seventeenth birthday, Peter expected to be collected by his new parents; instead, he was put on another train. This journey was, curiously, much longer than he had expected. Bournemouth, he had been told, was just a few miles from Swanage. Why were they passing through so much countryside? When his carriage pulled into Liverpool Street Station, Peter asked what was going on. There had been a change of plans, the chaperone told him. Peter was now headed to the north of England. The authorities had traced an uncle who had come to Britain some years earlier. There was to be no choice in the matter. The teenager would move in, regardless of how those involved felt about the arrangement.

VI

THE BASEMENT AND
THE JUDGE

THERE WAS NEITHER A WARM welcome nor a joyous reunion awaiting Peter in the rain-pelted northern city of Manchester. Peter's uncle—his late mother Alice's elder brother—was stern and professorial by nature, but he also seemed inexplicably cold, even hostile toward the teenager. He asked no questions about his nephew's interests or Peter's escape from Germany. Instead, Peter was gruffly shown to the spare room and informed that, when visiting the bathroom, he was not to touch the family's toilet rolls, but was instead to make use of the sheets of old newspaper that had been laid out for him.

Fascism creeps in, step by step, in increments of tyranny just small enough to be ignored by those who have invested too many of their years, too much of their wealth, too deep their relational and emotional ties to flee the situation. Peter's uncle, Walter Deutsch, had been one of the first to overcome the psychological and administrative barriers to exile. In 1933, shortly after Hitler's rise to power, Walter took his family out of Germany.

As a university lecturer in physiology at Düsseldorf's Medical Academy, Walter was one of the first to lose his job when, on April 7, 1933, the newly instated Nazi Party enacted the *Gesetz zur Wiederherstellung des Berufsbeamtentums*—the Law for the Restoration of the Professional Civil Service. This, the first step in the so-called *Säuberung*—cleansing—of German universities, enabled the party to remove academics from their posts for one of three spurious reasons: "inadequate training," "political unreliability" or, simply, for being a "non-Aryan"—defined as anyone who had a Jewish parent or grand-parent.

The purge, which Bertha Bracey described as an "absolute blasphemy," began immediately. Within six weeks, 164 teachers had been dismissed from their posts or had resigned in protest. Having lost his job so early into the regime, Walter Deutsch had few ties holding him back.

His family's escape was aided by a serendipitous meeting, in May 1933, between a young Hungarian physicist named Leo Szilard—a close friend of the physicist Albert Einstein—and Sir William Beveridge, director of the London School of Economics. Szilard had fled Germany for Austria, and there checked in to a Viennese hotel. On arrival he looked over the guest list to see if he knew any of his fellow residents and spied Beveridge's name. It was precisely the kind of fortuitous opportunity Szilard had hoped for; he left a note for Beveridge with the front desk requesting an audience. When the pair met, the Hungarian laid out an ambitious proposal to establish a university run entirely by refugee scholars—an ingenious way to take Jewish academics out of Germany and provide them with employment.

Beveridge was sympathetic, but realistic about the challenges involved in building such an institution from scratch. He returned to England resolved to see whether it might be possible to offer displaced scholars roles in existing British universities instead.

Beveridge was persuasive and soon secured the support of numerous university vice-chancellors, who together pledged to find vacancies for the sacked professors. The organizers of the scheme took over two office rooms in the Royal Society building and, on May 23, 1933, a press release appeared in the *Times* announcing the formation of the Academic Assistance Council, a group that would bring more than a thousand scholars to Britain between 1933 and 1939—10 percent of the eleven thousand refugees who came to Britain prior to the war—including Peter's uncle, Walter Deutsch.

WHEN PETER ARRIVED ON HIS uncle's doorstep, Walter had already spent five years in Manchester, a liberal city that accepted a greater number of refugees than most. He had changed his family's name from the unhelpfully Germanic "Deutsch" to the softer "Dale," and split his time between lecturing at Manchester University and working as a biochemist at the Christie Hospital and Holt Radium Institute. The unanticipated arrival of this skinny, estranged Jewish boy with a thick accent and poor grasp of English threatened the Dales's carefully cultivated aura of respectability. Walter did not hide his disinterest.

"He did not want to know me," Peter said.

Eager to learn something about his mother, whom he did not remember, Peter asked questions that might fill in the void of details surrounding his parents' personalities and fate. Walter was evasive. Peter was safer than he had been at the orphanage, but paradoxically, living here among his relations, he felt more isolated than ever. What had, at first, seemed like a serendipitous opportunity had become an episode of freshly wounding rejection.

With no income and only a few pieces of silver cutlery in his possession, Peter was dependent on his uncle's goodwill. Having little else to do in a city he did not know, where locals spoke a version of English he struggled to understand, he began to write weekly letters to Germany, in an attempt to reach those few people that he knew cared about him: Echen, heiress of the Kempinski empire; Jonas and Selma Plaut, directors of the Auerbach orphanage; and his grandfather's housekeeper, who had hidden him from the Gestapo. Walter promised to stamp and send the letters. When Peter's back was turned, he threw them away.

THE EVENTS OF *KRISTALLNACHT* HAD heightened the British public's interest in the country's response to the German persecution of Jews.

Keen to hasten sympathy into action, Bertha Bracey proposed an appeal to raise £5,000, funds that could be used to support the various organizations working to rescue yet more children and families. On December 8, 1938, less than a week after the first *Kindertransport* delegation arrived in England, the former prime minister, Lord Baldwin, launched Bertha's appeal on the radio, now with his name on the label, calling it the Baldwin Appeal. The British people, he urged, must donate to provide "a hiding place from the winds, and a covert from the tempest" for those who were most in need. The appeal exceeded all expectations. More than a million donors raised over £500,000. From her original goal it was, as Bertha described it, "rather a nice progression."

A portion of the money was immediately used to bring the various refugee organizations now working with subsets of refugees into a single building, where they could better support one another. Bertha and the other leaders of the refugee organizations chose the Palace Hotel on Bloomsbury Street in London, close to the British Museum. The lease allowed for a change of name: Bloomsbury House. Bertha and her staff began the challenging task of transporting their eighteen thousand case files to the third floor of the new building, a mile away.

Politicians, keen to ensure their policies matched the public mood, drew opposing conclusions from the appeal's display of national generosity. Prime Minister Chamberlain—who, in a letter to his sister, once described the Jewish people as "rich, clever and un-loveable"—believed its success showed the British people wanted further admissions of refugees. The home secretary, Sir Samuel Hoare, claimed the opposite. Debate raged as to the wisest course to follow in balancing Britain's humanitarian obligations with the increasing concern among those responsible for maintaining the security of the realm at the numbers of German and Austrian nationals now living in Britain.

IN THE SUMMER OF 1938, a few months before Peter's arrival, a number of sealed envelopes arrived on the desks of chief constables and immigration officers across Britain. Each was marked with a portentous instruction: only to be opened on the eve of war. Inside was a list of names of individuals living in Britain whom MI5, the British domestic intelligence service, considered to pose a meaningful threat to the country. If war came, the letter explained, these named individuals were to be immediately subject to arrest and imprisonment without trial.

The list—which contained the names of men who were demonstrably fascist or demonstrably communist—had been compiled by the office of Sir Vernon Kell. A former army captain now in his mid-sixties, Kell had worked as an intelligence officer in Shanghai during the time of the Boxer Uprising, while moonlighting as a foreign correspondent for the *Daily Telegraph* newspaper. In the months leading up to the First World War, he and a small staff worked alongside the Special Branch of the Metropolitan Police to identify suspected foreign agents.

The day before Britain entered the First World War, Kell and his team directed the arrests of at least twenty spies, many of whom were convicted and subsequently executed. The operation was hailed as a great success; the Home Office boasted it had "broken up the spy organisation [that] had been established before the war." Regardless of the truth of the statement, the operation secured the reputation of both Kell and his nascent intelligence agency.

Now responsibility for identifying residents in Britain who might pose a threat again fell to MI5's cofounder; using his newfound resources, he was able to expand the agency's remit from counterespionage work to something approaching mass surveillance. Any group deemed to be politically hazardous became the subject of MI5's attention, leading to the creation of a vast card index recording the names and addresses of suspicious individuals in Britain.

This list formed the basis of the letters sent to police stations across Britain in the summer of 1938. The names contained represented a diverse group: journalists, hunger marchers, pacifists, people who had signed petitions opposing book censorship in Britain, businessmen suspected of having Nazi sympathies. Most shared a common factor: they were foreigners. The letter's instructions were simple. In the event of war, those individuals who were named were to be summarily arrested and sent to prison, from where they would be passed to one of twenty-seven internment camps established to house potential spies.

Many names were included for dubious reasons. During a visit to Britain in 1933, George Gercke had written a fiercely anti-Nazi piece for the *Independent* newspaper, in which he presciently wrote: "A proper Nazi wouldn't mind exterminating all the Communists, Socialists and Jews rather than give up power." When he returned to England five years later with his homesick English wife, the *Daily Mirror* ran a short profile on Gercke, who, at a time of widespread unemployment, had resorted to selling ice creams from a tricycle. The story mentioned, in passing, that Gercke's father had been a U-boat commander in the last war. That Gercke had stated his anti-Nazi views in the British press was not enough to save him from a place on MI5's list.

It was not the first time that questionable decisions had been made while preparing for internment in Britain, a weapon used in wartime by governments to protect their citizens against resident foreigners of enemy nationality. During the First World War a total of twenty-nine thousand German and Austrian men were arrested and sent to internment camps on the Isle of Man, an island in the Irish Sea that by 1916 had become, as an observer put it, "one huge enemy prison camp." The project, which the island's government took on hoping to profit, was riddled with errors and misjudgments.

A supply of potatoes infested with wireworms was used, over a two-week period, to make buckets of disgusting stew, which guards forced internees to eat. The winter weather caused tents to blow away, huts to rot, and living quarters to become flooded, all of which compounded the misery of thousands of men. After lunch on November 19, 1914, internees at Douglas camp staged a protest in the dining hall and began to smash crockery and overturn tables, jeering and booing at the kitchen staff. The scene was rowdy, not dangerous, but nonetheless the military reservists and volunteers guarding the men loaded their rifles and fired indiscriminately into the packed hall.

Five internees were immediately killed, and another died later from his wounds.

When the last internees left the Isle of Man in September 1919, the government departments that had been embroiled in the chaos and scandal vowed never again to repeat the disaster. Deportation, not internment, would in the future prevail as government policy. As late as September 1938, the Home Office wrote to chief constables to inform police departments that "in the event of a war emergency" it is hoped that "as many aliens as possible would leave the country."

Yet *Kristallnacht* had complicated the matter. Thousands of those "enemy aliens"—a term that forced estrangement onto its subjects, conferring otherness and unbelonging—were refugees who had come to Britain to escape persecution. The notion that in the event of war these individuals and families might either be deported or imprisoned was unspeakable. The supposedly dangerous men identified by MI5 would have to be interned. But there would be a public outcry if the government sent individuals like Peter Fleischmann, who just a few months earlier had been offered sanctuary in the country, to camps.

The Home Office proposed a compromise. While, in the event of war, refugees would still be classed as "enemy aliens," it was decided that most "can be presumed to be more favourably disposed to this country than to those they have been forced to leave." Therefore, every enemy alien over the age of sixteen would be allowed to state his case via a tribunal. Those who could prove that they posed no risk to Britain would be allowed to remain.

MI5 was incensed. In the summer of 1939, the agency's director of counterespionage, Guy Liddell, had just thirty-six officers with which to thwart German intelligence. Liddell calculated that it would take at least eight months for his staff to interview every German and Austrian living in Britain and weigh his or her loyalty to Britain.

"In the meantime," he wrote, "the Germans will have every opportunity of working on enemy aliens in this country and organising them into some kind of intelligence agency."

Internment, that imperfect but effective tool of the First World

War, was, for Liddell, the swiftest, simplest, and most effective solution. As he wrote in his diary, "From an MI5 point of view, it would be far preferable to have [all enemy aliens] put away."

Tribunals, expulsion, or internment: the fate of Peter Fleischmann and tens of thousands like him would, to a large degree, be decided in the court of public opinion. As a precaution, the Home Office ordered the War Office to increase its potential accommodations for internees to eighteen thousand. And Vernon Kell, founder of MI5, sent his list of names to police stations across the country so that, when war came, the apparatus of the state was suitably prepared.

FRESHLY MISERABLE IN MANCHESTER, Peter Fleischmann was desperate to move out and move on. Walter was just as eager for his nephew to leave the family home, lest Peter tell one of his risqué jokes at the dinner table around visitors. First, Peter needed a job, preferably one related in some way to his calling, and preferably one that paid him enough to gain some measure of independence. Like all the children arriving in England, Peter's prospects were limited by the stipulations of his immigration permit, which forbade employment, paid or unpaid, while in the United Kingdom.

His uncle was equally keen for the teenager who had been imposed on his home to become financially self-sufficient. As Peter later put it, his uncle "fought bitterly" to see to it that the boy could leave as soon as possible. On January 16, 1939, three weeks after he had arrived in Manchester, and shortly after his seventeenth birthday, Peter either left, or was expelled from, the house that, momentarily, had promised to provide him with a family. Alone in a foreign country and with only a tentative grasp of English, he was vulnerable. He moved into a series of lodging rooms, first at 5 Maple Street, a run-down house in a deprived area of Manchester, and then, a few months later, into a shelter for young Jewish refugees on Balliol Street in Crumpsall.

One of the paradoxes of Peter's life was the way in which the circumstances of his birth enabled him to move between the world of extreme wealth and extreme poverty. His experiences living with his grandfather and later staying with the heiress Echen and her children had given Peter the deeply useful but often overlooked gift of feeling comfortable in the full range of social situations, a sense of belonging in settings of both affluence and need. Even so, the conditions on Balliol Street, a notorious slum area, formed a new category of poverty for him.

"I saw sights I had never even read of in books: the kind of things talked about or made into films became a living thing," he said.

The house had been built without guttering so that when it rained the water would cascade to the ground. The rooms were furnished not with beds but with blankets; the entire street shared a single outdoor toilet.

Peter was not alone in his view that British poverty occupied a distinct tier of severity. Before she graduated from university, Bertha Bracey worked as a volunteer for the social services.

"British poverty in those days stank," she said. "It was ragged. It was dirty. It was unkempt. It was smelly." When she later arrived in Vienna to provide aid to impoverished families, Bertha was astonished to find the Austrian homes clean, orderly, and well-swept by comparison, nothing like the desperate conditions at home. But while his standard of living had plummeted, in his new home Peter nevertheless felt the breeze of adolescent freedom that accompanies any person's first step toward self-determination. His new life reeked, but at least it was his own.

Peter learned there was, around the corner, a company called Progress Limited, one of two British studios that specialized in a kind of artistic work peculiarly of the moment. The owner, a thirty-year-old salesman named Albert Ripkin, would knock on the doors of families who were known to have lost a loved one in the First World War and inquire whether the family had any photographs of the deceased in the house. So many had died in the Great War that often the family would produce a treasured portrait of the young man dressed in his uniform. Ripkin would then offer to take the monochrome picture away to convert it to color.

Seeing Peter's folder of commissioned artworks, and spying an opportunity for some cheap labor, Albert immediately hired the young Berliner, not only to color the photographs but also to retouch them to render the subject more handsome or chiseled by redrawing the mouth or filling out the cheeks.

When Peter arrived for his first day's work on Cheetham Hill Road the conditions were "indescribable," as he later recalled. The artists worked in the murky basement, hunched over desks in the half-light, transforming the photographs into color, the only sound that of the rats "humping around" on the beams and in the shadows. Peter considered his title of "photographic artist" laughable. The work involved painting directly onto the photograph to create a "frameless" memento for the bereaved. There was little artistry involved. Still, his employment came with two substantial benefits. Depending on how many works he completed, Peter received at least £6 a week—around £340 today—more than most boys of his age could expect to earn.

The job also came with accommodations. Ripkin invited his newest employee to move in with him and his wife, Gertrude, on Downham Crescent in Prestwich, a detached two-story house on the border of the picturesque Heaton Park. With the sense that his circumstances were improving, Peter arrived at his new employer's home with his bag and folder of art materials under his arm. Inside, religious pictures lined the walls; the Ripkins were Seventh-day Adventists, and their adoption of Peter was inspired, it seemed, by the chance to gain not only comparatively cheap labor, but also a potential convert.

ON SEPTEMBER 1, 1939, TWO days before Britain declared war on Germany, police forces around the country received the order to unseal the envelopes sent by MI5 and arrest those individuals named within. In London, officers escorted the internees to the Olympia exhibition hall on Hammersmith, which had been set aside as a clearing center, even forcing the men to pay for the taxi ride. By the end of the week, 350 individuals had been arrested across the country and delivered to

Internment Camp No. 4, an out-of-season seaside resort at Clacton-on-Sea in Essex, just fifteen miles away from the *Kindertransport* camp at Harwich.

Despite months of investigation and planning, this first wave of arrests—intended to capture only the most dangerous Nazi sympathizers and fervent communists—was characterized by mistakes and misunderstandings. Eugen Spier, Alex Nathan, and Dr. Bernhard Weiss, all Jews and staunch anti-fascists, were among the first men arrested and taken to Olympia, where they were herded alongside bona fide Nazis such as Hitler's friend Ernst Hanfstaengl. Weiss was the former Berlin police chief and had become famous in Germany after he sued Joseph Goebbels, Hitler's minister of propaganda, more than forty times for libel and won every time. It was difficult to imagine a less likely suspect for a Nazi spy.

With those MI5 had deemed highest risk interned, the question of what was to be done with the thousands of other "enemy aliens" living in Britain immediately arose. In the House of Commons on September 4, the MP Arthur Greenwood put the following question to the home secretary, Sir John Anderson, who had been on the job only a day: "What steps [do you] intend to take to deal with aliens in time of war?"

For the first time in public, Anderson began to explain the government's plans.

"A number of aliens whose suspicious activities have been under observation are already under detention," explained Anderson. Others, he said, would now have to report to the police and obtain permits for change of residence, travel, and the possession of items such as cameras and motorcars.

"A large proportion of the Germans and Austrians at present in this country are refugees, and there will, I am sure, be a general desire to avoid treating as enemies those who are friendly to the country which has offered them asylum," Anderson continued. "At the same time, care must be taken to sift out any persons who, though claiming to be refugees, may not, in fact, be friendly to this country."

Here was the essence of the problem facing the British government. In a letter to the foreign secretary, Sir John Anderson explained that "It was felt . . . it would be wrong to treat as enemies [those] refugees who are hostile to the Nazi regime, unlikely to do anything to assist the enemy and often anxious to assist the country which has given them asylum." And yet, there was a risk that there could be enemies posing as refugees, spies who had already entered Britain under the cloak of asylum.

On September 29, Cordell Hull, the US secretary of state, sent a telegram to the American embassy in London warning of the moral dangers inherent in a policy of mass internment. Hull referenced the lessons of the First World War, when "the rigorous . . . internment of enemy aliens" caused "widespread and seemingly unnecessary suffering to thousands of innocent persons." Copies of the message were also sent to the American embassies in Berlin and Paris, a pointed sign of US neutrality at this stage of the war.

For now, however, the threat of mass internment seemed both remote and mitigated by the plan for the tribunals that, between October 1939 and March 1940, would deliberate no fewer than 73,353 cases, including that of Peter Fleischmann. Most were refugees, and the others long-established residents or people who, by chance, were in Britain at the outbreak of war. Nevertheless, the reliability and loyalty of everyone would be examined by a panel. If suspicions remained, they were to be interned.

Not everyone condoned such a magnanimous approach. Guy Liddell, MI5's head of counterintelligence, summed up his view of the decision to forgo mass internment with a single word: "Farce."

ON NOVEMBER 14, 1939, ELEVEN months since he landed in Britain, Peter headed to the tribunal that would decide his fate. He felt hopeful. Not only had the orphanage where he lived in Berlin been the subject of an attack by Nazi Party members, he had come to England via the *Kindertransport*, deemed a vulnerable case.

When Peter arrived for his tribunal, however, he was met by the foreboding sight of Lord Chief Justice Rayner Goddard, one of the most senior judges of the courts of England and Wales. The sixty-two-year-old Goddard had a formidable reputation for being a punitive interpreter of the law. He regularly donned a black cap prior to sentencing a man to his death and, according to his clerk of many years, would sometimes become so aroused when passing a death sentence that he would require a fresh pair of trousers.

Goddard, who, like each of the 122 tribunal chairmen, was paid two and a half guineas for every half-day session, would have to ascertain, through a combination of questioning and examination of the evidence, which of three categories outlined by the Home Office best fitted Peter. He would be aided in his decision by paperwork supplied by the volunteer organizations, which had been compelled by the government to hastily produce reports on the tens of thousands of individuals due to be examined in this way.

Those who presented a significant risk to the nation—such as individuals who displayed obvious sympathy toward Nazi ideology, who were past or present German army officers, or who had special knowledge of munitions or bomb making—were classed as category A and would be subject to immediate arrest and internment. Individuals who were not judged to pose a serious threat to Britain, but over whom concerns remained, were to be placed into a compromise class known as category B—not to be interned, but forbidden from owning a car, a camera, or a large-scale map, or from traveling more than five miles from their home.

Those considered to be refugees from Nazi oppression, or who had lived in Britain for some time and could produce "evidence of character associations and loyal intent," were judged as category C. They were free to continue living in Britain at liberty, albeit subject to a strict midnight curfew.

Despite extensive guidelines produced for the chairmen of the tribunals, there was sufficient room for interpretation to allow for wildly different regional outcomes for aliens of otherwise similar circumstances. Reigate and Leeds labeled most aliens a category B. The Croydon tribunals opted, almost universally, for category C.

There were no guarantees, however. While those running the tribunals were well-versed in legal matters, a government inquiry later judged that their "[lack of] knowledge of Continental affairs, laws, politics, the sense of the war, its reasons and geography" made them woefully ill-equipped for the task at hand.

"Why did you leave Germany in April 1933," one witness recalled being asked by Ronald Burrows K.C., the chairman of the Aliens Tribunal No. 8, held in London, "[when] Jews could carry on there still in 1933 and 1934?" Besides, Burrows continued, "Did not the Jews advocate the access of Hitler to power?"

Tone-deaf and insulting, the tribunals were often hasty in their pronouncements.

"Very often the chairman did not listen to the alien and sentenced him after two minutes to be interned," wrote one eyewitness. Not only did the tribunals routinely judge individuals as category A for spurious reasons such as, for example, having "friends of the opposite sex without being married to them," the inquiry also found that they lacked the experience to uncover a bona fide Gestapo agent.

It wasn't only the subjects of the tribunals who gave voice to accusations of carelessness. Lionel Birch, the English staff editor of *Picture Post* magazine, accompanied Jewish film producer Fred Weiss from Vienna to give a character reference at his friend's tribunal. Weiss's character was unimpeachable: in 1930 he had produced the anti-Nazi film *The Vagabond*. Weiss had lectured in the United States against Nazi ideology, was married to a Scottish woman, and had, in his back pocket, a written reference from the film censor Lord Tyron.

Birch watched, to his astonishment, as the chairman of Weiss's tribunal refused to read the reference and proclaimed that he did not want to hear from Birch.

"The true Nazi sympathisers had neutral passports or had married English women," said Klaus Hinrichsen, the art historian who was reported by a neighbor who believed the rhythmic tapping of his lovemaking contained a secret Morse message. "Certainly, they were not running around with a passport with a 'J' in it . . . It would have been much too much work to infiltrate real refugee groups."

Eva Neurath, cofounder of the book publisher Thames & Hudson, whose second and third husbands were both destined for internment in Hutchinson camp, put it most straightforward: "[The magistrates] were out of their depth."

Peter's case was heard alongside three others. The men were not allowed legal counsel but could bring a single friend, and could present as much evidence as they had in the form of letters of recommendation from welfare agencies or reputable British subjects to help their case. Peter went alone.

Despite the reputation that Goddard would later develop, that day the judge appeared friendly.

"He talked to me like an uncle or relation might," Peter recalled. "I was a juvenile, a boy."

Goddard's pronouncement was swift and benevolent. The teenager's Certificate of Registration was stamped with the following endorsement: "Refugee from Nazi Oppression. The Holder of this certificate is to be exempted until further order from internment."

For the moment, along with the other 64,243 enemy aliens who were judged to pose no threat to Britain, Peter was free.

In Whitehall, Sir John Anderson, the home secretary and minister of home security, believed that while he had for now managed to strike an even balance between ensuring the security of the realm and maintaining the basic rights of the private individual, the situation might not hold indefinitely. Faced with invasion, would the British people be so accepting of the tens of thousands of foreign nationals living freely among them?

"It is very easy in wartime to start a scare," Anderson wrote in a letter to his father. "People are easily worked up, and a spy scare can be started at any time as a 'stunt.'"

VII

SPY FEVER

At first, Hilde Marchant, star reporter for the *Daily Express*, doubted the sailor's story. Two nights earlier, the man explained, he had stood on the deck of his ship, loaded with British nationals headed to England, and watched as a confetti of parachutes drifted across Rotterdam harbor. Dangling from each silhouetted disk, the sailor insisted, were German soldiers dressed, not in Nazi uniforms, but in women's skirts and blouses.

Hilde, who was born in Hamburg to an English father and German mother, grew up in the north of England before she moved to London to make it as a journalist. Waifish and snub-nosed, her common sense and considerable experience were widely recognized by Fleet Street colleagues—even if, through envy and snobbery, she was also the subject of interminable patronizing remarks. At a time when most women journalists were encouraged by their editors to cover fashion, Hilde was drawn to conflict. She had worked as a foreign correspondent in Spain, France, Poland, Sweden, and Finland in the lead-up to the war, learning to chew gum to steady her nerves during air raids. Later, her eyewitness reports of the blitz of Coventry, during which she climbed the tower of the city's smoldering cathedral, would be issued to British embassies around the world at Winston Churchill's instruction.

Described by one of her editors as "the best woman reporter who ever worked in Fleet Street," Hilde had been poached by the editor of the *Express*, who offered thirty guineas a week plus expenses to defect, five guineas more than the paper's chief reporter. At twenty years old, she was one of the best-paid journalists in London, man or woman. By the time of the Nazi invasion of Holland, Hilde was used to sifting fact from embellishment.

She quizzed other eyewitnesses to check the sailor's story. Not only did they verify that they, too, had seen Nazi parachutists disguised as women, but they also added further outlandish particulars. Some of the paratroopers were disguised as priests, said one. It wasn't clear, another source told Hilde, whether the skirt-wearing paratroopers were men in disguise or women sent as "decoys." But either way, each one carried a submachine gun.

One witness claimed that he watched a paratrooper disguised as a policeman land, then proceed to direct a group of Dutch troops to a neighboring street. When the soldiers rounded the corner, German troops mowed them down with machine-gun fire. Most troubling was the testimony of the survivor who claimed to have seen residents wearing German uniforms creep from their homes. These traitorous individuals, the witness claimed, had previously been declared as refugees.

Any reservations the reporter felt about these reports of refugee spies and blouse-wearing Nazis was surely offset by the fact that Hilde knew these testimonies would make for stupendous copy. On May 13, 1940, two days after the invasion of the Netherlands began, the *Daily Express* published Hilde's story under the headline "Germans Dropped Women Parachutists as Decoys." To provide a little reputational insurance, the newspaper staff added, in small type, a pretext surely designed to prise some distance between Hilde and the claims laid out in her story: "English people, bombed as they left Holland, say . . ."

Peppered throughout Hilde's story, which made page three, was the term "fifth columnist"—which, just a few months earlier, would have been unrecognizable to most of her readers. Hilde was one of the first people to adopt the phrase, coined during the 1936 Spanish Civil

War as shorthand for "traitors poised to support an enemy invasion from within." She had been on assignment in Madrid during the siege of the city, and had, therefore, seen firsthand the havoc that could be caused by such an enemy. The term was immortalized by the American writer Ernest Hemingway in his 1938 play about the siege, *The Fifth Column*. British newspapers had adopted the phrase after the German invasion of Norway in early April 1940, when reports circulated that fifth columnists had been installed in the country to aid the German invasion. By the time Hilde's story ran, there wasn't a reader in Britain unaware of the term or its meaning.

The story's claims of treachery—which expanded the following day to include tales of poisoned wine and chocolates—were, it would transpire, overstated. Still, the image of the double-crossing immigrant would prove indelible, and not only among the readers of newspapers. The British minister to the Dutch government, Sir Nevile Bland, also witnessed the landings of the German paratroopers just before, like Hilde's sailors, he escaped the country via ship. When Bland reached London on May 14, the day after Hilde's story broke, the foreign secretary, Lord Halifax, asked him to draft a report on what he had seen. Bland's account, like those published the day before, was equally vivid and fearful, and inflated to mythic proportions.

Bland titled his account "Fifth Column Menace." The title made plain the document's overarching claim: that the paratroopers were each armed with a list of names of officials and Allied sympathizers to be "shot on sight"—a death list supplied by a secret network of Dutch residents who had passed intelligence to the Germans. "Every German or Austrian servant, however superficially charming and devoted, is a real and grave menace," Bland wrote. Britain should expect similar treatment. When the signal is given to invade Britain, Bland continued, "there will be satellites of the monster all over the country who will at once embark on widespread sabotage and attacks on civilians." Britain, Bland concluded, "cannot afford to take this risk. ALL Germans and Austrians, at least, ought to be interned at once."

Bland's feverish report was widely distributed in Whitehall, where one colleague noted it was "damned good stuff." A copy reached King George VI, who summoned the home secretary, Sir John Anderson, for a meeting at Buckingham Palace.

"You must take immediate action against political Fifth Columnists and other enemies of the State," he reportedly told Anderson. "Men and women."

Having reached the highest levels of the British establishment, the contents of Bland's report were next broadcast by the BBC, lending the rumors the luster of state media endorsement. The news had an immediate and transformative effect on the British public's attitude toward refugees, and Jews in particular, which until now had been broadly characterized by fragile tolerance.

Before May 1940, not a single person interviewed by the polling group Mass-Observation suspected the refugees of espionage or suggested that they should be imprisoned or interned. To that date, only 569 individuals had been interned, either through MI5's initial roundups or as the result of tribunals. Some critics had always maintained that Anderson's policy had been too weak. In April 1940, Colonel Henry Burton, Conservative member for Sudbury, asked members of the House of Commons if it would not be "far better to intern all the lot and then pick out the good ones." This view had begun to spread through the Conservative backbenchers and now, with the news from Holland, it was taken up by the newspapers, which carried the clarion call for mass internment.

"Act! Act! Act! Do It Now!" blared a *Daily Mail* article by G. Ward Price on May 24, arguing that "the rounding up of enemy agents must be taken out of the fumbling hands of local tribunals" and "all refugees . . . should be drafted without delay to a remote part of the country and kept under strict supervision . . . You fail to realise," Ward wrote poisonously, "that every German is an agent."

On May 26, the *Sunday Chronicle* published a story under the headline "The Fifth Column" that stated: "We ought to have interned the lot. We have not interned anything like the lot . . . The letters readers send about Germans who are going free in their own district would make your hair stand on end. Particularly the women."

The reports of the disguised Dutch paratroopers and fifth columnists had hastened and solidified an ongoing shift in attitudes. They had an "immediate and alarming effect" on the public imagination:

> Now the enemy in our midst is easily visualized. The always latent antagonism to the alien and foreigner began to flare up. Nearly everyone, as previous research has shown, is latently somewhat anti-Semitic and somewhat anti-alien. But ordinarily it is not the done thing to express such sentiments publicly. The news from Holland made it quite the done thing, all of a sudden.

A widespread ignorance of the true numbers of foreigners to whom Britain had offered asylum hastened the change in public attitudes. One poll asked British citizens to estimate the number of refugees who had come to Britain from Nazi Germany in the previous six years. Respondents put the number at anywhere between two and four million. The figure was, in fact, just 73,500.

Anti-Semitism contributed to the United States' restrictive policy toward refugees from Nazi oppression, too. There, a bill to admit twenty thousand European children did not advance beyond a congressional committee, where some argued that accepting refugees without their parents went against the laws of God. Such decisions had catastrophic effects. In 1939, President Franklin Roosevelt denied an ocean liner from Hamburg, the MS *St. Louis*, permission to land. Of the 937 passengers aboard, 254—the majority of whom were refugees from Nazi oppression—are known to have subsequently died in the Holocaust.

In Britain, most citizens acknowledged the injustice inherent in mass internment, but felt that it was nevertheless an appropriate, justifiable measure.

"You can't say which is good and which bad," said one respondent to another poll, which found that more than half of people interviewed favored the internment of all enemy aliens. "Some of them is very nice people, but it's safest to pull them all in."

Hysteria smothered logic. Most refugees spoke thickly accented

English, were unaccustomed to British social norms, and would make ineffectual spies. Fifth columnists, if they existed, were far likelier to come from the ranks of British fascists. As the Labour politician Herbert Delaunay Hughes wrote pseudonymously at the time: "It is lamentable how quickly people seem to have forgotten who exactly the refugees are and how it is that they came to this country."

Major Victor Cazalet, the Conservative member for Chippenham, was blunter still. There was, he noted dryly, a "tremendous public demand for the internment of practically everyone whose family has not lived here for a hundred years."

LIKE EVERY OTHER RELOCATION IN his brief life, Peter Fleischmann's moving in with his new employers had gone neither smoothly nor well. The Ripkins's detached house on Downham Crescent was spacious and comfortable compared to his previous rooms in Manchester's slums. Across the road, the expansive Heaton Park provided Peter with space to walk and, after the long days spent toiling in the murk of the basement squinting at old photographs, a place to recalibrate in the evening sunlight.

It was clear, however, that while they appreciated their newest employee's work, the Ripkins were more disheartened on the question of Peter's soul. Before their first meal together, Albert and Gertrude Ripkin bowed their heads in a prayer of blessing for the food. Peter broke the silence to explain that he did not believe in God and would not participate in the grace. Just as his lewd jokes had soured the atmosphere at the dinner table during his brief stay at his uncle's home, now his faithlessness caused disharmony with his employers. As the weeks progressed and Albert and Gertrude realized they were unlikely to gain a convert in Peter, the portions of food they offered him grew smaller, even as they continued to exploit his talents in the workplace.

Peter's experience of provisional kindness was common for many *Kindertransport* children, who were subject to efforts to convert them to whichever stream of Christianity their rescuers followed. Fear, loneliness, and the desire to belong led many Jewish children to convert, although Bertha Bracey and the Quakers were more sensitive, ensuring that their charity was unconditional.

A lack of faith was not the only issue Peter faced. He did not know it, but to save costs, his employers had hired Peter to replace a more expensive artist at the company. When the disgruntled employee learned that he had been replaced by a German refugee who did not have the right to work, he reported Peter to the police, hoping perhaps that the Berliner would be deported. While Peter had begun to speak English with a thick Lancashire accent, it was clear to the officer that he was far from fluent and had been taken advantage of. On December 23, 1939, the date of Peter's eighteenth birthday, the Manchester Employment Exchange stamped his document with permission to work at the job Peter had already held for much of the year.

Despite the decent pay, by the time he received official work clearance, Peter had come to despise the job.

"I'd rather paint shop signs for 25 shillings a week," he'd grumble to colleagues.

The misery of his home and work life was offset by the arrival of a friendship that would come to mark the rest of Peter's life. In the Dickensian murk of the basement, Peter began chatting with an English boy a year or two older named Donald Midgley. When Midgley heard Peter's story—the death of his parents, his escape from Berlin, his uncle's rejection, the judgmental dinners with the Ripkins—he took pity on the bespectacled artist and invited him to stay with his parents in the Yorkshire town of Halifax on the weekends.

The Midgley family was not wealthy, but they were generous and provided the young refugee with his first authentic experience of family since he left his housekeeper's home on the outskirts of Berlin. Like so many benisons in Peter's life, however, the period was fleeting. When Donald was called up to serve, Peter accompanied him to the recruitment center to see if he, too, could join the air force. He was too young. The two men parted ways. Once again, Peter Fleischmann was alone, a refugee with no friends and few connections, living in a country that was becoming, by the week, increasingly hostile toward people like him.

DURING HIS FIRST CABINET MEETING as prime minister, three days after the momentous debate in Parliament that led to the ousting of his predecessor, Winston Churchill agreed to the internment of all male enemy aliens between the ages of sixteen and sixty currently living within the seacoast counties of Britain. This "protected area" was where, in the event of Nazi invasion, a spy could cause significant harm. These men were to be interned regardless of the category the tribunals had bestowed on them a few months earlier.

The following day, on Sunday, May 12, 1940, Scotland Yard's fleet of motorcars roared from police headquarters. Many of the officers dispatched to make the day's arrests had been unaware of their task until they arrived at work that morning.

"The arrests were made so suddenly that the men concerned had no opportunity of making any arrangements," the *Daily Telegraph* reported. By the end of this first mass roundup, around two thousand refugees had been taken into custody and handed to the military authorities for internment.

Three days later, on the morning of Wednesday, May 15, Churchill's War Cabinet met at 10 Downing Street to discuss whether to extend the measures to other areas. The final point on the agenda was titled, simply, "Invasion of Great Britain: Danger from parachutists and Fifth Column elements."

Lord Halifax, the foreign secretary, recounted details from Nevile Bland's report on "the elaborate organisation for co-operation between German parachutists and Fifth Column elements in the Netherlands."

"A German woman," Halifax said, "who had been employed as a maid servant and had returned to Germany, had been landed by parachute with a party of men with the express purpose of leading them to a particular house."

The home secretary, Sir John Anderson, was still opposed to mass internment, a position that he hoped to hold "unless the war begins to go badly." His report, titled "Invasion of Great Britain: Possible Cooperation of a Fifth Column," emphasized that the majority of the seventy-three thousand Germans and Austrians living in Britain were refugees opposed to Hitler. Now, faced with the apparently imminent threat of enemy invasion, and with the newspapers ablaze with reports of foreign spies and fifth columnists patiently awaiting their moment, he was forced to concede that there were "various bodies and groups of persons in this country against whom action would need to be taken," including refugees.

Fear now threatened to trump reason. Through the tribunals established by Anderson, no fewer than 55,457 of those interrogated had been classified as refugees from Nazi oppression, their victimhood verified by the state. Now it seemed these displaced men and women, many of whom had lost their wealth and livelihoods and who were vulnerable, were at risk of imprisonment without further trial. Even the *Manchester Guardian*, usually a staunch defender of civil liberties, lent its voice to the chorus calling for mass internment, stating: "No half measures will do."

In the cabinet meeting that day, Churchill listened to his ministers in silence before issuing his conclusion.

"There should be a very large round-up of aliens and suspected persons in this country," he pronounced. Internment would, he added, "probably be much safer for all German-speaking persons themselves since . . . public temper in this country would be such that such persons would be in great danger if left at liberty."

This argument—that internment was, in fact, in the best interest of the internee—precisely echoed that made by the Nazi officials to justify the arrest of the party's political opponents a few years earlier. In a speech delivered in March 1933, shortly after the opening of Dachau, the first Nazi concentration camp, Heinrich Himmler reasoned: "I felt compelled [to make these arrests] because in many parts of the city there has been so much agitation that it has been impossible for me to guarantee the safety of those particular individuals who have provoked it."

The Nazis used a euphemistic term for this category of arrest—
Schutzhaft (protective custody)—a term that now applied to Britain's
own policy toward Jews. Men and women who had survived arrest in
Germany only to be interned in Britain felt the cruelties of the internment saga more sharply than most; some, such as the Austrian politician Emil Maurer, survived not one but two Germany camps—Dachau
and Buchenwald—only to be sent to the Isle of Man by his supposed
saviors.

Having allowed the popular press to whip up jingoism and hatred,
instead of taking an enlightened lead, the government now used public
opinion as justification for strict measures. The threat posed to national security by the so-called enemy aliens in Britain seemed real. A
surge of public sentiment, combined with the looming threat of enemy
invasion, clouded any sense of moral clarity. Among Londoners "some
sort of neurosis had taken grip," Klaus Hinrichsen noted. "Anyone who
was German was considered to be a Nazi." The refugee organizations
were so desperate to help refugees assimilate, they published a book
filled with advice, urging individuals to "refrain from speaking German in the streets," or from pointing out "how much better this or that
is done in Germany" (even if "it may be true"), and to avoid becoming
conspicuous in "manner or dress." It was not enough. There now came
a crescendo of measures against the refugees.

On May 15, Anderson ordered the arrest of male enemy aliens between the ages of sixteen and sixty who had been judged by the tribunals to be category B, regardless of where they lived. Seven days later, on
May 22, the government added a paragraph to Defense Regulation 18B
granting the home secretary the power to intern any person whom he
believed to be in sympathy with the enemy. That night police arrested
Oswald Mosley, leader of the British Union of Fascists, and thirty-five
of his followers, individuals who would have certainly supported Hitler's invasion of Britain from within. Here, the powers Anderson had
gained had been defensibly used. They also laid the pathway to mass
internment; those with the power to plot a new course were now beyond persuasion.

Britain's strategic position had become precarious and now bordered on disastrous. On May 26, the British Expeditionary Forces began to evacuate from Dunkirk, and the German occupation of the Channel ports laid England open to the menace of direct attack for the first time since Napoleon. The next day, under pressure from the War Office, Anderson agreed to the arrest of all women in category B ("Is not the female of any species generally more dangerous than the male?" Sir Thomas Moore had asked in the House of Commons three days earlier), while the chiefs of staff presented a list of fourteen further recommendations, including a call for the internment of all German and Austrian passport holders resident in the country. On May 28, Belgium capitulated to the Nazis. Now that German units surrounded French troops, an invasion attempt seemed both likely and imminent. Engaged in a helpless retreat on the continent, the chiefs of staff turned their focus to those Germans over whom they still held uncontested power: the refugees.

That day the cabinet approved the proposal that Chamberlain should establish a committee for the preservation of domestic security. Viscount Swinton headed this clandestine group, known as the Home Defense (security) Executive, which held near-unrestricted powers in the name of national defense. Decisions about the fate of refugees had been moved away from the cabinet, from MI5, and from the War Office, and placed in the hands of a tiny group of unelected officials, separate from the framework of democratic accountability.

On May 31, the Home Office sent a letter informing local police constables that they now had the power to arrest and imprison any German and Austrian man or woman of category C. All the diligent work of the previous winter's tribunals had been undone, as well as Britain's centuries-long adherence to the principle of habeas corpus—the right not to be imprisoned without trial. No one in Britain was safe from the threat of immediate arrest and indefinite internment based on their nationality, ethnicity, religion, or political beliefs.

* * *

ON SUNDAY, JUNE 4, WINSTON Churchill, who had been prime minister for less than a month, addressed the House of Commons to announce the government's new powers:

> There is . . . another class, for which I feel not the slightest sympathy. Parliament has given us the powers to put down Fifth Columnist activities with a strong hand, and we shall use those powers . . . without the slightest hesitation until we are satisfied, and more than satisfied, that this malignancy in our midst has been effectively stamped out.

Churchill acknowledged that the orders would affect "a great many people . . . who are the passionate enemies of Nazi Germany." There was, he said, nothing to be done. "I am very sorry for them," he added, "but we cannot . . . draw all the distinctions which we should like to do."

A week later, the day after Italy declared war against Britain, Britain's prime minister ordered the police to "endeavor to round up *all* enemy aliens as quickly as possible." The time for equivocation was over. Those under sixteen and over seventy were to be excluded, as were the infirm. Otherwise, the police were ordered to "collar the lot." Internment was, for the majority, the punishment for exile.

THE REFUGEES' TRANSFORMATION FROM ASYLUM seekers to enemy suspects was complete. A spattering of arrests became a torrent. The writer Rene Levy was one of those arrested. After a miserable week imprisoned at Kempton Park Racecourse, surrounded by a "luxuriant vegetation of barbed wire," he would spend the remainder of the year interned on the Isle of Man. Spy fever was the driving force for the arrests, of course, but Levy noted that these measures also helped the British government to look decisive and strong: "Prisoners taken in the successful raids on the enemy positions in Hampstead and Golders Green were," he wrote drolly, "the biggest haul the British had made up till then."

When word of the mass internment reached Hitler, he seized the opportunity to show how Germany and Britain were not so unalike after all.

"The enemies of Germany are now the enemies of Britain too," he said. "The British have detained in concentration camps the very people we found it necessary to detain. Where are those much-vaunted democratic liberties of which the English boast?"

DOWNHAM CRESCENT WAS DARK AND empty when, in the early hours of July 5, a Black Maria police car pulled up at Albert and Gertrude Ripkin's home. The punky slam of the car door was the only sound in the sleeping street as the two police officers strode up to the house. Peter Fleischmann awoke to the sound of sharp knocking, the purposeful, foreboding sound pronouncing the arrival of authority that he was used to hearing about in Nazi Germany, not Manchester.

Albert Ripkin was not yet up, so Peter tripped down the stairs to open the door. The officer's instruction was curt and urgent.

"Get your clothes," he ordered. "Come with us."

Others arrested that night were given an hour or two to gather their things. No such luxury was afforded to Peter Fleischmann.

Neither soldier nor criminal, Peter, one of ninety aliens and refugees arrested by the Salford police that morning, was denied the civil rights that even convicts enjoy: no charge, no trial, no bail. None of his story mattered: not the fact he had been orphaned and made homeless by the Nazi regime. Not the fact that he was brought to England as a destitute child, nor that he had been carefully interviewed by one of the most senior judges in the land and deemed to pose no security risk to his adoptive country.

In this new reality, subject to the British government's panicked measures, only Peter's nationality—the same nationality the Nazis hoped to strip from all German and Austrian Jews—had led to this nighttime arrest. The teenager sat in the back of a British police car, en route to the Oldham jail. Buffeted along a twisted road by the gale-force winds of geopolitical history, Peter was, once again, rootless, unwelcome, de-homed.

VIII

NIGHTMARE MILL

MAJOR ALFRED JAMES BRAYBROOK SURVEYED the damp crowd while an attendant placed a wooden crate once used to transport oranges at his feet. Without the aid of this makeshift podium, the forty-five-year-old retired army officer whose domain, until recently, stretched no further than the newsagents he owned in suburban London, would struggle to be seen by the crowds of dejected men in front of him. Braybrook climbed onto the crate, steadied himself as it wobbled on the greasy floor, then tucked his marching stick under his arm, stuck out his chest, and took a breath.

Peter Fleischmann watched with quiet amusement. It was as if, the teenager thought, a *Punch* caricature had hopped from the magazine into this disused cotton mill in northern England. The backdrop to the display was anything but cartoonish. Massive, decaying, derelict, Warth Mills cast a brutish silhouette on the Lancashire horizon. Its proprietors had been forced by recession to abandon the premises—built in 1891 on the banks of the River Irwell—ten years earlier.

Warth Mills had been abandoned in haste: the floor, a mixture of cobblestones and wood, was viscid and slippery with old machine oil, the smell of which mixed with the acrid stench of the canal that ran alongside the building and stuck in the throat. Transmission belts hung like nooses from rafters. Crankshafts, partly dismounted, dangled at Damoclean angles. Clumps of rotting, moldy cotton decorated the floor, and shafting cobwebs suggested that skittering monsters ruled the shadows. A series of cast-iron columns crowned with intricate Corinthian capitals, high up in the vaulted murk, supported a glass roof, the sole source of light inside the building, which was pocked with broken panes that let the drizzle indoors.

The building, three stories tall at one section, had sat empty and dampening until the British army moved in on June 5, 1940. Warth Mills was to become a transit camp for internees. The first men arrived seven days later. They'd had ample time to take in their new home's thuggish frontage. From Bury station the internees were marched the four miles or so along Manchester Road to the building. It was a walk of shame; hostile onlookers watched the men, in what was the first time, for most, that they had been paraded in front of the public as prisoners.

"To be marched like a bloody prisoner of war, with people watching . . . that really hurt," recalled Peter Katz, a pastor in his mid-fifties who had been one of the first arrivals. "I felt degraded."

When Peter Fleischmann arrived four weeks later, Warth Mills was packed with internees. There were dozens of men loitering behind two rows of barbed wire in the small gangway that had been left around the walls for exercise. While armed guards from the Lancashire Regiment led Peter and the others through the litter-strewn entrance, the men grimaced and shouted from behind the wire. The whole thing, as Peter put it, was "a nightmare."

Now, in the 150-by-120-foot spinning hall, which could accommodate five hundred people, Peter and the others were gathered into groups of twenty-five to listen to Braybrook's speech. The commandant outlined what was expected of the internees, as well as the broader purpose of the camp as a temporary holding place for them while they were processed to be sent on to permanent camps. An interpreter translated what was said into German. Penned in and perspiring under the weight of confusion and luggage, a few audience members fainted and had to be roused and supported back up to their feet by those close to them. As Braybrook's speech wound to a stentorian conclusion, Peter felt an arm settle on his shoulder.

"Don't worry," a voice said. Peter turned and saw the speaker was dressed differently than the other loitering refugees. Most wore suits and jackets. This man appeared to be a sailor, a member of a captured German U-boat crew, Peter assumed. Via one of the thousands of administrative errors that soon characterized the organization of mass internment, it seemed German POWs had been mixed in with the clerks and bakers, the farmhands and chefs.

"We will soon win the war," the man assured the young Jew, "and set you free again."

A phalanx of British army officers sat behind a row of tables, ready to check the men's belongings. The internees lined up behind ropes. Each man smelled the stench of heavy disinfectant and listened to the sounds of captive men while he waited to be called forward. When Peter's turn came, he approached, and a private grabbed his bag and tipped the contents onto the table. As the soldier sifted through Peter's belongings, a seated officer thumbed through his wallet. Peter assumed the men were searching for any items that might be used as weapons, but it soon became clear that anything of value was in danger of confiscation. Just as the Nazis had systematically robbed many of these men of their valuables, so the British officers now took chocolate, cigarettes, writing paper, and typewriters, distributing these items among themselves in full view of the looted.

The confiscation of razor blades was justifiable, and a case could possibly be made for the seizure of gold sovereigns to preclude black-market trading. Other choices seemed indefensible: watches, books, medicine. One soldier took insulin from a diabetic. For some internees, this was a familiar experience. Many had passed through Ascot and Kempton Park, holding camps that Major Braybrook had also overseen. At Kempton Park, a young tailor, Kurt Treitel, lost both his watch and money to larcenous officers.

The breach of privacy revealed not only what each internee had considered sufficiently important to pack during the harried moments of his arrest, but also the range of vocations represented among the captives. Doctors watched bewilderedly as the soldiers pocketed their stethoscopes. Academics argued with the soldiers that they should be allowed to keep their textbooks. Artists pleaded to keep their drawing paper. It was clear that the newly instated internment policy respected neither status nor achievement. Here, on the sticky floor, the Oxbridge don was subject to the same indignities as the orphan apprentice.

For many of the men, the ransacking crowned a brief period that had devastatingly transformed their view of Britain, and their place within it.

"[We] went around breathing injustice and feeling very sore about all kinds of things," wrote Uri Hirsch, who was arrested alongside a number of other young Orthodox Jews, most of whom had come to England via the *Kindertransport* program. "Since gloom only serves to increase one's loquacity, [we] soon became unbearable to ourselves."

Some of the men at Warth Mills had already experienced great drama in their escapes to England. Two days after the war's outbreak, Gotfried Huelsmann successfully crossed the German-Dutch border disguised as a greengrocer, driving a van filled with vegetables. To be interned by the country of their salvation, after such acts of derring-do, was hurtful; to be robbed by those in whom they had staked their trust, unthinkable.

"I remember very clearly—and this was the dominating thought— the feeling of insult," noted Claus Moser, who later became chairman of the Royal Opera House. "The whole operation was panicky and cruel."

THE GUARDS LED PETER AND the others up shadowy staircases and through the mill's catacomb-like corridors to a hall on the ground floor that had been converted into a kitchen. Once the internees had been fed porridge and tea from tin containers, the guards ordered them to collect their beds. Peter picked through a horsehair blanket, so full of lice and chewed by vermin that it was almost unusable. Some men requested newspapers to wrap around their arms and legs, believing this would provide a more effective guard against the cold. When the internees were then told that they were to lie on old wooden boards, an argument broke out.

"You will not treat us as criminals," shouted one of the incensed internees, who demanded that the men be allowed to take some of the spare straw mattresses from the sick bay. At length one of the officers relented and led the men to a storeroom filled with palliasses, ordering them to take three.

Carrying his blanket under one arm and his bag under the other, Peter searched for an empty space in the main room to lay his bed, while sentries stood watching from the perimeter with bayonets fixed to their rifles. He spied a vacant spot where, in the next space along, a striking-looking man with a craggy head and giant hands sat removing the slats from his bed in slow, patient movements. Peter squeezed along the narrow, fourteen-inch walking space between each line of beds and watched.

At first, Peter assumed that the man, who looked like a craftsman from the Middle Ages, was sharpening the slats to make a weapon. When the man noticed the teenager watching him work, he introduced himself as Ernst Müller-Blensdorf. A doctor's son, forty-four-year-old Müller-Blensdorf was a sculptor of considerable repute. He had fled to Norway after Hitler's regime took aim at modern art, classing any work that did not conform to Nazi aesthetic ideals as "degenerate." Artists who wanted to continue working in ways that were not sanctioned by the party were forced to emigrate. Müller-Blensdorf's exile was hastened after Nazi Party supporters destroyed his workshop, where he had been working on a memorial to the Norwegian polar explorer Fridtjof Nansen.

Müller-Blensdorf was familiar with life in captivity; he had spent four years of the First World War interned in South Africa after the capture of the freighter on which he crewed. A committed pacifist, the stone war memorials he carved in Germany avoided the glorification of war, instead representing grieving mothers and children—work that was systematically smashed by the Hitler Youth, who then buried the pieces in different locations.

Peter watched the sculptor use the tools sharpened from the metal slats to carve the wooden parts of the bed. The work was primitive, but in Müller-Blensdorf's massive hands there was the unmistakable flex of a master craftsman. Internment may have derailed the orphan's ambitions, but it had brought him into the orbit of a genuine artist.

* * *

ANY SENSE OF WONDER AND surprise at the evidence that Warth Mills might house, among its two thousand–odd inhabitants, gifted men was offset by the suffocating conditions of the building and the gnawing uncertainty of one's fate. To ensure no skin touched the filthy blankets, no man undressed to sleep. Besides, the oppressive atmosphere meant that every internee felt the need to be ready at any given moment to respond to an emergency. As darkness fell, the stifling, echoing atmosphere created a sense of haunted unreality.

On his first night, a young actor, Otto Tausig, was awoken by the cries of a group of German monks who had been drenched by rainwater pouring into the building through the broken ceiling.

"Water!" shouted one of the monks.

"Fire!" replied a jokester from somewhere deep in the murk.

This cry startled a man with learning difficulties, who should have been exempted from internment. In a panic, the man stood to his feet and began to run through the hall, trampling on the beds and bodies of those on the floor. In the ensuing chaos, an older internee who had volunteered to escort anybody who needed the bathroom to and from the hall, lit his candle.

"Put that light out!" screamed a guard.

Individuals suffering from serious illness were supposed to be exempt from internment, yet Warth Mills was home to more than fifty men who were "gravely ill," including individuals suffering from tuberculosis, diabetes, and cancer. Separated from their instruments and drugs, the German doctors among the internees were unable to provide much in the way of comfort or relief to these men.

One of the camp's most famous inmates, Rudolf Olden, had collapsed soon after his arrival to the mill. When the Oxford professor Paul Jacobsthal visited Olden's bed, he was astonished by the depravity of Warth Mills' sick bay.

Olden was a lawyer and journalist who had become one of Germany's leading public voices in his former role as political editor of the

Berliner Tageblatt, one of Germany's two leading liberal newspapers and home to a constellation of star journalists. In the mid-1920s Kurt Tucholsky, a commentator on the intellectual life of the Weimar Republic, described Olden as one of the two hundred or so "really significant" men in Berlin. No person in Warth Mills better exemplified the absurdity and impulsiveness of mass internment. Not only was Olden so vociferously anti-Nazi that the party had revoked his German citizenship, but also, prior to the war's outbreak, he had been recruited by British Intelligence to write propaganda scripts to be broadcast to Germany. Olden's prescence in the depraved conditions of Warth Mills' sickroom was, Jacobsthal wrote in his diary, "easily the most depressing sight in the camp."

IN WARTH MILLS TWO THOUSAND internees shared a single bathtub and eighteen water taps—a limitation that, soon enough, forced almost every man to give up on shaving and encouraged some to rise as early as four o'clock in the morning in order to avoid the mass hustle for the facilities. Laundry could be washed in an empty room but without soap or drying facilities, clothes and blankets often emerged as dirty as before. There was no sewer system in place, and the lavatories amounted to sixty buckets housed outside, beneath an oblong tent. As the day progressed, the stench became unbearable. The latrines became so choked that, toward the end of the day, men would simply relieve themselves in a quiet corner. Jacobsthal described seeing "men of European reputation in an act which is not normally performed in public."

The undignified lavatorial arrangements showed internment as a leveler: the eminent must live as the insignificant. Braybrook's soldiers offered a reward to anyone willing to pull on the protective clothing and volunteer for the retch-inducing work of transferring the contents of the latrine buckets to a neighboring cesspool. Ernst Manasse, a thirty-five-year-old farmhand who had been arrested and brought to the mill from Wilcote Grange Farm in Oxfordshire, volunteered in exchange for the luxury of a shower-bath and a special meal. In this upturned world order, the cleaner outranked the professor. The old hierarchies failed to map to this new reality.

These rudimentary cleaning measures were considered, by the numerous German doctors among the inmates, to be insufficient to ward off disease. They wrote and cosigned a memorandum of complaint to Major Braybrook. Dr. Simon Isaac, a former professor at the University of Frankfurt who had overseen makeshift hospitals on the Russian Front, wrote that he had never seen a place less fit for the accommodation of human beings. It was a week before the internees were given lime to pour into the lavatories to stave off dysentery.

Warth Mills, or "Wrath Mill," as one internee revealingly misspelled it, was, for most of the men, home for only a week before they were moved to one of the permanent camps. The experience still managed to leave an indelible impression.

"Never," wrote Paul Jacobsthal, "have I spent a week in a place and left it with the feeling of a month." The academic claimed that he never forgot "the smallest detail" of this "hellish labyrinth," which reminded him of the Italian painter Giovanni Piranesi's etchings of imaginary prisons filled with impossible stairwells and looming gallows.

To be imprisoned in a building "not even fit for beasts," as another internee wrote, had a profound effect on the men's view of the country that had offered them sanctuary. "Many [have] ceased to believe in the British spirit of humanity which before they had acclaimed," he continued.

The indignities of isolation from friends and relatives, meager food rations, wet palliasses, lice, and inadequate sanitary arrangements led many internees to draw parallels between the mill and the Nazi concentration camps from which they had fled. A former member of the German Foreign Office held in the mill claimed conditions were much worse than those of the notorious French prisoner of war reprisal camps he experienced during the First World War. According to an official Ministry of Information report, two men, both of whom had previously been incarcerated in Nazi concentration camps, died by suicide.

With the grim realization that, when it came to the treatment of prisoners at least, the British did not appear so different from the Nazis, many men glumly accepted their fate, settling into a fug of fatalism. There were some, however, of a rowdier temperament who chose to protest against their situation. Hermann Fechenbach was another artist of repute among Warth Mills' population. Fechenbach, a painter from an ultrareligious family in the small town of Bad Mergentheim who worked in a style known as *Neue Sachlichkeit*—New Objectivity—had already endured a great many setbacks before he washed up at the mill. While serving Germany during the First World War, he was the only survivor of a grenade attack that resulted in the amputation of his left leg.

Temperament and circumstance made Fechenbach an irritable internee, quick to hold a grudge, slow to cool and, as one fellow internee put it, "permanently slighted by almost anybody." Rather than acquiesce to his treatment, the painter announced that he was staging a hunger strike to protest about conditions. It wasn't difficult to abstain from the camp's meager and miserable meals. Without a dining area, food was eaten in the men's billowing dormitories. Breakfast consisted of coffee or tea without sugar and bread without jam. Lunch usually consisted of stew, beans, and rice—occasionally herring. Without soap to wash the bowls, the flavor of herring would infuse the next day's food.

"How could you get rid of the taste from the metal bowl with earth as the only detergent?" wondered the Warth Mills internee Otto Tausig.

"We were always hungry," recalled another internee. Thirsty, too: "We were warned not to drink too much of the water, as it was not drinking water." Still, Fechenbach's decision to abandon this welcome interruption to the gnawing mundanity of the daily routine was courageous, if short-lived. To prevent the mutiny from spreading, he was arrested and taken to cells in Liverpool, to await shipment to the Isle of Man.

THE FULL DEPRAVITY AND HORROR of the Holocaust was yet to be fully revealed to those who had successfully fled Germany prior to the war. And while the ultimate purpose of the British internment camps and the Nazi concentration camps differed, the internees were not the only ones to draw comparisons between the physical conditions at the institutions. Third parties also bore witness to the psychological and material indignities visited upon the refugees.

Mass internment had swept in a cataclysmal tide of novel issues for the refugee organizations at Bloomsbury House. Overnight, their focus switched from seeking employment and housing for refugee families to a mass of personal problems arising from internment: the storing of furniture, the sending on of clothes, the settling of businesses, paying small debts, and answering inquiries from anxious parents about their children.

To mark the shift in focus and demand, the various refugee organizations combined to form a Central Department for Interned Refugees, with Bertha Bracey as its chairperson. The committee met, for the first time, on June 13 1940. Its remit was simple: to advocate for interned refugees, regardless of race or creed, and to campaign for adequate conditions, sufficient provisions, and swift release.

One of Bertha's first jobs in this new role was to review the conditions in which internees were being held. On July 10, 1940, a few days after Peter arrived at Warth Mills, Bertha sent her friend and colleague William R. Hughes to carry out an inspection. Hughes was better prepared to inspect conditions than practically any other person in Britain at the time; in 1935 he had visited Sachsenburg, a Nazi concentration camp for dissidents established in an abandoned four-story mill in Saxony. That same year he had prepared a report for one of Hitler's secretaries calling for the release of internees. Hughes was appalled to see the parallels between Warth Mills and the Nazi camp, and how, at both locations, inmates "brooded in discomfort."

Hughes spent five hours touring the camp. He recorded that, apart from the group of German merchant seaman, the majority of the eighteen hundred internees were "friendly aliens of class 'C', ranging from Boy Scouts of sixteen to elderly Oxford professors and well-known men like Rudolf Olden." Hughes was unflinching in his assessment of the camp, which he described as dirty, overcrowded, and "certainly worse than any I have seen." Heavy rain the previous night had contributed to the dour conditions, which Hughes described as "cruel and punitive."

The Quaker described the men he spoke to—who had "no news, hardly a book among them, no occupation, no visits, no opportunity to help themselves"—as "almost uniformly miserable and indignant." The camp, Hughes concluded in his report, should be "cleared at once" and permanently closed.

Hughes's dismay was further compounded when he learned that scores of Warth Mills' internees had previously been held in Nazi camps, only to experience the same treatment at the hands of their supposed rescuers.

"I saw you in Sachsenburg," said one internee as he approached Hughes. Several more claimed that the conditions they had experienced in Dachau were "better than in Bury."

FOR PETER, THE MISERY OF Warth Mills was as much psychological as it was physical. The presence of German sailors led to speculation that internees might be classed as prisoners of war and thereby exchanged against British prisoners in Germany. The thought of being returned to the country from which he had fled, by the very authorities who had promised him sanctuary and refuge a few months earlier, caused considerable distress to Peter and the other refugees. Some even put the question to a visiting representative from the Red Cross, who returned with a response from the commandant that "the question was not yet decided."

Major Braybrook sensed the opportunity to turn the internees' preoccupation with their release to his advantage. While Whitehall had promised to review the cases of every internee in order to release those they judged, beyond all reasonable doubt, to pose no threat to Britain, the mechanisms, guidelines, and forms needed to begin this process were weeks, if not months, away. Braybrook sidestepped this administrative vacuum and announced from his orange crate that any internee interested in making an application for release could do so using whatever scrap of paper they could find. The suggestion caused a rush of frenzied activity; some men scrawled their arguments on scraps of toilet paper. Braybrook's proposal, however, was a bad-faith ploy simply to keep the captives occupied. He threw away every application that reached his office.[*]

Braybrook's behavior—for which he would be later called to account—had one minor positive effect.

"After Warth Mills," as one man put it, "anything was alright."

In the second week of July 1940, Peter was told to collect his few meager possessions and report to the duty officer. Any hope that this was all a terrible misunderstanding—that the British authorities had acted rashly and would isolate refugees from Nazi sympathizers, reverse their decision, and release anyone already declared as harmless by tribunals—was gone. The question became, simply, where next? To another camp with another corrupt commandant or, worse still, to another country in ships forced to run the gauntlet of the U-boat–infested Atlantic, separated from friends and family somewhere across the distant horizon?

Again, serendipity worked against the young orphan. He was told that he was destined for yet another temporary holding camp, close to the railway city of Crewe. Müller-Blensdorf, Fechenbach, and a host of other artists, those with whom Peter had just started to become acquainted, were headed to the Isle of Man, to become the first residents of the newest camp on the island. Once again, Peter had been diverted from the people to whom he felt drawn, the vocation to which he felt called. For now, the island and all it would come to represent, remained distant.

---

[*] Braybrook was not the only British officer accused of foiling internees' formal applications for release. Evidence presented for a government inquiry into tribunals and internment describes an incident in which Colonel Blimps, commandant of Seaton camp, summoned an internee to his office and, in front of him, tore up the man's application for release with the remark: "Go back to Germany."

PART TWO

"Never before or since have I met such an
extraordinary collection of people in such a small place."

Fred Uhlman

THE MISTED ISLE

THE ISLAND
JULY 12, 1940

WHENEVER AN UNFAMILIAR BOAT SAILS into the Isle of Man's waters, so the legend goes, Manannán mac Lir, son of the sea, necromancer, the first ruler, stands atop the tallest mountain and unfurls his great cloak, the *féth fíada*. As the garment settles, the island's cliffs and shores, hills and hamlets melt from sight, like a photograph undeveloping. Far below, among the white-maned, champing waves, the ship's skipper sails by, and the island is once again spared the touch of foreign feet.

There was no such meteorological ruse tonight. Forced to follow in the zigzagged wake of a minesweeper, the vessel carrying Klaus Hinrichsen, a twenty-eight-year-old art historian from Lubeck and around a hundred other foreigners made slow-patterned progress. A journey that in peacetime conditions took a little over two and a half hours would tonight take four. There was no doubt where it was headed.

The atmosphere on the boat was partylike. Someone had smuggled a guitar aboard and the lower deck resounded with the sound of young men singing the hit songs of the day. Not everyone appreciated the revelry. A group of older men glared accusingly at the youngsters: How could anybody embrace frivolity amid such indignity? These internees preferred, instead, to sit in anticipatory grief.

It was the height of blazing summer; in Liverpool, Hinrichsen and the other passengers had boarded the ship bound for the island at dusk. His arrest a few days earlier had been farcical. When the police knocked on the front door of the boardinghouse where he lived in the leafy north London area of Hampstead, Hinrichsen had been out at work.

"We have come to arrest Walter Bergmann," the officer explained to Hinrichsen's bewildered landlady. Bergmann, however, had already been taken the previous day.

"Any other Germans living here?" the officer asked glumly.

The landlady offered up Hinrichsen's name to the officers, who duly returned to collect him that evening.

On the Liverpool dockside any sense that he was here as the result of clerical error, rather than in his new degrading status as an enemy alien and possible spy, was corrected when a group of young Liverpudlians began to shout abuse and hurl stones, accusing Hinrichsen and the others of being fifth columnists. On the ship, only the youngsters seemed able to shrug off any feelings of resentment or disappointment at being treated as enemies of their adoptive country.

One of the younger guards used the time to disassemble and clean his rifle. Hinrichsen and a few others watched the young man struggle to fit everything back together again. Some offered suggestions until, finally, one of the refugees gently took the weapon from the guard and, with a practiced hand, reassembled and returned it to the soldier. It was the first of many signs to come that the relationship between captives and captors on this island would be far from typical.

As Hinrichsen explored the ship, he spotted, crouched under one of the lifeboats, a striking man with spiked, mouse-colored hair and rimless glasses. He was carefully drawing in a small red notebook. Hinrichsen took a breath of salty air and said hello.

The man introduced himself as Erich Kahn, an expressionist painter from Stuttgart. Though he was handsome and fresh-faced, the artist also appeared to carry a world-weariness beyond his thirty-five years. It was a shrewd observation; Kahn, who was a young prodigy and graduate of the Stuttgart Arts and Crafts school, had only recently emerged from Welzheim, a particularly brutal Nazi concentration camp. Having escaped one injustice, he was beset with anxiety as he now entered another. Kahn explained to Hinrichsen that he had positioned himself by the lifeboats as, in the event of a torpedo strike, he wanted to be first to safety.

Hinrichsen warmed to the anxious man, whose sketch suggested to the art historian a major talent.[*] Which other luminaries, the art historian wondered, might be counted among this haggard boatload?

THE SHIP PULLED INTO DOUGLAS harbor at ten o'clock at night. Six weeks earlier on May 27, Bertha Bracey had watched the arrival of the first 823 captives, the first internees sent to the island since the First World War. Like the furious Liverpudlians who had seen Hinrichsen off, many of the islanders had hurled insults and clods of earth. Others, anticipating imminent invasion by the Wehrmacht, took a more self-interested approach. One cried out: "Be kind to us when the others arrive."

Even the camp commandants were seemingly yet to appreciate what kind of men had been sent to their nascent camps. One was overheard saying to his adjutant, in a puzzled voice: "I never knew so many Jews were Nazis."

The attitude of the Manx islanders reflected that of their leaders. A local politician, E. W. Fargner, had summed up prevailing suspicions on the island during a session at the island's parliament, Tynwald: "They plead persecution; they tell us they had to flee from Germany; they assure us they are now anti-Nazi. And we, who are the most gullible people in the world, believe it . . ." The governor of the Isle of Man had endorsed his colleague's comments, adding theatrically: "There is only one good Hun: a dead Hun."[†]

---

[*] Hinrichsen's judgment was sound; after the war the eminent art critic Professor J. P. Hodin, winner of the first international prize for art criticism at the Venice Biennale, described Kahn as "undoubtedly one of the best artists in [Britain]."

[†] There were some notable exceptions. A Mrs. Gribbon, who lived at 1 Upper Church Street, less than a mile from Hutchinson camp, offered accommodations for the wives of prisoners who

A combination of the late hour and the waning novelty of the incoming ships laden with foreigners meant there was no crowd of locals to watch and jeer as Hinrichsen and the others disembarked. In the gloaming twilight the internees struggled to locate their belongings, then began to crunch up the steep road into the deserted murk.

Earlier that day the governor had issued a regulation forbidding public access to the roads that bordered Hutchinson Square. The internees marched through dead streets. Presently, the men arrived at a long stretch of double-barbed-wire fencing, ending at a high gate on the corner of Drury Terrace and Marathon Road. Under spotlights they filed through the gate, flanked by soldiers bearing fixed bayonets.

A smartly uniformed man emerged from the gloom. The officer, Regimental Sergeant Major Ambrose Harry Potterton, was a former constable for the Metropolitan Police and one-time head porter of the prestigious Dolphin Square apartment block in London. Gesticulating with his brass baton—a gift, he claimed, from Indian natives—Potterton briskly counted Hutchinson's first prisoners as they filed past, occasionally halting the line to divide the men into smaller groups.

When the boisterous youngsters who had sung songs passed Potterton, he distributed the boys among the other groups to dilute the risk of troublemaking. Hinrichsen calculated that there were only enough men to fill three of the houses, around thirty-five men per building. With a certain professional interest, as well as a natural human inclination to support a man who seemed so bereft, the young art historian stood close to Erich Kahn. The ploy worked: they were placed in the same group, to be billeted together in House 3.

Potterton selected one man in each set to function as housefather. For Hinrichsen's group, he chose a foreign correspondent for a German newspaper who was dressed in the kind of smart blazer and gold buttons that suggested he was management material. Potterton announced that morning roll call would take place at 0730 hours sharp,

---

came to the island to visit their husbands, and refused to accept any payment from those women who stayed in her home.

after which the internees would meet the camp commander for "P" camp's official opening. Armed soldiers escorted each group to their appointed house.

As they filed in through the front door, Hinrichsen noticed that there were no curtains and that, while the majority of the lightbulbs had been removed, those that remained had been daubed with red paint.

"Blimey," said one of his housemates. "We have been billeted in a brothel."

FORTY-TWO OF THE FIFTY BOARDINGHOUSES within the barbed-wire perimeter of Hutchinson camp had been set aside for the accommodation of internees. They were similarly built, with nine small rooms (including an attic bedroom), a fifteen-by-fifteen-square-foot common room with two tables, a kitchen, bathroom, and toilet. The house was frowsy and sparsely furnished, but livable in, and had running water. There was even a small garden to the front and rear, an astounding luxury to those men who had come from Warth Mills.

The table was laden with sandwiches, and soon a sizable kettle was put on to boil. First, however, there was the issue of sleeping arrangements. The army had placed two double beds in each of the rooms on the first and second floors intended to serve three men each. There was no linen; instead, internees aged fifty-five or under were given two horse blankets; those over the age of fifty-five were allocated three. It was up to the men to decide who slept where.

It was immediately clear that the journalist whom Potterton had selected as housefather had no leadership skills. An elderly Austrian followed him around the house, complaining that as a former military officer, he should not be expected to share a bed. Meanwhile, the younger men moved their bags into the top-floor rooms without discussion, dismantled the bedsteads, and placed the parts in a loft recess. Then they spread the mattresses on the floor in such a way that they formed a continuous carpet suitable for both walking over, sleeping on, and staging pillow fights.

While the other residents argued over who would sleep where, a distraught and elderly retired doctor boldly announced that he was headed home. He strode out of the house and up to the fence where, as he attempted to prize apart the wires, his white beard became entangled in the barbs. When he heard the commotion, Hinrichsen and his new housemates dashed outside. Rather than aid the trapped doctor, the housefather—perhaps fearing that he would be punished for failing to maintain order—admonished the elderly man for leaving the house during curfew. Some of the young housemates snipped at the man's beard, while, on the other side of the fence, the guards held up torches to guide their hands.

Hinrichsen listened to the creaks and groans as the house settled on its frame. Just as he was drifting off, he again heard manic commotion. Frustrated by his fruitless search for a sleeping tablet, one of the housemates had begun scratching the red paint from one of the lightbulbs with a kitchen knife. Noticing the glow of white light, the air-raid wardens had raced to the house and unscrewed the bulb from its holding.

At last, calm fell. On the top floor, the younger men cracked open the skylight and watched the stars through the gap from their sea of mattresses. There was, for the young men, the frisson of an unexpected holiday, even adventure, to the day's happenings. The older men, who better understood the precariousness and uncertainty of their situation—imprisoned without charge or trial, subject to the outrageous accusation of being a member of the regime that precipitated their exile, and with no idea how long they would be held—found it harder to sleep. These were holiday homes, but this was no holiday.

THE MELLOW, INSISTENT CALL OF a bugle, the signal for the morning's roll call, woke Hinrichsen at 0730 hours. He shuffled from his bunk and lined up with the other housemates in the front garden, in untidy rows of six. The newly appointed housefather, still wearing his blazer, repeatedly counted the men in his charge, arriving each time at a different number.

"Start by counting yourself, at the end count yourself again, and then deduct one," suggested one of the boys from the top floor, a mathematics student named Werner. The housefather dubiously tried the method and reliably arrived at thirty residents with each counting.

Soon RSM Potterton arrived at House 3, flanked by a corporal with a clipboard. Ignoring the housefather's count, the officer began his own count while Potterton explained to the housemates that, at eleven o'clock sharp, every internee was to gather at the highest point of the quadrangle for an address by the commandant. Satisfied with the count, the soldiers moved to the next house, leaving Hinrichsen to explore the confines of his new community.

HUTCHINSON CAMP CONSISTED OF TWO parallel rows of houses to the west side of a sizable grassy rectangular area, and one row to the east side of the square. The bordering pavement fell inside the barbed wire, while the road fell outside, remaining accessible to the residents of nearby houses. The lawn gently sloped toward the Irish Sea, a decent stretch of which was visible beyond the rows of red-tiled roofs that led down, like a coastal shelf, to Douglas harbor. There the men spied a saluting lighthouse and, beyond that, Conister Rock, a tiny reef that holds a baby castle built to provide shelter to the shipwrecked—"a tower of refuge," as William Wordsworth wrote in 1833 during his visit to the island, "built for the else forlorn." On a clear day it was possible to just make out the Cumbrian coastline, an alluring horizon for any man who longed to escape.

Flower beds, shrubs, and the odd lonesome tree punctuated the terraced lawn, which was almost as long and wide as a soccer field. The area was well-kept, with stone seats and wooden banks, an orderliness that bespoke the lightly menacing aspiration of a middle-class English garden.

Forty-two of the houses that bordered the square were allocated for the accommodation of internees although, today, most stood empty. Numbers 34 and 35 had been prepared as the camp hospital, while four other addresses had been set aside for, respectively, the camp laundry, the canteen and chapel, the shower (or "decontamination" block), and, most significantly, the "Office House," which would, in coming days, assume the multifunctional role of post office, bank, library, and much more.

The houses dated from the late 1800s. Hydrangeas bloomed in every front garden, while palm trees stood, drawn tall and frondy from the ground by the warm winds of the Gulf Stream. In peacetime, each building housed ten lodgers, a capacity that had been ambitiously tripled for the internees.

The buildings' older proprietors remembered the chaos and confusion of internment during the previous war. They had balked at the news their houses were to be again requisitioned in this war. Others reluctantly welcomed the arrival of these curious-looking foreigners whose room and board would be paid for by the British government—albeit at a low rate—providing some meager recompense for the wartime loss of tourism.

Since the inaugural race in 1907, the Isle of Man had become synonymous with the Tourist Trophy, a series of motorcycle races staged on its serpentine public roads. The event attracted both competitors and paying spectators from around the world. War had canceled what had become one of the most important and profitable weeks on the calendar.

"Finally," wrote one local journalist in May of the news that the grim business of internment was, once again, coming to the island, "[a] welcome indication that . . . a move is being made towards replacing something of the loss entailed by the cessation of the visiting industry." The boarding-house owners would have to find furnished accommodations into which they could move, but at least, the journalist added naively, "there is no intention to repeat the large-scale internments of the 1914–18 war."

JUST BEFORE ELEVEN O'CLOCK, HINRICHSEN made his way to the top end of the lawn. More internees appeared to have arrived in the camp throughout the morning; the gathered crowd now numbered 415 men. Through the barbed-wire fence that ran along Hutchinson Square Road he could see the commandant's office, and to the right of that, the intelligence officer's building, both situated in their own secluded compound. Storerooms filled with provisions occupied the remainder of the space within this segregated area, accessible via the camp's north gate.

At eleven sharp, RSM Potterton and a group of officers marched into the camp ahead of Hutchinson's commandant, Captain Hubert Daniel. The internees craned to see the man in charge; everyone knew well how the character of the commandant defined the camp's culture. Captain Daniel, compactly built, middle-aged, had an air of easy authority. During the First World War he had delivered food to the frontline trenches. There, among the gaunt and horrified men, he had caught smallpox. He was nursed by a woman from the Voluntary Aid Detachment who, in 1916, became his wife. No longer fit to fight, Danny, as he was known to his friends, became the director of National Service, handling army recruitment for the Manchester area. He carried these people-management skills into his professional life, first at the paper importer Westwall, then when he founded his own paper merchants in 1922. After a stint at the advertising firm Lever Brothers, where he ran promotions for the Wembley Exhibition Centre, working on campaigns for a seawater aquarium and Pears Palace of Beauty, he managed a fleet of no fewer than 750 ice cream tricycles across London. Captain Daniel was used to large-scale administration of people.

When war broke out again he had returned to the world of advertising, working at the consumer goods giant Unilever, commuting to work from his home in Putney in south London. In January 1940, he was recalled to the army. A few months later, Danny, his wife, and their two sons arrived at the island, where his seniors believed his talent for management would be well-suited for the task of internment.

Another factor, unknown to his superiors, made Daniel an ideal candidate for the role of caring for men who had lost everything. His father had died when Daniel was three, and his mother when he was eight (his wife, Margery, was also an orphan by the time they met). While tragedy had surely contributed to the officer's drinking habit, a longing for relationships also made him personable and eager to be liked. As the men would soon discover, Captain Daniel would rule Hutchinson not with an iron fist, but with an open hand.

"As Officer-in-Charge of this Internment camp, I want to assure you that I am responsible for your safety and well-being, and that you will be treated in accordance with the Geneva Convention," Captain Daniel began, his voice carrying to the assembled crowd.

Having been stationed on the island for several weeks, it was clear he had considered the general character of the average internee more closely than his superiors in Whitehall. The boys in their uniforms, the limping elderly, the well-dressed businessmen, the ruffle-haired intelligentsia, the religious men wearing skullcaps or fur hats in midsummer: either the Nazis had orchestrated a comically inventive set of disguises for their spies or, much more likely, the British authorities had arrested thousands of men who were exactly as they seemed: innocents tangled in the mess of live history.

"To avoid becoming demoralized by idleness and boredom, it is most important to stay physically and mentally alert," he said. "This square is ideal for exercises and especially for running any distance. I will contact my colleagues at the other camps on this island to arrange football matches." The commandant then recommended that internees who were fluent in English teach those who were not, and pointed out that, as there were several pianos in the requisitioned houses, musicians might consider arranging performances.

Daniel's understanding that he was not, in fact, commandant of a camp filled with dangerous agitators had clearly softened his rhetoric. To the gathered internees, their chief jailor seemed both "humane and sincere."

"It is important not to submit to apathy," Daniel continued. "You have to keep pride in your appearance and look after your personal hygiene. I now hand you over to Lieutenant Jurgensen, the camp's intelligence officer."

* * *

Caspar George Jurgensen, a forty-two-year-old Norwegian, seemed quite unlike Potterton and the other British officers Hinrichsen had met so far. He walked, the art historian noted, "like a civilian dressed up in a uniform." Having served as a private in the Middlesex Regiment during the First World War and worked as an interpreter at the Port of London Authority, Jurgensen also spoke pristine German, a fact that reassured many of the refugees.

"I hope you have recovered from yesterday's long boat trip," Jurgensen began, before inviting the men to sit on the grass. Where Captain Daniel had emphasized the virtues of cleanliness and industry, Jurgensen opted, instead, for empathy. He explained that throughout the morning he had spoken with internees and discovered that most had previously been classed as category C; he understood their frustration at being arrested as such, having already been judged to be victims of Nazi oppression who posed no security risk.

For many of the assembled men, it was the first recognition from an authority figure that, not only were they here through no fault of their own, but there was also a case to be made that they shouldn't be here at all.

"He seemed to be a human being," Hinrichsen noted. "Possibly even intelligent."

"We, the British army, are only the instrument of implementing that decision, as were the police when you were arrested," Jurgensen continued. "We are here to guard you, nothing else. We will endeavor to do that in a responsible and humane manner, but we need your co-operation."

Jurgensen explained that the internees were free to confirm or deny the appointments of their housefathers made by RSM Potterton the previous night. Then, each of the three streets must elect a *Reihen Vater*—a street or rows father—and above him, a *Lagervater*—camp father—who would occupy the most senior position within the camp's emergent hierarchy.

"We will interfere as little as possible," he said. "Soldiers will enter the camp only twice a day for roll call. You will entirely administer yourselves, but regularly meet the commander or myself to iron out any problems. It is up to you to elect representatives."

This system of self-governance had been developed by the British army to facilitate the smooth colonizing of indigenous groups. It was cannily designed to invest a community in the orderly and peaceful organization of its own captivity. As well as empowering internees to self-moderate, the arrangement minimized contact between internees and their captors; no man was allowed to approach the military authorities directly; instead, he must pass requests or queries up through the hierarchy. By granting the captives the autonomy of self-governance, the British would be free to concentrate on security and external relations, and their charges would remain occupied and usefully invested.

Jurgensen next explained that each man would receive two printed cards. On one he should sign his name and address, which would be used to inform loved ones of his whereabouts. On the other card the men should fill out the name and address of next of kin, to be used in the event of an emergency. Each internee would also be given one sheet of letter paper, on which, under War Office regulations, he was allowed to write no more than twenty-four lines. Jurgensen was clear: he would read every letter sent from the camp.

"I am not a blue-pencil man and will not cross out anything," said Jurgensen, "but I will call in the writer to discuss any reservations I may have." The paper, he added, had been chemically treated to reveal invisible ink.*

Radios were forbidden in the camp. Recognizing that the men would surely be eager for news of the progress of the war, on which their fate would surely depend, Jurgensen explained that discussions were underway in the relevant government departments to provide internees with newspapers.

---

* In one of the many ironic twists of the internment story, the Cambridge University student Walter Wallich was interned in Huyton, Liverpool, alongside a Nobel Prize–winning chemist who claimed to be the inventor of this paper, which he had developed for the German army during the First World War. The inventor explained to his fellow internees how they could, in fact, use invisible ink to leave secret messages—although, according to Wallich, none tried.

"Nothing is worse than unsubstantiated rumors which may cause panic or despair," he added.

Lastly, Jurgensen made an appeal for translators, typists, accountants, and clerks.

"We can only pay one pound per week," he said, "and there are no paid holidays. But some of you might like regular hours and congenial work. For your and your families' sake I hope that our acquaintanceship will not be a lengthy one." He ended on a conciliatory note: "Once you are free, I hope you will remember [internment] as a wartime measure, and one during which you were treated fairly and with dignity."

As the officers left the lawn, there was an astounded silence among the crowd. Here was a man who appeared to recognize the nuances of the internees' predicament, to understand history, who spoke German, and who was aware of the business of tribunals and classifications and the cruel overturning of those verdicts. For Hinrichsen, Jurgensen was the first person in a position of power who appeared to be both knowledgeable and sympathetic toward his charges.

RELIEF NOW COMBINED WITH RECOGNITION as men discovered school friends, colleagues, and even relatives among the crowd. The Berlin lawyer Curt Sluzewski, who prior to internment had practiced international law and claimed the Vatican among his clients, discovered two friends with whom he had played in a classical trio for years and who, prior to this morning, he believed had emigrated.

There was heated discussion of the officers' speeches and the implications of what had been said. As well as practicing lawyers, there were numerous legal scholars among the internees, such as Dr. Max Grünhut, former professor of law at Bonn University, more recently of All Souls College, Oxford. Captain Daniel had mentioned the Geneva Convention. Grünhut pointed out that international agreements only covered prisoners of war, not civil internees. Despite Captain Daniel's reassurances, there was no guarantee that the various provisions and protections afforded to a captured Nazi soldier would extend to an interned refugee.

While it was clear that Hutchinson's guards were well-meaning, there was also concern that cooperation with the camp authorities might indicate acceptance of the internment measures. As well as letter writing, some internees discussed whether noncooperation might influence the government to reverse its decision. Others cautioned that noncompliance might simply hasten their deportation.

The one-legged painter Hermann Fechenbach was seen as something of an expert in such matters: his hunger strike in Warth Mills had proven so disruptive he had been expelled from the camp and sent to prison cells. Perhaps, Fechenbach suggested, Hutchinson's internees might demonstrate their noncooperation by refusing to speak or understand English, absenting from roll calls, breaking the nightly curfew, flouting blackout regulations, even leaving the bins containing the daily rations to spoil in the sun.

"In which case we won't need a hunger strike: we will starve anyway," replied one skeptic.

Many internees shared Fechenbach's sense of anger and betrayal, but most concluded that, as the commandant had no power to release anybody, there was little point in making his job unnecessarily difficult.

While the dialectical discussions raged on, Hinrichsen was eager to see if the surge wave of internment had deposited any other notable men in this coastal prison. He was not disappointed. Just as during the past eight years the German government had forced hundreds of eminent academics from their positions, so the Nazis' war on the arts had forced thousands of artists, musicians, architects, writers, photographers, fashion designers, and critics out of work and into exile. They had first been obliged to register at the Reichskulturkammer—the Reich Chamber of Culture. Membership was required for anyone who wanted to produce, exhibit, or sell artwork; it was also granted only on presentation of a so-called "Aryan certificate." This structural exclusion of Jews from culture was deliberate; Nazis believed modern art's various movements, predominantly spearheaded by Jewish artists, represented an assault on German civilization.

Having lost their ability to work, many came to Britain. Some were aided by the Artists' Refugee Committee, a group cofounded by the surrealist artist Roland Penrose shortly after *Kristallnacht*, which found artist refugees the host families and guarantees of employment required to secure immigration visas. Diana Uhlman, daughter of the MP Sir Henry Page Croft, had become the group's first secretary.

While it was a deliberate policy of persecution that had caused at least three hundred painters, sculptors, and graphic artists to flee to Britain, it was coincidence that brought a disproportionate number of these cultural luminaries to Hutchinson camp. Diana Uhlman had special interest in the immured men. Ten days before the camp opened, she had given birth to her first child. The child's father, Manfred—better known as Fred to his friends—was a thirty-nine-year-old lawyer-turned-artist from Stuttgart who had been arrested just prior to the birth. Like so many of the exiled artists, he had been brought to Hutchinson.

As well as Uhlman, the dream-haunted Erich Kahn and the paddle-handed sculptor from Warth Mills, Ernst Müller-Blensdorf, Hinrichsen spied a number of familiar faces on the lawn, both rising stars and established luminaries of the German and Austrian art worlds, each reduced to the status of muddled prisoner.

There were the Austrian sculptors Siegfried Charoux, whose monumental baroque sculptures stood in many towns in Austria—and later greeted visitors to the Royal Courts of Justice and the Royal Festival Hall in London—and Georg Ehrlich, who in 1937 was awarded the gold medal at the World Exhibition in Paris, and whose work stands in the gardens of St. Paul's Cathedral. Both men were forty-three and had been arrested from almost-neighboring houses in Hammersmith.

There was Paul Hamann, who studied at the Arts and Crafts school in Hamburg and with Rodin in Paris, before he came to London in 1936 at the invitation of the English diplomat Harold Nicolson. Prior to his internment, Hamann developed a process of making "life masks" of live models, and created the likenesses of well-known English figures such as the writer Aldous Huxley, the playwright Noël Coward and, astonishingly, considering his current predicament, Prime Minister Winston Churchill's wife, Clementine.

As well as the hunger-striking painter Fechenbach—whom Hinrichsen believed had taken a dislike to the young art historian[*]—there was Hellmuth Weissenborn, a former professor at the Leipzig Academy of Fine Arts and a master printmaker, and Carl Felkel, a society portraitist who had settled in England long before Hitler's rise to power.

A constellation of stars from other creative industries studded the lawn. There was the celebrated set designer Ernst "Este" Stern, a frequent collaborator with the theater directors Max Reinhardt and Noël Coward, whose work for the Charell Revues had defined expressionism in both theater and cinema. There was the fashion designer Otto Haas-Heye, founder of the successful Berlin salon Alfred-Marie, whose clothing set trends in the 1920s. There was Harald Mahrenholz, friend to Pablo Picasso, Christian Dior, and Gabrielle "Coco" Chanel, whose clientele at his Mayfair fashion house later included Her Royal Highness the Princess Margaret, the Royal Ballet dancer Margot Fonteyn, and the Hollywood actor Vivien Leigh.

Dozens of writers and journalists stood among the crowd, too, including two former staff members of the Berlin newspaper *Vossische Zeitung*. Rudolf Kästner was a friend of the composer Gustav Mahler and a nephew of Thomas Mann, and had been the paper's music critic. His colleague Leo Freund—who since his arrival in Britain had adopted the more Anglo-friendly moniker Michael Corvin—had been a culture reporter for the same newspaper. There was also the poet Count Franz Josef von Matuschka, a former professional tennis player whose two volumes of published poetry had been described as "the most exquisite written in recent years."

Alongside these, there were film directors and actors, such as Philo Hauser, who would later star alongside James Bond's Roger Moore in two episodes of *The Saint*, and Wolf Frees, who would depict the Nazis from whom he'd fled in *The Guns of Navarone* and appear in Alfred Hitchcock's *The Man Who Knew Too Much* and David Lean's *Doctor Zhivago*. There were architects such as Karl Franck—later known as

---

* Later, Fechenbach offered to paint Hinrichsen's portrait. The painter refused to show the art historian the work until it was complete. When Hinrichsen finally saw the painting, he understood why: "The picture was [of a] very large house and in the top room was a very, very small window [where] I was looking out." Perspective had been deployed as a weapon, seemingly.

Carl—who helped change the silhouette of British cities at the influential firm Tecton, as well as leading doctors and surgeons, such as Oskar Fehr, who pioneered the operation to fix a detached retina. There was even a young athlete wearing an Olympic jersey who claimed to have represented, four years earlier, Great Britain in the Berlin games.[*]

It was as if a tsunami had deposited a crowd of Europe's prominent men onto this obscure patch of grass in the middle of the Irish Sea. These were the "distinguished" individuals who, three days earlier, the MP Osbert Peake referenced in the House of Commons during a debate on the current predicament of thousands of refugees who might otherwise be useful to Britain's war effort.

"Whenever we have set in motion any general measure of internment," he said, "we have invariably found that we have had very quickly to arrange for the release of those who were contributing to our war effort in a way which nobody else could replace."

For now, however, Hutchinson's luminaries loitered on the lawn. Regardless of their previous accomplishments, each now shared the same miserable status of "interned enemy alien," robbed of place, robbed of purpose.

Hutchinson camp, Hinrichsen concluded, housed perhaps the most extraordinary set of captives ever assembled. The collection highlighted the preposterousness of the policy that had united them. It was farcical, but also mildly comforting. As well as safety in numbers, there was a feeling of safety in *eminence*. Surely the British government could not keep such a brilliant, self-evidently useful group locked up for long?

In Whitehall, few shared this optimism. As Eleanor Rathbone put it dryly in the House of Commons just three days earlier: "It is about as easy to get a man out of an internment camp as it is to pull a camel through the eye of a needle."

---

[*] This individual is mentioned in sources both unpublished and, as in Fred Uhlman's 1960 memoir, *The Making of an Englishman*, published. Of the 171 men who represented Britain in the 1936 Olympic Games, however, not one appears to be recorded in the official Home Office records of internment. Two accounts suggest that the young man in the jersey was of Italian origin and may have been a swimmer, but there are no further details to verify whether the man was the international athlete he claimed to be or, if not, how he came to wear the jersey. Months later the Austrian skier Hugo Kuranda, who would later represent his country in the 1948 Olympic Games, arrived at Hutchinson. The camp had, then, at least one verified Olympian among its alumni.

X

THE UNIVERSITY OF BARBED WIRE

DRAWN FROM HIS CANVAS TENT by the chug and boom of nearby bomb fall, Peter Fleischmann watched the glow of distant fires soak across the night sky. The guy ropes caught the light like tracer fire. The teenager had a few more weeks to endure before he and many of his camp mates would join Klaus Hinrichsen and all the other brilliant men on the Isle of Man. For now, his home was here on Prees Heath, a temporary, tented camp situated on a forest-lined common sixteen miles southwest of Crewe, a city currently under attack.

A few weeks earlier, thousands of soldiers, weary from their evacuation from blazing Dunkirk, cluttered the city's pavements, awaiting transfer from one of Britain's busiest railway stations. By the time Peter arrived, the soldiers were gone, as if chased by the incoming German pilots, who now traced the railway tracks below almost nightly in search of the factories building the engines for British planes. A nearby trench, dug by the internees, promised feeble cover if the bombs came too close to Prees Heath. For now, with moonlit faces, the men gazed upward, heard the guns grumble, and felt the distant ground dent.

After the indignities of Warth Mills and its thieving commandant, the camp at Prees Heath Common—a favored peacetime spot for local picnickers—had a bucolic charm. Surrounded by restoratively green woodland, it was here, among the trees and fauna, that more than twenty thousand men had been trained in trench warfare during the First World War before leaving for the front line in France. Two decades later, the camp's purpose had switched from a place of commission to one of containment.

Eight men slept in tents built for four, lying, as one internee wrote, "like slices of cake," their feet protruding from the canvas. For those internees who could "still appreciate the romance" of camping, life under tent had an appeal. For anyone suffering from poor mobility or back conditions, however, the lack of basic comforts and facilities presented a novel but no less onerous set of difficulties to Warth Mills.

The men were grouped according to their perceived risk. Captured merchant seamen were assigned one section; civil internees another. Had a passing German pilot peered down, he would have spied the pools of canvas forming an archipelago of islands among the green foliage, much like a summer camping park. At ground level, however, a perimeter of barbed wire encircled the settlement, while internal fences divided it into compounds. Despite the fine weather, the clean air, and the uninterrupted view of the stars, this was just another prison for men yet to face charge or trial: the most basic legal norms of arrest and imprisonment that are acceptable in a constitutional democracy.

BY THE TIME PETER ARRIVED, Prees Heath had mostly emptied of older men. The camp's commandant, Captain Muirhead, had successfully argued to his superiors that tented accommodations were inappropriate for the bewilderingly large number of internees suffering from illness or infirmity, men who should, according to government guidelines, never have been interned. Accordingly, most above the age of fifty had been transferred elsewhere. Despite the relative youth of those left behind, cut off from the outside world and forced into stifling proximity with strangers, misery—both physical, emotional, and intellectual—was commonplace.

The tents were overcrowded and noisy. The days were warm but, even during the summer months, the nights were cold and the men desperately needed warm clothes, stockings, and boots. Hundreds of internees, hungry and tired, roamed restlessly through the camp with little to do. Some busied themselves with washing, placing their clothes in a large metal drum, adding soap and water, then pounding the material with long sticks. To stave off the creeping irritation derived from living too close, among too many, some of the internees introduced a schedule of silent hours. Visitors were kept away from tents by polite but curt notices fixed above the entrance. The first shadows of depression began to fall. In a letter to his wife written shortly after his arrival at Prees Heath, Professor Ludwig Marx, who would later issue energetic lectures at Hutchinson, wrote: "My soul is sad." The following week his mood had darkened further. "[After] weeks of bitter experiences, life seems so senseless."

Yet, the peaceful surroundings of Prees Heath also awoke, in some, the imagination. One day the lawyer and writer Walter Zander—who soon became a key figure at Hutchinson—sat, "full of sad and longing thoughts," with a group of friends and watched two young horses frisk in the meadow beyond the barbed wire. Another man produced from his suitcase the pocket score of Brahms's string sextets. There were no instruments to hand, but there were enough music readers among the group to, between them, sing the harmonies.

As the chorus sounded, Zander noticed one of the men lift from his slump. Leo Wurmser had worked as a repetiteur at the Dresden and Vienna opera houses before immigrating to Britain in 1938, where, at the time of his arrest, he had been employed by the BBC as an accompanist and conductor. Denied music and freedom, Wurmser had withered in internment. Grasping an opportunity to support his friend, later that day Zander persuaded a guard to smuggle into the camp plain-paper books from his daughter's school. The guard duly passed a pile of these blue exercise books to Zander, who began to fill the pages with empty musical staves.

Zander presented Wurmser with the hand-drawn manuscript

paper. What might, in another context, have seemed like a measly gift, had a transformative effect. Wurmser spent the next week transcribing Beethoven's opera *Fidelio* from memory into the exercise books. When he had completed the score, the young conductor gathered his friends. Together they performed, in front of the other men, the opera's mournful yet determined "Prisoners' Chorus."

> *Oh, what joy, in the open air*
> *Freely to breathe again!*
> *Up here alone is life!*
> *The dungeon is a grave.*

In the context of the camp, the lyrics assumed a new potency. The performance, Zander said, was not the best he had ever seen, but it was, without doubt, the most powerful. For the musician who, in Zander's estimation, "had been very near to a complete breakdown," it was a turning point. "He recovered visibly." When, later that month, the internees staged an open-air performance of *A Midsummer Night's Dream*, Wurmser composed the music accompaniment, which he later developed into a work for full orchestra.

Wurmser was not alone in his emergence. Some men formed a theater group. A professor in medicine gave a lecture. Others, such as the violinist Peter Schidlof, performed in the evening, until darkness fell and the men retired to their tents, where, without electricity, they would listen for the zip and whistle of hostile planes.

Jostled and enlivened by the creative endeavor around him, and not knowing for how long he was to be a prisoner, Peter also began to fill his time with artistic pursuits. Having watched how the sculptor Ernst Müller-Blensdorf improvised materials at Warth Mills, Peter began to approach any man who received a parcel from outside the camp to ask if he might have the brown wrapping paper, which he would uncrumple, pat down, and use as a canvas.

Prees Heath would be closed before the end of summer, and many of these men, including Zander and Wurmser, transferred to Hutchinson. For now, it provided a foreshadowing of all that was to come: both the lingering desperation and gloom of internment, and the creative awakening it could inspire.

KLAUS HINRICHSEN AWOKE TO THE smell of bacon, eggs, and fresh coffee curling into his bedroom. Since his arrest, he had eaten only gray porridge for breakfast; the notion of a cooked breakfast felt like an old dream. The art historian plodded downstairs and into the kitchen common room, arriving at the same time as House 3's newly elected housefather, who had replaced the hapless, gold-buttoned journalist, who had moved to a different house. Hinrichsen saw a broad-shouldered man with a towel draped around his neck reclining at one of the room's two tables. A stooped barber fussed at the man's face, who was dictating a letter, taken down by a soberly dressed middle-aged internee standing in the corner of the kitchen. On the table rested a boastful plate, laden with illicit foodstuffs: sausages, bacon and, not one, but two eggs.

"What the hell is going on here?" asked the housefather.

With a grin the man gestured to an empty chair at the table.

Dressed only in a tracksuit and running shoes, Ludwig Warschauer cut a rather different figure from the camp's besuited academics and frizzly artists. The forty-two-year-old had the face and swagger of a prizefighter and, it seemed, the winnings to match. When he moved into House 3, after Captain Daniel's inaugural address, two bodyguards—"assistants," as he referred to them—carried Warschauer's luggage into the house, where he demanded a bedroom be cleared for him and his associates. Some residents protested; another spied an opportunity and offered to sell his spot, pocketing a five-pound note and moving into another overcrowded bedroom.

Warschauer did not bear any signs of ordeal, but seemed giddily jovial, as if party to a joke those around him were not. He had only been arrested on July 12 and arrived at Hutchinson the following day. Having evaded the thefts and billowing dereliction of Warth Mills, his brief experience of internment had been comparatively soft.

"Breakfast," said Warschauer, gesturing at the plate. "Join me."

The housefather declined the invitation and instead demanded to know where the man had acquired the ingredients. The Isle of Man was not yet subject to rationing. Still, while food was comparatively plentiful, luxury items such as these were unseen in the camp. After lunch each house dispatched a team of five "bin carriers" to collect their next allocation of supplies, placed in large metal bins, with prominently displayed house numbers. The men would carry them to their respective kitchen, then, by ten o'clock the following morning, return the empty bins to the stores to be cleaned in preparation for the next day. Eggs and sausages had not been a part of the previous day's allocation.

"Anybody can buy this stuff from the soldiers and through a hole in the wire," explained Warschauer. "The cost is hardly higher than on the open market."

It was not, in fact, the first time that extravagant foodstuffs were found inside one of the island's camps. One of the first internees to arrive at the island was a twenty-eight-year-old student known as Count von Lingen. At the time of his arrest Lingen was a history student at Cambridge University, studying under the esteemed historian G. M. Trevelyan. Described by a fellow internee as a "paragon of propriety . . . perfectly groomed, polite and tactful," Lingen shrugged off questions about his past. Soon after his arrival on the Isle of Man, he began to receive luxury hampers from Fortnum & Mason, the upmarket London department store—rations that he shared among his fellow internees.

Skeptics were right to suspect Lingen's backstory. His real name was not Count von Lingen but Friedrich Georg Wilhelm Hohenzollern, also known as Prince Frederick of Prussia, a great-great-grandson of Queen Victoria. Hohenzollern had been sent to England by his grandfather Kaiser Wilhelm II to establish contact between the British and the former German royal family. The alias Count von Lingen had been, he claimed, suggested to him by King George V, and the hampers paid for and sent by Queen Mary.*

Warschauer's illicit breakfast was something else, however. During his opening address, Captain Daniel had explained that Hutchinson was to be a camp of equality: regardless of his wealth no man was permitted to withdraw more than ten shillings a week.

"In this camp the Oxford professor will not be treated any better than the scavenger among you," the commandant had said. Black-market dealing, of the sort Warschauer had apparently engaged in, undermined the principle.

By way of explanation, Warschauer revealed that he was an accomplished engineer, owner of a clutch of patents, including one for a powerful recording device that would be of great value to the British war effort. So great were his talents, he continued, that his presence in Hutchinson camp must have been the result of an administrative error.

"I can't help laughing," Warschauer bragged, "when I imagine the scene in London: the buzzing telephones between the Ministry of Aircraft Production, my friends Brendan Bracken, Lord Beaverbrook and the Minister for Munitions all asking each other, 'Where is Warschauer?' I really am enjoying this holiday. Alas, I will be on my way home this time tomorrow."

Hinrichsen was immediately put off by Warschauer's supercilious manner, as if the latter was the only one around to see the truth of the situation and as if, to him, the rules did not apply. Later, the internee who had been transcribing the letter for the engineer over breakfast explained to Hinrichsen that he was a printer from Bremerhaven who, like so many others in the camp, had been forced to leave his business and flee Germany. In England he had started up a small printing press. Warschauer

---

* The prince was deported to Canada on the SS *Ettrick* on July 3, 1940, ten days before Hutchinson opened, and remained incognito throughout his internment. In his unpublished account, Hinrichsen claims that the prince was interned at Hutchinson. If true, it was a fleeting visit on his return from Canada; Hohenzollern was among the first deportees to return to Britain, on January 11, 1941. He was freed eighteen days later, on January 29. Regardless of his precise whereabouts, Hohenzollern's mannerly silence spared both the state and the Crown considerable embarrassment.

had promised to invest in his printing press and pass on substantial orders if the printer assumed the role of his secretary inside the camp.

While the engineer's boasts were provocative, they were well-founded. The MP Sir Herbert Williams had recently become chairman of the company financing the development of Warschauer's recording device. Williams had written to the War Office to say that he "had not the faintest doubt of [Warschauer's] complete sincerity." Prior to Warschauer's arrest, Sir John Anderson had even visited the engineer's home office to watch a demonstration of the invention. What better candidate could there possibly be for release than an acquaintance of the architect of Britain's internment policies?

ACROSS THE CAMP, WHILE AWAITING news of how they might extract themselves from this predicament, distraction came to Hutchinson's captives by way of an election for the role of camp father, the man who would function as liaison between the internees and their keepers. The chance to vote for a leader, even in the weightless elections of internment, had an energizing effect; most of the internees, as Jews, had been barred from the electoral registers by the Nazis. Even those who recognized that this power was mainly a jailor's ploy to maintain order and docility were, nonetheless, swept up by feelings of longed-for autonomy.

Some older men in the camp wanted to fix a minimum voting age, but one outspoken internee, Friederich Wittelshöfer, a former Prussian ministerial director who had helped organize elections during the Weimar era, insisted that every resident in the camp, from the youngest to the oldest, should be allowed to vote for his representative. The lobbying began immediately. One faction favored a political appointment. Others argued that fluency in the English language was of primary importance when dealing with the British authorities. A further group wanted a businessman who could secure paid work for the internees, and perhaps extend their comforts.

The initial set of candidates was soon whittled down to two men: Rudolf Munster, a thirty-seven-year-old lawyer, and Friederich

Burschell, a writer and a former Cambridge University don. Burschell, a close friend of Rudolf Olden, who had by now sufficiently recovered at Warth Mills to be transferred to Hutchinson, was a former private secretary to the Nobel Prize–winning author Thomas Mann and spoke pristine English—"much better than Captain Daniel," Hinrichsen noted. He was well-suited to the task of consulting with the British ruling classes, a group with which Burschell, with his lolling pipe and unflappable attitude, seemed to already belong.

The votes were counted and Wittelshöfer assembled the internees on the lawn and pronounced Burschell the winner. The don appeared at the first-floor window of the administration building overlooking the lawn and waved to the men he now represented. Then, following a meeting with Captain Daniel—the first of what would become a once-daily rendezvous—Burschell allocated departments to the various rooms in the office building and department heads to oversee their smooth running of the camp bank, post office, welfare department (which distributed clothes and money to the so-called "destitute" in the camp), and a labor exchange. To protect the camp father and his staff from accusations of impropriety, Burschell finally appointed Robert Gold, a twenty-five-year-old chartered accountant, to be camp auditor, overseeing and logging all "official" financial transactions.

Each official was paid a pound per week and wore a white plastic rosette fastened to his lapel with a safety pin. Only Burschell, possibly viewing himself as above such crude symbols of authority, eschewed wearing the badge of office. In time some internees, like Hinrichsen, would come to vaguely resent their newly instated leader, who could often be seen in a position of lordly recline. "He overestimated his friends' reliability, and underestimated his foes' slyness," his friend the journalist Michael Corvin would later conclude of Hutchinson's first camp father's reign. In time, Burschell would also lament his decision to run for office. "Even a god would not be able to conform to all the wishes of all these men," he'd write. For now, he had performed his duties with swift efficiency; Hutchinson had an administration worthy of an upstart town. One issue remained. What would the internees do with all this time?

* * *

ON THE SECOND DAY HINRICHSEN watched a small group of men emerge from one of the boardinghouses, each carrying a chair onto the terraced lawn. Each man selected a location around the square sufficiently distant from the next, nestled his chair into the soft ground, and tentatively clambered onto the seat. Some efforts had been made by internees to occupy themselves at their previous holding camps; the overriding atmosphere, though, had been one of demoralizing inactivity and wastage.

"[We] long to have the chance to DO something," wrote the master of Modern Languages at Rugby School in a letter to the *Times*, published on July 13, the day of Hutchinson's opening. Devoid of occupation, the men were at risk of slipping into feelings of "disillusion and despair," as one observer put it, a sense of despondency familiar to anyone who has been hounded from society. With such a high concentration of luminaries in Hutchinson, a collective awakening of imaginative possibility was not only more likely, it was inevitable.

Each lecturer stood on his chair and began to hold forth on his specialist subject—everything from Greek philosophy to explorations of the industrial uses of synthetic fibers to explications of Shakespeare's sonnets. Drawn by the noise, pools of men started to gather around each speaker. Soon the square was filled with various audiences wandering between the attractions, a scene reminiscent of Speakers' Corner in London's Hyde Park.

Hinrichsen stood next to Bruno Ahrends, one of his housemates in House 3, and together the pair watched the developing scene with keen interest. Ahrends was an architect whose practice—Salvisberg, Büning, and Ahrends—had designed Berlin's influential modernist housing estates, built for soldiers returning from the First World War, such as the quietly imposing six-story towers at the Weisse Stadt in Reinickendorf. As a former director of the Association of German Architects, the sixty-two-year-old was also an experienced speaker, having lectured at the Bauhaus, the celebrated art school. He was eager to evaluate the character and quality of this group of self-selecting teachers.

With so many accomplished academics among the camp's population, the speakers' expertise was unquestionable. The format was, however, another matter. On July 15, two days after the camp opened, an additional seven hundred men had arrived at Hutchinson, bringing the camp's population to eleven hundred. With such large crowds, internees would swarm one speaker for a few minutes before moving on to join a neighboring lecture. Emboldened by numbers, some had even taken to heckling. Professor Friedrich Heinemann, a lecturer in philosophy at Manchester College, Oxford, proved especially disruptive, wandering around and correcting, with a "nasty cackle of laughter," anyone who misapplied a term. The scene was utterly chaotic.

Ahrends, who had organized lessons for the schoolboys in his previous transit camp, felt a professional impulse to impose order. He asked Hinrichsen to accompany him to Captain Daniel's office to seek permission to organize a formal schedule of lectures. The idea appealed to Daniel, whose military training had instilled in him the belief that order begets harmony. There was one problem, however. Might not some of these men, loudly proclaiming on his lawn, be demagogues, rallying the internees to violent protest at their internment, he asked?

To assuage Daniel's concerns, Ahrends proposed that every lecture would be delivered in English, allowing British officers to eavesdrop for signs of mutiny. The compromise was sufficient. Captain Daniel offered the two men a room on the first floor of the camp's administration building, where they could draw up a schedule of weekly lectures, organize theater and music performances, and, most urgently, arrange lessons for the sixteen- and seventeen-year-olds in the camp to prepare them for the school exams they would, hopefully, be taking after their release.

Ahrends christened the outfit, officially founded on July 17, 1940, four days after Hutchinson's opening, the *Kulturabteilung*—the Cultural Department. Captain Daniel, however, insisted that it be known as Hutchinson University, or, when he wanted to claim a degree of ownership, My Hutchinson University, an institution of which he considered himself, naturally, the chancellor.

Hinrichsen and Ahrends asked the members of each house to appoint yet another representative, a *Kulturwart*—a cultural liaison officer—who would attend a meeting every morning and then report the department's plans to his fellow residents. And just as Burschell had appointed department heads to oversee the running of the camp administration, so Ahrends appointed cultural heads to oversee the various branches of education and entertainments.

Dr. Hans Rothfels, a historian at St. John's College, Oxford, was chosen to oversee the schedule of academic lectures. Hinrichsen would be responsible for the so-called "popular lectures," on softer subjects. Rabbi Max Eschelbacher took charge of Jewish cultural programming, while the bilingual Heinfried "Heinz" Beran, taught English to those refugees who hoped to one day make Britain their permanent home. The music critic Rudolf Kästner would organize a schedule of musical performances in the camp, and Ahrends appointed a twenty-seven-year-old editor, Ernst Sänger, as games master, in charge of organizing chess, bridge, and boxing tournaments. Kurt Böhm, a teacher at St. Christopher School in Letchworth, volunteered for the unlikely role of gymnastics instructor.

As coeditor of *Liddell and Scott's Greek-English Lexicon*, the Oxford professor Dr. Paul Maas was the ideal candidate for the role of Hutchinson University librarian, organizing books donated by the Oxford University Press, the British Council, the London publisher Victor Gollancz, local island libraries, and even the office of the chief rabbi, who sent ninety copies of two books that he had authored. There were no mahogany bookcases in this library; Maas would have to make do with arranging the books on the floor, at least until the canteen could donate some empty orange boxes to be used as shelving.

The eleventh and final position on the Camp University committee, the nebulous role of "representative of the audience," went to Professor Heinemann, the heckling Oxford philosopher. Any internees who felt the cultural schedule was in any way lacking would, it seemed, have a sympathetic ear for their complaints.

The committee worked quickly, posting a weekly timetable on a board erected in front of the camp's post office. Lectures immediately ranged from the courageously broad (Dr. Cohn: "The Culture of China") to the fiercely specialist (Dr. Simchowitz: "Radium and X-rays and Their Use for the Treatment of Cancer") to the manifestly utilitarian (Dr. Renner: "Brown and White Bread and Their History"). Whatever their passion or speciality, and regardless of their professional status, the refugees had a place to share their experience, knowledge, and talents for the enlightenment of their community.

"There wasn't a subject in the world that wasn't discussed," said Fritz Hallgarten, a lawyer–turned–wine dealer who gave a lecture on wine. As the artist Hellmuth Weissenborn put it, "[I]t was a miracle of the human will to live and to work, changing a miserable prison camp into a kind of university."

The lawn—or, as it was rather grandiosely referred to in the weekly schedules, the "Lawn-Amphitheatre"—came to represent "a nucleus of an almost bygone humanism and culture," as one internee wrote at the time. With its unimpeded views over the barbed wire toward the sea, in its evergreen newness, it became a place where "one could dream in the bright sunshine beautiful fairy-dreams, far remote from reality."

WITH SO MANY ACADEMICS FROM prestigious institutions, however, rivalries were inevitable. Paul Jacobsthal, a former professor of classical archaeology at the University of Marburg, who had now joined Christ Church, Oxford, arrived in Hutchinson on July 17, the day of the Cultural Department's founding. Jacobsthal judged the majority of the lectures to be, as he wrote in his diary, "cheap" and "delivered by dilettantes."* While he was eventually persuaded to deliver a talk of his own, he was eager not to be counted among the "ghostlike professors, selling their old German stuff again after the years that they had been muzzled."

---

* Jacobsthal made an exception for a series of lectures on English humanism delivered by his friend and housemate Rudolf Pfeiffer, titled "Aspects of English Life," which he considered "*masterly* . . . serious and very good."

Jacobsthal had especially robust feelings toward those talks given by some members of the Camp University committee. In his diary, written in his room on the upper floor of House 24, Jacobsthal described Professor Kästner's introductions to musical performances as "boring," "stupid," and "inadequate," while he deemed the heckling Professor Heinemann to be "conceited," noting, ruthlessly, his colleague's "dwindling audience."

Regardless of any individual's feelings about the cultural schedule, the lawn soon became the camp's omphalos. On any given day one might find men putting golf balls, sunbathing as if they were at the beach on holidays, or tending to the surrounding flower beds. There would be a group of chattering walkers, individuals sitting on benches learning, studying, while another group of captivated chess lovers, their legs dangling over the walls, watched two players absorbed in a game.

When a lecture began, there was a frequency of interest and engagement perhaps unmatched in any other university. For internees who had given up on their education—or had seen it cut short by the Nazis—here was an opportunity to learn from some of the best-regarded scholars in Europe, teachers who required nothing more from their students than open minds and ears.

"It was rather a touching scene," noted Hinrichsen. "Grown men, who, perhaps due to inflation, had left school at sixteen to work and support their families" now had the chance to sate "a thirst for knowledge, which they could not still."

For the professors, too, here was an electrifying proposition: not only the chance to teach their fellow countrymen after years of enforced silence, but also the bracing knowledge that while their audience was, in one sense, captive, the students were also free to wander off if the lesson failed to hold their interest. Hutchinson would provide honest and immediate feedback on the performance of any professor, unbiased by his stature, position, or formal qualification.

By the end of July, fourteen "official" open-air talks had been staged on subjects ranging from philosophy to geography, music to law. Each had attracted audiences of no fewer than a hundred and fifty, and as many as four hundred. Lectures with smaller audiences had been given in various houses. Egon Wellesz, the musicologist and composer who had fled Germany to teach at Oxford, was convinced that nobody wanted to hear him speak on Byzantine music. In fact, so many internees were eager to hear Wellesz speak that he had to repeat his talk three times, watching in astonishment as groups of men "eagerly discussed the finer points" of his niche subject.

Every evening a scurry of men carrying chairs could be seen emerging from the houses to congregate on the lawn. Sunday night was concert night, and, as well as the option to take a daily walk through the local countryside under armed escort, there were twice-weekly sojourns to the beach, where internees were even allowed to swim. To an outsider, Hutchinson camp appeared to be a modest utopia.

ON JULY 20, A WEEK after its opening, Hutchinson received its first inspector: Rabbi Solomon Schonfeld, director of the Chief Rabbi's Religious Emergency Council, who had been involved in the organization of the *Kindertransport* initiative that brought Peter to Britain. Even at this early stage, a rivalry had developed between the commandants, who were eager to prove to Schonfeld that their camp was the best. Captain Alexander, commandant of Mooragh camp, pointed to the quality of cooking in his camp as incontrovertible evidence of its superiority. The claim seemed justified to Schonfeld until he arrived at Hutchinson and met the "enthusiastic" Captain Daniel, who took the rabbi on a tour of the camp and showed off Ahrends's astonishing cultural program, complete with plans for theatrical performances, marionette shows, and live concerts.

The visit proved persuasive. In his report Schonfeld wrote that Hutchinson's internees were "co-operating . . . in organizing every possible cultural, social and educational activity." The camp was, he added, "a model community." The truth was more complex.

"Lest this all sounds too rosy a situation," noted Hinrichsen,

> let me assure you that all these frantic activities were entered into as a means of distraction from the ever-present anger at the injustice of being interned . . . the constant worry about wives and children left without a provider and under almost nightly bombardment in London and other towns . . . from the lack of communication and, of course suffering from the cramped living conditions and the lack of freedom of movement.

All the frenetic organization and schedule making masked, for many, a seething sense of fear, betrayal, hurt, and anger. The fevered activity distracted from the underlying state of enforced aimlessness. Some of Hutchinson's internees had an additional trauma to contend with: two weeks before the camp had opened, more than a thousand internees and prisoners of war—purportedly some of the most dangerous men residing in Britain—boarded a ship in Liverpool, bound for Canada, the second consignment of captives Britain had attempted to offload.

Midway across the Atlantic the SS *Arandora Star* encountered a U-boat. The ship never reached its destination. Hundreds died. By the time of Hutchinson's opening, the disaster was well on its way to becoming a scandal for the British government, which was desperately trying to find out the truth of what had happened. In Hutchinson camp some of the men had firsthand knowledge. They had been there, in the freezing water, only to wash up, two weeks later, on the Isle of Man.

XI

THE VIGIL

MICHAEL CORVIN SAT AT A wooden table, flanked by two rows of candles. The mood was somber as Corvin shuffled the sheets of paper in front of him in the wriggling candlelight. In early July the former journalist for the Berlin-based newspaper *Vossische Zeitung* had seen firsthand, and with a reporter's eye for detail, the tragedy that would become emblematic of the cruelty of the British government's internment measures and, in time, the catalyst for the long and complicated process of undoing the mess. Corvin was one of a handful of survivors of the sinking of the SS *Arandora Star* now imprisoned in Hutchinson.

To process his ordeal Corvin had followed professional habit and recorded, in exacting detail, all that he had witnessed. Any urge to keep his account private was overcome not only by a writer's innate instinct to seek communion with a readership, but also by the knowledge that he was not the sole survivor at Hutchinson camp. Perhaps his account might help others process the enormity of what they had witnessed? So Corvin had approached the Cultural Department's secretary, Bruno Ahrends, and asked that he might be allowed to read his eyewitness account as part of the camp's cultural schedule.

Ahrends booked a room and listed the event as "Michael Corvin reading from own writings"—an innocuous title for an event that held the first key to the internees' longed-for releases. Either as a show of solidarity or out of morbid interest, some of the artists Corvin had befriended, as well as a few other survivors, had gathered to hear the story.

It was not the first time that, in some quiet corner of Hutchinson, men had begun to share their distress. The Oxford professor Paul Jacobsthal had watched a group of six Orthodox Jews huddle in the front garden of one of the camp's kosher houses to recall, in turn, the events of *Kristallnacht*. When each man had finished his account, the group sang in unison a mournful Hebrew lament. Tonight's gathering was led by a journalist, not an adherent, but would be no less grave and, as Corvin began to read from his account, no less affecting.

TWO WEEKS BEFORE HUTCHINSON CAMP opened, Corvin looked up at the ship in thickening dusk on the Liverpool dockside while his fellow captives nattered in an assortment of accents and tongues. None knew where he was to be taken. On the journey to Liverpool Corvin had hoped he was bound for the Isle of Man, where his son, Assar, was a student at the King William's College boarding school. Now, however, as he looked over the colossal ship, the journalist knew that he was destined for a more distant port.

After fleeing the family's comfortable flat on Berlin's Hohenzollerndamm, leaving their German shepherd, Prince, and an enviable library of books, Corvin had sailed from the Spanish island of Ibiza to England in 1936. He was accustomed to traveling long distances by boat and could see that, at more than five hundred feet in length, and with no fewer than seven decks, the SS *Arandora Star* was a cruise liner designed to cross oceans, not channels.

In fact, the ship, built in Cheshire in 1927, had made frequent trips to the Pacific and Caribbean, carrying wealthy passengers toward the winter sun. With electric elevators, an onboard cinema, and an above-deck tennis court and swimming pool, the SS *Arandora Star* offered the height of luxury sailing to its paying passengers. Advertised as the "world's most delightful cruising liner," previous passengers included the writer George Bernard Shaw, the comedian Max Miller, and King Carol of Romania.

Today, on June 30, 1940, more than a thousand men drawn from a variety of holding camps around the country gathered on the dockside—men who had been hastily selected for this, the second ship to deport internees and prisoners of war. Corvin had been brought just a few miles, from Huyton camp in Liverpool. Another of the captives, the BBC reporter Uberto Limentani, let out a cry of recognition; years earlier he had seen the ship moored in Venice opposite St. Mark's Square and thought how lovely it would be to take a cruise in such a handsome vessel.

At that time the ship had been known by its nickname "Wedding Cake," due to its brilliant white paint and blue bunting. For today's journey the SS *Arandora Star* looked quite different. The twin funnels, crimson red, black-topped, and stamped with bright lode stars of the Blue Star Line remained, but the hull had been repainted in gunship gray, the portholes a furtive dark blue. Menacing coils of barbed wire tumbled around the decks and lifeboats, a measure, Corvin guessed, to dissuade prisoners from making a swan dive toward freedom. A hulking twelve-pound antiaircraft gun pointed skyward on the aft deck, and soldiers, not white-suited stewards, patrolled the decks.

As EARLY AS MAY 24, even before the British government introduced the mass internment policy, Churchill had remarked to his cabinet that he favored the deportation of all internees from Britain. To this end, the government had attempted to persuade its trading partners and colonies—Canada, Australia, and New Zealand—to take its captives. On June 14, Canada agreed to admit 2,633 German category A internees; 1,823 prisoners of war; and 1,500 pro-fascist Italians. Officially, everyone on the dockside was a political extremist. Corvin, whose newspaper had been closed by the Nazis for its oppositional beliefs, knew this was not true.

The risks posed to transatlantic shipping were considerable; German U-boats had been attacking Allied ships with increasing success. Regardless, the first ship filled with internees bound for Canada, the *Duchess of York*, departed on June 21. Now, nine days later, the SS *Arandora Star* was set to follow, carrying its cargo of supposedly high-risk Nazis to Newfoundland.

One by one the queuing men began to walk the gangplank onto the ship. The slow rhythm of embarkation gave Corvin the opportunity to size up his fellow passengers. The Corvins were professional noticers; in Berlin, his wife had worked as a society reporter who carried a tiny Minox camera with which to take candid shots of personalities. He saw that, on the dockside, the men had naturally grouped according to nationality. While they may have been political opponents, many of the 473 German and Austrian passengers—123 of whom were German merchant seamen—recognized one another from the holding camps where, prior to today, they had been held. The 86 German prisoners of war stuck together, as did the 734 Italian men who formed the largest contingent of passengers.

It was an untidy and fractious crowd. These men were supposed to represent some of the most dangerous enemy aliens living in Britain at the time. Certainly, there were Hitlerites present; the War Office had selected a group of high-risk category A internees known as "R group," or "Ringleaders," for the day's journey. The selections had, however, been made in great haste: the War Office was given just six days to decide who among the thousands of enemy aliens interned across the country should be deported. In order to make up the numbers, Jews and other refugees from Nazi oppression had been assigned to the ship, men now forced to mingle with their oppressors in even closer proximity than at the camps.

There was Kurt Kaminski, a Jew who had been a foreman at the Sachsenhausen concentration camp before the Quakers aided his escape to England. There was nineteen-year-old Ernst Seemann, brought to Britain by the British Czech Refugee Trust Fund. There was Willi Blumens, against whose internment representatives of the Jewish Refugees Committee had fruitlessly protested, and Karl Liebel, a doctor's son brought to Britain on a *Kindertransport*, then promptly interned a fortnight after his sixteenth birthday—"for your own sake," as the chairman of his tribunal put it.

There were men of repute, too, such as Dr. Josef Ötvös, an Austrian doctor who had dual British citizenship and had accompanied many of the *Kindertransport* children as a chaperone; Dr. Kurt Regner, a Jewish lawyer and refugee from Austria; and Kurt Winkler, an artist, also known as "Kurwin," who, before he was interned, painted the portrait of one of the royal princesses for the *Queen* magazine.

As one internee later wrote of the sorry mishmash of deportees standing on the quayside: "The martyrs, the victims, the hunted Jews, helpers of this country, who fled to find refuge . . . herded together with their slaughterers."

The Italians, too, were far from a homogeneous group of fascists. There had been no time to hold tribunals for the thousands of Italians living in Britain, so mistakes were widespread. Italian fascists mingled with mild-mannered fellow countrymen and leading chefs from top London restaurants. The incongruous passenger list personified the chaos of the government's mass internment policy; the selection process for the day's deportation had been as mistake-riddled as the early tribunals, characterized by what one member of the House of Lords would later describe as "mismanagement, lack of foresight, forethought and consideration."

Canada's offer had been gladly received in Westminster, where many senior officials, especially inside the Home Office, believed there were far too many refugees in Britain and any opportunity to offload some to other countries should be embraced. There was particular eagerness to rid Britain of those internees who had been judged to pose the greatest risk to national security and, on July 21, the first deportation liner, the SS *Duchess of York*, carried 2,096 category A internees and 529 prisoners of war to Canada. There was pressure to find further candidates for deportation, and selections were made in haste and without sufficient deliberation.

Even the police officers responsible for the arrests knew that the reasons behind many selections were at best spurious, at worst senseless. Robert Mark, a Manchester-based police officer, visited the house of Ernani Landucci, a waiter who lived on Ruskin Avenue in Moss Side, a few days earlier. Mark explained that Landucci was being arrested, while the man's wife and British-born daughter became increasingly distressed.

"Even to my tired eyes this poor chap looked absolutely harmless," Mark recalled. Before allowing himself to be led to the police car, Landucci beckoned the arresting officers to his cellar. There he pulled out three glasses, which he solemnly filled with white wine. Landucci distributed the drinks, raised his glass, and proposed a toast: "Bugger the fascists."

While his wife and child wept, Mark glumly drove Landucci to the cells.

"It was a needless internment," the officer later said. At the station Mark inquired as to why, precisely, he had been sent to arrest Landucci, only to be told that the prisoner owned a small patch of land in Southern Italy and was required to pay a tax to the Italian consul. This had been enough, apparently, to force Landucci's deportation.

AS THEY CAME ABOARD, EACH man was counted by two guards, recently returned from the horrors of Dunkirk, either side of the exit. Embarkation took six hours. The *Arandora Star* was not so much at capacity as foolishly beyond it. In peacetime the ship typically carried 450 passengers and a crew of 200. Today, Italian, German, and Austrian internees combined with the ship's crew and British guards to form a load of more than 1,500 individuals.

The ship departed Liverpool at 4:00 a.m. on Monday, July 1. The captain, Edgar Moulton, plotted a zigzag course through the Irish Sea. At first light, early risers watched the ship trail past the coast of Wales and, shortly thereafter, on the starboard side, the easy slopes of the Isle of Man. Corvin's hopes that he might be reunited with his son there were dashed as the vessel surged toward the vacant horizon.

Hitler was yet to declare unrestricted submarine warfare around Britain, hoping to starve the country into submission by preventing the passage of food and supplies into the country. Nevertheless, the early months of war had been marked by numerous U-boat attacks. While there was no Royal Naval escort to ward off would-be attackers, a British submarine tailed the SS *Arandora Star* for a while, and later a flying boat checked in on the ship's progress, exchanging the time of day via light signals.

Many of the internees aboard were genuine refugees from Nazi oppression, some of whom had allegedly seen their classification "bumped" to qualify for deportation; but there were many genuine Nazi sympathizers. Prior to embarkation, at Seaton camp, Wolfgang Kittel had led a group of internees in pro-Nazi songs while on marches through the town and during their morning gymnastics ("Today we possess Germany, tomorrow all the world"). Not only had he killed anti-Nazis, Jews, and religious Christians, but Kittel bragged that he had been among the murderers of Rosa Luxemburg, the revolutionary antiwar activist shot by members of a German paramilitary group of proto-Brownshirts in 1919.

Word spread among the refugees that some of the merchant seamen quartered in the ship's ballroom had hung a Nazi flag and sung party anthems—behavior that resulted in the guards escorting the entire group out of the ballroom to switch bunks with a group of Italians. Some British soldiers responsible for maintaining order on the deportation ships felt stronger kinship with the Nazi Germans aboard than with the German and Austrian Jews, however. Lieutenant Colonel William Scott, who commanded the guard on another transport ship, wrote in an official report that he considered the Nazi Germans to be "honest, straightforward, and extremely well-disciplined." The Jews, he continued, "can only be described as subversive liars, demanding and arrogant . . . definitely not to be trusted in word or deed."

As in Warth Mills, depression descended on many of the refugees, who feared that the presence of individuals such as Kittel and other prisoners of war aboard meant that there was a strong chance they were destined for Germany, to be exchanged for British prisoners. For the thirty-three-year-old opera singer Alfons Blumenthal, the pressure was too great to bear. He hung himself from one of the ship's railings. Still alive when the soldiers cut him down, Blumenthal dropped into the sea. The ship did not stop to recover him.

After the past few weeks of stress and confusion—eighty-eight of the Italian passengers had come straight from Warth Mills—the relaxed pace and circumstance provided a welcome change. The ship's doctor shared cigarettes with some of the internees in the easy breeze. On the evening of July 1, stewards served pink gin and beer.

As the sound of the gramophone trailed from the ballroom out into the night, Corvin watched as the ship rounded Malin Head, the northernmost tip of Ireland, and plotted a course due west, into the Atlantic.

At that precise moment, Günther Prien, the first of the so-called German U-boat aces to rise to prominence, chugged at a speed of nine knots toward a gap between the Shetlands and the Faroe Islands, a route that would lead him home to Germany. It had been a fruitful thirty days at sea for the crew of *U-47*, who had sunk eight ships on this, their sixth patrol of the war. Thirteen of the U-boat's fourteen torpedoes had been fired. One remained.

Prien spotted the liner headed toward his position at 6:29 British Summer Time, on the morning of July 2. The U-boat, which had been traveling on the ocean's surface, dived and switched from its air-huffing diesel engine to its electric motor. For twenty-five minutes Prien observed the liner through his periscope. At first it was not clear from its markings whether the ship represented a legitimate naval target. The ship's abrupt tacking pattern, known as "zig-zag number ten" was the tell Prien was looking for. "I recognise her as enemy from her zigzags," he wrote in his logbook.

At two minutes to seven, from an ambitious distance of one and a half miles, Prien fired *U-47*'s last torpedo toward a ship that, unbeknownst to him, carried hundreds of his fellow countrymen, a mixture of both supporters and victims of the Nazi regime. For ninety-seven seconds Prien and his crew waited for the telltale plume of water that would signal a direct hit, a notch on the scoresheet of naval warfare and the attendant tragedies.

MICHAEL CORVIN WAS AWOKEN IN his bunk by a growl, a shudder, and the sound of breaking glass. His cabin, like every other room on the ship, had been thrown into darkness. The last of *U-47*'s torpedoes had struck the SS *Arandora Star* on the starboard side, at the aft end of the engine room. Both the main and standby generators were instantly destroyed. Robert Connell, the ship's Glaswegian chief engineer, tried in vain to reach the wrecked engine room, where, within two minutes, the water had risen to sea level.

Using his torch, Connell directed Corvin and other men to safety, away from the ship's stern, which had begun to settle into the sea. The stress of late departure, and the exertion of managing so many disparate and opposed groups of men, meant that none of the ship's crew had been practiced in emergency stations, and none of the military personnel or internees had been instructed in the use of life jackets. There had been no drills. Without a coordinated plan for where they should congregate in the event of an emergency, most internees gathered on the upper deck, a mass of bodies that hampered the crew's attempts to organize the orderly filling and launch of lifeboats.

Even if these measures had been in place, the SS *Arandora Star* was ill-equipped to deal with disaster. There were twelve working lifeboats aboard, with a combined capacity of a thousand—five hundred fewer than the current contingent of passengers. The torpedo had destroyed Lifeboat No. 7, however, and the falls and davits on Lifeboat No. 5 were damaged. As guards lowered the vessel, the ironwork came loose, dropping the lifeboat into the water, injuring or killing its occupants.

Of the remaining ten lifeboats, three were positioned behind barbed-wire barricades and inaccessible. The ship's captain had complained about the barbed wire in Liverpool. His argument, that it "greatly hampered" the crew in its work, went unacknowledged. Without training, the guards were unaware that there was a special method for loosening sections of the barricade to provide access to the lifeboats. The troops attempted to prize away the clamps securing the wire with bayonets and rifle butts, even tearing at the wire with their bare hands, to no avail.

The sheer number of bodies on the upper deck confounded any attempt to orchestrate a mannerly exodus. About half of the ninety upper-deck rafts, designed to provide buoyancy in the water, were hurled overboard. The crew urged able-bodied internees to jump after them, but none volunteered.

At 8:15 BST, an hour and a quarter after the torpedo struck, the list to starboard dramatically increased. The ship's gun was torn from its mooring and crashed into the sea, violently tugging a trail of barbed wire behind it, which hooked and dragged victims into the ocean. The proud funnels broke from their fixing and plummeted into the water, while Corvin heard a series of muted blasts as the ship's boilers exploded, somewhere deep in its belly.

Captain Moulton coolly asked for a glass of water, which he drank from his position on the bridge, encircled by barbed wire. Even as the ship began to sink, many of the older Italian internees—residents of rural mountain areas of Italy who had never learned to swim—refused to jump. As the water rushed up to meet the bows, the ship's doctor stood and saluted his captain. The vessel sharply turned over. The forty-eight-year-old Major Christopher Bethell of the Royal Tank Regiment was seen to hand his life jacket to one of the internees, then assume a position next to the ship's captain, an act of kindness one survivor described as "the finest thing I have ever seen."

The last men seen on deck were fifty-four-year-old Captain Moulton; Father Fracassi, an interned Italian priest; and Otto Burfeind, a German prisoner of war who, eight months earlier, had survived the sinking of his cargo ship, SS *Adolph Woermann*.

The SS *Arandora Star* settled stern-first. A massive beam tore loose and swept the ship's side, swatting the men who dangled on the ropes in its trajectory. There was a mechanical groan, then a frothy roar. A geyser of steam fired a hundred feet into the air. Then, swirling silence.

SOMEHOW MICHAEL CORVIN LOST HIS shirt in the commotion. Semi-naked, he managed to cling to a life raft sufficiently far from where the ship sank to avoid being dragged down. The water was cold, but not murderously so, and Corvin, who at forty-three was neither young nor old, was strong enough to keep his head above water. Around him in the eerie, sad scene, others exhaustedly gave up hope and struggle, to slip beneath the oil-marbled water.

Eventually, a lifeboat drew sufficiently close to Corvin, its presence announced by the lazy slapping of water; through a mixture of his own effort and that of its occupants, he climbed aboard. Others who managed to swim to the side of one of the lifeboats weren't so welcomed; it took Uberto Limentani two hours to reach the lifeboat he'd spotted on the horizon. When he finally grasped the side and called out for help in Italian, one of the passengers told him that they could "only take on British survivors." The SS *Arandora Star*'s twenty-nine-year-old third officer, W. H. Tulip, overruled and ordered the other passengers to make room.

For survivors, a period of shivering, sorrowful reflection began. One had seen men grasp at ropes and slide down them into the water to moderate their fall, only to let go as the skin was torn from their hands. Their agonized screams were cut abruptly short as they plunged into the water. For another internee the dominating image was of a man in the water crying, "*Aiuto!*"—Help!—while his head fell open like the "leaf of a book."

AT 10:30 BST, TWO HOURS after the ship sank in the water, Michael and the others heard the approaching chug of an engine somewhere in the sky. A Royal Air Force Sunderland flying boat began to drop rations, first-aid outfits, cigarettes, and matches in watertight bags. It was another four hours before the Canadian destroyer HMCS *St. Laurent* arrived on the scene and began to collect the sodden, bedraggled survivors. The wind had pushed debris across a three-mile area to the west of the sinking, and wreckage intermingled with the bodies of the living and the dead. Few of those in the water had the strength to pull themselves up; they had to be hoisted aboard via line, where each man was given a sip of rum and handed a blanket and a cigarette. The work was "painfully slow." As the number of survivors who were left in the water dwindled, the Sunderland plane flew overhead, pointing out men who had drifted away.

At 16:55 BST, the last of the living had been taken aboard and the Sunderland returned to base. When, an hour later, the British destroyer HMS *Walker* arrived on the scene, the crew found no remaining signs of life. With the plane's support, 850 men had been saved by the HMCS *St. Laurent*. Two internee doctors—Dr. Ernest Ruhemann, a German, and Dr. Josef Ötvös, an Austrian and evangelical Christian—worked throughout the night, administering aid to their fellow survivors.

The rescue ship sailed into Greenock on the River Clyde on the morning of July 3. Four men who had been pulled from the water died before they reached land. Those in need of medical attention, including Michael Corvin, were immediately driven to Mearnskirk Hospital near Glasgow. It would prove to be one of the largest ocean rescue missions of the Second World War and one of the greatest losses of life, too: 446 Italians, 117 Germans, and 24 Austrians were missing, presumed drowned. Five men of unknown nationality died, along with fifty-eight crew members and ninety-five British soldiers between the ages of nineteen and forty-eight, many of whom had survived the evacuation of Dunkirk just a few weeks earlier. Four days after he raised a toast with his arresting officers, Landucci, the Italian waiter wrongly accused of being a fascist, was among the dead.

THE FIRST REPORTS OF THE disaster reached the public the following morning. The *Times* newspaper's initial story centered not on the multipronged tragedy of the event, but on the supposedly disreputable behavior of the internees. "Germans and Italians fight for lifeboats," blared the subheading, while in the main text the anonymous reporter wrote that there was "panic among the aliens . . . especially among the Germans, who thrust aside Italians in their efforts to reach the boats first."

The following day a second story developed the scene: "When the Germans made a wild rush for the lifeboats and fought with the Italians for precedence, scores were forced overboard in the struggle." British officers were made, the report continued, to split the fighting men apart, thereby wasting "valuable time that might have been devoted to rescue work." The fighting, the piece claimed, continued all the way to Scotland, proof, if proof were needed, of the dubious character of those who had been chosen for deportation.

These sensationalist claims were immediately disproven by the official firsthand reports collected from surviving officers by the Admiralty's Shipping Casualties Section.

"There is absolutely no truth in the statement that German prisoners were pushing the Italians out of the way, nor did I notice any fighting between the Germans and the Italians," Frederick Brown, chief officer and highest-ranking survivor, told his interviewer.

Regardless of what had happened on deck during the ship's last moments, at a War Cabinet meeting on the morning of the HMCS *St. Laurent*'s arrival in Scotland, ministers agreed that the tragedy should in no way interfere with the policy of deporting refugees. The remainder of the ships scheduled to carry internees across the Atlantic would proceed. Survivors would not be exempted; they would again be deported a few days later, this time to Australia.

Either through serendipity, or a rare instance of bureaucratic benevolence, Michael Corvin was sent, not to Australia on the HMT *Dunera* along with most other survivors, but to the Isle of Man. It was a fortuitous decision. There, as a resident of Hutchinson camp, Corvin would be close, not only to his son, but also to a unique collection of movers and shakers whose friendship and influence would alter the trajectory of his life.

These were the faces that Corvin saw as he finished his reading and looked up. To Hinrichsen, it was clear that Corvin was wracked with survivor's guilt. The vigil was somehow an attempt to express remorse at having lived while others had perished. Corvin slowly extinguished each candle, leaving just one flame on the kitchen table. In the almost dark, some members of the audience, perhaps fearing that a similar fate had struck their sons or friends, wept. Other survivors of the disaster sat in silence.

XII

THE SUICIDE CONSULTANCY

WITHOUT RADIOS OR NEWSPAPERS, Hutchinson's internees were exasperated by their enforced ignorance, not only of the ongoing debates about their fate in Parliament, but also of the general progress of the war. The War Office planned to produce a news bulletin to be distributed within the camps, but the first issue was yet to be circulated. Into the vacuum created by a lack of information swarmed "ghastly rumours and gnawing anxiety," as one of Hutchinson's internees wrote.

A backlog of letters at the sorting office meant that most internees did not know what was happening to their loved ones, many of whom were entirely dependent on their husbands' earnings prior to internment. To René Elvin, "the ensuing distress, heartbreaks, and . . . catastrophes were certainly not intended, but, in effect . . . [were] almost as cruel as the deliberate and systematic brutality of the Gestapo."

Many sought solace in books. Within three weeks the camp library had more than 130 available to borrow, some donated, others, including Pelican editions of works by H. G. Wells and George Bernard Shaw, were bought with the library's modest budget and marked as camp property with an official stamp. The librarians estimated that around 60 percent of internees used the library, the most popular texts including Lewis Carroll's *Alice in Wonderland* and Daphne du Maurier's

Rebecca. Literature offered its precious gift of escapism. Even here, however, there were reminders of the outside world; one of the librarians, the eighteen-year-old tailor Kurt Treitel—who, like Peter, fled to Britain on a *Kindertransport* train—found Nazi propaganda hidden among the pages of the books that had been sent by the German government. He threw the pamphlets away, but they served as a pointed sign of the forces that had both brought the refugees to Britain and now placed them in captivity.

All but the most optimistic or occupied internee felt some degree of distress from the absence of news. Most of the men understood that the catalyst of their arrest had been the risk of German invasion. On a cloudless day, Hutchinson's internees could see the Cumbrian coastline on the horizon, which some assumed to be Ireland. A rumor whipped around the camp that the country had fallen to the Nazis, who were now poised to invade the Isle of Man. Many fully expected to wake up one morning and discover their guards had switched from British to German.

Even if Captain Daniel flung wide the gates as the enemy landed, the captives would have no place to go, and would find little help from the generally hostile Manx population. The Gestapo would surely assume control of the camps, so helpfully filled by the British with their political and cultural opponents. There was plenty of space in the hills of the island for mass graves. It seemed certain that any man whose name was included in the Nazis' notorious "black book" would be returned to Germany, tortured, put on show trial, and executed.

These fears were well-placed. Two weeks before Hutchinson's opening, on June 30, the Nazis occupied the island of Jersey, which, like the Isle of Man, is a self-governing British Crown dependency. Jews living on the island were immediately registered, had their businesses appropriated, then their homes, and were finally deported to Nazi concentration camps. Islanders who weren't born locally were deported to Germany, where many died in prisons and labor camps, as did some of those who resisted the occupation.

In Hutchinson there were widespread discussions about what each man would do if faced with a comparable situation. The wine merchant

Fritz Hallgarten and his friends planned to cut through the wire, steal a boat, and attempt to drift across the Atlantic. If no vessel could be found, they vowed to fight.

"We didn't want to be caught like rats in a cage," he said. "We might have died on the Isle of Man, but we would have died fighting."

Others contemplated a different path. In Germany, suicide had become prevalent, particularly among Jews, where it had become an act of defiance, not of capitulation. In the days that followed *Kristallnacht*, suicide became so common that the authorities turned off the gas supply to Jewish homes in the town of Mainz. The idea that self-annihilation was preferable to state-annihilation had come with the refugees to Britain.

By the time of Hutchinson's opening, six men had hung themselves in Liverpool's Huyton internment camp, following the example of a Mr. Schiff, the first to die, in the camp's cloakroom on July 3. The police refused to listen to another refugee, a sixty-two-year-old chemistry professor, when he explained he was working on a process for utilizing sisal waste in submarines and had an exemption from internment. Before they returned to collect him, he swallowed a vial of poison.[*] A builder, Arthur Just, went missing on the ferry bringing him to the island; it seemed he had drowned himself rather than face internment.

The author Heinrich Fraenkel was among the men at Hutchinson who were willing to endure internment, but not an invasion. On one sunny afternoon on the lawn, he admitted that he had stowed a particularly sharp razor blade in readiness for invasion. If his life absolutely had to be taken, Fraenkel reasoned, then he would be the one to take it.

"Razor-blade be damned," countered a working-class German, who had previously been tortured by the Gestapo. "If those swine should catch me again, I wouldn't do their job for them. I would bloody well make 'em spend one of their precious bullets on me—and by God, I should use that last minute to tell 'em what I think of them."

---

[*] According to the MP Eleanor Rathbone, who recounted this story in the House of Commons, at the inquest one of the officers asked the widow whether her husband was a Jew. "No, he was of Jewish origin, but baptised a Christian," she answered. The officer, believing that this would have been grounds for exemption from internment, turned to his colleague and said: "What a pity. If we had only known before."

Feeling a professional duty to equip the men in Hutchinson with the most effective and straightforward way to take one's life, a clinical pathologist and a retired funeral director in the camp established a unit dubbed the Suicide Consultancy. The group, whose existence was hidden from Camp Father Burschell and his assistant, Wittelshöfer, offered lessons to any interested parties on the best and most painless way of killing oneself in the event of invasion. The pair offered demonstrations—one of which proved almost fatal to a volunteer—on how to make a reliable hanging noose from either a washing line or a pair of twisted trousers.

While the men in Hutchinson deliberated how they might leave the camp by any means necessary, in London different but no less desperate discussions regarding liberty were taking place.

ONE WEEK AFTER THE SURVIVORS of the *Arandora Star* landed in Scotland, on the morning of July 10, 1940, a group of some seventy German planes crossed the glittering waters of the English Channel and entered British airspace. It was the first skirmish in what would become known as the Battle of Britain, the fight for dominance over England's southern skies, and, it followed, the nation's future. In the House of Commons the debate focused not on the air assault, but on the ongoing fate of the thousands of men, women, and children—mostly refugees, mostly Jews—currently languishing behind barbed wire.

British internment policy had, thus far, been unmoved by the sinking of the *Arandora Star*, which Churchill later described as, merely, an "unpleasant incident." Despite the fact that the testimony of the surviving officers discredited the sensationalist press reports about German internees fighting to save themselves, the government had good reason to disparage the dead.

"All the Germans on board were Nazi sympathisers and . . . none came to this country as refugees," the shipping minister, Ronald Cross, had assured colleagues in the House of Commons. It was a claim that would have surprised Michael Corvin and the other refugee survivors.

Cross intimated, falsely, that the number of lifeboats and life rafts had been "more than sufficient to accommodate all passengers and crew," and that the high number of casualties was solely due to the misconduct of the passengers.

Fretful about the threat of imminent invasion, and aware of the mounting losses of merchant ships in the Atlantic, the idea that British seamen should have to give their lives to chaperone Nazis was understandably unpopular. Even so, earlier that week a poll found that only 27 percent of British citizens wanted a more discriminate internment policy; more than half the population still favored mass internment.

In Whitehall, however, there was a gathering realization that, in a mood of haste and hysteria, nuance may have been lost, ramifications left unconsidered, and injustices wrought by mass internment. The measures had been designed to protect Britain from an enemy within. It was increasingly clear that the policy threatened to damage the nation's position on the global stage. The German propaganda machine had wasted no time in claiming that Britain, by imprisoning so many Jews—80 percent of internees were Jewish—had willingly adopted Nazi policy. In response, a number of American newspapers had published articles condemning "Britain's concentration camps."

Any stories about the mistreatment of Jewish refugees in Britain risked alienating powerful potential allies—especially when the US secretary of state had specifically warned of the moral dangers inherent in a policy of mass internment prior to its introduction. Moreover, by interning most of the brilliant scientists and academics whom Britain had welcomed during the past few years, had the state not immobilized a source of invaluable support to the war effort?

That such a debate should take place at such a momentous stage in the war showed the beginnings of change in prevailing attitudes toward mass internment. But while the Spitfires fought German planes in the coastal skies, there was little consensus in the House of Commons.

"If a man is a victim of Nazi oppression, he is a friend of this country," Eleanor Rathbone told Parliament during the debate, restating a series of facts that should have prevented thousands of innocent men from internment. "He [has been] first combed out carefully by the tribunal after he has been watched for months and sometimes for years by refugee organisations, who see him every week, and after he has lived in hostels under reliable British guidance, and after he has had guarantors. What greater guarantee can you have?" For the young Conservative MP Major Victor Cazalet, the internment of refugees ran contrary to British values. It was, he said, "totally un-English."

The indignity and inconvenience to the interned innocents was, the Labour Party politician David Logan countered, a reasonable cost when it came to matters of national security. "Why should we trouble if one or two, or a thousand suspects are interned if this land of ours is safe?" he said. Some members of Parliament and the British public were, in fact, increasingly troubled.

"Would it not be better to make inquiries first rather than intern people and subject them to these indignities?" asked MP Glenvil Hall with pointed straightforwardness.

"At one time the feeling in the country and in this House was entirely in favour of the refugees," argued Osbert Peake. "That feeling changed in the early days of May. Today it is swinging back in the other direction."

Peake's analysis was perceptive. It would be the observations of a young British army officer made later that same night that forced the pendulum to swing fully in favor of Peter Fleischmann and the rest of the interned innocents.

SECOND LIEUTENANT MERLIN SCOTT, a twenty-one-year-old Oxford undergraduate, had always had a keen eye for detail. A hobbyist lepidopterist before he put his studies on hold to join the army, he had spotted a famously elusive butterfly, the marsh fritillary—the first recorded sighting in Britain since 1864. On the night of July 10, 1940, a few hours after the debate in the House of Commons, Scott was posted to Liverpool dockside to help oversee the embarkation of more than two thousand internees onto a ship that, just like the *Arandora Star*, was bound overseas.

It was dark and wet, but Scott had a clear view of the men as they traipsed dejectedly up the gangway onto the eleven-thousand-ton troopship HMT *Dunera* destined for Australia. Scott watched as, when each man crested the plank, his suitcase was snatched by a guard. Michael Corvin, headed to the Isle of Man, had been spared the night's cruelty. The majority of the *Arandora Star*'s survivors were not. In a state of shock and disbelief, the men returned to Liverpool via train, then filed onto the ship—indignant, incredulous. Having survived a torpedo attack in the mid-Atlantic, they were now to be forced into a similar journey with equivalent risks.

Any man who attempted to hold on to his bag was shoved with a rifle butt. Soldiers, some of whom appeared to be drunk, slipped watches into their pockets. The looting was indiscriminate: wallets, spectacles, fountain pens, toiletries were all removed. That which wasn't pilfered by the guards was thrown onto a gathering pile in the rain. Scott watched as a police officer, who had come to monitor the departure, picked items of clothing for himself from the dampening hoard, in full view of the owners waiting to board. When one internee politely requested that the soldiers stow his violin somewhere dry, the instrument was pulled from his hands and, in the ensuing scuffle, one of his nails torn off. No lists of valuables were made, no receipts given.

When the last of the internees boarded, Scott returned to his room and, in a state of angered disbelief, composed a letter to his father, a civil servant at the Foreign Office by the name of Sir David Montagu-Douglas Scott. He described what he had seen: the violent searches, the looting, the jeering, the thieving policeman.

"It was," his letter concluded, "a thoroughly bad show."

Scott's father read his son's letter with dismay, then shared its contents with his colleagues. Setting aside the behavior of British soldiers, it seemed that nobody in the Foreign Office had known that many of the *Arandora Star*'s survivors had been again loaded onto a troopship and sent into the gauntlet of the ocean less than two weeks after their ordeal. A representative from the Home Office declared that his department had also been unaware of the plan to deport survivors. United in their dismay, the Foreign Office and Home Office coauthored a letter of complaint addressed to Sir John Anderson, incorporating details from Scott's eyewitness account.

Regardless of who was to blame, the unmistakable fact was that many in government were unaware of the decisions that had been taken relating to internment, or that thousands of refugees from Nazi oppression were currently languishing in British camps. A clerical error heaped further cruelty upon the families of those involved: survivors had been recorded as deceased, and the deceased as survivors, leading some mothers to grieve for sons who were, in fact, still alive and interned, and others to celebrate the survival of loved ones who were dead. The doubt already cast on the government's version of events quickly curdled to outrage.

Compounding the looting of internees bound for Australia on the HMT *Dunera*, there were now reports of gross mistreatment of prisoners aboard the ship, where refugees had been beaten, deprived of food, and packed together in cramped, unhygienic conditions. Five thousand internees had been deported by the British government to camps in Canada, Australia, and other dominions. No further internees were sent abroad after the *Dunera* set sail, but the economist John Maynard Keynes, an adviser to the government who had taken up the cases of several interned economists, claimed that he had "not met a single soul, inside or outside government departments, who is not furious at what is going on."

IN HUTCHINSON TENSIONS BEGAN TO run high among these men forced to live in close proximity to strangers, offered no official route to protest their innocence, and with no idea how long they were to remain imprisoned. People whose lives had been buffeted by international-scale politics now found themselves embroiled in domestic-scale politics. In

House 2, a fracas between two men who had been forced to share a bed reached sufficient proportions to necessitate the establishment, by the other housemates, of a "Privy Court of House Arbitration."

It was claimed that, at night, Georg Kohlberg, a forty-seven-year-old textile merchant, would shove his bedfellow, Alex Cohn, against the wall in an effort to stop his snoring. The resulting anguished cries made the matter of the two men's sleeping arrangements a house-wide concern, yet neither man would volunteer to change rooms. The housemates finally ruled that Kohlberg must find somewhere else to sleep.

Hellmuth Weissenborn, a former professor of graphic design at the academy at Leipzig, was well-liked by most of his housemates in House 28, who benefited from his skill as house cook. Weissenborn was, as Hinrichsen put it, able to transform "any fish into salmon, any potato into a culinary feast, beautifully served."

When asked what a particular dish consisted of Weissenborn usually answered, *"Ausgekochte Scheisse"*—boiled shit—with the kind of self-deprecation that enamored him to many of his fellow intern-ees. Not everyone was charmed, however. One morning a man who had taken a dislike to Weissenborn went downstairs to breakfast and, upon seeing his housemate, exclaimed: *"Scheisse!"* With enviable quick-wittedness, the artist bowed from the waist and replied in a dis-play of mock-introduction: "Weissenborn."

AS THE DAYS TURNED TO weeks, the internees soon found where they best fitted; communities formed around the camp, men drawn to one another through common interest, profession, religion, and what-ever arcane compatibilities spark friendship. Weissenborn united his housemates around food, but it was his pioneering window art that first brought the artists in the camp together.

The ship that had been carrying blackout material to the island was sunk in enemy action according to an official report. So Hutchinson's windows were either covered with polymer film or simply painted with black or blue paint, which made the interiors "intensely depressing," as Bertha Bracey described the ambiance after she visited the camp in the early autumn.

One day Weissenborn took a razor blade to the polymer film, cutting a mythological scene into one of the windows of House 28. The image, an inverse silhouette, welcomed light and fantasy into the drab rooms and awakened the imaginations of subdued, cloistered minds. When none of his fellow housemates complained, Weissenborn began to cut more: centaurs, a unicorn, a dolphin rider and, in the kitchen window, plates of food and fruit. Seeing the artist's work, a group of Orthodox Jews in a neighboring house asked Weissenborn to produce a similar tableaux on their windows, albeit this time depicting scenes from the Hebrew bible.

Weissenborn's use of this unlikely canvas soon spread, moving from house to house, allowing residents to mark their building with images that expressed their collective character or interests. In House 19 the sculptor Ernst Müller-Blensdorf, whom Peter watched dismantle a bed at Warth Mills, engraved two naked women lying on a beach while a seagull lasciviously hovered overhead . Another intrepid artist attempted to replicate a section of the Sistine Chapel. Others simply adorned their house windows with worldly objects of penitentiary longing: whiskey, lobster, cigars.

Amateurs participated, too. Anton Löwenthal, a twenty-year-old textile designer, carved images of Adam and Eve carrying an apple bearing a price tag that appeared to accuse the camp canteen of profiteering. The upper of the sash windows showed a sun and a half-moon, and when opened, Adam became silhouetted against the sun and Eve against the moon. Johann Neunzer, a fifty-year-old animal trapper and, at the time of his arrest, the lion tamer at the Burnt Stub Zoo, cut exquisitely expressionistic wild animals into the bay window of House 40—a rhino, a giraffe, a camel, and the backside of an elephant—each stylized and rendered in crisp, sharp lines. In Hinrichsen's view, the amateur's work was the camp's best.[*]

___

[*] It was not the first time that internment had produced such unexpected fruits on the island. Twenty-six years earlier, in 1914, a young German named Joseph Pilates was traveling through England with his circus. After the government instituted its first mass internment policy, the po-

The artists interned in the camp, as well as other assorted art-minded writers and poets, found themselves inexorably drawn to one another, the sense of community accelerated by the arrival, four days after Hutchinson's opening, of a true celebrity of the art world.

IT WAS SHORTLY AFTER BREAKFAST that the residents of one of Hutchinson's houses heard a rap on the front door. The visitor was a large man in a buttoned-up, three-piece, gray-striped suit. He had a soft, loose mouth, and thinly tousled gray hair, a few strands of which trailed down to a pair of bright blue eyes. While the man was as tall and broad-shouldered as Ludwig Warschauer, he held his body not in the manner of a streetfighter but in that of a benign vagrant, an effect compounded by the old, stout boots—at least one size too large—and socks pocked with a galaxy of holes. In his hand, he carried a bucket filled with slop.

Few would have recognized the strange figure as Kurt Schwitters, the renowned associate of Dadaism, the avant-garde art movement of the 1920s that celebrated nonsense and absurdism, which, for its participants, seemed the only appropriate artistic response to the catastrophic loss and destruction of the First World War. Schwitters was not Jewish, but his work was sufficiently despised by the Nazis to have been included in the *Entartete Kunst* exhibition of so-called "degenerate" art.

Hinrichsen had attended the exhibition, which opened in Munich on July 19, 1937, where 650 paintings, sculptures, prints, and books stolen by the Nazis were displayed. The exhibition was deliberately laid out in a chaotic manner to elicit a sense of confusion and disorder in visitors. Scornful slogans, such as "An insult to German womanhood" and "Nature as seen by sick minds"—accompanied the works, alongside price tags that indicated how much money had been spent by Ger-

---

lice arrested Pilates and sent him to the island where, in the weeks and months that followed, he developed and taught his fellow internees the exercises that would later take his name. The Pilates stretches, the first of internment's manifold, unlikely cultural dividends, were, Joseph later claimed, based on those performed by the local, tailless Manx cats he had observed from behind the wire.

man museums on their acquisition. The party hoped these monetary footnotes would enrage those visitors who had struggled to feed their families during the recent depression, while the artistic elite spent millions buying these crude, deviant works.

One of Schwitters's collages, titled *Merz Picture 32 A*, was placed in Group 9 of the exhibition, a section titled *Vollendeter Wahnsinn*— Complete Madness—and a photograph in which Hitler was shown grinning inanely in front of Schwitters's artwork, deliberately hung askew, had appeared in German newspapers.

Framed in the doorway of the terraced house, today Schwitters cut a rather different figure from the revolutionary artist of reputation. He had been aged and reduced by a difficult escape from Germany, via Norway to Edinburgh, where he had spent his fifty-third birthday sleeping on a hard floor of a local pub, herded together with other refugees. The stress of internment, first at the York racecourse, then at Warth Mills, had triggered at least one severe epileptic fit before, finally, the artist arrived at Hutchinson on July 17.

Schwitters's immense powers of concentration had always enabled him to disassociate, somewhat, from the physical world; he would often forget to shave and neglect to wrap up on a chilly day. In a time of youth and plenty, this self-neglect passed as the eccentricity widely assumed to accompany artistic brilliance. Today, beleaguered by the toils of exile, Schwitters appeared merely haggard.

"Do you have any leftovers?" Schwitters inquired, nodding at the bucket in his hand.

There were always leftovers. For many of the continental refugees, the art of porridge making proved evasive. The rumor that the British authorities were adding bromide to the oats in order to stifle sexual desire in the camp added further disincentive to eat. When one housefather asked why, precisely, Schwitters was interested in their cold porridge, the artist replied that he intended to use the material to patch up some holes in a wall. He filled his bucket and loped away, on to the next house.

The author Richard Friedenthal, who later became chairman of the PEN club of German-speaking authors abroad, was the first to recognize Schwitters, whittling an abstract birch-wood sculpture the morning after his arrival at Hutchinson. Friedenthal led the artist by the arm and began introducing him around the camp as "the great Dadaist Kurt Schwitters." Hinrichsen, switching from student of art history to witness *to* art history, shook the artist's hand—"a surprisingly limp handshake"—and showed Schwitters around the camp.

"As soon as I can lay my hands on some paint and canvas, I shall paint this," Schwitters told Hinrichsen when he noticed the view leading down from the camp, across the red-roofed houses, and out to the little tower perched in the bay.

Schwitters walked gingerly, tracking the ground as if afraid of accidentally stepping on a cat's tail or a child's fingers. If he spied a lost bug or beetle, he'd guide it safely off the path. Whenever he came across an empty cigarette box, a torn-up envelope with a postage stamp, or the wrapper from a chocolate bar, he'd bend down, study the object lovingly, then place it in the deep pocket of his loden jacket.

Soon enough, those who did not receive a formal introduction were made forcefully aware of Schwitters's presence in the camp. One evening Fred Uhlman, the Stuttgart lawyer-turned-painter, arrived at House 19 to visit Schwitters, who was painting Uhlman's portrait. On the ground floor stood an elderly Viennese businessman, barking up the stairs at Schwitters, who stood on the top-floor landing, barking down.

"Woof-woof," barked the businessman in a manner that reminded Uhlman of a mastiff.

"Woof-woof-woof," answered Schwitters, assuming the role of a dachshund.

The call-and-response continued, a crescendo of barking, until both men became tired and, finally, the businessman sloped off to bed.

The barking, which on one occasion caused British guards to enter the camp in order to investigate the noise, appeared to be Schwitters recapturing former performances in freedom, in this case a Dadaists' tour of Holland, when he had interrupted the Dutch artist Theo van Doesburg's speeches with animal noises.

Hutchinson, it was clear, was having a revitalizing effect on the artist, who began to transform his attic bedroom with collages stippled with cigarette packets, seaweed, shells, pieces of cork, wire, glass, nails, and—as he began to bring the pails of leftovers back from his morning rounds—a mound of hardening porridge.

SCHWITTERS'S ARRIVAL AND THE CAMP trend of cutting images into Hutchinson's windows gave the art-minded internees a burgeoning sense of community. As well as commercial artists such as Willy Dzubas, a producer of exquisite art nouveau travel posters, and the cartoonist Adolf "Dol" Mirecki, there were more than twenty professional artists and sculptors at Hutchinson camp. The group began to self-organize.

In the camp's earliest days, any artist hoping to create work had swiftly learned to improvise. Lavatory paper—marked, to the delight of those internees able to find humor in the perversities of their new life, with the slogan "War Office Property"—became "elevated to a sort of illuminated scroll," as Hinrichsen put it. The linoleum used to cover the kitchen and corridor floors in many of the boardinghouses was used for linocuts, while Weissenborn, who via the blackout art had already shown himself to be one of the most industrious of Hutchinson's artists, pioneered the manufacture of printing ink by mixing crushed graphite from lead pencils with margarine.

Schwitters was used to working with unorthodox materials for his collages. He collected discarded cigarette boxes, stamps, and candy wrappers, dismantled tea chests for their plywood panels, and painted directly onto the staircase of the office building inside the camp. For those artists who were less industrious, or who worked in more traditional media, there was, however, a desperate need for materials.

The former Berlin art dealer Siegfried Oppenheimer became an unofficial spokesman for the group and met Captain Daniel in an attempt to cajole the officer into viewing himself as a patron of the arts in the camp, with the aim of securing some space and materials with which the artists might work. Oppenheimer was an overpowering character, liable to gross exaggeration, who constantly quoted Goethe and would address every artist as *Meister*.

"Listening to him one would think that the accumulation of talent in Hutchinson camp had only twice been equalled in history," wrote Hinrichsen. "In antiquity under Pericles, and in Renaissance Florence under the Medici."

"We have a number of very well-known artists here," said Oppenheimer in his opening gambit. "They are desperate for materials."

Captain Daniel did not take much convincing. Not only was the officer an amateur photographer, his wife, Margery, was also a keen artist. As a teenager, she had been forbidden from accepting a place in art college by her parents, who explained the profession did not fit their aspirations for their daughter's life. Having experienced the frustration of being unable to practice her creativity, Margery was sympathetic to the artists in the camp and duly encouraged her husband not only to donate and secure materials, which were distributed by the Cultural Department, but also to set aside studio space on the top floor of the office building, where artists could work and, later, host classes.

In return Oppenheimer, seeking to agitate Daniel's competitive streak, promised the commandant an art exhibition the likes of which had never been seen before in a British internment camp—the ideal event, perhaps, to which to invite his rivals on the island, particularly the commandant of Onchan camp, which had recently beaten Hutchinson's team at soccer.

JUST AS THE ARTISTS NEEDED space to work, they also needed space to socialize. One day, shortly after the camp's opening, Uhlman recognized the owner of a patisserie in Hampstead Heath. The pastry cook was an Austrian refugee who had run a successful café in Vienna, frequented by writers and artists. When Hitler annexed Austria, Nazi supporters ransacked the café; two days later, the man fled Austria to England, where he had opened what he hoped would become a similar establishment in London.

While living in Paris as an impoverished, beginner artist, Uhlman had spent much of his time at the Café du Dôme on Montparnasse; café life had become romantically associated with his personal creative awakening. So, in London, Uhlman had become a regular visitor at the pastry cook's new café.

The two men greeted one another, shared the stories of how they had come to the island, and reminisced about good coffee and conversation.

"What about a Hutchinson Café?" Uhlman suggested.

Soon enough, the pair located a venue: an extension, currently being used as a laundry room, built into the garden of House 15, an end-of-terrace house situated in the northwest corner of the camp, away from the square. With its whitewashed walls and bubbling paint, water taps and washboards, the venue had none of the sophistication of the continental cafés of Uhlman's vision. But the room was sizable and, when some trellis tables, chairs, and stools had been arranged inside, provided a relatively comfortable space for afternoon meetings, conversation, and even performances.

The establishment—which later adopted the name *Café Chez La Dame Absente*—would be, Uhlman decided, a member's club. There were no membership cards, no blackballing, and no outright rejections—anybody creatively engaged was welcome provided some existing member had recommended them. The rules, which developed with time, were few but enforced. There was to be no talk of "release," nor of "*Heimweh*"—homesickness—nor, later, of Christmas, topics that too easily inspired nostalgia and mourning. The café would instead provide an oasis of escape within the camp, where—for a moment—no man had to fret about invasion or contemplate suicide or worry about the fate of his loved ones on the outside.

The group attracted a diverse number of characters from a range of disciplines. As well as the painters Erich Kahn and Kurt Schwitters, and sculptors Paul Hamann and Ernst Müller-Blensdorf, members included at least two photographers, three architects, four musicians, and five writers. Bruno Ahrends, as head of the Cultural Department, was a founder, joined by the journalists Heinrich Fraenkel and Michael Corvin, and Curt

Sluzewski, the papal lawyer. As with any club, a certain cliquishness was inevitable. While some of the camp's best-known fine artists, including the tetchy hunger-striker Fechenbach and Ludwig Meidner, either refused to join the artists' collective, or arrived too late—many other musicians, composers, and actors were never, seemingly, invited.

Drawn by the promise of coffee and like-minded conversation, the Artists Café soon swirled with laughter and badinage. Miraculously, the café's proprietor served Austrian-style cakes and pastries studded with raisins and almonds. The men came from diverse backgrounds, different countries, different disciplines, yet were united in their experience of exile and their eagerness to remain at work behind the barbed wire.

If Schwitters felt any animosity toward Michael Corvin by way of the journalist's previous employer, the *Deutsche Volkszeitung*—which, in 1920, described Schwitters's best-known poem, "Un Anna Blume," as "the most revolting piece of writing in our time"—he did not let it interfere in his relationship with the writer. Professional jealousies dissipated here, in the leveled field of internment, where work stood on merit, not its maker's connections.

As well as offering games of poker, the café became a venue for memorable performances: the author Richard Friedenthal recited excerpts from his 1931 book *The White Gods*, a historical novel about the conquest of Mexico, from memory. Fred Uhlman recounted his time selling tropical fish in Paris, when a water shortage wiped out his livestock. And soon Schwitters began to hold court with a mixture of anecdotes imbued with magical realism, absurdist stories, and recitals of his poetry.

Like the anarchic thrum of 1920s Berlin, Hutchinson's unique set of circumstances provided its artists with a vibrant community, while their status as internees gifted a unifying perspective: the cognizance of freedom, an invisible state to all but those from whom freedom has been taken. A scene—that necessary context for any unifying artistic endeavor—had begun to emerge. Nazism had robbed Peter Fleischmann of his artistic training. Now fate and politics had conspired to prepare for him a community of mentors far beyond his means or imagination.

XIII

INTO THE CRUCIBLE

THE GLOOMED CARRIAGE RATTLED IN almost-darkness. It was the night before the Luftwaffe returned to bomb Crewe for the third time. Earlier that day Peter Fleischmann and two hundred or so of Prees Heath's remaining internees had been ordered to pack their belongings. The camp was due to be closed at the recommendation of Rabbi Schonfeld, with Peter and the others redistributed. Caught in this new riptide, there was little time to prepare for what was next, or to consider what was being left behind. One middle-aged businessman bagged a clutch of the foot-long tent pegs that had secured his bell tent to the ground. Peter's only souvenirs were those of his own making: the drawings scribbled on discarded envelopes.

The journey to Liverpool caught in Peter's mind in a series of sounds and stills, as if burned to memory via the intermittent flickering of streetlights through a train window. There was the groan of wood as the carriage leaned determinedly into a corner. There were the faces of his fellow travelers, ghosts in the quiet blue lightbulbs. There was the crumpled ribbon of material as a finger lifted the blinds a crack, then the instant, rageful admonishment of fellow passengers. Disembarkation; salt wind; rollicking ferry. The churn of the dockside approach. Ropes creaking in the dark. Gray-fingered rain. A trickling line of men crunching up a steep road. Barbed gates. Querying torches. A brass baton. And, finally, the step into the dusty warmth that marked the threshold of House 1, Hutchinson Square.

After dealing scores of blows, serendipity had at last smiled on Peter Fleischmann. For an orphan exile with artistic ambition in a foreign country, there was no place better suited than Hutchinson camp, where happenstance had gathered a group of some of the finest and most influential German and Austrian artists. On Monday, August 26, 1940, a journey that to date had felt like a tumble down a set of stairs had ended, for now, in the soft landing of opportunity.

THE NEXT MORNING, HIS CLOTHES still damply cloying, Peter and his new housemates congregated in front of their new home and awaited roll call in the hesitant light. After the misery of Warth Mills and the cramped discomfort of Prees Heath, Hutchinson, with its flower-bordered lawn, wooden chairs, tables, beds, china, decent rations, and semi-autonomy, felt like, as another of the Prees Heathers put it, "a return to civilization."

Hutchinson was six weeks old; Peter had entered a maturing universe. The internees had developed their daily routines—the favored mug, the preferred toilet cubicle, the ideal route to take when crossing the lawn—habits of minor, vital comfort. The camp's daily, immovable routine provided the semblance of a reassuring structure, too. For those who couldn't manage to rouse themselves for the optional dawn exercises held on the lawn square at 7:00, there was mandatory roll call at 7:30. Breakfast: 8:15. Lunch: 12:30. Supper: 7:00. Then, a final counting of heads at 9:30 in the evening.

Thanks to Ahrends and Hinrichsen's formidable powers of organization, the camp's schedule of intellectual diversions had grown and diversified, too. On the week of Peter's arrival, Hutchinson's timetable of cultural events listed no fewer than forty lectures. The subjects covered philosophy, bookkeeping, medieval history, and the nutritional benefits of fruit (Title: "Q. 'Why should we eat oranges?' A. 'Vitamins'"), as well as performances of Brahms and Schubert by a young graduate of the Royal College of Music, Hans Fürth, accompanied on violin by the impressionist painter Fritz Salomonski.

For internees who wished to practice their French, there was a weekly "Cercle Française" run by Dr. Arthur Bratu, a teacher who fled Germany for Belgium before escaping to Britain on a fishing boat. Anyone interested in photography could join weekly classes offered by Paul Henning, a member of the Artists Café. There were soccer games, chess tournaments, boxing matches, and local hikes—albeit under armed guard—through the island countryside, with its bowed reeds and ragwort. In the afternoons Peter could watch a kind of proto-aerobics session on the lawn: exercise set to music, led by Kurt Böhm, the school gymnastics teacher. For a young orphan from Berlin it was overwhelming.

"Artists? Painting? Concerts? For free? Every day? It was unheard of," Peter later recalled.

There was, in Hutchinson camp, no shortage for a man in search of diversion. There was opportunity for paid work, too. The Camp Bank consisted of one manager and a few clerks; the Post and Parcel Office employed a postmaster and four staff. Sixteen men made up the Fire Brigade and the Air Raid Precaution Services and had regular drills to practice using the portable reciprocating water pumps known as stirrup pumps. They were supplemented by one doctor and twelve stretcher bearers.

In the six weeks since its opening, the camp office had expanded its range of community services, too. It now housed two shoemakers, a laundry, a tailor, a pressing and ironing service, a shirt repairer, two hairdressers, and four watch repairers; services that had enabled some internees to return to the vocations they had been forced to leave behind in their homelands. At the suggestion of Bertha Bracey's man-in-situ, William Hughes, the members of this last group fixed watches owned by residents outside the camp at the trade union pay rate, on the proviso that the watchmakers did not train any fellow internees—presumably so as not to further threaten the livelihoods of British workers.

Those who preferred outdoor employment could apply to chop wood or work as farm laborers. One group of young men from Hutchinson helped to build the island's airport, digging ditches and laying cables.

Anyone could buy items from the camp canteen, managed by Hans Guttmann, the director of Hammond book publishing. Guttmann, supported by four shop assistants, would even allow any internee to purchase items on credit, provided they could prove they owned a bank account on the outside. In time, every prisoner of war and internment camp, including Hutchinson, received bespoke currency: generic notes stamped with the "camp of issue."

The camp had emerging opportunities for men who wished to exercise existing talents or seek out new ones. Few may have recognized Otto Haas-Heye, a distinguished clothes designer who, via his Berlin salon Alfred-Marie, helped shape fashion during the 1920s. After a dozen or so men joined his weaving school and began to produce exquisite rugs under his tutelage and direction, however, everyone recognized his work. A carpentry school taught woodwork, while another group made artificial flowers and stuffed animals. Some items were of a particularly high quality. Michael Corvin wrote of Leon Kuhmerker's talent for artificial flower making: "The [flowers] consist mainly of fine coloured leather and their appearance is amazingly vivid . . . no flower leaves the little shop which is not perfect in form and unique in making."

A shop was opened in Douglas to sell items made by the internees, including rugs from the weaving school and model boats made by the carpenters. In her role as chair of the Central Department for Interned Refugees, Bertha Bracey organized materials for most of the workshops and schools.

NONE OF THE PAID WORK was of interest to Peter, however. While he was counted among the small number of "destitute" cases in Hutchinson, with no income or funds to support life inside the camp, he had nevertheless realized that the budding artistic activity he had seen in Prees Heath was nothing compared to the hub he had now entered.

Shortly after his arrival in the camp, Peter had seen a strange-looking artist sitting in the corner of the square. He watched as the man stopped people as they walked past, offering to sketch their portrait in as little as five minutes for a fee. As commercially efficient as a Times Square caricaturist snaring passing tourists, the man priced his portraits on a sliding scale: £3 for a head and shoulders; £4 for head, shoulders, and arms; £5 for a half figure.

When someone informed Peter that the man in the loden coat was the famed Dadaist, he was somewhat surprised at the straightforwardness of the portraits, but immediately signed up for life-drawing lessons hosted by Schwitters, which were popular among those who wanted to learn to paint, or those who merely wanted a closer look at the celebrity. Under Schwitters's guidance, Peter painted still life canvases, depicting items in his immediate vicinity: his shoes, his knife, fork and plate, flowers. He continued his work outside the lessons, painting on the hardcover panels torn from books on loan from the camp library.

"I had always wanted to paint, and here was the opportunity," Peter recalled. "I had a chance, at last, to paint and to learn, from morning to night, every day."

Peter was a quick learner and, when his painting of his shoes won first prize in a camp art competition, he soon caught the attention of the other artists.

"I shared the conviction of the older artists that here was a natural talent, a born artist who just could not stop himself from working and learning," Hinrichsen noted.

Proximity to doyens of German and Austrian art only heightened Peter's longing for that which had been robbed from him, first by the Nazis and then by the British: an artistic education. Here Hutchinson began to provide a valuable, almost preindustrial grounding. In *The Ministry of Fear*, Graham Greene's wartime novel about a refugee who turns out to be a spy, he writes about the unique companionship shared by the exiled, those who, united in their tragedy, "always had friends." It was in Hutchinson that Peter Fleischmann first experienced this, the benevolent network of the oppressed.

Youthful enthusiasm and eagerness made Peter a useful apprentice to the older artists, who passed on their gifts. He learned to use toothpaste to size their painting grounds, and how to find and crush minerals, then mix them with the oil from sardine tins to create oil paints. He persuaded several bushy-eyebrowed internees to let him have a few hairs, which he made into brushes, later used by Fritz Kraemer to paint his delicate portraits.

Hellmuth Weissenborn, who started the craze for window silhouettes, taught Peter how to mix shoe polish and pencil lead with margarine for printmaking. Just prior to his arrest Weissenborn had managed to pack his engraving tools and some boxwood blocks. To produce prints he cut small pieces of linoleum from the attic of House 28, then he taught Peter how to adjust a clothes wringer to print linocuts. The sculptors Paul Hamann and Georg Ehrlich showed Peter how to smuggle clay dug while out on an escorted walk in the local hills back into the camp—an inverse process to the tunnel diggers in the prisoner of war camps and their soil shaken from trouser legs. The older men showed Peter how to separate the gritstone sand and, finally, how to cast. Ernst Müller-Blensdorf showed Peter how to carve using blocks of firewood. The training was practical and foundational.

"Everything thereafter," he said, "was just a recap."

The teenager was not the only one inspired to express himself. Others who had never shown an interest in artistic pursuits were drawn to simple forms of self-expression. Inspired by the example of the craftsmen in his house, Hans Gussefeld whittled the wooden tent pegs he'd taken as souvenirs from Prees Heath into crocodile-shaped letter openers. A young furniture maker, Frank Herbert Jacob, carved a wooden figure of a diving girl, a piece that showed, as one camp critic put it, "remarkable aptitude." Jacob was duly welcomed into the Artists Café.

Peter, however, was of a different category of talent—sufficiently gifted, in fact, to recognize that his work to date had been elementary and plainly representational. He yearned to move beyond the rudiments of depicting the relationship between objects and space, to begin exploring what that relationship might mean. To this end, Schwitters extended a rare invitation for the young artist to visit his attic studio in House 19.

Schwitters had no qualms about allowing Peter into the sanctuary where he kept his less traditional, more vulnerable work. His son, Ernst, was also interned, but he did not join his father in Hutchinson until he was transferred to the camp in November 1940. When he arrived, many of the other members of the Artists Café took an immediate dislike to the younger Schwitters, whom Hinrichsen described as an "arrogant and opinionated brat, visibly envious and hostile." Uhlman recorded that Schwitters's "ghastly son" may even have been "ashamed of his father." In Peter, who was three years younger than Ernst, Schwitters had an interested, appreciative disciple.

Peter arrived at an anarchic scene: the floor a slum of discarded plates, pieces of stale bread, and greening cheese. In one corner, the artist had built a blanket fort under a table, a mattress hidden inside. Elsewhere in the room there were stick figures carved from the legs of the performer Rawicz's collapsed piano. Peter was surprised to see a garret adorned with collages, nothing like the portraits that Schwitters hawked on Hutchinson's lawn and which, perhaps fearing the derision of his peers, he had showed only to the few he invited to his studio.*

Three tall, gray, aromatic towers dominated the space. As Peter looked more closely, he realized that they were made from old porridge studded with found objects: stamps, cigarette boxes, nails, pebbles, and shells. Built from the leftovers Schwitters collected in his bucket on his post-breakfast rounds, the porridge had acquired rainbow streaks of mold and now emitted a faint sickly smell.

Ignoring the boy's curiosity, Schwitters showed Peter how to mix paint. At his wife's urging, Captain Daniel had provided materials for

---

* If this was Schwitters's fear, it was well-founded. Even the painter's sober portraiture failed to convince the Oxford professor Paul Jacobsthal, who specialized in ancient Greek vase painting and Celtic art, and who witheringly described Schwitters in his diary as "an amateurish painter" and reciter of "infantile poetry." The carver Ernst Müller-Blensdorf was more forthright still with his feelings. In a letter to Schwitters he wrote woundingly: "I am sad for you to have produced such stupid stuff."

the artists; Schwitters, however, had learned through the disruption of recent months to take nothing for granted and thus believed self-sufficiency was a useful skill for any interned artist. He picked up a loose brick and began rubbing it to produce a ruddy powder. Once he had collected enough powder, he added linseed oil to produce a colored paste. Peter watched the artist, who was more than twice his age, work in the strange, jumbled surroundings of his gathered domain.

Not everyone was so enchanted by the artist's presence. The patience of Schwitters's housemates in House 19, first tested by Schwitters's barking, had snapped when residue from the porridge began dripping through the ceilings onto the lower floors. For these men the experience of living with an eccentric was proving an unenviable arrangement.

Art is often, among other things, the pursuit of stillness in the midst of chaos—the same stillness, as the novelist Saul Bellow described it, that characterizes prayer in the eye of the storm. For Peter, the training was not only a means to a vocational end, but also a way to access the intimate realm of creation, where the world can be ordered and processed, and, in some way, the riot stilled.

THE RIOT WAS, FOR MOST of Hutchinson's internees, closer to the surface. Once the men recognized that their immediate needs were to be met, for now at least, the systems of mental and physical adaptation—those short-term resiliencies that enable a person to survive in acutely stressful situations—eased. In their place came the insistent and unpleasant anxieties about everything in each man's life beyond the basics of food and shelter. No amount of sunshine and leisure could stave off the agonizing appreciation of the situation for men with wives and children or abandoned businesses who did not know how their families would endure without their income and who understood the precariousness of their position, and that of Britain more generally. The gestalt vibe was tetchy, irritable. In the words of Professor Jacobsthal, Hutchinson "seethed with anger and excitement."

There was simmering indignation at the *Absurdität*—absurdity—and *Groteske*—grotesqueness—of men and women who had been arrested and interned on suspicion of being sympathetic to the same regime that had persecuted them. Oswald Volkmann summed up the widespread feelings among the internees in a bitterly ironic poem titled "Loyalty," which pointed out that many of those interned had been fighting the Nazis while, prior to the war, Britain was misguidedly seeking some sort of appeasement deal with Hitler.

> We have been Hitler's enemies
> For years before the war,
> We knew his plans of bombing and
> Invading Britain's shore,
> We warned you of his treachery
> When you believed in peace,
> And now we are His Majesty's
> Most loyal internees.

The men's sense of anguish had been heightened by the fact that, while the imminent danger of invasion from German forces in France seemed to have eased, there had been no change in government policy to match.

"Some of us believed the reason for our sufferings lay in the period of acute danger through which the country was passing," wrote one internee. "But when the crisis was averted and we were still made to feel outcasts, many despaired."

Fred Uhlman had seen, from his time as a lawyer in Stuttgart, the way in which men convicted of a crime would experience acute anxiety while awaiting their sentence, only to "settle down miraculously" when the judge handed down the timescale of their punishment. For Hutchinson's internees, this lack of a time frame, the basic kindness afforded even to thieves and murderers, exerted a "special torture," as Uhlman put it. "I didn't know if I was going to be out in six days, six months or six years."

To maintain composure required a constantly nurtured conviction of innocence, an immunity to despair, and a pinch of genetic good fortune. Unusually, class, status, or wealth provided no protection here in the camp. Each day, Peter watched the poet, former tennis star, and scion of one of the oldest and wealthiest families in the Kaiserreich, Count Franz Josef von Matuschka—better known as "Graf" to his friends—mournfully trudge the perimeter of the barbed fence, in an impenetrable fug of depression.

The combination of worry and ignorance began to make men ill. Uhlman suffered stomach cramps and giddiness that he attributed to nervous tension caused by his predicament and a fear that "something in my Home Office file would prevent my release." He had reason to feel miserable. His wife, Diana, had given birth to the couple's first child shortly after his arrest. Every week spent away from a baby is a milestone missed. The losses felt profoundly unfair for Uhlman and the other men in the camp who, with the arrival of each envelope containing a censored letter from a loved one, saw their hopes raised, then inevitably dashed.

Uhlman was not alone in his private agonies.

"Confinement," wrote the Oxford professor Paul Jacobsthal in his camp diary, "means a break in the continuity of existence, an interruption of the normal flux of life." In short, he concluded, "it causes a trauma." Hellmuth Weissenborn claimed having to kill a soldier in the previous war was an easier burden to bear than internment, which was, he wrote, a "continuous torment."

Peter felt little of the animosity expressed by those men who were consumed with anxiety for their loved ones outside of the camp. After his uncle failed to post Peter's letters, his grandfather's housekeeper did not know whether the boy she had hidden had even made it safely to Britain. Peter had lost contact, too, with Echen, the heiress with whom he had spent his summer holidays. For Peter, not only was there nobody at home waiting for him, but there was also no home.

His friend and former colleague Donald Midgley was the only link to the outside world, the only person on whom Peter could spend his weekly ration of twenty-four written lines. To begin with, he wrote regularly to Donald, who had been posted to Burma with the Royal Air Force. In his letters Peter described the vivid and unlikely community of refugees into which he had landed. Each week, Peter hoped to receive a reply—eventually, one did arrive. It was nothing against Peter personally, Donald explained, but his commanding officer had queried why a British serviceman might be receiving letters from a German interned on suspicion of being a spy. Donald's CO had suggested that he should not have contact with any individual whose loyalty to Britain was in doubt. For now, Donald told his friend, the letters would have to stop.

Peter had learned to not bother counting time (later in life he could not even remember the year he came to England). "I didn't know what the future would bring, and I couldn't bring back the past," he recalled of his serene acceptance of circumstances. The closed environment of Hutchinson, where both his physical and intellectual needs were met for the first time, discouraged him yet further from keeping track of the months. We do not count the days we hope will last forever. The older artists were astonished by their new student's apparent unflappability.

"Peter seemed singularly unconcerned about the inconveniences and hardship of internment," Hinrichsen noted. "All he wanted was to draw and paint." In this regard, Peter was almost an anomaly. Among the artists, only Ludwig Meidner, who a contemporary critic described as the "hottest crater" in the "volcanic epoch" of expressionism, was eager to remain interned.[*]

Peter's attitude was not uncommon among the younger internees, however, who had less invested in the outside world and, therefore, fewer causes for concern or longing.

---

[*] For Meidner, whose work had been included in the Nazis' *Entarte Kunst* exhibition, internment provided not only an escape from the violence of war, but also, as a convert to Orthodox Judaism, an observant community from which to draw support. Some suspected he was also enjoying space from his younger wife and former artistic protégée, Else, with whom Meidner had a turbulent marriage. In 1941 the artist applied for a continuation of internment; the appeal proved successful. After a stint at Huyton camp in Liverpool, then Mooragh camp on the island, he arrived at Hutchinson in the autumn of 1941, where he remained until his final, reluctant release in early December.

"The camp here is quite wonderful," the seventeen-year-old Baruch Emmanuel wrote from Hutchinson in a letter to his aunt. For some working-class men, the chance to stay by the sea with full board was a luxury they might not have otherwise experienced. One elderly Orthodox Jew was overheard saying, while standing by the perimiter fence, staring out to sea: "Well, I could never have afforded this, could I?"

Those internees who could approximate to something of their previous routine and endeavor fared best. Unlike Kästner and Corvin, writers without a home for their work, the political writer Heinrich Fraenkel had built a successful career as a freelance journalist in Britain, setting weekly chess puzzles for the *New Statesman and Nation* under the pseudonym "Assiac"—Caïssa, the goddess of chess, spelled backward. Prior to his arrest he had met with the bon vivant and publisher Victor Gollancz to discuss the possibility of authoring a book about the experience of being an anti-Nazi German living in wartime Britain. Two weeks after Fraenkel arrived in the camp, Gollancz sent a telegram commissioning the book.

Captain Daniel, perhaps fearing what Fraenkel would write about him, provided the author with a typewriter, desk, a private room, and a generous supply of paper and carbons. For Fraenkel, internment was no more than a "little inconvenience"—an assessment clearly influenced by the fact that the commandant had excused the writer from both the evening curfew and morning roll calls. Routine and absorption in his work enabled Fraenkel to avoid the mental health issues experienced by many of his friends.

Another man had been a road sweeper in Vienna. In Hutchinson he could be seen each day gripping a broom and endlessly sweeping the roads that ran between the rows of houses. As with Fraenkel, this man took comfort from exercising his occupational muscle memory, unaffected by the change in scenery. Routine fostered resilience, the carapace of purpose.

"Work," as Uhlman wrote in his diary, "is the only help against *die Schwarze Sucht der Seele*—the black addiction of the soul."

* * *

IT WAS PAUL HAMANN WHO first offered Peter membership to the Artists Café, a semi-exclusive club that, up until that point, had maintained a
lower age limit of twenty years old. In the café Peter saw a mixture of fresh
and familiar faces. As well as Ernst Müller-Blensdorf, whom Peter recognized as the sculptor with the huge hands from Warth Mill, there was one
of his fellow residents in House 1, the young Oskar Wenzel, an art teacher
who taught window dressing at the Reimann School of Art and Design
in London. Fred Uhlman, the Stuttgart lawyer-turned-painter, was a
new figure and seemed to be a dominating presence; sucking on a meer-
schaum pipe, the artist struck the teenager as "emotional and romantic."

The washroom café was an impoverished imitation of the Berlin
and Viennese establishments many of the group once frequented. For
Peter, however, the feeling of belonging subsumed aesthetic consider-
ations of decor or ambiance. Peter was, after all, one of the few internees so destitute and unspoiled that the meager camp rations seemed
both abundant and delicious. Peter keenly watched Kurt Schwitters
in a mode of performance; since the Dadaist started frequenting the
café—lured, Hinrichsen suspected, by the promise of cake—he had
begun tentatively performing poetry recitals to the group, which he
hoped to soon take out to the wider camp audience. Peter watched
these intimate recitals with intense concentration, even committing
snippets to memory.

As well as discussions about art and Germany, conversation in
the Artists Café would frequently turn to the divisive figure of Ludwig
Warschauer, whose notoriety had only grown in recent days. Shortly
after his altercation with Hinrichsen, Warschauer had been seen to
stride up to Hutchinson's main gate and pass the guard a note addressed to Captain Daniel.

"Dear Sir," it read. "I must get in touch with Sir William Bottomsley and would be obliged for your arranging this."

Bottomsley was the chairman of Unilever, Captain Daniel's previous employer. Warschauer's ploy to circumvent the camp hierarchy in

order to secure a private audience was a success; assuming Warschauer must be an important individual, the commandant invited him up to his office. Just as Warschauer used coercion against those who he considered to be inferior, he employed charm and blandishments toward those in positions of power. After shaking the commandant's hand and flashing a smile that revealed a row of platinum-plated teeth, he made his pitch.[*]

"This war does not need more academics," said Warschauer, taking aim at Hinrichsen and Ahrends's highfalutin cultural schedule, "but practical engineers: young people who know how to accomplish things."

He then outlined his vision for a Technical School, to be established within the camp, which could be run as an educational facility, training young internees in various aspects of engineering. The project would not only cure idleness, Warschauer argued, but would also instill in Hutchinson's young men skills that would prove useful to them and to the war effort if and when they were released. Warschauer's current employer in England could provide sheets of mica to be used by the students for their projects, and, given time, the school might even bring some money into the camp.

In Warschauer's own words, Captain Daniel "did not like the scheme at all." What if the young people chose to use their newfound technical knowledge to cause difficulties, or even to help the enemy? Nevertheless, where the other internees had perceived a bully, Captain Daniel saw an industrious self-starter, impressed as he was by Warschauer's charm and self-assurance. Perhaps, Daniel suggested, a building could be found for Warschauer's enterprise. Until then, the engineer was to be given a position in the Cultural Department and there create a schedule of lessons that could be closely monitored.

* * *

[*] In an interview with MI5 agents, Warschauer repeatedly claimed to have lost the missing teeth when he was shot down while flying during the First World War. At various times Warschauer claimed that he was awarded either the Iron Cross First Class or the *Pour le Mérite*—the highest military medal given by Germany during the First World War—for his bravery. None of these stories were verified.

WARSCHAUER'S POSITION IN THE CULTURAL Department caused immediate friction. Its founder, Bruno Ahrends, resented the presence of this rogue faction within his meticulous organization. To Ahrends's frustration, Warschauer's daily program of lessons occupied students throughout the entirety of each day, leaving the young men no time to engage in other pursuits that might provide them with a more rounded education. Tensions became sufficiently high that Ahrends went so far as to accuse Warschauer of sabotaging the cultural education of the young men in the camp.

"When I hear the word 'Culture,'" Warschauer reputedly said, deploying an infamous quotation from Hermann Göring familiar to anyone driven from Germany for their artistic work, "I loosen my revolver belt."

To a community of men who had been first ostracized and then expelled from their country for their art, it was a wearyingly familiar attitude. Few, however, had ever heard a Jew quote a Nazi in such a way. Could Warschauer be a representative of that wispy group on whose existence their internment had been predicated: the fifth columnists? The truth of Warschauer's past would, for now, remain opaque. But for his fellow internees, there was little doubt of the kind of man he was.

"At heart and by temperament," Hinrichsen concluded, "he was a fascist."

If Warschauer was a subject of suspicion, there was firmer evidence still that the British had, using the expansive net of mass internment, hauled in a few of its enemies. Four doors down from Peter's bedroom in House 1, Dr. Heinrich Arnoldi was not only narrowminded and humorless, he was also a proud fascist. Fred Uhlman had seen Arnoldi gazing toward the horizon, and overheard him incanting the words *Heute fahren wir gegen Engelland*—Today we are driving toward England—as if summoning an invading force.

For a group of men suspected of being Nazi spies posing as refugees, here was a chilling realization that there might be genuine infiltrators in the camp. If this was true, how long would they be made to remain behind barbed wire, while the sheep were separated from the goats?

XIV

THE FIRST GOODBYES

THROUGHOUT THE WARM WEEKS OF July, as Hutchinson's internees appointed their leaders and cooks, drew up the schedule of lectures and entertainments, and learned to paint, a pile of suitcases sat in a corner of another internment camp in Devon, a few hundred miles away. Rescued from the wreck of the *Arandora Star*, these unclaimed effects were the somber luggage of the recently deceased. It was a smaller pile of belongings than those left at the doors to the Holocaust's shower rooms, but still emblematic of injustice. As the swollen bodies of the dead began to wash onto Irish and Hebridean beaches, so fresh details about the tragedy continued to emerge, casting further doubt on the official version of events.

On July 30, in the House of Commons, the secretary of state for war, Anthony Eden was asked whether the government had known for sure that, as previously claimed, everyone aboard the *Arandora Star* had been a Nazi sympathizer. By now, Eden knew for certain that this had not been the case.

"Fifty-three [Germans and Austrians aboard] were or claimed to be refugees, but had nevertheless been placed in category A," he conceded.

In Whitehall, the impersonal statistics were now clothed with the intimacies of story. Politicians learned that, among the dead, there was a

German sailor who came to Britain as an anti-fascist, only to be interned with a "mélange" of Nazi sympathizers; there was a metalworker who, after spending four years imprisoned in Nazi camps, escaped to Britain, was interned, then killed in the sinking; there was the blind pensioner who had been separated from his wife for the first time in his life.

The admission that refugees of Nazi oppression had been aboard the ship caused widespread outrage and called into question the wider policy of mass internment, which had begun to seem less like a rational security measure and more like victim-blaming on an industrial scale. The *Jewish Chronicle*, which just a few months earlier had defended a wartime government's "right to interfere drastically with the freedom of the individual," now likened the "disgraceful hounding of refugees" to "Gestapo methods." Readers agreed. "It seems strange that in order to defeat the Gestapo abroad, it should be considered necessary to introduce their methods at home," wrote Moya Woodside in a typical letter published in the *Northern Whig*. The public's attitude had changed. Policy would duly follow.

While still far from secure, Britain's general position in the war had shifted enough that, as Churchill put it to his cabinet, it was now possible to "take a somewhat less rigid attitude in regard to the internment of aliens." Arrests, which had continued at a rate of around 150 per day throughout July, were suspended. If a so-called enemy alien had thus far managed to avoid being apprehended, they would most likely remain free for the remainder of the war. Mass internment was finished.

"That tragedy may . . . have served a useful if terrible purpose," said Lord Faringdon of the *Arandora Star* in a speech to the House of Lords later that week. "For it may have opened the eyes of those responsible, and of members of the public, and of His Majesty's Government."

It would take months and years to unpick the tangled mess of internment. Politicians' efforts to justify and distance themselves from the episode were, by contrast, immediate.

"I always thought [the fifth column danger] was exaggerated in this Island," claimed Churchill on August 15, before adding a note of self-justification: "I should not have felt I was doing my duty by the National Defence if I had not taken these special steps to cope with Fifth Column activities."

Where Churchill chose denial and rationalization, Sir John Anderson, the home secretary who to some extent had opposed internment early on, expressed more straightforward remorse.

"Most regrettable and deplorable things have happened," he said in an address to Parliament on August 22. Mistakes were due, he argued, to the "inevitable haste" with which the policy was conducted. But so, too, he admitted, was "stupidity and muddle."

The Conservative MP Victor Cazalet declared that he would not be happy until "this bespattered page of our history has been torn up and re-written."

Certainly, by now the moral and material harm caused by mass internment was clear, not only to those caught up in the policy, but also to Britain's standing overseas. That week the *Spectator* reported that "nine London correspondents of leading newspapers in neutral European countries" had reported the "damaging impression created abroad by the spirit and methods" of the refugee internments. "Millions of sympathizers with Britain's case begin to doubt whether British ideals of humanity and justice prevail."

Anderson was forced to concede that it was indeed "a matter which touches the good name of this country." This was the closest to an official apology that any internee would receive. The damage done by the government's internment policy was irreparable in the case of those refugees who had lost their lives to drowning or suicide, or who had been spirited thousands of miles from their families. "Injustices have been committed that can never be repaired," concluded one letter to the editor, printed in the *Spectator*.

For now, however, no internee wanted an apology. They simply wanted freedom. For the eighteen-year-old Peter Fleischmann— hounded from his orphanage by Nazis, brought to Britain on a *Kindertransport*, then imprisoned by his rescuers on an island in the middle of the Irish Sea—freedom would be a long time coming.

* * *

HEINRICH FRAENKEL STOOD IN FRONT of the peeling white paint, the damp shirts and drawers strung from laundry lines, and began to read from the typed letter in his hand. The Artists Café had been a scene of noisier debate than usual during the week of Peter's arrival at Hutchinson. On July 31, shortly after canceling its policy of mass internment, the Home Office published a white paper that listed eighteen criteria under which an internee could apply for release. At first the news caused a delighted scramble: finally, the internees would be free. Elation soon turned to dismay.

Twelve of the eighteen categories merely restated those criteria that should have exempted individuals from internment in the first place: those who were too young or too old, too infirm, or who already had permits to work in positions of national importance would be freed. There was no provision for releases on the grounds of political sympathies, race, or reliability. Only those who could render services of special value for the conduct of the war were eligible for release. For the Jewish refugees, the stipulation that freedom was to be predicated on usefulness, not innocence, was painfully reminiscent of the world they had fled.

"In Germany today Jews . . . who are engaged in war work . . . wear an armlet with the inscription 'useful Jew.' Is this not the same principle?" argued the German legal scholar, refugee to Britain, and internee Gerhard Leibholz in a letter to the bishop of Chichester.

Scholars and academics could only apply for release if their specialization related to the sciences, much to the chagrin of the dozens of humanities-focused academics at Hutchinson. As one MP put it, under these classifications, neither the scientist Albert Einstein, nor the writer Thomas Mann, nor the conductor Arturo Toscanini would have been freed. (An Albert Einstein was, in fact, interned in Britain in 1940. This Einstein, however, was a year younger than the famous theoretical physicist, and worked as a manufacturer of artificial silk. He was released on January 30, 1941.)

Campaigners, politicians, and public figures responded with equal dismay. "[This] smells . . . of Hitlerism," stated the MP Rhys Davies. "Men should be let out of internment because they are innocent, not because they are useful." That releases were, seemingly, to be "the exception rather than the rule" was "profoundly disappointing," wrote one journalist. "The Cabinet is apparently convinced that, if the Home Office . . . releases a few hundred, the wrong done to over 73,000 will have been righted," wrote another. In a letter published in the *Times*, influential figures including H. G. Wells and Lady Violet Bonham Carter signed a letter arguing that as "wholesale internment was conceived in panic and is incapable of sober justification . . . a complete reversal of Government Policy is the only solution."

The process of applying for release remained unhelpfully arcane, too. No special form was provided to the internees, leaving each applicant to decide for himself what information might favorably influence the official who deliberated his case. The refugee organizations that had brought the majority of internees to Britain were, as the MP Eleanor Rathbone put it, "not merely ignored but implicitly barred from intervention." The procedure, she continued, was "calculated to ensure that only a few of the few nominally entitled to release will actually achieve it."

For the members of Hutchinson's Artists Café, there was little hope of being able to prove that their work as painters, sculptors, and poets was "of national importance." For these men the white paper was not so much a document of hope as a declaration of the futility of their situation. That same week the celebrated composer Ralph Vaughan Williams wrote in a letter to a friend of his despair that the arts had been overlooked in the white paper. "To fructify the life of the country *is* of national importance," he argued, adding that perhaps a joint letter might convince the government of "the fact that artistic and intelligent people who will spread the gospel of anti-Nazism are an asset to the country?"

Vaughan Williams was not the only one considering this route. While Heinrich Fraenkel had been feverishly occupied with the book he was writing from inside the camp, he felt just as frustrated as his friends and colleagues. The author suggested the group compose a letter expressing their indignation to Kingsley Martin, his friend and editor of the *New Statesman*. Earlier that month, a leader in the magazine had blamed the rashness of the mass internment policy on Churchill. If only the prime minister had given the matter deeper consideration, Martin argued, he would have "seen the military folly of locking up invaluable allies and destroying the force of his appeal to fight for the liberation of Europe."

With Martin as an ally, there was a good chance, Fraenkel told the group, that the magazine would publish a letter of protest from actual internees and bring their cause to a national readership. For a number of days, the group's members debated the wording of the letter. The tone and line of argument had to be right if the letter was to prove effective. When the agreed-upon draft was completed, Fraenkel read the text to those assembled in the café.

"Art cannot live behind barbed wire . . ." he began.

> The sense of grievous injustice done to us, the restlessness caused by living together with thousands of other men . . . prevent all work and creativity. We came to England because we saw in her the last bulwark, the last hope for democracy in Europe. We are asking our British colleagues and friends and all who are interested in art to help us obtain our freedom again.

When Fraenkel finished, the audience murmured in appreciation and agreement. Only Friedrich Burschell, the pipe-smoking camp father, expressed reservations. It was unusual, he pointed out—not unreasonably—for any artist to be provided food, accommodation, and studio space in which to work for free. Moreover, a brief survey of the art produced in the camp to date disproved the letter's crucial point, that captivity throttles creativity. If anything, internment had provided an energizing impulse. Besides, was it not a tenet of Dadaism that destruction feeds creation?

The men were used to spirited debates. By the time of Peter's arrival, Hutchinson had a fully realized debating society, styled on its Oxford University equivalent. Teams would take sides on controversial motions. Some, such as "That newspapers are a nuisance," or "That saving money is unwise," were relevant to the refugees' recent experiences. Others—"That beauty in women is of greater importance than intelligence," or, bolder still, "That slavery should be reintroduced"— while breezily expressed, were straightforwardly divisive.

Burschell's arguments today, however, pierced the realm of the hypothetical into the artists' immediate context. As a nonartist, he had the necessary distance and authority to say the unsayable and had articulated an uncomfortable tension recognizable to every man in the room: the tug between the elemental yearning for freedom and the artistic security of their current situation. Nevertheless, in turn the men signed the letter.

These philosophical debates over the role of art in captivity did not much interest Peter Fleischmann. After a life filled with loss, abandonment, and sorrow, he had at last found his people. Freedom as a legal status and moral concept was meaningless to a teenager who had found, inside the internment camp, many of the things denied to him on the outside. While he was surrounded with interesting people and opportunities, Hutchinson represented a positive force in his life, even if his sense of purpose and happiness was apparently contingent on the relative misery of his mentors.

"It was the beginning of my life," he said. "The making of my life."

SINCE THE PUBLICATION OF THE government's white paper, the subject of release became a habit of thought for almost every man. It dominated talk throughout the camp. "It must be accentuated over and over again that the release question is the prevailing feature of camp-life," wrote Bertha Bracey's colleague William Hughes in one of his reports. Walter Heydecker, a housefather in the camp, summed up the preoccupation in a poem, the first and last stanzas of which read:

O' Isle of bearded Man,
O' Isle of tailless cats,
Mice in the frying pan,
Release-tomorrow chats . . .

O' world of barbed wire,
Of Herrings, palms and "Why?"
Keep burning your home fires—
Cheerio, farewell, goodbye!

The first group of men had, in fact, left Hutchinson even before the publication of the white paper. For these men freedom had been accompanied by a significant condition: immediate deportation. The offer was extended only to married men whose wives were interned elsewhere on the island, in the women's camp. Couples were offered only one thirty-minute meeting, a brief, intense, life-defining encounter to decide whether to accept the unfathomable offer. When the couples were forced apart, there were "heart-breaking scenes."

Around thirty couples took the bargain. Those from Hutchinson left the camp on Tuesday, July 30, to be transferred to another internment camp near London and there await the next outbound ship. According to at least one report, the arrangements were so haphazard that some of these men were then sent on to their new countries of residence alone. Their wives were left loitering in London refugee centers, luggage piled up in the hall, "looking bewildered and unhappy"—an act of unimaginable cruelty via carelessness.

The publication of the white paper had only compounded tensions with its capricious definitions of who was chosen for release and who was passed over. The feeling was captured in a contemporaneous cartoon by David Low, the most famous political caricaturist of the period, which showed John Anderson turning the handle on a tombola as the name of an internee popped out at random.

Those left behind delighted in the news that the first man to have been unconditionally freed from the camp was, apparently, the elephant keeper from the London Zoo. After he was arrested, the elephants refused to eat—or so the story went. Fearing the animals might die, the zoo successfully petitioned the War Office to have the keeper returned to his post. This sweetly romantic tale, often repeated in later years by Hutchinson alumni, had a metaphorical resonance: here was a German refugee so needed by his English family of elephants that the government had been forced to free him. Perhaps other refugees, whose families needed them to come home and put food on their tables, might be similarly let go?

The details were only partially true, however. Gossip and speculation had spread misinformation that instantly calcified to myth. The man in question, Hans Honigmann, had worked for a brief period at the London Zoo, but he was no mere elephant keeper. A highly respected zoologist, Honigmann was the former director of the Breslau Zoo and an honorary member of the New York Zoological Society. He had come to Britain in 1935 at the invitation of the biologist Sir Julian Huxley and, like the Berlin chief of police, Bernhard Weiss, had the unenviable accolade of being named in the Third Reich's notorious black book, a list of individuals to be killed by the occupation forces in the event of a successful invasion of the British Isles.

Prior to his arrest, Honigmann had been employed as the official scientific adviser to the Dudley Zoo. Frantic bureaucratic busywork facilitated a review of Honigmann's internment. He left the camp on August 5, a little over two weeks after Hutchinson's opening, although, contrary to the rumors, by then the zoo had been closed and he no longer worked there.*

Fifty men sailed from the Isle of Man the same day that Honig-

---

* There was a widespread belief among the internees that Honigmann had been interned at Hutchinson camp. Official documents, however, do not identify where the zoologist was held during his brief period of internment, and his family has no documents to indicate the camp where he was kept. While the oft-repeated anecdote about the elephants was incorrect, Honigmann did, in fact, work closely with these animals. His son recalls an incident when his father performed an autopsy on an elephant—probably at the Breslau Zoo—by crawling inside the carcass to examine the organs. Honigmann emerged covered in blood, an unforgettable image.

mann was released, all category C risks. Each met one or more of the release criteria. These men were drawn from camps across the island, including Hutchinson. It was, for those campaigning to right the injustice of internment, nowhere near enough when an estimated fifteen thousand internees around Britain were now eligible for release—at least a thousand of whom were classed as infirm.

Rumors compounded fears of those left behind that the men chosen for this first release had been selected not because of what they believed but because of who they knew. According to speculation, one of the men freed from Hutchinson was a businessman who had somehow acquired a letter of endorsement from the pope. Another was the German orchestral conductor Hans Oppenheim. In 1936, King George VI's wife, Elizabeth, had attended a performance of *The Magic Flute* at Glyndebourne Opera House conducted by Oppenheim. She is rumored to have said: "Before I heard that opera I had no idea how heavenly life could be." Oppenheim's release was hastened, reportedly, by a royal letter of recommendation. What other man could compete with that? The rumors were correct. Release, for now, was contingent on a person's connections, not their attitude toward Hitler's regime.

"The average man who is 'only' loyal is completely ignored," wrote one exasperated internee. "His great misfortune is to be unknown."

EVEN THE MOST ANGUISHED CAPTIVE could not resent the news that the brilliant lawyer and speaker Rudolf Olden had been among this first group of internees freed. Olden had been a towering, inspirational presence wherever he went: first at Warth Mills and then, via the lectures he gave to audiences of hundreds, at Hutchinson.

Olden had applied to become a British citizen at the beginning of 1939, but his application had still not been processed by war's arrival. He wrote to a friend: "[The Home Office] has just declared me to be an 'Enemy Alien.' I deeply feel I did not deserve this." He was arrested on June 25, 1940, one day after his daughter sailed for Canada with a group of evacuee children. Oxford's loss was Hutchinson's gain. To be interned with Olden, Hinrichsen declared, was to live with "somebody who has been everywhere, somebody who had interviewed all the great politicians, and has a worldwide view and philosophic approach to everything." Olden so inspired the young actor Otto Tausig that he began to pray, not for his own release, but for that of Olden's.

Olden's friends outside the camp had not given up on him, either. In early July the philosopher Gilbert Murray sent a letter to Oxford University's vice-chancellor in which he argued: "There are many . . . refugees in the University whose release from internment is desirable . . . but I doubt there is anyone who has so devoted himself to the struggle against Hitlerism as his main interest in life."

While his fellow internees might have assumed it was Olden's social and professional connections that secured his release, it was in fact his heart condition. He had collapsed first at Warth Mills, then at Prees Heath, proof enough that he should not remain interned.

"Lo and behold," Otto Tausig wrote of his reaction to the news, "my prayer was answered. It was a miracle."

Before he left the camp, Olden sat for Schwitters. In the portrait Olden is depicted sitting cross-legged on a chair wearing a suit jacket, a scarf, and rounded spectacles, his long fingers extended, as if captured in a moment of professorial explication. It is arguably the most striking portrait that Schwitters painted in Hutchinson, the impact of its likeness strengthened by the energetic pose. There is a melancholy to the picture, too, the muted palette, a soft note of sadness in Olden's eyes that appeared to foreshadow tragedy.

The British authorities on the island were just as ill-prepared for the management of the releases as the police had been during the preceding arrests. To preserve the government's reputation, measures were taken that approached a cover-up. Some internees were forced to promise that they would not reveal conditions in the camps following release. Every man was made to sign a contract relinquishing all financial claims against the authorities. Releases were subject to lengthy delays whereby the internee was left to languish in the camp for as long as a month after the order for release was given.

When Bertha Bracey visited the Isle of Man in August, she was astonished to find there was no financial provision for the internees' return journey to their homes. During the visit she left £15 in cash with the officer in charge of welfare so that he might provide a few shillings to each man to cover the cost of his travel.

WHILE MOST OF THE TWELVE hundred or so men in the camp who were not selected for release felt frustration and anguish to varying degrees, few were as dismayed as Ludwig Warschauer, the black-market-dealing engineer who, since his arrival on the island, had maintained that his internment was a gaffe soon to be rectified. When it became clear that his name was not among those picked for release, Warschauer swapped his posturing for industry.

Charm and obsequiousness had ingratiated the engineer to Captain Daniel, whose initial misgivings about Hutchinson's Technical School had given way to feelings of pride that his camp should house this unique asset. Anything that gave Hutchinson an advantage over its rivals would be useful, the commandant believed, when the government came to choose which camps to close first.

Shortly after the first releases, Captain Daniel summoned Warschauer to his office and informed him that House 36 had been cleared and prepared to become the official, permanent home of the Technical School. Warschauer, his assistants, and a number of the tutors could move out of House 3 and live in the upstairs bedrooms.

On August 22, almost six weeks after Hutchinson opened, a crowd of internees, together with Captain Daniel, Captain Jurgensen, and RSM Potterton, gathered for the official opening of the Technical School. The windowpane above the front door had been decorated with a bespoke logo: an entwined *T* and *S* inside an *ohm* symbol. Elsewhere, a handmade poster displayed the institution's punned slogan: "Technical Knowledge Overcomes Any Resistance, Even Grumblers, Even Internment."

"Sir, my friends: today we are starting the Technical School for Engineers, thanks to the understanding and the help of the commander of this Camp," Warschauer began in his address to the crowd. Eight years earlier, he and some friends had invented a device to render the gramophone player "obsolete," he explained. The results of that experiment would revolutionize Britain's war effort. Having been struck on his arrival at Hutchinson by the "number of people who did not know what to do with their time," he had settled on a new venture, one that "may have the same or even greater effects" than his invention. Here at the Technical School, students would be taught "basic theoretical knowledge"—how to read switch diagrams, the workings of motors, transformers, and condensers, with lessons split into mathematics, physics, electrical engineering, and instillation—before progressing to practical work. In this way he would transform "enemy aliens," he said, into "valuable aliens."

"The work," Warschauer insisted, "will start in earnest when I shall have returned to London," revealing his persistent belief that internment was, for him, merely a fleeting setback. And with that, Hutchinson's Technical School was declared officially open.

The Technical School was immediately popular among many of the young men, who hoped that practical training would hasten their release. The eighteen-year-old Kurt Treitel left his job at the camp library to enroll in the school's twenty-hour syllabus, the majority of which was delivered in English during morning and afternoon sessions that ran from Monday to Saturday. Perhaps sensing his parents' displeasure at him having abandoned intellectual pursuits for practical training, he wrote to them to explain that he was continuing, twice a week, to attend a philosophy-themed study group run by Friedrich Heinemann, the heckling Oxford professor.

"I also go to as many lectures as possible because that is at least one way of getting something out of this lost time," Treitel added.

Among the members of the Artists Café, Warschauer provided a focal point for generalized feelings of resentment and anger. In Germany, each man had an obvious antagonist in Hitler, whose policies had forced their poverty and exile. In Britain, their adversary was less clear. Was it Churchill, who had ordered mass internment? Or Anderson, who had signed off on the policy? Was it the owners of the British newspapers, who had helped whip the public into a state of fearful xenophobia, creating the necessary conditions? Or was it more nebulous ideas and systemic structures without names and faces? Warschauer offered a useful embodiment, not of the architects of the internment measures, but of the kind of man who might justify them.

Apart from his apparent belief that the rules of internment did not apply to him, there was the question of how this Nazi-quoting engineer with a Jewish name had been able to leave Germany so close to the outbreak of war. His boasting thickened the clouds of suspicion. Someone in the camp pointed out that all of the industrialists with whom Warschauer claimed to be friends had been members of an illegal fascist German-British friendship organization. Further doubt surrounded Warschauer's flagrant displays of wealth: How had he smuggled so much money out of a country that had systematically stripped the other refugees of their wealth?

Curt Sluzewski, the papal lawyer, had harder evidence that Warschauer was not the man he claimed to be. Before he fled Berlin, Sluzewski said he had personally seen the engineer driving a Mercedes and frequenting restaurants, nightclubs, and cinemas long after legislation made it impossible for Jews to own cars and imposed upon them strict curfews. Moreover, the invention known as the Tefifon mentioned during Warschauer's speech had, Sluzewski claimed, been used by the Nazis to secretly record the conversations of Jews and other political opponents.

"I don't want anything to do with him," Sluzewski said before anyone had the chance to ask him how, precisely, he knew all of this. "I don't like his face."

XV

LOVE AND PARANOIA

At his desk in Blenheim Palace near Oxford, James Gregan Craufurd sat at his typewriter in studied concentration. Rakish with a neatly cropped mustache, kind eyes, and a bow tie that bordered on the foppish, Craufurd's genteel appearance belied the severity of his task as one of MI5's counterespionage investigators. While politicians had lurched back and forth on the issue of internment throughout the war to date, MI5's position remained resolute: intern all "enemy aliens" and keep them interned.

Now that some men were becoming eligible for release, there was a danger that those who posed a genuine risk to Britain might convince the relevant authorities that they should be freed.[*] While MI5 opposed the speed and scale of any such releases in the strongest terms, it had no powers to reverse the policy. It was imperative, then, that Craufurd and his colleagues in B4b—the unit responsible, in part, for investigating internees—work quickly to root out true enemies of the state.

Craufurd, who was fifty-four, was well-suited to work in the so-

---

[*] These concerns had been compounded by the news that, in April 1940, the Home Office authorized the release of Jürgen Kuczynski, a well-connected communist who had impressed his camp commandant—"he is . . . a thoroughly good sort." MI5 believed the commandant had been hoodwinked, and that Kuczynski remained "a very dangerous person."

called secret world, and the intelligence service was in desperate need of experienced men with the right sort of temperament and background. A graduate of University College, Oxford, Craufurd was a lawyer by training, used to conducting interviews, untangling truth from lies, and compiling his findings into meticulous written reports. Moreover, he had already been engaged in "War Trade"—a widely used euphemism for intelligence work—during the First World War.

In recent weeks Craufurd, together with his friend and colleague John Noble, had become increasingly focused on one of Hutchinson camp's residents. This man, an engineer from Berlin, had brought fourteen sound-recording sets known as Tefifons with him when he fled Germany for Britain. These devices could be connected to a microphone, telephone, or radio to make a permanent record of the message or speech, which could be played back instantaneously. The engineer claimed that the device was being widely used in Germany, including by the Gestapo. British tests, however, showed that the device did not work properly and required significant development before it would be fit for production.

The tests cast doubt on the engineer's entire story. So Craufurd had been assigned to investigate Ludwig Warschauer, currently interned at Hutchinson, where he had already secured a house of his own and gained a large group of young, impressionable devotees.

To assist his investigations, Craufurd had used the simmering disquiet in Hutchinson to his advantage, recruiting trustworthy internees as informants. There were at least three internees in the camp—referred to in MI5 reports as Informants D, E, and X—who passed on information about fellow internees to the intelligence service. There was neither financial compensation nor the promise of early release for those who accepted the role, leaving the primary incentive as the desire to make a valuable contribution to the war effort or, in some cases, to exercise personal grudges or political enmities.

The informants were, in some cases, not merely eavesdroppers, but proactive sources. Henry Wuga was a sixteen-year-old internee who had come to Britain via the *Kindertransport*, only to be classed as a category A risk for exchanging letters with his relatives in Germany, and ordered to appear before a judge at the High Court in Edinburgh on a charge of corresponding with the enemy. One day a man arrived at the door of his room at Peveril camp on the island and introduced himself as Wuga's new roommate. Later that week, the newcomer plied Henry with alcohol and, when the boy was drunk, began asking questions about his family's Nazi connections. When the investigation proved fruitless, the informant promptly moved out of the room.

In Hutchinson, Craufurd's informants did not have to wait long to find intelligence on Warschauer. A born bragger, the engineer had boasted not only of his connections to the British establishment but also of those within the Nazi Party. He frequently told a story of how, during a supper with Himmler, the leader of the SS had patted him on the shoulder and told him that nothing would happen to him. The cuff links on his shirt, Warschauer claimed, were a gift from the head of the German intelligence service, Helmuth von Moltke, and, most alarmingly, he claimed to have personally installed one of his Tefifon recording devices in Göring's office, to enable the Nazi to record relevant telephone conversations. One informant at Hutchinson said that Warschauer had boasted that he had "so many friends in the Gestapo" that he would be safe, whatever the outcome of the war.

These facts alone would have been enough to bolster Craufurd's report recommending that Warschauer remain interned no matter what, but his own investigations had found additional reasons why his subject should not be trusted. Not only was Warschauer's father the former director of the Secret State Archives in Danzig, Warschauer was himself, it seemed, a German ex-intelligence officer. Until these details and the information from the informants could be verified, it was imperative that Warschauer remain safely interned.

Craufurd concluded his report with a clear recommendation: "It is not desirable that he should be exempted from internment on any ground."

* * *

CAPTAIN DANIEL, IN FULL COMPLEMENT of medals, attempted to look suitably dignified as he stood in front of the orderly room outside the wire perimeter of Hutchinson camp, and held one corner of the baldachin aloft in the wind. It was cramped inside the billowing tent, which currently housed the thirty-four-year-old groom, Dr. Ernst Bodenheimer, of House 12, his fiancée, Clementine Eisemann, and presiding over the ceremony, one of the camp's captive rabbis. Several hundred Hutchinson internees had gathered on the camp side of the fence to watch the couple, the rabbi, and the four tent bearers surrounded by garlands of wedding flowers provided by one of the camp doctors, Captain Robert Marshall.

Wives and girlfriends were not typically allowed to visit the camp. Clementine had been granted special leave from the Home Office to travel to the island for today, September 4, 1940, her wedding day. For the afternoon ceremony she wore a brilliant white dress and veil, providing an archangelic vision for Hutchinson's gawkers. The promise of freedom was, in part, the driving force for the union; the couple had secured visas to Cuba, which could be used only once they were married. Earlier that morning the couple were officially married at a civil ceremony performed at the Civil Registry Office in Douglas. This afternoon's service was, in part, for the benefit of Bodenheimer's friends and housemates.

The Orthodox Jewish ceremony unfurled in all its arcane ritual—murmured blessings, spoken chants—until Bodenheimer lifted a wineglass in the air, then flung it at the ground. The unexpected sound of breaking glass caused Captain Daniel to flinch, his confusion deepening as the bride and groom stomped on the crystal shards, signifying that only when the glass could be fitted back together would they be free to break their marriage vows. A cheer went up from the gathered onlookers. The rabbi, the bride, the groom, and three of the four tent bearers began dancing as Captain Daniel stood stoically in the center of the revelry.

Next, the bride was driven along the fence, around the northwest corner of the camp, and along the road that bordered the backs of the row of houses that stretched from Peter's home at House 1 to the Artists Café in House 15. Bodenheimer, who had to return to the camp to await his imminent release, stood in the back garden of House 12, and he and his housemates whooped and danced "as if possessed," as Hinrichsen put it. That evening, at seven o'clock, at the invitation of the lawyer and wine merchant Fritz Hallgarten, a select group of invitees joined the house residents for "a little celebration."

The camp wedding provided a moment of wistful escapism for many of Hutchinson's internees. The idea that romance could persist even in an internment camp offered a flicker of sunny hope or, at very least, a basic distraction from domestic obsessions—as Jacobsthal put it, the "trivial facts of food, health, digestion, sleep, furniture . . . discussed and discussed"—and fears about the wider war.

In September the Luftwaffe began to bomb Liverpool in an effort to obliterate the port where Britain's essential food imports arrived in a never-ending procession of transatlantic ships. At night, not only could the internees hear the drone of German planes lining up their approaches and the deep thud of the jettisoned bombs, but they could also watch the sky glow with the light of fires along the Mersey docksides, a reminder of the violence that encircled the lonely island and that constantly threatened the camp's uneasy peace.

For those internees who had left behind wives and girlfriends, the loneliness of internment was exacerbated by the longing for romantic contact. The set designer Ernst "Este" Stern decorated every wall in his room with a frieze of lubricious, gaudily colored dancing girls. When Kurt Schwitters's son, Ernst, discovered that his wife had made an application to the War Office threatening to file for divorce if they refused to release her husband, he joked to other internees that she was afraid her teeth would fall out in the absence of sexual satisfaction. Peter, who had no girlfriend waiting for him on the outside, developed a fascination with a young woman who walked past the wire fence every day on her way to work. Separation increased her appeal.

"To me, behind the barbed wire, she was beautiful," he recalled.

When, however, Peter tried to speak to the woman he was ordered by a guard to back off. "A hopeless situation," he called it.

JUST AS SOME MEN ENTERED the camp in the throes of young love, inevitably some arrived at Hutchinson with their marriages in more complicated states. Paul Hamann was forced to share his weekly letter allocation between his wife and his photographer lover and, Hinrichsen observed, possibly other women besides. At the time of his arrival at Hutchinson, the marriage of Hellmuth Weissenborn—the professor of art who had pioneered the camp trend of blackout art—had all but disintegrated.

Weissenborn, who was neither Jewish nor particularly politically active, had been forced from his post at the Leipzig academy through marriage. His wife, Edith Halberstam, came from a family of wealthy, cultured Jewish fur traders. Even though Weissenborn was a professor at a well-regarded institution, Edith's parents considered him to be a deficient match for their daughter. Following the couple's marriage in April 1931, the Halberstams severed relations with Edith, who gave birth to Weissenborn's son, Florian, eight months later. When their maid threatened to report the couple to the Gestapo, Weissenborn and his young family fled to England, further separating Edith from her resentful parents.

Before he even reached Hutchinson, Weissenborn knew that Edith wanted a separation. The pair began a fractious, wounding correspondence. In August, while Weissenborn was contributing to the *New Statesmen* letter, he was also sending his wife furious, even manipulative private letters "blaming me, threatening me . . . with suicide and going mad," as Edith told her sister.

As is commonplace for any couple experiencing the collapse of their marriage, each party lunged between feelings of empathy and bitterness toward the other. Recognizing how much her husband must be suffering from the curtailment of his freedom, Edith attempted to have him freed on at least one occasion. She also applied for a visa for her and Florian to immigrate to Argentina, where she planned to join her sister and brother-in-law. Resolve overcame commiseration when, just as Clementine had secured permission to come to the island to be married, Edith secured a special permit to visit the island in order to serve a divorce petition.

Absence also strained some relationships, which prior to internment appeared to be strong, past the breaking point. Wilhelm Feuchtwang was particularly hard-hit by events precipitated by his internment. In Berlin he had been arrested by the Gestapo. His wife, a resourceful young woman named Eva, borrowed money from friends to pay for his bail and, as soon as they reunited, the pair moved from house to house, evading the police, until they were able to escape to Holland and, from there, to London.

The pressure of escape bonded the couple but, following Feuchtwang's arrest in London and his transfer to Hutchinson, Eva found herself impoverished with a young child to feed and care for. In the camp, Feuchtwang made friends with another internee, Walter Neurath, who was the director of books at a print company called Adprint, which produced the popular Britain in Pictures series.

When Neurath was told he was to be freed to continue his work, which had been deemed useful propaganda by the Ministry of Information, Feuchtwang asked his new friend to check on his wife and son when he reached London. Neurath kept his promise. He arrived at Eva's apartment close to Primrose Hill, presented her with an orange, and invited her out to dinner. The meeting turned into an offer of employment, which eventually turned into a love affair. Eva left a heartbroken Feuchtwang, still languishing in internment, for his former Hutchinson camp mate. The new couple cofounded the publishing house Thames & Hudson.

Romantic love, surely, bloomed between some internees, too, but in a country where homosexuality would remain illegal for another three decades, any such relationships had to be discreetly maintained. Gossipy stories of rebuttal were more likely to spread. Professor Haas-Heye, founder of the weaving school, soon earned among internees the nickname "Q of Q"—Queen of Queers. One afternoon Klaus Hinrichsen passed Haas-Haye, who was married to Viktoria Agnes, the countess of Eulenburg. The professor swung around, placed his arm over Hinrichsen's shoulder, and whispered: "Dear boy, let us never talk about it again, but you remind me of my daughter."

A more consequential pass was made by Count Franz von Matuschka, the tennis player and depressive poet. Midmorning one day, Hinrichsen, who had by now been promoted to the position of housefather, heard cries for help coming from a room on the first floor. As he rushed up the stairs to see what was happening, he passed the poet on the way down. Matuschka held one shoe in his hand and wore none on his feet.

In the bedroom upstairs, Hinrichsen found one of the younger housemates in a state of distress. The young man explained how while sitting on the green with the count, he had told him that he, too, was writing sonnets to his girlfriend in Birmingham. The count insisted he read them and accompanied him to the younger man's house. Inside the room Matuschka had, the man alleged, locked the door, removed his shoes, and forced a kiss. Hinrichsen returned the single shoe to the count, whom he "liked very much," along with a note quietly requesting that he not visit the house again.

ANOTHER GROUP OF HUTCHINSON'S INTERNEES had to cope with the anxiety concerning not only their own release, but also that of their wives who were interned just a few miles away, at the women's camp on the island. The Rushen women's internment camp had opened on the island's southern peninsula on May 29, incorporating two small seaside resorts: Port Erin and Port St. Mary. Despite the considerable number of women held there—close to four thousand, three hundred of whom were pregnant—security was laxer than at the men's camps. A single barbed-wire perimeter encircled both resorts and, while the women had to apply for a permit before they could visit each other's houses, they were free to walk between the two sites without hindrance.

At first the Hutchinson men whose wives were interned on the island had to send letters via the usual route to the backlogged censor's office in Liverpool, where delays often meant their messages were long out-of-date by the time they arrived. From the moment the first internees arrived on the island, Bertha Bracey had pressured the government to establish a separate camp for married couples. Convincing the relevant departments to make such an expenditure was proving difficult.

In lieu of a married camp, Hutchinson's intelligence officer, Captain Jurgensen, announced in late autumn the first monthly meeting between husbands and wives interned on the island. The rendezvous, he explained, would take place at the Port Erin branch of Collinson's Café.

On the morning of the first meeting, a group of around fifty men, wearing their finest clothes and, in some cases, carrying bunches of flowers, gathered in readiness to leave the camp and be reunited, for a fleeting moment, with their imprisoned wives. A few hours later the men returned to Hutchinson. Many looked dejected. Werner Klein, one of Hinrichsen's neighbors who had gone to meet his wife, explained to his friend that the psychological conditions in the women's camp were even more strained than at Hutchinson. His wife had told him that Rushen was riddled with Nazi sympathizers, who had been whipped into a state of obstinate zeal by their self-appointed leader, Wanda Wehrhan, wife of a Lutheran pastor based in London and an energetic fascist. There had been no consideration of race or political allegiance when allocating women to Rushen's houses. In some cases, Jewish women had been forced to share beds with fervent anti-Semites.

The Nazi women, like many of the male internees, believed that invasion was imminent. In some houses, Jewish women were banned by their Nazi housemates from the common room and forced to remain in their bedrooms. When one refugee entered the local Methodist church, one of the Nazis said, loudly: "Oh there is a bad smell, a Jewish smell, in this church."

The women were permitted to leave the camp to shop twice a week. One of the landladies whose house had been requisitioned recalled overhearing a group of Nazi-supporting women discussing which of the local houses they would take for themselves when Germany won the war.

Rushen camp's commandant, Dame Joanna Cruickshank, was seemingly ill-equipped to deal with these sensitivities and conflicts. Cruickshank, a former matron in chief of both Princess Mary's RAF Nursing Service and the British Red Cross, had enjoyed a distinguished career in military nursing appointments. She had formidable powers of organization, but no understanding—or apparent willingness to understand—the situation of the women in her charge. She hired Nazi women to work on the camp staff, granted them access to camp records and, intent on preserving impartiality, ordered Jews and Nazis to collaborate on the production of the camp's newspaper, of which only a single issue was produced.

Unaccustomed to being questioned by intelligent women from civilian life, Cruickshank became entrenched when challenged on her decision-making. When Klein's wife, a non-Jew, had proposed to her camp commandant the separation of Jews and Nazis, Cruickshank said: "You are all enemy aliens, and that is the end of it."

Still, the meeting between husbands and wives passed without incident, so the island's commandants decided to repeat the rendezvous as a twice-monthly, two-hour-long fixture hosted at the Palace ballroom. The regular opportunity for female contact was so alluring that, soon enough, the single young men in Hutchinson devised schemes whereby they could accompany the married men, claiming they had, for example, an "aunt" on the island—a single young woman whose photograph they had picked out from the selection one of the married men brought back to the camp.

Soon so many men were traveling to the meetings that the monthly cost of transport for them came to £270. Undeterred by a crackdown on the scheme, engagements between young men and women on the island became rife, another loophole that enabled these fleeting moments of contact.

* * *

INTRIGUE AND CONFLICT WERE NOT limited to the women's camp on the island. Most internees had come from a world where suspicion flavored one's interactions, where a smiling neighbor, bank manager, or pastor could, in fact, be a secret adversary. Refugees brought their watchful habits to Britain, and the fear transposed from continent to island. Those internees who had come via Dunkirk, stealing across the channel on fleeing British boats, were viewed with special vigilance by their camp mates, as were the survivors of the *Arandora Star*, who were understood to have been high-risk captives according to the government's claims.

"We, as Jews, had no confidence in any non-Jew," Fritz Hallgarten said about the feelings of those internees who had seen the indifference and even duplicity from many of their neighbors. "We had to find out for ourselves: What did he think? What did his family think?"

A rumor, possibly spread by a communist agitator, blazed around the camp that the thirty-seven-year-old Rudolf Munster—one of the camp's three rows fathers, and a Gentile—had appeared in Leni Riefenstahl's 1935 film *Triumph of the Will*, saluting at a Nazi rally. Soon the gossip had Munster pegged as an SS officer, arrested in London at the outbreak of the war. Few asked how he might have bluffed the tribunal to gain a category C rating or why, if he was indeed a spy, Munster would seek such an influential position in an internment camp.

(Munster was not, in fact, a Nazi. The source of the rumor was, according to Hinrichsen, a conversation that had been overheard between one internee and his interned father. The younger man, a film technician who had been a runner on Riefenstahl's film, had pointed at Munster and said to his father: "Leni fancied strong blond men; she would have made a beeline for this one.")

For the professional journalists in Hutchinson, these routine flare-ups of rumor and intrigue provided a reminder of the work of reporting and verifying that many had been forced to leave behind in Germany. It was Michael Corvin who, with the encouragement of other members of the Artists Café, first mooted the idea of a camp newspaper that could provide not only a record of camp goings-on, but also an outlet for internees' letters and opinions, and a place to publish the work of the writers, poets, and even artists within the camp.*

A duplicating machine was found and Captain Daniel offered Corvin a supply of paper and use of a room on the first floor of the main office building. Corvin, who would be editor of the paper, appointed as publisher—responsible for the laying out of the pages—Wilhelm Feuchtwang, the man whose wife would soon leave him for his fellow internee. The newspaper would, Corvin decided, be given the prosaic title *The Camp* and published fortnightly.

The decision to publish only English-language articles was hardfought. Internees typically fell into one of two sides: those who viewed their exile as temporary and who planned to return to Germany as soon as it was safe to do so, and those who sought to make a new life in Britain. For members of the former group, it was of paramount importance to preserve German tradition, culture and, particularly, language, even if doing so might attract suspicion. The assimilators, by contrast, believed it was crucial to demonstrate their allegiance to the country of, confusingly, both their refuge and their arrest, by publishing in the language of their adoptive homeland.

Corvin, who would later immigrate to North America, fell into the latter group. Moreover, publishing articles in English had the added benefit of speeding the publication's passage through the camp censors. So Corvin and his team began to prepare the first issue, slated for publication on September 21, ten weeks after the camp's opening.

The Camp's editor solicited contributions from internees, who began to submit articles and letters. He sagely invited Captain Daniel to provide an introduction for the front page, and began writing his own submissions, including an absurdly flattering review of the camp's newly installed shower block, written in an ironic high style

---

* In an article for *The Camp* published in late 1941, long after most of the men involved in its early editions had been freed, Warschauer claimed that the newspaper had been his idea. That Warschauer founded the paper "three days after the opening of this Camp," is highly doubtful for a range of reasons.

("the pretty green of the dividing canvas harmonises with the cool and refreshing concrete floor").

In Berlin Corvin had worked on the literary side of his former newspaper, and coverage in *The Camp* skewed toward his tastes: gentle essays, art criticism, and short stories. For the first issue Corvin solicited reviews of a camp variety performance, where songs were sung and skits performed ("The actors did their best, being most natural and without any shyness"), and a write-up of the first, tentative attempt at a camp art exhibition, where, among others, works by Schwitters, Fechenbach, Kahn, Weissenborn, and Uhlman were placed on display ("[a] most promising start").

It was shortly prior to publication of the first issue of *The Camp* that some authentically newsworthy information reached the journalist's office. The beloved Rudolf Olden—also a former newspaper editor—had left the camp in early August. Shortly after he returned to his home in the university city of Oxford, Olden's ex-wife Mädi and half-brother Peter found a job for him at the New School for Social Research in New York City. On September 13, at Liverpool's docks, Olden and his wife reluctantly boarded the SS *City of Benares*, a ship carrying, among others, ninety evacuee children.

Four days later in the mid-Atlantic, Kapitänleutnant Heinrich Bleichrodt, commander of the German U-boat *U-48*, fired three torpedoes at the ship, which he and his crew had been tailing. Two missed. The third struck its target. The ship sank quickly. Of the 407 people aboard, 260 lost their lives. Olden and his wife were among them.

News of Olden's death was gravely received at the camp office, which apparently held the information back for a formal announcement in the paper. Friedrich Burschell, the camp father who had corresponded with Olden after his friend's release, wrote a tribute, which was printed on the back page of *The Camp*'s inaugural edition.

"Rudolf Olden was one of the outstanding personalities of the German emigration," wrote Burschell. "His loss is irreparable."

* * *

FOR PETER FLEISCHMANN, THE ELEVATED discussion of whether or not *The Camp* should be written in English or German, the debates about the merits or otherwise of its loose political focus, and the loss of Olden, who had left the camp three weeks before his arrival to Hutchinson, all passed him by. He was content to busy himself with his lessons, soaking in the benevolent presence of the artists who had drawn him into their group, a bystander to their debates. When discussion turned to the spicier subject of whether or not Corvin should print the commencement address by Ludwig Warschauer, founder of the Technical School, in the first issue of the newspaper, the tone of the discussions changed, and Peter listened more carefully.

Warschauer had cemented his position of influence in the camp administration. The Technical School had begun to install a speaker system throughout the camp. The system—codesigned by Dr. Hans Rothfels from St. John's College, Oxford, consisting of 2,700 yards of wire, which fed fifty-three speakers in each house's dining room—enabled the broadcast of radio programs from the BBC, among other pieces of audio.

One of the first transmissions was the October 21 broadcast from Prime Minister Winston Churchill, a message of encouragement directed to the French people. Churchill was ultimately responsible for the internees' current predicament. And yet, as Kurt Treitel wrote to his parents later that week, "it made a great impression on us to be able to hear the trusty old voice of the Premier . . . once more. It gave us a certain feeling of togetherness with the wider world from which the barbed wire separates us."

Soon internees used the radio system to broadcast talks, English lessons, and even entertainment written and performed in the camp. Occasionally, vinyl records were played in lieu of an evening concert. The twenty-one-year-old journalist Pinechas Cargher was among Hutchinson's younger internees. Using the pen name "John," Cargher wrote for *The Camp* newspaper about the transformative effect that music played via the wireless system had on his well-being: "Truly it is wonderful, this invention. The whole world can listen to the great statesmen of our day and the whole world can shine in the reflected glories of the great artists who lose none of their power through being transmitted over thousands of miles."

The system also enabled the commandant to relay messages from his desk to the entire camp. Captain Daniel warmed to his role of radio announcer and would routinely announce the latest cricket scores to the bewildered European internees. Sometimes, tipsy from afternoon drinks, he would address the men with conspiratorial familiarity, in garbled officer's English that many of his prisoners struggled to parse. For Daniel, this impressive technology was a testament to Hutchinson's organization, the skills of its internees, and the commandant's wisdom in allowing the establishment of the Technical School.

Warschauer took the credit, but the keen-eyed internees noticed that he took no practical part in its installation. This struck the camp's intelligence officer, Captain Jurgensen, as curious. Why would Warschauer not participate in the work that he had apparently pioneered at home?

"As long as I am interned, I will do nothing in my own line of work," Warschauer told Jurgensen, implying that his aloofness was a form of protest. "Everything else: yes. That: no."

While Warschauer gave the impression that he was fully engaged in his work at the Technical School, behind closed doors he spent most of his time gambling; he had been overheard boasting that his luck and skill were so great that he was making between two and three pounds a week just from playing cards. Aside from his group of camp "cronies," as one report described them—a clique of nineteen men whom MI5 described as "definitely unsatisfactory from a security point of view"— Warschauer was disliked by the majority of internees. His bullying behavior and dubious reputation combined with his rising position of power in the camp administration also made him feared.

In one report, Captain Jurgensen wrote that, as "organiser of workshops, [the] Technical School, outside working parties and almost every other phase of camp corporate life," Warschauer had become "in effect, the camp leader." It would "hardly be too much to say," he added, "that every activity seems to revolve round him."

* * *

IN THE ARTISTS CAFÉ, SOMEONE mentioned that Warschauer had recently boasted that not only was he a friend and acquaintance to the British ruling class, but that his wife was also famous, too. Peter took notice of this.

"Who is she?" another member asked.

"The only millionairess in Berlin," came the reply. "A Kempinski."

Peter balked. It could only be Echen Kohsen, heiress to the Kempinski empire, a woman who had showed such kindness to Peter over the years that he had come to call her "aunt." Peter, who had spent time at Echen's home, and accompanied the family on skiing holidays, knew that Echen was not married. At last, he had something to bring to the conversation.

"That is not true," Peter said. "I have stayed with her family many times."

For Warschauer's doubters, this was a significant and welcome development. Here, at last, the man appeared to have been caught in an extravagant lie. Emboldened by the outrage of his father figures, Peter decided to confront the founder of the Technical School.

"You are a liar," he said.

Warschauer met Peter's indignation with an equally forceful denial, explained that he and Echen had been married for close to a year. He had, among his effects in the camp, a towel stitched with the initials E.K.—Echen Kohsen. How would he come to own such a thing if the pair weren't romantically linked? You don't have to take my word for it, Warschauer continued. Echen was due to visit the camp the next day; the teenager would be able to see for himself.

Peter Fleischmann was not the only one with questions and suspicions; MI5's J. G. Craufurd and John Noble were just as eager to quiz the couple. The case of Ludwig Warschauer was quickly coming to represent one of British Intelligence's most expansive and detailed wartime investigations of an enemy alien. No person associated with the man's past or present fell outside suspicion, not even Peter.

PART THREE

"Trying to get justice out of this internment business
is like climbing up a mountain of feathers for a star."

Helen Roeder

XVI

THE HEIRESS

BERLIN
JUNE 26, 1939

ECHEN KOHSEN HEARD THE MUFFLED crunch of an approaching vehicle. Through the window she watched her father's chauffeur, Boggum, park her father's car. During the past six years, the family's restaurant empire had been systematically stripped of its wealth. There was still, however, enough residual money and loyalty for the driver to stay on call. While the heiress still had her home, her finery, and her driver, the window of opportunity to flee Germany had narrowed to a sliver of possibility.

The past year had been characterized by painful separations. Echen's daughters, Anita and Monica, with whom Peter Fleischmann had played during his holidays, had followed him out of Berlin on a *Kindertransport*. The goodbye was traumatic. After waving the girls off, Boggum drove Echen and the children's nanny, Irene, on to the next station to continue the farewell when the train passed through. Her younger daughter was saddened by the reappearances of her mourning mother; her elder was galled by the disordered separation.

Echen's parents had fled to London. So, too, had her uncle Hans, who left during the Berlin Olympics, when travel restrictions were begrudgingly eased. A family of diamond merchants with whom Echen was close had filled their pockets with jewels and skied across the border into Switzerland. Echen's plan to rendezvous with her friends and family in London would be less cinematic, but no less treacherous. Everything depended on this morning's mission.

Echen left her breakfast things on the table and gathered herself while her boyfriend ferried his seven suitcases to the waiting car and Boggum loaded the trunk. In the front passenger seat of the car, a shadowy figure sat watching the activity in the rearview mirror. The trunk closed with a metallic kiss, and the car left for Tempelhof Airport. Echen sat in the back seat in private contemplation of the events that had led to this moment.

THE EXPLUSION OF HER DAUGHTERS from Berlin had provided a crowning misery to a decade's worth of loss. Born "Elisabeth," in November 1930, Echen had divorced Walter Kohsen—a family friend, the lawyer for the Kempinski business, her husband of seven years, and the father of her two children—on account of his infidelity. Walter had left his daughters in Berlin and fled to France, ostensibly as a protest against the Nazis, but also, surely, to escape the debris of his life. Later that year, he parked his car on the side of a Parisian boulevard and shot himself in the head. Through chance or spite, Walter killed himself on the eve of Echen's thirtieth birthday.

Echen had loved Walter, but he was not her first love. As a young woman she had first fallen for a young doctor, Kurt Werner—an educated man, but a dentist. Considering Kurt to be an unsuitable match for his daughter, Echen's father had discouraged the union. (He was practiced at dissuading his daughter from pursuing her interests; he once convinced her to abandon her ambition to apply to medical school in exchange for a kitten; for her twenty-first birthday he bought her a sewing machine rather than the car for which she had asked.) After the divorce from Walter, Echen rekindled the flame with Kurt, who, in the intervening years, had also married. Kurt left his pregnant wife for Echen, but the relationship was doomed by guilt and Echen moved out after nine months.

By her early thirties Echen Kohsen—who had reassumed her first husband's distinguished surname—was once bereaved, twice divorced, separated from her children and parents, and in the process of being prized from her fortune by the inexorable force of the Nazi state. She was desperate. So, when a charming, broad-shouldered engineer, to whom the tightening restrictions and persecutions of life in Berlin did not seem to apply, stepped into her life, Echen sensed an opportunity.

THE LOOTING OF THE KEMPINSKIS was the story of the looting of any other Jewish business in Berlin, except on the grandest scale imaginable. The Nazis, eager to preserve the appearance of legality, ensconced industrial theft in the language of taxation. The empire diminished in slices, a miserable chapter to a story of inspiring enterprise. Echen's grandfather, Berthold Kempinski, began his career as a traveling wine salesman, selling Hungarian wines from a wagon to local landowners and pastors. At twenty-nine he moved to Berlin and opened two restaurants in quick succession, which, in addition to a fearsome array of wines, offered oysters, crayfish, and other seasonal delicacies at equitable prices.

Berthold Kempinski wanted to democratize the experience of eating food and drinking wines usually reserved for the wealthy. He introduced affordable set menus and, for those to whom these, too, were out of reach, half-portion plates. By the time of Berthold's death in 1910, M. Kempinski & Co. was not only the most successful wine importer in Berlin, but also, thanks to the diversification of the business, a major property owner in the city.

Under the stewardship of Echen's father, Richard Unger, the Kempinksi family brought fine dining to Berlin. So great was the family's success that, as a child, Echen attended the opening of one of the family's latest restaurants in the company of Kaiser Wilhelm II, the guest of honor. The business grew inventive spin-offs. At the tearoom Haus Vaterland, footage of a thunderstorm played on a continuous loop, allowing diners to experience the electric wind and rain without fear of injury. At another outlet, customers could buy sandwiches, drinks, and desserts from vending machines.

By the mid-1930s, the family was forced to appoint an Aryan to take control of the Kempinski business. Richard found a candidate in one Dr. Lisse, a man he had met in the chamber of commerce. Lisse was in his late fifties with gray hair, clear blue eyes, and a thatch of dueling scars across his face. Was he a Nazi? Like many hoping to find a way out of Germany, Echen did not feel she had the luxury of asking such a difficult question. At her father's urging, Echen and the other stakeholders passed Dr. Lisse power of attorney.

The Kempinski empire was not Dr. Lisse's only business interest. He was also a major investor in a supposedly revolutionary listening-in device—a kind of continuous-running Dictaphone. One day, in the spring of 1938, Dr. Lisse visited Echen's house to demonstrate the new device. Lisse did not come alone; he was accompanied by a man who claimed to be the creator of the machine. Echen was transfixed not by the invention but by the inventor.

Ludwig Warschauer, she discovered, was the son of respectable parents. He had been educated at the Friedrich-Wihelms-Gymnasium in his hometown of Posen, a city on the Warta River in western Poland. He seemed like something of a catch. And the chance to marry into the Kempinski family business, even in a state of siege, was attractive to Warschauer, whose concealed debts had all but reduced his mother to poverty.

While she wore the fearsome armor of high privilege, Echen inspired a protective urge in men. At five foot one she was childlike in frame; her nickname, Echen, meant "Little E." Mutual interest soon blossomed into something more. Warschauer's brazen confidence and the unique freedoms he seemed to enjoy around the city, despite his Jewish heritage, provided a frisson of mystery.

Desperation played its role in repressing any difficult questions Echen might, in other circumstances, have been inclined to ask. In early 1939, when Warschauer told her that he could secure her two children places on a *Kindertransport* for a price, she paid him what he asked. Then, in April 1939, when he offered to arrange her parents' escape for another substantial sum, she again agreed. Finally,

Warschauer offered to smuggle Echen out of Germany, to reunite her with her family. This time the price had increased: he wanted her hand in marriage.

When faced with such an offer at such a moment, any doubts Echen might have harbored vanished. She accepted. Warschauer accompanied her to the Fremdenpolizei in Berlin, where her passport was miraculously reissued and an immigration permit granted. Warschauer explained that he would travel to England ahead of her by plane. She would join him a few weeks later. When she landed, he told her, they would marry.

As the car approached the airport, Echen heard the man in the front seat quietly order Boggum to pull over; he turned to the couple in the back and explained that he would walk the remainder of the way and meet them inside. At the terminal, Warschauer embraced Echen and reassured her that they would soon be reunited. She watched him approach passport control, only to disappear into a side room. Eventually, Warschauer emerged on the other side of the gate. His bags, it seemed, were not going to be searched. As he passed through the barrier that led to the airfield, Echen tearfully waved.

Six weeks later, on August 7, 1939, Echen arrived in London. She had made it just in time. In three weeks' time, Britain would declare war with Germany and all visas granted to German nationals would be declared void. She kept her promise. Three days after she landed, Echen Kohsen became Echen Warschauer at the St. Marylebone Register office. The newlyweds moved into 3 Circus Road in St. John's Wood and began a honeymoon that glowed brightly against the grim backdrop of war.

It was no mere marriage of convenience. Echen loved the man whose powers of charm were considerable, as evidenced by his close allyship with Hutchinson's commandant, Captain Daniel. When their mother was with Warschauer, Echen's daughters believed she was the happiest they ever saw her. Then the police came to collect her husband. Once again, Echen was forced to say goodbye.

* * *

IN HUTCHINSON CAMP, PETER FLEISCHMANN watched the unmistakable diminutive figure of Aunt Echen file into the intelligence office on the other side of the fence. Warschauer, the teenager realized, had been telling the truth. Visits from internee's wives were highly irregular in the camp's early months. Bloomsbury House advised Fritz Hallgarten's wife to not even attempt to visit unless someone was seriously ill or in imminent danger. Whatever justification Echen had for coming to the camp must have been serious.

There was no chance, however, for Peter to say hello, or ask how, exactly, a woman he had last seen in a palatial Berlin apartment had arrived on the Isle of Man, now wife to a man that everyone in the camp seemed to despise. Peter knew that he had been wrong to call Warschauer a liar. Still, Ludwig Warschauer's boast that he had married into one of Berlin's wealthiest families, represented, as usual, only the flattering part of the story.

The sight of a familiar face around the camp was a cold reminder of the truth of Peter's situation. In early September Lord Halifax, the foreign secretary, had warned in a speech that "there will be . . . many [internees] who are, in fact, devoted to our cause, but who nevertheless are not let out." At this time, only 616 of the 27,200 internees across the British Isles had been released—fewer, damningly, than the 650 who had been drowned while being deported on the *Arandora Star*. Only a hundred of these had been freed from Hutchinson specifically. The prospect of months, possibly years behind barbed wire was distressing, yet inescapable for everyone who fell outside the government's narrow release criteria.

Faced with this reality, letters from loved ones provided one of the few salves—a psychological connection to the real world, the reassurance to each man that he was not forgotten. They often came with items of sustenance, too. In the post Kurt Treitel received coffee, bread, shaving cream, chocolate, jam, biscuits, cheese, sardines, and even a sausage, which arrived half-nibbled by a mouse. Klaus Hinrichsen received packages from the German Red Cross, at least one of which contained biscuits cut in the shape of swastikas. (Hinrichsen immediately saw the comic potential in the situation and hung the provocative biscuits from his shirt.)

Peter received none of these boons. Ostracized by his uncle in Manchester, he had nobody thinking of him, no one, as he put it, "waiting or pining for me."

The tragedy of his situation drew the artistic community closely around him to offer support and protection. Fred Uhlman regularly sat with Peter and told him about the world outside England. Schwitters increasingly became a surrogate father. A few of the artists saw their younger selves in this eager would-be apprentice.

"Some were reminded of their own beginnings, forever drawing, painting or sculpting, desperately hoping that somebody would show genuine interest and encouragement," Hinrichsen noted.

Peter's potential as an artist was not all that ingratiated him to the older artists. They knew that, on the outside, they had intercessors working for their release—people, many from the art establishment, who believed a person's freedom should be contingent on their innocence, not their utility, and who were willing to take the government to task repeatedly. What hope was there for Peter Fleischmann, a student with no school, an artist with no reputation, a teenager with no family?

AFTER SHE GAVE BIRTH TO her first child, Fred Uhlman's wife, Diana, had passed her work as secretary of the Artists' Refugee Committee onto the painter Helen Roeder. Before the war, the group, cofounded by Roland Penrose in November 1938, had worked to orchestrate the rescue of artists from the continent. Now, under Helen's direction, its focus had necessarily shifted along two key lines. First, to ensure the comfort of the interned artists, that they had sufficient materials with which to continue their work, and "to encourage English people in every walk of life to do the same." And second, to expand the categories outlined in the white paper to enable artists of distinction to apply for release, while simultaneously campaigning for a change in policy so that "a man's innocence and that alone shall secure his release."

As well as writing to various organizations such as the National Union of Journalists, the PEN club, and the National Council for Civil Liberties, Helen was eager to join forces with groups who represented other professions in the camps, most notably the Society for the Protection of Science and Learning and the Musicians' Union. Tremendous pressure was being put on the Home Office by all these groups to enable people of distinction in science and art to apply for release.

"If this method fails," she wrote, everyone involved agreed that a "mass protest meeting should be called at the Albert Hall."

Like Bertha Bracey, Helen was a tireless campaigner for justice. She compiled a list of every artist supported by the committee and sent it to her friend Kenneth Clark, director of the National Gallery.[*]

"I'm afraid it's not exactly cheerful re-reading," she wrote. "They are all brave people and deserve all the help we can give them."

The list, Helen continued, did not include those artists who were not currently receiving financial aid from the committee.

"The list of those who have applied to us from the internment camps for help," she added, "would fill pages, some of them are very distinguished, and most of them tragic."

Helen's letter moved Clark. He put in a call to the *Times* suggesting an article about the situation.

"Trying to get justice out of this internment business is like climbing up a mountain of feathers for a star," wrote Helen in a letter thanking her friend for his efforts. "Please go on making them sit up and take notice. They need it."

---

[*] Helen first met Sir Kenneth, whom she called "K" or, pleasingly, "His Nibs," on January 1, 1940, when she visited his London flat to interview for the position of his secretary. Sir Kenneth gave Helen a tour of the various original artworks that hung on his walls. The pair stopped in front of a Degas of a woman in a bathtub. "It's wonderful," he said. "But I sometimes feel it's a little obscene." Helen blurted out: "It's not the picture that's obscene; it's being imprisoned in this room. In a bare studio it would be magnificent." She did not get the job, but the pair became close friends thereafter.

Just as Helen worked for the artist internees and Bertha Bracey for the destitute, so Esther Simpson, secretary of the Society for the Protection of Science and Learning, began to stage her assault on government policy on behalf of the academics interned at Hutchinson and elsewhere.

Much to the dismay of those academics who worked in the humanities and the arts, the government's white paper only covered scientists whose work was considered most likely to be useful to the war effort. Those spurned professors wrote dozens of letters to Tess, as she was known to friends and acquaintances, a woman who had played a pivotal role in bringing each of the academics to Britain in the first place.

Like Bertha Bracey, Tess had trained as a teacher, only to move into humanitarian work. She joined the Academic Assistance Council (by now known as the Society for the Protection of Science and Learning) on July 17, 1933, at the behest of its cofounder, the Hungarian physicist Leo Szilard. Together, the pair worked out of a small office room on the top floor of Burlington House in London, sifting through the names of scores of displaced academics hoping to find a role for them at a university in Britain. They worked until ten o'clock every night, when the building was locked and they were forced to go home. It was thanks to Tess's determined efforts that so many academics had fled to Britain in the first place, rather than relocate elsewhere. It was Tess who had organized the immigration of Peter's uncle and helped arrange his post at Manchester University.

In the summer of 1940, Tess found her role had shifted from attempting to spare academics from German concentration camps to attempting to free academics—many of whom had become her friends—from British internment camps. It was a preposterous turnaround. In May 1940, she emphasized in a letter to the Home Office that many of the European scientists and scholars in Britain were well known to the society, which could vouch for their integrity to spare them from internment. The Home Office did not respond. Her pleas ignored, Tess had been forced to begin the exhausting work of preparing no fewer than nine copies of each internee's application and supporting documents for each of the 532 academics applying for release.

Tess was not alone in her petitions. The Nobel Prize–winning physiologist Archibald Hill provided moral and material support. As well as asking awkward questions of the home secretary, Hill had a knack for generating useful publicity. On December 3, 1940, he addressed the House of Commons with a speech in which he complained about the delays in correspondence between internees on the Isle of Man and the Royal Society. One application for release, he pointed out, took forty-two days to arrive, a speed equivalent to "a quarter of a mile per hour, or less than the speed of a tortoise."

Three days later the *Daily Telegraph* took up Hill's quip when a columnist pointed out that the winner of the world's only tortoise derby, Pebblestone, was able to walk 150 yards per hour. In fact, the columnist corrected drolly, "[the] department moves three and a half times faster than a tortoise."

Hill responded by saying that he was referring to Greek tortoises, not to those who hailed from Oklahoma.

"Poking fun at the Home Office," Hill wrote in a letter to Tess, "may do more good than getting angry with them."

These combined efforts quickly took effect. On September 5, two days before Marjan Rawicz gave his matinee performance at the camp, Helen received a letter containing good news from Kenneth Clark about the plight of the refugee artists. Under mounting pressure, the government had decided to expand the categories for release, to be included in a new, forthcoming edition of the white paper.

"Artists and I think musicians, [will be] among the categories to be exempted," Clark wrote, adding a dampening footnote that this would apply only to those who had achieved, nebulously, "distinction" in their chosen field. This threshold would be determined by all new tribunals. It was, nonetheless, "a welcome development."

Helen responded with characteristic wit: "I hope the Royal Academy won't be asked to decide who has achieved distinction in the arts, otherwise the only people released will be those who are too old for internment anyway."

Despite the efforts of these honorable intercessors, the desperation felt by many internees made them vulnerable to exploitation. So-
called "touting agents" promised to make personalized petitions on
their behalf to the Home Office in exchange for exorbitant fees. So
many internees fell foul of these moneymaking schemes that the Central Department for Interned Refugees distributed informational posters warning of the scam.

On October 8, 1940, Sir John Anderson, both architect and mod-
erator of the policy of mass internment, left his tortured post as home
secretary. It was clear that Anderson's handling of internment would
be his defining legacy. That day the MP Aneurin Bevan addressed the
House of Commons and issued a damning summary of his colleague's
record.

"The right honourable Gentleman's handling of the internment of
aliens was, and remains, a disgrace to the country," he said. "There are
many examples of the appalling consequences of the way in which that
matter has been managed . . . Even now, the categories of aliens still in
internment are a disgrace."

Anderson shook his head in mournful denial.

His successor, Herbert Morrison, not only inherited a vast administrative mess from Anderson, but also now became the focal point for
anger and questioning from his colleagues in the House of Commons.
Morrison was immediately besieged. In the same session, he was asked
about specific "monstrous" cases relating to deaths aboard the *Arandora Star*; about why internees who had been successfully sent to Canada had now been given the status of "prisoners of war"; about why a
reputed broadcaster for the BBC, Paul Gottschalk, was interned; and
why, precisely, it was taking so long for internees who applied for release under the criteria of having a history of being anti-Nazi to have
their cases examined.

Nine days later, on October 17, Morrison published the third
and final revision to the white paper, outlining three new categories

by which an internee could apply for release: students; those who had been living in the United Kingdom for at least twenty years; and, crucially for many of Hutchinson's residents, persons eminent in art and learning.

Distinguished bodies including the Royal Society, the Royal Academy of Arts, and the Royal College of Music would nominate committee members who could judge which refugees met the criteria. For Helen Roeder it was a longed-for moment—even if the fact that an artist had to meet some vague standard of "distinction" seemed, to her, a preposterous requirement. As she wrote in a letter to Kenneth Clark: "Do you think [the criteria could] be stretched to include the poor souls who have been too busy being hunted to achieve distinction in the arts?"

EIGHTY-FIVE PERCENT OF THE FOURTEEN thousand internees still imprisoned in Britain resided on the Isle of Man. The news provided a new glimmer of hope. For some, however, it came too late. By mid-August, three men had died while interned in the Isle of Man's various camps.

On arrival at Hutchinson camp on September 5, Sigmund Stiegel immediately died of a heart attack. A fellow passenger on Professor Jacobsthal's ferry died of exhaustion before the boat docked on the island. With winter approaching, the chief rabbi's office, anticipating more deaths, purchased a half-acre plot—with room for an estimated fifty burials—on the north end of Douglas Borough Cemetery, "on account of the large number of Jewish internees at the camps in the Isle of Man . . . and the advanced age of many." The Douglas Borough Council even rented out a room in the caretaker's house to be used as a Jewish chapel for funeral services at a rate of £7 per year.

At least forty-five men died in the Isle of Man camps. To die in internment was a compound injustice. Internment to interment, without interlude. Forty-six-year-old Simon Guttmann was one of the unlucky few sent to Australia on the notorious HMT *Dunera*. When he returned from Sydney to Britain sixteen months later, Guttmann was sent to Hutchinson, where he was twice refused release. On September 6, 1942, having survived two world crossings by ship as an internee, Guttmann died of a heart attack, possibly brought on by his considerable ordeal. Or there was Kurt Schier, an ice-skating instructor, who, like Guttmann, was refused release on two occasions; he took his life at Hutchinson. Men like these, who never left the camp, were permanent victims of a policy that, while not strictly malicious, was indisputably panicked, disorganized and, via that combination, cruel.

Those internees who, for one reason or another, had no job and no papers, still faced a near-insurmountable challenge in convincing the authorities that they posed no threat to the British state, let alone that they qualified in any way as eminent.

The thirty-year-old Hutchinson internee Oscar Norbert Gugenbichler was a typical case. Despite his muscly Germanic surname, Gugenbichler (he later truncated his name to Gugen) was born in Paris where, as a dual French-Austrian citizen, he lived during the invasion of France. As the German troops advanced, Gugen destroyed his papers. A professional diver, Gugen ably swam the mouth of the River Loire in Nantes and climbed aboard a British destroyer, which was in the process of evacuating troops. Having obscured his German nationality, Gugen was welcomed and taken to Britain, where he was summarily arrested and sent to Pentonville Prison and, finally, to Hutchinson. Unable to prove his identity or his loyalties, Gugen would remain in the camp until its closure in March 1945, occasionally teaching the other internees French, while those around him left, person by person.

Men like Gugen fell under the classification "Unsponsored Cases" and represented some of the most tragic and disregarded individuals in the internment saga. Most of these cases became the responsibility of Bertha Bracey at Bloomsbury House. She and her department did their best for these men, providing emergency grants for a few days' board and lodging, but without documentation it was impossible to register any individual who came to Britain in this way as a refugee.

One man known only as "Mr. von D" had arrived in Britain by hiding as a stowaway in a wine crate on a ship from Bordeaux. He spoke no English and, having been born in Hungary but spent his life in Germany, was unable to even identify his own nationality. His only documentation was a letter of employment, dated 1923, identifying him as a champagne salesman for a Bucharest-based firm. Mr. von D explained that, after a stint in a Nazi camp, he fled to France in 1935. Bracey provided the man with a small grant and regularly visited him in prison. In early July 1940, separated from his family, his homeland, and his identity, Mr. von D was deported to Canada. He died on the *Arandora Star*.

Peter Fleischmann was, likewise, categorized as an unsponsored case, and certainly destitute. When word of the expanding categories of release reached the Artists Café in Hutchinson, the initial rush of excitement and relief was quickly replaced with concern over how, exactly, the tribunals would establish who among them were artists of distinction. For Peter, however, there was nothing to consider. An artist with no place of study outside of Hutchinson, he was neither student nor professional, and certainly not yet distinguished. His only hope for release was to secure a place at a British art college. For that, he would need work that demonstrated his ability, alongside a letter of recommendation. Against all odds, Hutchinson camp had provided Peter with the luminaries who might be able to vouch for him. And the chance to exhibit in the forthcoming second art exhibition provided the excuse to assemble a portfolio.

XVII

ART AND JUSTICE

ERNST MÜLLER-BLENSDORF APPROACHED THE DOOR of Hutchinson's pristine new hall under the cover of darkness. Prisoners of war in camps both in England and in Germany would, throughout the war, stage their escape attempts in the dark. Müller-Blensdorf's aim on this chilly November night was the opposite, however. He hoped to break *into* a camp building, not out of one. Müller-Blensdorf's attempt was being made considerably more difficult by his accomplice: a pregnant giantess. Müller-Blensdorf had named this huge statue, made from clay and cast in plaster, *Figure of a Woman*. His plan was straightforward: to smuggle her into this, the newest Hutchinson camp building, ahead of its official opening.

Situated next to the camp laundry and above the canteen, Hutchinson's newly built, heated hall was a generously sized venue. The main auditorium was designed to house musical and theatrical performances, and the chairs could easily be pushed to the sides for indoor sports events. Before the year's end, it would become home to a ping-pong table and double as a place of worship; some Jewish internees would fashion an altar from an upturned orange box covered by a tablecloth, while both Protestant and Roman Catholic contingents peacefully negotiated bookings.

Every group and club had plans on the space, so they impatiently anticipated the building's opening. As one internee wrote in *The Camp*:

"How long will its erection take? Let us hope that it will be done more quickly than the installation of an electrical light in our present hall." Two months earlier, between September 15 and 17, Hutchinson had hosted its first art exhibition arranged in the houses, a three-day-long affair that, by all accounts, had failed to match the significant promise of the camp's distinguished cadre of artists.

"It was too early," Klaus Hinrichsen said. "Not enough work was ready."

As well as the paucity of works, there was too little space to properly show them off. The new hall building provided both inspiration and opportunity: now the artists could stage a more ambitious and accomplished exhibition worthy of their talents. The members of the Artists Café scheduled a second exhibition for mid-November, to coincide with the hall's opening ceremony.

Captain Daniel hoped the quality of work on show would reveal to visitors that his was the best-run camp of any on the island (and therefore less likely to be picked for closure when the time came to consolidate camps due to falling internee numbers). The artists hoped that the quality of work on show would demonstrate to visitors the idiocy of the mass internment policy, which had locked up those most dangerous classes of refugee: the whittlers and paintbrush-wielders, the portraitists and landscape observers.

For that majority of internees who had been passed over for release, here was a new category of distraction, too. Now that some of the most notable and celebrated men had been freed, concerns that those who remained were to be forgotten had been somewhat assuaged by the visit of Lord Lytton, a former Olympic tennis player and keen artist, who had taken a camp tour in late October. In a recent broadcast on the BBC by the aristocrat Lord Cecil, he had admitted that "the great mistake was treating all refugees as enemy aliens," which would have been more comforting if the men left behind at Hutchinson knew their release was imminent.*

---

* As early as July 1940, the prime minister conceded in the Commons that "it is fully recognised that many such persons are not hostile to this country and that in referring to them it is better to use such a phrase as 'persons of enemy nationality,' but it is not always possible to avoid the term

An art exhibition, then, would at least help to elevate the mind to higher things.

Klaus Hinrichsen assumed the role of curator. With modest power came modest misery. It was Hinrichsen's privilege and burden to choose which works by which artists could be shown, while ensuring that the space did not become overcrowded, all without bruising the delicate egos of the competing artists who were, when it came to exhibitions, used to having things their own way. It was, in short, "a nightmare," as Hinrichsen put it. "No artist is ever satisfied with the number of his works accepted, nor with the space where they were shown."

Müller-Blensdorf had been more successful in his petitions than most. Hinrichsen accepted seven of his drawings and three wooden plaques, carved from the mahogany panels he had taken from the piano that had been wrecked by Rawicz's playing. This was not enough to sate the carver's appetite. Suspecting that *Figure of a Woman* would be considered too large to include, Müller-Blensdorf had decided to smuggle her into the building without permission, perhaps hoping that she would prove too cumbersome for anyone to later evict.

For Peter, the event presented an opportunity to produce and exhibit work alongside many of Europe's finest artists, an unimaginable prospect outside the camp's warped reality. Peter may not have been the orphan prodigy of literary cliché, but, to the right person, tenacity is a gift of equal value to genius. He, like many of the other professional and burgeoning artists in the camp, turned his focus to what he might make and show at the forthcoming event. Poverty necessitated invention. Peter cut the collars from his shirts and sewed them into his sweaters, in order that he might use the material for canvas.

While Müller-Blensdorf chose subterfuge to maximize his space in the exhibition, Peter decided he would be entirely straightforward in

---

'enemy alien.'" It took three years before a distinction between "enemy aliens" and "refugees" was made by government departments, in October 1943, when the words "does not include a refugee alien" were added to the definition of "enemy aliens" in the national security regulations. This came, for almost everyone concerned, far too late to be meaningful.

his submission. He would offer just four pieces for consideration. Their inclusion would be won on merit.

THE NEW HALL WAS NOT the only upgrade Hutchinson's internees had enjoyed to their living conditions. Thanks to the attention and care of the Quaker William Hughes, whose regular written reports on camp conditions had been keenly read at all levels of government, conditions in Hutchinson camp had steadily improved. By autumn, a building situated between the camp laundry and canteen had been turned into a bathing facility with thirty-six showers and dressing cubicles. The showers, which each internee was permitted to use once per week, had not been paid for by the Home or War Office but by one of the three local breweries on the island. The camp administration had shrewdly played the three companies off against one another to see what they might offer in exchange for the exclusive "licence" to sell their beer in the camp.

The winning brewery offered the shower block in return for the contract, believing that a camp of twelve hundred bored men with few things on which to spend their money represented a lucrative opportunity. When, however, the canteen began to stock beer on October 5, 1940, it became immediately clear this had been a poor investment. Many internees abstained from alcohol, and most had limited funds, which they would prefer to spend on food. Those who did drink were limited to one pint per day. The majority were Jews who, as Hinrichsen observed, "you only ever find . . . drunk in extremely secure surroundings."

As one writer put it in *The Camp* newspaper: "If the authorities thought to end the whining of our moan-men by permitting the sale of wine in this place, they were on the wrong tack."

The only alcohol regularly seen around the camp in the early months were the bottles of sherry presented to Captain Daniel whenever he attended a camp event. From late October, internees were allowed to order bottles of wine at the canteen, much to the chagrin of those who thought it quite preposterous they could order a bottle of French Sauternes but not fresh milk, brown bread, cheese, or chocolate.

Bertha Bracey, via the Germany Emergency Committee, had also organized the provision of tools, musical instruments, seeds for planting in the gardens, and various textbooks for students. She had also pressed for the reuniting, wherever possible, of fathers and sons interned in separate camps on the island. The fruits of her campaign, while welcome, had unintended effects. The improvements to food, drink, and facilities at Hutchinson led many of the men to become increasingly institutionalized to their predicament, intensifying the contradictions they felt between the injustice of their imprisonment and the modest comforts it provided.

"Slowly and imperceptibly," wrote the Oxford academic Paul Jacobsthal in his diary, "we [have] lost every feeling of the fantastic reality of this life, of its absurd rhythm and *nomos*." Every other day Jacobsthal went on the scheduled soldier-escorted walks outside of the camp, across the Manx hills, nodding and waving to passing islanders as they rambled.

"We [are] hardly still aware that only two months ago we had lived an existence like that of the people we met," he wrote. Jacobsthal concluded that the men of Hutchinson were becoming as zoo animals, inured to confinement, the sensations of freedom increasingly remote.

CAPTIVITY HAD PROVEN A PARTICULARLY complicated context for Hutchinson's celebrity artist Kurt Schwitters. Here he enjoyed artistic kudos at having had his work exhibited in the notorious Nazi exhibition of degenerate art. He had, in the Artists Café, a sympathetic group who would listen to his absurdist anecdotes and to whom he could recite poetry. Schwitters even had a keen understudy in Peter, whose eager presence provided a reaffirmation of his identity as a doyen of the art world, a position that had slipped in Germany in recent years.

Schwitters desperately missed his wife, Helma. While he wrote to her regularly, he had received no response since he left Norway in the spring. When, on October 5—the same day the canteen received its beer—Schwitters celebrated his silver wedding anniversary by eating chocolate cake while wearing a crown of silver foil, there was surely a tide of sadness rolling somewhere beneath the revelry.

Alone in his room Schwitters drew a heart on a windowpane in white chalk—an adolescent expression of longing—that, he told Helma in a letter, represented "our future . . . forever and all eternity."

Two weeks after the anniversary celebration, on October 20, 1940, Schwitters made his first application for release under the expanded categories outlined in the white paper.

"I paint since 1909," he wrote as his plea. "I am not able to carry on with my work while interned."

Like almost every other internee Schwitters was eager to leave internment as quickly as he had entered. The claim that captivity had blocked his creative output was demonstrably untrue, however. Schwitters was one of the most productive artists in the camp, generating, in addition to his porridge sculptures, the abstract designs that adorned the stairwell of the office building, ink studies of local flowers, collage works of objets trouvés, and abstract paintings. Despite the artist's claims, captivity had not sealed the well.

Most of Schwitters's efforts had focused on his popular line in mannerly portraits of internees, which had, over the weeks, made him a wealthy man in Hutchinson. He was able to build up a collection of wines, pay other internees to conduct his house chores, and even hire the camp tailors to cut him a suit. The artist did not choose all of his subjects for financial reasons, however. He painted the pianist Marjan Rawicz and the writer Rudolf Olden for their stature, and did so gratis, partly to help attract more paying customers. Others, like Bruno Ahrends and Friedrich Burschell, he painted because they were significant figures in the camp. Some he chose simply by virtue of their faces.

"I hear lectures on philosophy and art and concerts and paint very interesting heads," Schwitters wrote in a letter to his mother.

He also painted some men as repayment for favors; in Klaus Hinrichsen's case, the portrait was an appeasement gift from Schwitters, who used the young art historian's office as a studio space—partly because it was quiet, partly because it had an electric heater that could keep both artist and sitter warm. One day Hinrichsen had wandered into his office to an unsettling scene: a man stood under the heater fully naked, his face red from the electric fire, his feet blue from the ambient cold. When Hinrichsen explained that if Schwitters planned to paint live nudes he could no longer use his office, the artist offered to paint Hinrichsen's portrait by way of apology.

This was not the only time Schwitters's work in the camp was motivated by an electric fire. On another occasion, Peter was watching Schwitters paint a portrait when the sitter's clothing caught fire (Schwitters was so preoccupied in his work that he did not notice the flames until Peter cried out). Schwitters later happened upon a man in the camp with the surname Schaltenbrand—a pun on the German term for "fire switch"—and he playfully insisted that he paint the man's portrait as his name implied he was flameproof.

Schwitters even made portraits of the family members of fellow internees, whom he drew from photographs. Anneliese Sluzewski, the daughter of the Vatican lawyer Curt Sluzewski, was among the outsiders Schwitters drew from within the camp. Many eminent academics and businessmen employed his services hoping to shore up their reputation in a place rife with status anxiety.

Among others, Schwitters painted Alfred Sohn-Rethel, the secretary of the Egyptian chamber of commerce; Dr. Alfred Guttmann, the director of the Parlophone Records factory; the author Dr. Harald Landry; the pastor Alfons Schultes; and the camp's medical officer, Dr. Robert Marshall. Schwitters painted or sketched an equal number of working-class men without reputation, such as Hans Terner and Rudolf Meyer, both motor mechanics in their early twenties. While Schwitters's portraits were widely celebrated, they did not convince everyone. Professor Paul Jacobsthal described Schwitters in his diary as "an amateurish painter." This judgment was seemingly biased by Schwitters's relationship with another Oxford academic, Robert Eisler, whom Jacobsthal despised.

Eisler, a Jewish-Austrian polymath, had published books on subjects ranging from Christianity to astrology, and had, before his arrival

at Hutchinson, spent fifteen months imprisoned in Dachau and Buchenwald before fleeing to England, only to be interned. The excruciating
journey, which left Eisler with a heart condition from which he never
recovered, did nothing to temper Jacobsthal's appraisal of his colleague,
whom he considered to be "the perfect type of intellectual imposter." It
is unclear what Eisner did to earn his colleague's scorn—although perhaps a pinch of envy was involved: Jacobsthal refers to the "enormous"
audiences who gathered for his colleague's "muddle-headed" lectures.

Jacobsthal particularly objected to a portrait that Schwitters
painted of Eisler, which he considered to be nobler than the subject
deserved. With great relish Jacobsthal recorded that Eisler had borrowed the gown he wore for the sitting from the daughter of the camp
doctor, Captain Robert Marshall. She was, Jacobsthal gleefully wrote, a
mere "undergraduate."

Each man of distinction who paid for his portrait inspired the
next, until anyone with the means and desire had employed Schwitters's services. It was, then, inevitable that Ludwig Warschauer's appetite for status and respect would be similarly agitated in this culture
of self-memorialization. So Warschauer sat for Schwitters, wearing a
thick and dark roll-neck sweater, and with a large pipe emerging from
the side of his mouth. The pugilist's chest fills the frame; through tone
and angle Schwitters portrayed in a flattering light a man whom the
camp population knew instinctively not to mess with.

Regardless of what anyone else thought, Schwitters chose to enter
a selection of the portraits he had painted into the second art exhibition. The portraits would help sell more work—and, surely, attract less
drive-by criticism—in a way that his more provocative *Merz* collages
would not. Underneath the list of artists and artworks in the exhibition
catalog, designed by Hellmuth Weissenborn and Erich Kahn, he added
the invitation: "Place your order for a portrait."

MICHAEL CORVIN ANNOUNCED THE SECOND art exhibition in the
eighth edition of *The Camp*. This was not, he argued, to be a rarefied

exhibition only for the elites at Hutchinson. Rather, its purpose was to inspire everyone, whatever their profession, to "go on with your work as well as you can." Creation, Corvin assured his readers, is "not limited to the great things; as a miner you create no less than as an artist, and your humble help in farming is not less valuable than a contribution in art." View the exhibition in these terms, Corvin urged, and "it will help you not only to keep your chin up, but strengthen your mind and your resolution to overcome everything by creating in the way given to you."

Corvin's inspirational editorial was well-timed to provide solace and focus. Many of Hutchinson's captives had by now bade goodbye to friends they had made in the camp, and were in need of some encouragement. Schwitters had lost a number of close associates. Marjan Rawicz, the pianist who gave the memorable matinee performance on the lawn, was freed on October 18 after Ralph Vaughan Williams made a petition on his behalf. The night before his departure, Rawicz played to a small group of friends in his house, including the tune "Smoke Gets in Your Eyes," which had become something of a hit within the camp.

Before Rawicz left, Schwitters gave his friend a list of London contacts and, Hinrichsen later recalled, a Player's Navy Cut cigarette packet that the artist had decorated with eyes, a nose, and two church steeples. The rear of the packet was addressed, in Schwitters's affected stuttering style, to "*mmmeinem Freunde, Roland Peppenrose . . .*," the man better known as Roland Penrose, the art collector and cofounder of the Artists' Refugee Committee.

Send-off parties were often grand affairs, especially for popular internees. When housemates learned that one of their number was to be released, the men would save flour in order to make a leaving cake. While these farewell events were jubilant, they were confused by the usual feelings of sorrow that accompany any final parting and, below that, the shadow of a resentful question: Why him and not me? The art exhibition and opening of the new camp hall, then, represented an opportunity for internees to divert their thoughts away from the ever-pressing anxiety about release.

* * *

AT FOUR O'CLOCK IN THE afternoon on Tuesday, November 19, Captain Daniel entered the first room of the exhibition, flanked by RSM Potterton, and trailed by his staff of officers in the manner of royalty attending the opening of a national gallery. The atmosphere was one of high ceremony. To mark the occasion, Hutchinson's new camp father, Erich Bruckmann, had written a speech to set the tone, thanking the commandant for fostering an environment in which artists could work and flourish.

"For many of us it is exactly twenty weeks today that we have been interned," Bruckmann began. "[Your] really friendly assistance has made it possible that the works which you find here could come into existence. The artist, more than anyone else, suffers under the stress and strain of adverse circumstances. He might have stupendous and even divine inspirations, but he wants an atmosphere of kindness and friendliness around him, shall that mysterious transmutation materialise: from thought and imagination into a work of art. Well, I hope that our artists have shown that they can work in spite of difficulties and quite natural depression."

Having flattered the commandant, Bruckmann, with lawyerly slickness, shifted tack. "We know, Sir, just how interested you and your officers are in our cases and that you do all in your power to help us to get our early release . . . Let me wind up this little speech by expressing my hope that this will be a very successful exhibition, but also our last."

THE COMMANDANT DECLARED THE EVENT open and it fell to Klaus Hinrichsen, as curator, to introduce the artists to the delegation of officers. The exhibition, which wound through a number of rooms, featured more than ninety works. For the young art historian, the tour presented a chance to play the satisfying role of educator to men who were, in the camp hierarchy, his superiors. Hinrichsen's knowledge combined with the fact that, as he put it, "all German styles were represented" allowed him to take his jailers on a tour, not only of the premises, but of German art history—from classicism to expressionism, impressionism to *Neue Sachlichkeit*—new objectivity.

Hinrichsen had set aside his personal tastes in favor of a magnanimous approach. As well as his preferred artists, he selected pieces from those whose work he enjoyed far less, such as Fritz Kraemer, whom Hinrichsen considered a better bridge player than artist. He had also widened the scope of the exhibition by including crafts such as marquetry boxes, a chess set, and the *Kasperle* figures first used six days earlier in House 23 for a Punch and Judy puppetry show written by *The Camp*'s editor, Michael Corvin, and produced by Hermann Fechenbach.

The businessman Hans Gussefeld, who had whittled his Prees Heath tent pegs into crocodile letter openers, had been encouraged by Fechenbach to enter the designs into the second art exhibition. Hinrichsen welcomed this expression of folk art and hung the pegs in a crescent splay at eye level next to one of the doors.

For the camp's commandant, the exhibition was a testament to the creative environment he had fostered in the camp at his wife's urging. He was, as Fred Uhlman recorded in his diary that day, "very pleased," and appeared to warm to the role of patron, so much so that, during the tour, he began to make critical pronouncements of the work.[*] The commandant disliked the distorted limbs that could be seen in Erich Kahn's drawings and etchings; Uhlman's gloomy gray scenes of imprisonment featuring a child clutching a balloon were, he said, rather depressing. Schwitters, Captain Daniel concluded, was the undisputed master of the exhibition; he urged the other artists to learn from his portraits.

---

[*] This was not the only time Daniel assumed the role of art critic in the camp. The following month he summoned Hellmuth Weissenborn to his office. Weissenborn had created a linocut that showed, as he put it, "the spirit of Christmas flying over the camp." When Daniel first saw the image, he had assumed the piece was a pointed critique of life in Hutchinson, the angel of death representing "a cloud of discontent." Weissenborn was therefore forced to explain his work to defuse the situation.

For this, the opening ceremony, the artists had been invited to stand by their work so that Hinrichsen could introduce Daniel and his entourage to the artists behind the art. For Peter Fleischmann it was a moment of supreme pride. His artistic efforts had been recognized and rewarded by Hinrichsen, who, despite being only a decade older than the student, had adopted a fatherly attitude toward the Artists Café's youngest member. As the entourage of officers traipsed around, Peter stood next to his work—two portraits, a representation of the camp houses, and a still life—no longer a mere aspiring artist, but an exhibited one.

THAT EVENING IN LONDON, THE civil servant Sir Frank Newsam sat down to write a letter. These had been difficult weeks for the government, which had once again been forced to deal with fresh and scandalous revelations about mass internment. On November 1, a man at Palace camp, which was situated a few hundred yards from Hutchinson and was where many of the Italian internees were kept, had been attacked and left severely injured by two fellow internees. The victim, Signor Cosomati, was a well-known cartoonist. A number of his anti-Mussolini cartoons had just been reprinted in a British newspaper. His attackers were fascist supporters. The failure to separate innocents from fascists in internment camps had been a recurrent criticism of the government, and this latest incident further damaged both its reputation and that of the policy.

Further embarrassment had been heaped upon the government with the publication of two books about the ongoing internment situation, *The Internment of Aliens* by François Lafitte and *Anderson's Prisoners* by "Judex." Both texts were highly critical and spared none of the gruelling details of hardship caused by its policy of mass internment. To counter some of this bad publicity, the government had pledged to increase aid to the various organizations working in the interest of refugees and internees. Critics argued that these funds would only extend the amount of time for which innocents could be imprisoned.

"They do not want your £375,000," Colonel Josiah Wedgewood told Parliament. "They want justice."

Newsam was, then, eager to find anything that might cast the internment debacle in a more favorable light. He had recently returned from a tour of the island's camps to check on conditions. There he had spent time with Captain Daniel, who had proudly showed off the first few issues of *The Camp* newspaper, described the imminent art exhibition, and even showed him a collection of watercolors and etchings that he had been gifted by the internees.

"I venture to suggest that the Secretary of State might be interested to see some of [this] work," Newsam wrote to Sir John Moylan, undersecretary of state at the Home Office. It might, he suggested, be used to improve the public's view of the internment debacle. "It seems a pity if at the end of the war the work of the internee should be dispersed among private individuals," he added. "Ought not some sort of museum be established?"*

While Newsam penned his letter in London, Hutchinson's internees gathered in the main auditorium of the freshly painted hall. That night, the Luftwaffe began a nine-day bombing raid on Birmingham, which would leave eight hundred dead and more than twenty thousand homeless. Here, inside the cozy surroundings of the new hall, Hutchinson's internees could, for a moment, forget about the war that brought them here. Stefan Pollmann, a professor of music from Vienna, sang eight pieces of Schubert, accompanied by Hans Fürth who, following Rawicz's release in mid-October, had become Hutchinson's resident pianist.† Fürth was then joined by the sculptor Paul Hamann and the lawyer Curt Sluzewski, who each played violin for a Bach interlude.

---

* The grandeur of the second art exhibition was not to be repeated in the camp, but on January 14, 1941, there was a third artistic display, in House 37, exclusively in honor of the work of Ernst Müller-Blensdorf, the carver who Peter first met in Warth Mills, and who was known to everyone in the camp for working on his sculptures in the front garden of House 19.
† Fürth later emigrated to North America, where he eventually became, not a professional musician, but Professor Emeritus of Psychology at the Catholic University of America in Washington, DC, specializing in developmental psychology.

Finally, Pollmann returned to the stage for the evening's final segment of Brahms.

Klaus Hinrichsen ended the day with the satisfaction that he had played midwife to a rich commemoration of the quality of work produced in these, the unlikeliest of circumstances. The project might not bring the plight of the artists to wider attention, but no visitor could have left doubting the talent of those men who had displayed their work.

"The mystery at last got lifted," he wrote in a short, sweetly naïf poem, later printed in *The Camp*, "how many people here are gifted . . ."

It had been an enjoyable day for the artists, though on some level had surely thrown the extent to which their professional horizons had shrunk into dizzying perspective. Men who had exhibited their work in Berlin's finest galleries were reduced to jostling for wall space in a remote island boardinghouse, to be appraised by an inexpert advertising executive. Peter's experience was the exception. Here was the tangible fulfillment that to him captivity represented an expansion of opportunity, a heightening of prospects, a ballooning of hope. That Peter had been able to exhibit was also testament to the care and support he had found in Hutchinson camp.

Having been abandoned by his family members through death or indifference, here Peter found a group of adults apparently willing to look out for him and nurture his talent and ambition. And now, with an exhibition to his name and the support of Hutchinson's professionals behind him, he just needed to find a way to springboard from camp to college.

XVIII

HOME FOR CHRISTMAS?

THE SOUND OF MUFFLED SHOUTING broke the atmosphere of quiet industry. Hutchinson's administrative staff put down their papers and exchanged glances. Each man strained to listen to what was being said. The office was not usually a place of raised voices. It was here they spent most of their time patiently checking through their fellow camp mates' applications for release. It involved work of grave responsibility—the slightest mistake could delay an internee's hearing by months—and, since the British government had expanded the release categories, the workload had become overwhelming. More than a hundred applications arrived each day. There was no time for quarreling.

The shouting came from the intelligence office. Everyone recognized the two parties involved: Captain Jurgensen and RSM Potterton. Snatches of sentences offered clues as to the nature of the dispute—wine, a restaurant, fish. Nobody was surprised to hear one internee's name repeated again and again: Ludwig Warschauer.

Since the opening of the Technical School, Warschauer had ingratiated himself to the British officers charged with his containment. James Craufurd and John Noble, the MI5 agents who had been watching Warschauer with ever-keener interest, noted that he had become one of Captain Daniel's "pet" internees. While they doubted the engineer's story, he was still viewed as a pillar of the camp community among Hutchinson's guards.

"There can be no doubt as to this man's loyalty to our cause," wrote a War Office security liaison officer stationed at Douglas. "During his stay here, he has been one of our most solid supporters of discipline and order."

Warschauer had numerous incentives to build up the work and status of the Technical School. It enabled him to establish a direct line to Captain Daniel, to secure a building separate from the other internees to live and work, to gain a position of responsibility—and, therefore, power—over the other prisoners, and free labor for his business interests outside the camp, much to the frustration of other members of the Cultural Department. Warschauer's primary motivation, however, was to present himself as trustworthy and useful to those considering his increasingly desperate applications for release.

Warschauer's self-publicity had proven effective. He regularly received "mysterious visitors from London," as one eyewitness put it. It was rumored these individuals were from Scientific Intelligence, come to pick the engineer's brilliant mind. This was untrue—the visitors had come to pick at his dubious backstory—but the Technical School was proving to be a compelling way to build myth and settle the concerns of casual onlookers.

Warschauer's school had become a state within a state, out of bounds even for elected camp officials. Those who distrusted Warschauer suspected that the schedule of lessons was a cover for the main thrust of the institution's work: exploiting young men to cut mica for Warschauer's company outside the camp. There were rumors that Warschauer and his associates took rations from the students, who were prepared to exchange food for the promise that he would help hasten their release and offer them lucrative employment thereafter. Whatever the truth, Warschauer's status with Captain Daniel appeared secure. Before his release, the camp father Friedrich Burschell had collected proof that matters he had raised with the commandant were later discussed with Warschauer, whose advice seemed to carry more weight than his own.

Today's argument in the camp office, however, provided definitive proof that Warschauer enjoyed unique privileges at Hutchinson. He had previously been permitted to leave the camp in the company of a corporal in order, purportedly, to visit ironmongers and tool suppliers in the local town center. The internees knew that he had used these excursions to shop not only for equipment for the Technical School, but also for personal items; once, he returned wearing a new Harris Tweed jacket and a brightly colored tie.

As the camp office workers listened to Jurgensen's remonstrations, however, it became clear that a line had been crossed. Warschauer had been seen by a camp guard in town in the company of RSM Potterton. The moneyed Warschauer had, it transpired, invited Potterton to lunch at a fish restaurant. An off-duty guard reported seeing the pair dining and drinking white wine together.[*] The camp office staff could only imagine Potterton's red face and quivering lip as he received this unprecedented dressing-down from the usually mild-mannered intelligence officer, who made it clear that the officer was never again to accept hospitality—especially alcohol—from a prisoner.

WARSCHAUER'S LUNCH WAS EXCEPTIONAL, but formal trips for internees outside the camp had become frequent. As well as the scheduled walks to the promenade, there were regular trips to the beach for both the male and female internees. Millicent Faragher, one of three police officers dispatched to the island from London to provide support to the local force, was scandalized by the Austrian and Italian women who would sunbathe, as she put it, "continental topless." One of Faragher's jobs was to police this behavior.

"We would walk up and down the beach in our heavy navy-blue king's uniforms saying 'Tops! Tops!," she said. "And they'd put their tops on, and, of course, take them off as soon as we'd passed by."

---

[*] According to MI5 documents, the primary source of Warschauer's wealth at this time was not his wife, but rather the generous monthly salary of £40 paid to him by the Tefi company during internment, only £20 less than his full managerial salary prior to arrest.

Another of Faragher's unexpected roles was to chaperone the women internees to the local cinema every Tuesday and Thursday afternoon ("Money for jam," she later put it). Hutchinson's men were given a similar opportunity. On the same day as the opening of the second art exhibition, around six hundred of Hutchinson's internees—at least half the camp's population—enjoyed their first trip to the local cinema. The film of the day was surprisingly fitting: Charlie Chaplin's *The Great Dictator*, the pratfalling comedian's satirical depiction of Hitler. As with so many matters within the camp, even the simple question of a visit to the cinema became the subject of fraught debate. A number of the older internees declined to partake.

"Hitler was the sole cause of all their misfortunes, including internment," recalled Hinrichsen. "Even showing that monster as a comical figure could make him appear human." Others argued that it was important to support a film that characterized Hitler as an undereducated maniac with vainglorious pretensions, as the depiction might convince the British fascists and category A internees of their misplaced loyalty.

The walk to the cinema along a short stretch of the grandiose sweep of the promenade gave internees their first close-up sight of the town, whereupon they realized that Hutchinson was not the sole camp situated in Douglas, but rather one of many. Hutchinson's men realized their good fortune to have been interned in the relatively salubrious square rather than crammed into one of the seafront hotels.

The film was preceded by newsreel footage, shorts that showed scenes of devastation in the British capital and how Londoners—at least those chosen to be filmed for this morale-boosting propaganda—had met the challenge with bright positivity. Hinrichsen's review of the day's expedition in *The Camp* newspaper noted: "[T]he Internees express[ed] their feelings by storms of applaud [*sic*] and cheers."

After the showing the men traipsed back to Hutchinson Square in a state of elation. The event, Klaus Hinrichsen wrote, had been "comparable to a schoolboy's excursion," with a "delightful effect on the spirit."

The mood blackened as soon as the group reentered through the main gate, however. Those who had stayed behind explained that, as soon as the cinemagoers had departed, the first row of Hutchinson's houses, including Peter's, was blocked off by soldiers, who searched the premises for contraband. Neither the commander nor the intelligence officer had been present for the search, leading to speculation that it had been organized by an outside authority. Regardless, as some of the internees noted, there was a certain irony to the fact that the raid had taken place during a visit to a film that pilloried dictatorial behavior; most of the refugees were familiar with Gestapo searches as a means of intimidation.

There were opportunities, too, for those who wanted to work outside the camp. From September 1940, the younger camp members were permitted to take on local farmwork.* After roll call, volunteers would meet by Hutchinson's gate and wait for news as to whether one of the local farmers required help that day. If they were fortunate, the young men would be collected and—under armed guard—set to work picking and sorting potatoes; pulling out carrots, beets, and turnips; threshing; or spreading manure.

The feeling of leaving the camp was "something like liberty," as one volunteer put it. "Standing on the field, looking at the hills, plains and forests around you, amidst all the beauty of the nature with a wide sky above you and the free soil beneath your feet, doing a useful job and so connected with the free people, you forget your sorrows and feel yourself free." These excursions brought contact with the islanders, whose sympathetic reaction revitalized the mental health of men who had lived under the cloud of suspicion for the past few months.

"You bring home the conviction that the population of this island, men you have spoken to, are far from believing the stupid accusations of this island's newspapers who pretend not to know that we are victims of Hitler and his friends," wrote the volunteer. "The way we are

---

* On December 19, 1941, the *Isle of Man Examiner* reported that, in a speech delivered to the Douglas Rotary Club, the Home Office representative to the alien internment camps, Mr. T. Angliss, stated that no fewer than 750 internees worked on farms, market gardening, and reclamation schemes on the island during the summer of the previous year.

treated by the farmers proves that they realise the mendacity of such accusations."

The volunteers were given produce, including butter, as recompense, which they brought back to the camp. Two weeks into the scheme, however, Captain Daniel discovered that profiteers had started paying the young men for butter by the pound, to sell it on for double. The commandant canceled the opportunity and placed the profiteers in isolation. Hellmuth Weissenborn was more fortunate. The chicken that one of his young housemates smuggled into House 28, which he roasted for his housemates, evaded detection.

As trips outside the camp became more commonplace—a group of Hutchinson internees attended a theater production in Douglas on at least one occasion—the likelihood of an escape attempt grew. When Hutchinson's linocut artist Hellmuth Weissenborn discovered that one of his former students, Denis Megaw, was the brother of the curator of the local Manx Museum, the internees requested to be allowed to visit.

After some deliberation, Captain Jurgensen agreed to the plan, and the internees competed for one of ten places on the trip, scheduled for October 27. Jurgensen allocated one spot to an elderly former resident of the Isle of Jersey who collected fossils. During the excursion the battery in the man's hearing aid failed and he missed the call to return to the coach. When he finally emerged from the room that housed the museum's fossil collection and saw his group had returned to the camp, the man panicked, fearing that it would be assumed he was attempting to escape. He approached a taxi driver and asked to be taken to Hutchinson Square.

"You can't go there," the driver explained. "That is an internment camp."

The internee explained what had happened and the taxi driver agreed to deliver him to the camp's entrance to clear up the situation. The car arrived to a great kerfuffle. A Manx man of a similar age and build to the deaf internee had been herded onto the coach by mistake.

Right: Herschel Grynszpan, shortly after his arrest on November 7, 1938, for the attempted murder of the German diplomat Ernst vom Rath in Paris. Herschel's actions that morning set off the chain of events that led, later that week, to *Kristallnacht*.

1

2

Left: Peter Fleischmann, a Jewish orphan and aspiring artist, photographed here as a teenager in Berlin in the 1930s. After *Kristallnacht*, Peter was given asylum in Britain. Then, when war broke out, he was arrested and sent to Hutchinson camp as a suspected Nazi spy.

3

Above: Following Ernst vom Rath's death in Paris on November 9, 1938, Nazi supporters commenced attacks on Jewish properties in Germany, including synagogues, during the pogrom that became known as *Kristallnacht*.

Below: Dawn rose on the morning of November 10, 1938, to reveal the scale of the previous night's destruction and a landscape that had been profoundly changed. One Berlin jewelry store, Margraf, reported losses of 1.7 million marks.

Right: Peter Fleischmann, art folder under his arm, arrives in Harwich on December 2, 1938, as part of the first delegation of children brought to Britain as part of the *Kindertransport* initiative. Three weeks shy of his seventeenth birthday, Peter only just met the criteria for rescue.

4

Above: In May 1940, the British government began to round up so-called "enemy aliens"—mainly refugees from Nazi oppression suddenly suspected of being foreign agents.

Right: The painter Hermann Fechenbach staged a hunger strike to protest the dank conditions at Warth Mills transit camp, where he briefly stayed en route to the island. He made this print in 1943, two years after his release.

Below: A satirical cartoon by artist David Low, published in the *Evening Standard* during the height of the arrests questions where the real danger lies.

8

9

Above: The photographer Paul Henning developed a talent for making linocuts at Hutchinson. This print, created at the camp, shows the square where internees staged dozens of lectures and musical performances.

Below: The British army compelled the internees to establish a hierarchy of leaders to self-govern. Soldiers only entered the camp in the event of an emergency—of which there were, admittedly, many.

10

Top Left: Captain Daniel was a benevolent camp commandant, dedicated to providing his charges with distractions and endeavors. He became proud of Hutchinson, which he believed to be the finest of the island's ten camps.

Top Right: After realizing that Hutchinson was home to a raft of eminent painters and sculptors, Margery Daniel (*center*), herself a thwarted artist, persuaded her husband to provide studio space and materials.

Bottom Left: Regimental Sergeant Major Ambrose Harry Potterton conducts early-morning roll call in 1940, his brass-tipped baton tucked under his arm.

Bottom Right: In a cartoon published in Hutchinson's newspaper, Adolf "Dol" Mirecki, depicted Potterton as a larger-than-life authority figure, to whom the internees are forced to look up.

15

Above: A crowd of Hutchinson's internees wait to collect their respective house's daily allocation of food rations, stored in large metallic, numbered rubbish bins.

16

Left: Ludwig Meidner depicts the scale of the chores required in a house numbering around thirty men.

17

Right: Hellmuth Weissenborn produced numerous woodblock pictures of domestic scenes at the camp. These were made using a laundry wringer modified for the task by Peter Fleischmann.

1   2

Above: The famed Dadaist Kurt Schwitters painted dozens of portraits of his fellow internees at Hutchinson, including those of Bruno Ahrends (*left*), founder of Hutchinson's Camp University, and Klaus Hinrichsen (*right*), its secretary.

Bottom Left: The pianist Marjan Rawicz gave a memorable matinee performance on Hutchinson's lawn using a hired grand piano.

Bottom Right: Rudolf Olden was a brilliant lawyer and fierce opponent of Nazism. Olden died soon after his release, when a U-boat torpedoed the ship carrying him and his wife to a new life in America.

3   4

Right: Adolf Hitler standing in front of a work by Kurt Schwitters at the *Entartete Kunst*—"degenerate art"— exhibition, which opened in Munich on July 19, 1937.

5

6

7

Left: Aerated V was one of at least two hundred works Schwitters produced at Hutchinson. This mixed-media painting features driftwood from the beach, and a ping-pong ball from the new hall.

Right: Two years after his release, Kurt Schwitters performed "*Ursonate*" in London, a poem he previously recited at both Warth Mills and Hutchinson.

8

9

Above: Ludwig Warschauer, the founder of Hutchinson's Technical School, was the subject of a multiyear investigation by MI5, which kept copious files on the purported inventor, including this photograph (*left*). Warschauer commissioned Kurt Schwitters to paint his portrait (*right*), a work identified by his stepdaughter during the writing of this book.

10

Left: The lawyer James G. Craufurd became MI5's lead investigator into the case of Ludwig Warschauer.

Below: Warschauer formally opened Hutchinson's Technical School building in House 36 on August 22, 1940.

11

12

13

Top Left: Blackout material provided a novel medium for those internees who were inspired to create artworks. Among them was the lion tamer Johann "Brick" Neunzer, who produced detailed silhouette images.

Center: The professional artists formed a café club in the laundry room at House 15, as per Fred Uhlman's illustration.

Below: The second art exhibition opened on November 19, 1940, to coincide with completion of a new hall facility in the camp. The majority of Hutchinson's professional artists exhibited, vying with one another for wall space.

14

Above: Numerous women advocated for the rights and the release of internees. Helen Roeder, secretary of the Artists' Refugee Committee (*left*; painting by Carel Weight, 1938), interceded for the artists, while the MP Eleanor Rathbone (*right*; painting by Sir James Gunn, 1933) championed the rights of all internees, regardless of profession.

Below: No campaigner did more for refugees from Nazi oppression in Britain than the self-effacing Bertha Bracey who, as chairman of the Central Department for Interned Refugees, worked tirelessly to improve camp conditions and to petition for the release of the wrongfully accused.

17

18

Above: Echen Kohsen (*front row, second from the right*), heiress to the Kempinski restaurant empire, cared for Peter Fleischmann during the school holidays in Germany and, just prior to the outbreak of war, agreed to marry Ludwig Warschauer in return for her safe passage to Britain.

Bottom Left: As a young child, Echen—seen here in the white dress—attended the opening of a Kempinski restaurant alongside Kaiser Wilhem II (*center*)—a measure of the stature and importance of the business during the early twentieth century, before its looting by the Nazi state.

Bottom Right: Ludwig Warschauer, desperate that his wife continue to petition for his release from Hutchinson, attempted to demonstrate his affection by making her this cross-stitch square from within the camp.

19   20

Above: After his parents' disappearance from his life, Peter moved in with his well-to-do grandfather, Alfred, and their housekeeper, Elizabeth (*left*). While working as a translator for the British army, Peter continued to develop his artistic skills (*right*).

Below: Beginning in November 1945, Peter worked as an interpreter at the Nuremberg war trials, providing interpretation for the former Nazi foreign minister Joachim Ribbentrop (*middle row, third from the right*), with whom he once played hide-and-seek in the wine cellars of the Kempinski restaurant.

24

Left: Peter painted this, his first self-portrait, inside Hutchinson camp. His few surviving works from the camp represent the only period during which he signed his paintings "Peter Fleischmann." Shortly after leaving the camp he assumed the surname of his friend and fellow artist Donald Midgley to become Peter Midgley.

Below: In 1976, Peter received an invitation from the Berlin Arts Festival to return to the city of his birth and present an exhibition of his work at the Rathaus Neukölln Gallery. At the opening of the exhibition, an interviewer asked Peter whether his paintings contained any special meaning. He replied: "They have a message if you are prepared to receive it, to feel it." Two years later he produced this final self-portrait.

25

The guards had ignored his protestations that he was not a German, nor an internee, and that his daughter would be tremendously worried when she came to collect him from the museum and found him missing.

"I took ten men and I brought back ten men," spluttered the sergeant who had supervised the expedition. "How should I know whether they were the same?"

The most curious and successful field trip outside the camp was organized by Professor Gerhard Bersu, an eminent archaeologist who had lost his job as director of the Römisch-Germanische Kommission in Berlin and come to Britain to direct digs at Little Woodbury, an Iron Age archaeological site near the city of Salisbury. Unlike the camp's artists, lawyers, philosophers, and musicians, Bersu did not have a vibrant community of like-minded specialists with whom to socialize, celebrate, and commiserate. Rather than languish in the uncertainty of his fate, Bersu decided to exploit the fact that he had been imprisoned on an island of major archaeological significance, and that the curator of the Manx Museum, Basil Megaw, was a distinguished archaeologist.

Bersu convinced Captain Jurgensen to put him in contact with Megaw. On November 4, 1940, the archaeologist, accompanied by a group of internees, including Fred Uhlman, left the camp for an exploratory recce in search of "burrows and manganese." Shortly thereafter, the museum informed Bersu he had permission to excavate a hilltop that, it was believed, may have once been the site of a Viking roundhouse.* Bersu would be allowed, under guard, to take around a dozen helpers with him, and the museum would supply a coach and driver to fetch and deliver the men. There was no shortage of volunteers for such an interesting proposition. Captain Jurgenson vetted all applicants and made the final selection.

Hutchinson's dig team set out from the camp in a mood of high adventure. The coach journey took around twenty minutes, and the

---

* Almost certainly this was the Braaid, a site of Iron Age and Norse architectural remains situated between Braaid hamlet and Mount Murray, a ninety-minute walk from Hutchinson Square. Bertha Bracey's Germany Emergency Committee donated £25 to help fund this archaeological work.

site provided the internees a magnificent view of the surrounding hills. The volunteers, which included an architect, a geologist, an expert in medieval languages, and a fossil-collecting banker, were ordered not to wander from the dig site, nor to carry any cash—presumably to prevent the purchase of contraband.

The intelligence officer's precaution was not entirely watertight. Soon after the team began its work, they were spied by a passing Manx milkman. The man made a detour and drove his car up along the unmade road that led to where the men were working. The enterprising milkman asked whether anyone wanted to buy any bread, butter, milk, or eggs. Before the group could explain that they were without money, the banker produced a blank check, drawn on a Manx account that, he explained, he had opened a few years ago. His fellow archaeologists could buy whatever they wanted from the milkman; he would make a note of the purchase, and they could reimburse him back at the camp.

The milkman, happy to accept a check, began taking orders, not only from the internees but also from their guards and coach driver. When one of the internees asked whether the milkman sold boiled eggs, he offered to bring some with him the next time he came. A scheme soon developed. The milkman would pass by the hill at around one o'clock in the afternoon. If the internees wanted to buy any produce, they would hoist a Union Jack flag, visible from the base of the hill, as a signal for the milkman to drive up to them.

This quiet trade with Hutchinson's archaeological team was burgeoning when a senior British army officer, who happened to be visiting the island, spotted the flag flying atop the hill. He surveyed the scene through binoculars and, curious as to what precisely this group of men was doing at a strategic location with clear views of the island, ordered his driver to approach along the potholed road and onward up the dirt track.

"What is going on here?" the officer asked as he climbed out of the car and surveyed the measuring equipment and cardboard boxes filled with broken rocks and stones. One of the guards explained that the men were internees from Hutchinson, digging for a Viking fortress.

"Who is Hutchinson? Should I know him?" asked the officer.

IN EARLY DECEMBER, MEMBERS OF the camp's administration, including Michael Corvin, visited the dig to see the progress that Bersu and his volunteers had made. There, while eating ham sandwiches and fruit and drinking cups of tea, they listened to an update from Bersu's assistant, Ernst Nassau. To the romantic Corvin, the trip, during which the camp officials were drizzled on by wintery rains, "gave everybody a feeling of freedom and being cared for as well as ever possible" in addition to, more philosophically, "proof of the goodwill from the side of the authorities, so often misunderstood and not rightly acknowledged."

Despite these opportunities, none of Hutchinson's internees seemed particularly interested in plotting an escape attempt.[*] Heinrich Fraenkel, by contrast, was desperate for volunteers to help him execute a plot to smuggle an item out. By the winter of 1940, the manuscript of his book for Victor Gollancz was almost complete. Free of distraction, with an isolated place to work and a special dispensation to ignore curfews, Fraenkel had been able to write quickly and, as he put it, "smoothly."

The book aimed to prove to readers that a great many Germans stood against Hitler and his policies. Interned with men from various political groups, Fraenkel had been able to obtain official statements from various anti-Nazi groups to bolster his case, including even the Communist Party, thanks to the presence of Hugo Gräf, a former Reichstag deputy who was interned at Hutchinson. Eager to publish the book before events overtook its premise, Gollancz had also exerted a consistent pressure on his author; every two to three days Fraenkel was collected from his private room by RSM Potterton and marched

---

[*] The following year, three Dutchmen plotted for two months an escape attempt from the nearby Mooragh camp. On October 15, 1941, they cut through the wire and rowed out to a moored yacht, which they managed to sail into a stormy Irish Sea. The RAF sighted the yacht the following day, and the men were arrested and imprisoned for six months. It was the closest any internee came to escaping the island.

to Captain Daniel's office, where the commandant would glare at the author and shove yet another telegram across the desk.

"Another one from Coblenz," Daniel, unable to pronounce "Gollancz," would groan.

On one of these occasions, Daniel inquired as to what Coblenz wanted this time. Fraenkel explained that he needed a selection of four or five potential titles for the book.

"What does Coblenz want five titles for," Daniel asked. "Surely, one will do?"

Fraenkel explained that the publisher wanted several options to choose from, and that he had already come up with six suggestions. His preferred title—*Help Us Germans to Beat the Nazis!*—was clearly designed to make Fraenkel's anti-Nazi stance public, a prerequisite for release.

Fraenkel delivered the sheaf of papers to Daniel's office, neatly bound in a cardboard folder. The commandant took the manuscript and weighed it suspiciously in his hand.

"What a lot of stuff," he said. "I suppose it would take me quite some time to read all this. I'd better have it shipped off right away."

This was a tremendous relief for Fraenkel, who had been concerned that his manuscript would be snared on the censor's desk. When he left the building, however, a postpartum cloud of paranoia descended. He convinced himself that the typescript could spend months in transit so that the book would be "out of date before it ever reached the printer, and all the frantic work of the last few weeks would come to nought."

Anxieties about a book becoming obsolete prior to publication are typical of the conscientious author, whose work cannot hope to match the churning rhythms of the news cycle. This vocational symptom was heightened, however, by what Fraenkel referred to as "barbed-wire disease," the combination of powerlessness and inertia that comes from imprisonment. Something, Fraenkel concluded, had to be done about it.

The author had already made some carbon copies of the manuscript, which he planned on entrusting to internees due for release to deliver to Gollancz's office. This was not enough, however, to quell

Fraenkel's worries. He enrolled the help of several co-conspirators, and over the next three days, they worked in shifts to produce six or seven legible copies on extremely thin paper. Fraenkel then approached one of the camp's potters and purchased a pair of long vases that could be used to conceal one of the rolled-up manuscripts.

"No one would suspect me for sending one of our pretty vases to my wife, and the other to Gollancz's secretary, Sheila Hodges," Fraenkel reasoned.

The risk of the document being discovered was further diminished by the fact that a member of the group worked in the camp post office; he was chosen to slip a copy of the manuscript into each vase after it had been inspected for contraband by the British officer in charge.

The success of the plan energized the group, which continued to dispatch copies of the manuscript "by devious routes and methods, some of them very subtle and complex." After a week or so of this frenzied subterfuge, Fraenkel received a telegram from Gollancz confirming the safe arrival of the "official" manuscript. Following his release on January 15, 1941, Fraenkel was finally able to visit Gollancz's offices, where the publisher explained that the smuggled typescripts were still arriving at a rate of about two or three per week.

CAPTAIN DANIEL WAS KEPT BUSY dealing with the handling of release applications for those internees who, like Peter Fleischmann, were too young to apply themselves or who had not, for whatever reason, filed the relevant forms. It seemed to Daniel that Peter had a clear case. That he was a refugee from Nazi oppression could not be in doubt: his escape had been facilitated by the British government itself. The official response to the formal application, though, was bewildering. Daniel summoned the teenager to his office and explained the extraordinary circumstances: either on the way to or from Liverpool, Peter's documentation had been lost, or stolen. His application for release could not be processed because there was no record of his ever being interned. In the realm of officialdom, Peter Fleischmann did not exist.

A few days later, Peter was once again summoned. This time he was met by a representative from the Home Office, who had an offer for the eighteen-year-old. If Peter agreed to join the British army, the problem of his internment would, the man explained, simply go away. No longer an internee, he would be considered a soldier, and, with this fresh identity, he would become a documented person in the government's records.

Peter had friends in the camp who had already signed up for a similar deal of freedom in exchange for service. The first recruitment officers appeared at Hutchinson camp in the late autumn. They came looking for young, able-bodied internees to join the only unit in the British army open to enemy aliens, the Auxiliary Military Pioneer Corps.

The Pioneers were considered the dregs of the British army, but since the unit began to accept so-called enemy aliens, they had proven useful, not least as part of the British Expeditionary Force. For internees, concerns over prestige fell far below the compelling fact that acceptance into the Pioneers offered one of the speediest routes to freedom. As Helen Roeder, secretary for the Artists' Refugee Committee, put it: "It's quite a good loophole of escape for people who have not achieved distinction in anything in particular."

Bernard Davidson, a member of the Jewish Refugees Committee, led the recruitment drive in Hutchinson. Upon his arrival at the camp, internees were gathered into the camp hall. When everyone was seated, the guards closed the doors behind them.

"My friends, I come here in order to discuss with you the question of joining the army," said Davidson. "We know you have been interned here on a precautionary measure . . . but there is one sure way to get out: joining the army."

Davidson's speech became firmer as it progressed, with the implication that the alternative to joining would be to remain interned for the duration of hostilities.

"No one leaves this room before he has signed up for the army," he concluded.

At the outbreak of war, Parliament passed the National Service (Armed Forces) Act, which imposed conscription on all British men between the ages of eighteen and forty-one. Conscientious objectors had to appear before a tribunal to argue their reasons for refusing to join up. In this context, the Pioneer Corps offered a suitable way in which refugees could display their loyalty to Britain. Still, not everyone responded favorably to the strong-arm approach, nor to the fact that the army's readiness to accept internees to its ranks made an utter mockery of the idea that these refugees had been interned in the first place. As one exasperated internee put it to Bertha Bracey during one of her visits to the island, "[E]nlistment in the Pioneer Corps would be quite illogical if the view of our enemy status were still maintained."

Outraged at what he considered to be blackmail, Fritz Hallgarten stood to his feet and marched up to the doors at the rear of the hall. When one of the guards refused to let him out, Hallgarten raised his voice: "You can't lock me in here."

An officer nodded at his subordinate, and Hallgarten was let out. Hallgarten was an anomaly, though. The promise of swift freedom, as well as the chance to prove their loyalty to Britain and enmity toward the Nazis, inspired scores of men to put their names forward. For many young men, there were few other options.

"It became clear that we had two basic options: wait for Parliament, or join the army," said one internee. By early December, 1,273 of the 8,000 internees who had been released across Britain had applied satisfactorily under category 12 for entry to the Pioneer Corps—the second largest category, exceeded only by category 3: the "invalid and infirm." Most of those past their twenties, however, were considered too old or too unfit, and had their internee cards stamped with the rather wounding judgment: "Rejected from A.M.P.C. on Medical Grounds."

While internees from other camps who were selected for the Pioneers were sent to train in Ilfracombe, Devon—where assault courses, obstacles, and gun positions were set up along the beach—this was not the case for Hutchinson's recruits. They received their initial training from RSM Potterton, just outside the camp wire, in full view of

252 THE ISLAND OF EXTRAORDINARY CAPTIVES

the other internees. For those men who had undergone military training in Germany, one of the first tasks was to relearn how to march, in the British style. "The step is shorter, quite natural, not beating the ground," noted Michael Corvin, *The Camp*'s editor. "The carriage is firm, but elastic . . . sporting, but sporting in a military way."

Having completed basic training, the first of Hutchinson's Pioneers left the camp on October 5, 1940. By the end of November, a trickle had become a stream, and dozens of young men had left the camp, including an Orthodox Jew who left on Yom Kippur with the blessing of a camp rabbi.

For Peter Fleischmann, however, the idea of joining the Pioneers as a means to secure freedom seemed unethical.

"I cannot agree to your offer under these circumstances," he told the civil servant in Daniel's office. Although he was obviously an anti-Nazi and a documented political refugee, Peter said that he could not, under what he saw as "sheer blackmail," join the British army conditionally.

"I would be glad to do so voluntarily," he continued. "But not under these circumstances."

Peter's stance meant that he left the commandant's office a nonentity with an indefinite sentence. When his fellow artists learned of what had happened, there was collective outrage. Peter's best chance of release, they decided, was to find a place at an art school. Once he was a student, the British government would be required by their own policies to release him. On December 8, 1940, two weeks after the closure of the second art exhibition, the artists drafted a letter of recommendation, addressed to Maria Petrie, care of Abbotsholme School in Staffordshire.*

---

* Petrie, born Maria Sophia Zimmern, was a German sculptor who studied at the Städel Art Institute in Frankfurt for three years, and then became a pupil of Aristide Maillol in Paris. She moved to Britain following her marriage to the British schoolteacher and England rugby player Francis Steinthal in 1913, and was best known for her 1926 portrait bust of her friend, the English writer G. K. Chesterton, now held in the National Portrait Gallery collection. While Petrie has been relegated to a barely legible footnote in art history, the celebrated war poet Wilfred Owen once described her as a "mighty clever German sculptress who had studied under modern masters."

"In this camp we have made the acquaintance of a young student of art, a fellow-internee whom we consider to possess really great talents as a painter," the letter began. "Being only eighteen years of age, he, Peter Fleischmann, is of course still very much in need of further systematic training, although he had studied at an art school for some years already . . . The only chance for him to be released from internment is to find a School of Art willing to accept him as a student."

Hutchinson's artists chose Petrie for her German heritage, her artistic nous, and the fact that she had recently entered the world of education and published the book *Modelling for Children* in 1936. They asked Petrie to assist them in "finding a school willing to accept [Peter]," preferably one prepared to give him the chance for a scholarship. Before signing off, the artists suggested that they were willing to send Petrie some of Peter's work that he had already exhibited in the camp. To witness a written letter of endorsement, signed by these figures, was to receive a validation of enough force that it might seed in a young man a lifelong self-belief. For now, there was nothing for Peter to do but join in the season's celebrations and hope that Petrie might take an interest in his case.

In London, German bombs had fallen for fifty-seven consecutive nights, forcing the capital's population to take nightly shelter on the floors of its Underground stations. The Blitz showed no sign of abatement as Christmas approached; thoughtful Londoners brought Norway spruces onto platforms as the warm subterranean wind breathed through the tunnels. Three hundred miles away at Hutchinson camp, the lead-up to Christmas and Hannukah represented, if not a perilous time, then a psychologically traumatic one.

The sculptor Siegfried Charoux had been released on September 4, under the white paper's category 6—"work of national importance"— but by early December the majority of the Artists Café's members were still awaiting news of their fate. In the early months of internment, the fact that so many brilliant men of self-evidently anti-Nazi beliefs had been interned highlighted the absurdity of the situation. By winter, however, any sense of perverse delight had clotted into dismay and bitterness as, one by one, the camp had been emptied of celebrated individuals whose presence had initially brought comfort, but whose absence now brought disquiet.

"The weeks until Christmas and after seemed to be just one endless gloom and depression," Fred Uhlman wrote. "Every day I waited in fear and hope till 5pm when the names of the released were announced, only to crawl back to my room too miserable to eat."

Schwitters, for all his creative output and commercial hustling, experienced pendulous mood swings.

"Haven't I lost enough?" he mourned in the poem "*Gefangen*" (Captured), in which he refers to himself as, variously, a dried leaf, a man lying in the valley of death, and someone punished for the mere crime of existence. In another poem, "*Für Dich*" (For You), written for his wife, Schwitters described the grim monotony of the life of indefinite confinement: "I am a prisoner. The days and the long nights fly bleakly past in the prison camp . . . always the same people, whom I don't hate, don't love."

Every effort was made to help Hutchinson's internees celebrate their first festive season as a salve for the despair. Dr. Max Kossmann staged a series of readings of Charles Dickens's *A Christmas Carol* in House 25, while Bertha Bracey arranged a donation of £250 to be split among the camps for "Christmas festivals." For the Jewish internees, Chief Rabbi Schonfeld, a regular visitor to the camp, organized the delivery of ninety-six boxes, each containing forty-four candles, for the celebration of Hannukah, which ran from December 24 to New Year's Eve that year. Perhaps fearing house fires in the camp, of which there had already been at least two, Captain Daniel made the decision not to distribute the candles among the internees. They were instead placed into storage. (The following year the rabbi's office asked for them to be returned due to a national candle shortage.)

On Christmas Eve, Schwitters attended a camp service. It was one of the artist's most cherished celebrations of the year; in Hanover, Schwitters and his wife, Helma, would host a notoriously decadent

Christmas party, where carols were played on a gramophone while young women lit their cigarettes from the Christmas tree candles.

Pining for his family, Schwitters entered the church building in a state of despair, unable, as he wrote to Helma later that night, "to believe in love."

For all the relative success Schwitters had experienced in Hutchinson, he felt robbed of faith. The stress of his flights from Germany and Norway, which had forced him to abandon his serious artistic projects, and his subsequent arrest and internment in Britain had triggered epileptic fits.

Schwitters saw five candles lit on the Christmas tree in the church. As the service progressed, a gust of wind snuffed out one of the lights, an image that Schwitters, in his melancholic state, found ineffably sad. As the men around him sang the old, familiar carols, Schwitters, unable to add his voice to the chorus, wept.

XIX

THE ISLE OF
FORGOTTEN MEN

ECHEN WARSCHAUER OPENED THE FRONT door of 51 Linden Lea in the Hampstead Garden Suburb in north London, the house where she now lived with her two daughters. A police inspector and two besuited men loomed on her doorstep.

"Good day, Mrs. Warschauer," said Inspector Hoare of the Special Branch. "May we come in?"

Echen was by now used to unfamiliar people visiting her home. In the sunny months following her marriage to "Lutz," as she now affectionately called Ludwig, important men would stop by for conferences on the main floor, which had been converted into an office. Prior to her husband's arrest, no less a figure than Sir John Anderson had visited. Then a different kind of stranger had come knocking, either to ask questions or to sift through the couple's belongings. She recognized one of the men today: a few months earlier he had conducted a search of the home and carried off boxes of her husband's correspondence.

James Craufurd already knew a great deal about Echen, and still more about her interned husband. During his investigation, Craufurd and his team had confirmed what Echen had long suspected: that her husband had cut a deal with the Nazis to secure her and her family's freedom. While this is where Echen's suspicions ended, Craufurd had reason to believe that Ludwig Warschauer had done more than bribe officials. The investigator's purpose today was to obtain from Echen a description—maybe even a photograph—of the man believed to be Warschauer's handler, a Gestapo agent known by the pseudonym Dr. Hans Sauer. Sauer, Craufurd believed, had facilitated Warschauer and his new family's escape to Britain not in exchange for money, but in exchange for services.

WARSCHAUER HAD FIRST COME TO MI5's attention in early 1940, after the chief constable of the Special Branch, Scotland Yard, received a letter from the former head of the German Jewish Aid Committee, the thirty-seven-year-old Hubert Pollack, who claimed to have helped Warschauer obtain the immigration permits for Echen and her family. Pollack explained in his letter that, while he had known Warschauer to be an acquaintance of high-ranking Nazis, he had had no reason to suspect his loyalties at the time. In recent weeks, however, he had learned of Warschauer's involvement with a sting operation in Berlin.

The ruse, Pollack claimed, went like this: Warschauer would invite a Jewish acquaintance whom the Gestapo wanted to arrest to lunch in a public restaurant. At some point an Aryan woman would join them at the table. Warschauer would excuse himself, and the moment he left the table, Gestapo personnel would enter and arrest the man for fraternizing outside of his race. Pollack felt compelled to alert the British to this information, adding that while Warschauer owed him money, this was not his motive for writing.

Sir Vernon Kell, then director of MI5, read the letter with keen interest. This was precisely the kind of suspicious activity—with "a Gestapo flavor"—that Kell had been looking for among refugees in Britain. MI5 duly opened a file that, thanks to the informants in Hutchinson, had now grown to a weighty document.

Information had come from various sources. A private serving in the Pioneer Corps claimed that Warschauer had masterminded a profitable blackmail operation in Berlin. The soldier claimed that the engineer had an arrangement with a pretty barmaid. Warschauer would go out drinking with a target; then, once they were blind drunk, deliver the individual to a room at his accomplice's bar. In the morning the man would awake to find the barmaid next to him in bed. Warschauer would then extort the target for money in exchange for discretion. Men now in Hutchinson may have been victims of the scheme.

Even if Britain were not at war with Germany, it would have been almost impossible for Craufurd to verify these accounts of overseas extortion, blackmail, and embezzlement. But the pattern of accusations appeared to reveal something about Warschauer's moral character. It was not, however, sufficient grounds to keep the man indefinitely interned, especially considering the support that his various applications for release had attracted from powerful figures in Britain. MI5 needed proof that Warschauer had come to Britain on a secret mission. The answer seemed bound up in the shadowy figure of Dr. Hans Sauer, who, according to the informants in Hutchinson, had seen him off at the airport and ensured that his bags weren't checked.

If Warschauer was, indeed, a spy, then everyone in his orbit became something of a suspect. At Hutchinson camp, Hermann Rahmer, whom Klaus Hinrichsen described as Warschauer's "bodyguard," had become so beset with worries that he had been hospitalized on the island. Rahmer told the camp's intelligence officer, Captain Jurgensen, that he was being blackmailed by Warschauer. Craufurd and his colleague, John Noble, needed to discover how far this went—whatever *this* was. Unsure of Echen's loyalties, and therefore not wanting to arouse in her any suspicion, Noble began by asking straightforward questions: "When were you born?" "Who are your parents?" "When did you first meet your husband?"

Craufurd took careful notes. When Noble turned the conversation to Dr. Sauer, Echen freely admitted that she had visited him and met his wife and children on more than one occasion. She could remember only a few details about him, however. He was around forty years old. Sporty. He spoke many languages, she recalled, reaching for details. No, she couldn't remember whether he had a mustache.

"His eyes, I think, are dark," she said. "He is not fat like my husband. I think he is against the Nazis."

Echen's openness quelled the agents' fears that Warschauer's spouse would prove as slippery as the subject of their investigation.

"In contrast to her husband," Craufurd wrote, "she appears truthful and sincere."

The agents concluded Echen knew little of her husband's sinister activities. As the three men stood to leave, Noble told Echen to contact Inspector Hoare if she recalled any information that might be pertinent to their investigation. Then they bade her goodbye.

IN HUTCHINSON CAMP, LUDWIG WARSCHAUER was not the only man feeling miserable about his continued internment, a mood deepened and darkened by the envy and dismay involved in bidding goodbye to friends and acquaintances. The third and final draft of the government's white paper had prized open the door to freedom for many of the artists and professionals from creative industries. As Michael Corvin mournfully put it in the first 1941 issue of *The Camp*, by the start of the new year the tide of release had "swept away many of the artists in this camp."

For Corvin, the release of so many of his artist friends represented not only an emotional wound but also a professional challenge: Where to find replacement illustrators for his newspaper? Corvin and his team had closed 1940 with a special *Almanac* edition of *The Camp*, a bumper issue featuring a blend of fiction and nonfiction, interspersed with drawings by camp artists such as Hellmuth Weissenborn, Fred Uhlman, Erich Kahn, and a full-page sketch of Corvin drawn by Kurt Schwitters.

The pressure Corvin felt had intensified with the news that copies of *The Camp* were to be archived at the London School of Economics, the librarian of which, Dr. Dickinson, had written to the Home Office in December to request copies of every issue of every publication created in the internment camps. While he would never again have so many potential illustrators to commission, Corvin ensured there was a balanced mix of words and drawings in subsequent editions, leaning heavily on one of the camp's most prolific cartoonists, the thirty-one-year-old amateur illustrator and member of Hutchinson's Artists Café, Adolf Mirecki.*

As weeks turned to months, the sense of loss and sadness that accompanied each goodbye soon gave way to keener feelings of misery for the remnant. By March 1941, 12,500 internees had walked free, representing almost half of those who had been interned the previous summer. This loss of his friends and collaborators drained Corvin of his enthusiasm for his work. In May 1941, Corvin transferred to the married camp, passing editorship to Carlo Pietzner. "Euologies can't equal the simple fact of the loss to the cultural life of this camp by his transfer," his replacement wrote. There were still many in the camp, however, who did not seem to fit any of the government's categories for release.

The men left behind revealed something of the old and enduring privileges of class, education, social standing, and connection; the camp had emptied of the distinguished, leaving behind the forgotten, the vulnerable, the stateless. The sense of misery and hopelessness was captured in a letter written by a group of internees at Promenade camp, close to Hutchinson: "A man who is neither scientist, priest, rabbi, key-man, too young, too old, or too ill, who perhaps hates Hitler but has had no opportunity to show it in accordance with category 19, who is not skilled, nor can enlist in the Pioneer Corps because he may be ill, or has lost three fingers at work . . . the trader, the businessman, the artisan and the clerk have no chance and no hope . . ."

For Peter, too, freedom seemed remote and unreachable. The letter the artists had written to the sculptor Maria Petrie had gone unanswered. His refusal to join the Pioneer Corps was a black mark; his options were now severely limited. Three times, Hubert Daniel, the camp commandant who by now had been promoted to the rank of major, and who, as a

---

* Mirecki, who signed his drawings "Dol," was, like so many of the refugees, an accomplished survivor. Born in Ukraine, at the age of fourteen he had traveled on foot to Austria, where he became a jobbing artist, before moving to Hamburg, where he opened a furniture store. Mirecki claimed to have escaped Germany by clinging to the underside of a train carriage. When he reached Coventry in England, he established a small business making pots and pans shortly before his arrest and internment. In the early spring of 1941, Mirecki, too, was released.

fellow orphan probably felt doubly responsible for Peter's fate, appealed on his behalf. Three times the appeal was met with flat refusal.

"People were leaving the camp left, right and center," Peter said. "Under what category would I fit?" Unlike many of his friends, who had wives, family members, and professional bodies petitioning for their release, Peter had no one fighting for his freedom. "Other people cared very little about me."

Having experienced a life characterized by the comings and goings of guardians and peers, the feeling of being left behind was intrinsic. In this way, Peter was better prepared for these familiar cycles of abandonment than most. And yet, there was a shard of hope. The young art historian Klaus Hinrichsen cared about Peter greatly. Before he left Hutchinson camp, on June 18, 1941, three weeks shy of his first anniversary there, Hinrichsen promised Peter he would do something.

AS HUTCHINSON DRAINED OF ITS academics and artists, the camp's cultural life flagged to the extent that, in late January, the Cultural Department suspended its program. An influx of new internees—men returning from the Canadian camps to which they had been deported the previous summer—revitalized and reshaped the character of Hutchinson's cultural output. "The new intake," Hinrichsen wrote in his printed weekly announcement on March 5, 1941, "enables us to continue our work and to revive several branches of Science and Learning which might be of general as well as special interest."

While there were few artists among the Canadian returnees, there were numerous aspiring actors, such as the young ballet dancer Hans Wolfgang Barczinski, young men whose enthusiastic presence had an immediate effect on Hutchinson. Cabaret had been one of the first entertainments at the camp, spearheaded by the Austrian librettist Peter Herz. In addition to being a celebrated lyricist, Herz had helped run a cabaret in Vienna, and was quick to found what he labeled the *Stacheldrahtcabaret*—the Barbed-Wire Cabaret—for his fellow internees.

The first serious actors had arrived at Hutchinson from Prees

Heath at the same time as Peter. The early theatrical performances in the camp were modest affairs, isolated scenes from plays such as William Shakespeare's *A Midsummer Night's Dream*; Jaroslav Hašek's *The Good Soldier Švejk*; *Der treueste Bürger Bagdads* by Jura Soyfer, a young playwright who had died the previous year in Buchenwald; and, in late October, a recital of George Bernard Shaw's one-act play *Over-ruled*. The first major production, an adaptation of John Steinbeck's *Of Mice and Men*, opened a week later, on November 5, 1940.

The group of actors from Prees Heath included Otto Tausig, an eighteen-year-old student who, in time, became one of the camp's best-loved performers, assuming title roles—both male and female—in various productions. Tausig had been awakened to the possibilities of performance in captivity even before he arrived at Prees Heath, during a brief stint at the miserable Warth Mills. One morning, in a bid to find a moment's respite from the groaning crowd of prisoners, Tausig had begun to explore the mill's warren of corridors in search of a quiet corner where he might be alone. He spied a staircase and took the stairs to the upper floor. Tausig emerged into a hall, completely empty but for two men.

The shorter of the two sat on a stone in a corner. Facing him a man in a high-necked green shirt performed for his listener a poem of primordial sounds: screams, whispers, coos, and chirps that seemed to have been dredged from an ancient pool, situated somewhere pre-language, the sphere of tongues.

> Lanke trr gll
>> pe pe pe pe pe
>>> Ooka ooka ooka ooka
> Lanke trr gll
>> pii pii pii pii pii
>>> Züüka züüka züüka züüka
> Lanke trr gll
>> Rrmm
>> Rrnnf

Tausig had happened upon Kurt Schwitters's first performance in internment, a recital of his 1932 poem "*Ursonate*," or "*Sonate in Urlauten*" (Sonata in Primordial Sounds), which soon became a staple around Hutchinson, after Schwitters performed it to a packed hall.

TO DEPICT AN OLDER CHARACTER, Tausig dusted his hair with white flour to age himself into the role, an act of ingenuity that drew spirited applause from the audience when he first appeared onstage. In Hutchinson Tausig had volunteered to collaborate with the cobblers and had learned how to nail or glue replacement soles onto shoes. After work, he would take the glue to the theater group and use it to stick on fake beards. The glue was exceedingly strong, and when the beard was ripped off following a night's performance, it tore at the skin. Tausig became sufficiently celebrated for his antics onstage and off that one day Schwitters offered to paint the young actor's portrait.

In all areas of theatrical production, ingenuity had to compensate for deficiency. As one anonymous contributor to *The Camp* newspaper, writing about Hutchinson's first full production, put it: "The story of the difficulties they had to overcome is one of the minor epics of stage history."

Some of the technical-minded members of the group fashioned stage lights out of old jam jars, which had a silvery reflective surface on the inside. The crew installed this phalanx of lights along the front of the stage. In lieu of a dimmer switch to control the output of these lights, the stagehands connected a strip of additional lightbulbs to the same circuit, which were kept in the wings, out of sight. The brightness of the stage lights could be controlled by screwing and unscrewing additional bulbs into the circuit, enabling the lighting team to create the effect of a sunrise or sunset.

Another lighting effect used two wires and a ceramic pot filled with salt water, with a metal plate attached to the bottom. When the wires touched the metal plate a bright light fired onto the stage. When

the wires were raised, the salt water still had weak conductivity, causing the stage to grow darker.

There was less scope for ingenuity when it came to costumes.
To circumvent the difficulty of staging period plays without period
clothing, the Hutchinson actors reinterpreted a number of the plays
in contemporary settings, with modern clothing and props: roll-neck
sweaters instead of livery, machine guns instead of swords in an early
example of dressing actors in contemporary fashion for a period play.
The Mayfair-based dressmaker Harald Mahrenholz, also interned in
Hutchinson, made many of the costumes.

While most productions were staged in the new hall, it was difficult to find times to rehearse, particularly because the venue doubled
as a sports facility during the daytime. As one of Hutchinson's performers mournfully put it: not only was there sure to be somebody
playing ping-pong in the hall, but there were also always "four pianos
going off at the same time."

The youth and inexperience of the actors was made up for by the
professional experience of the camp's leading director, Fred Weiss: a
bona fide filmmaker. Weiss had survived the sinking of the *Arandora
Star*, an ordeal that sent him into a spiral of depression.* The theatrical
opportunities at Hutchinson appeared, however, to draw him from the
fug of hopelessness; he was a natural leader for the actors and performers in the camp's midst. In March 1941, he adapted G. K. Chesterton's
novel *The Man Who Was Thursday* into a stage play consisting of no
fewer than twenty scenes, the first of numerous plays he directed in
the camp during the remainder of his internment. As well as bringing
professional expertise to Hutchinson camp's theatrical productions,
Weiss's associations to the film industry brought a frisson of glamour.
After keeping a low profile in 1940, he became more involved in the
cultural schedule with the arrival of the young actors from Canada—

---

* When first interned at Prees Heath, Weiss was called forward for release. While the release
document stated Weiss's internee number correctly, his first name was listed as Felix, not Fred.
It was an obvious clerical error—there was no Felix Weiss at the camp—but the filmmaker was
denied release nonetheless, a setback that compounded his misery. For the crime of a typo, Weiss
remained interned for close to three years.

identifiable by the POW jackets they had been forced to wear in the Canadian camps until new clothes could be found for them—hosting a film group and delivering lectures on various parts of film production under titles such as "From Story to Film," "Film Art," and a three-part series titled "On the Making of a Film."

As well as informing his audience about the practical elements of film production, Weiss also expressed his frustrations with the film business, complaining how directors are "not too often able to bring their own plans and ideas because they are all influenced by various factors such as the bank, the censor and the moving picture industry." Weiss's cynicism would not dissuade his audience from pursuing a career in film; the Canadian returnees Erwin Jacoby and Hellmuth Mirauer would both appear in films produced by Weiss after the war.

Meanwhile, inspired by the influx of performers, Kurt Schwitters began to stage performances of his own poems, which he was able to recall from memory. His stories became something akin to comedy routines in the camp, repeated with minor variations and drawing huge audiences in the new hall. When Schwitters recited his most famous prewar poem, "*An Anna Blume*," he changed the subject of the poem's name to "Eve Blossom," as "Eve," like "Anna," is a name "as beautiful forwards as it is backwards."

His most striking Hutchinson performance, however, was a newer composition involving props, often used to conclude a recital. Alone onstage in front of a packed audience, Schwitters lifted a cup and saucer from where they had sat throughout his performance. He placed the cup on its side, touched the rim of the saucer, and began to slowly rotate his hand. Over the timid tinkle of the china, Schwitters whispered the word "silence" over and again. As the audience craned to see and hear, he accelerated the spinning movement of the cup, simultaneously raising the volume of his voice: "Silence, silence, silence."

In a crescendo, Schwitters flicked the cup upward off the saucer, where it hung in the air for a split second. Then, as the crockery began falling to the floor, he thwacked the cup downward using the saucer, simultaneously screaming, "Silence!" Broken pieces of crockery scattered across the stage. "The audience was stunned," Klaus Hinrichsen wrote. "Screaming the word 'Silence' was perverse, but this madman had even wantonly destroyed a cup and a saucer, irreplaceable items in the camp."

After a moment's pause, the audience broke into frantic applause. All the anger and frustration of being considered an enemy to their new country, of being interned, of having to live in such cramped conditions, had found expression in this one authority-defying gesture. "It was," Hinrichsen wrote, "a cathartic moment."

HUTCHINSON CONTINUED TO BECOME A more comfortable camp for its internees in material terms, too. A camp laundry had opened on December 2, 1940, with prices set to half of those of the town launderette, enabling internees to increase their standards of cleanliness. The library was now well stocked with books and copies of the *Daily Telegraph*, the *Manchester Guardian*, and the *Times*, as well as a local island paper. A members-only reading room had been opened in House 35. Here, and for a weekly subscription of sixpence, internees could read, in addition to daily papers, periodicals such as the *Economist*, *Reader's Digest*, the *Jewish Chronicle*, the *Spectator*, and *Life* magazine. As Bertha Bracey noted during another visit to the camp on New Year's Day: "[C]onditions . . . have improved enormously."

The camp authorities had become more capable at managing any internee's special requirements, too. In the spring of 1941, Major Daniel agreed to allow the money saved on bread (1,267 pounds) and flour (211 pounds) during Passover to be spent by the 196 practicing Jews inside the camp on matzo, unleavened bread.

While the schedule of lectures had undoubtedly narrowed since the camp's early days, the influx of internees from Canadian camps as well as British camps, including Huyton, Central, Sefton, and Onchan, delivered some replacements willing to share their knowledge. Hutchinson's community welcomed each new delegation warmly, even if the number of lectures on offer inevitably fell.

"We are glad to have you here," wrote the new editor of *The Camp*, "not because we enjoy gloating over the destiny of those in a similar predicament to us, but glad—and sincerely so—because your arrival in Hutchinson camp indicates a trend of development . . . signified by the increasing number of releases coming through every day."

A few of the camp's defining characters remained. Johann "Brick" Neunzer, the animal trapper who had revealed a latent talent for illustration in his window etchings, was a favorite of the younger internees arriving from Canada.[*] He would pull up his shirt to reveal an enormous scar across his chest, the remnant of a lion attack, and, on his back, a fist-sized depression from where he had been pierced by the horn of a rhino, and as a party trick he would pick the heads from flowers using a small lasso.

There were dozens of clubs for special interests, including ones for Spanish, French, and Norwegian speakers, a *Collegio Dante* for fans of the Italian poet, and an English Section, run by the journalist Ludwig Elster, for those who wished to become "better acquainted with English Life and Institutions." There were possibilities for more practical self-improvement, too, with the offer of a first-aid course, complete with a St. John Ambulance certificate for any who passed the exam. A chess tournament involving no fewer than thirty participants was staged in the new hall, during the course of two days, drawing large crowds.

LUDWIG WARSCHAUER HAD LITTLE INTEREST in the camp's shifting variety of distractions. The net around him was tightening. His application to the Auxiliary Military Pioneer Corps had been rejected on medical grounds. At the end of January, he had received a letter from Tess Simpson, secretary of the Society for the Protection of Science

---

[*] Neunzer's nickname is, in some internees' recollections, rendered as "Blick." In the April 6, 1941, edition of *The Camp*, however, Neunzer signed an article on leopard attacks with the name "Hans Brick."

and Learning, informing him that the undersecretary of state had personally refused to authorize his release.

"I am afraid that there is nothing more that we can do," she concluded.

Warschauer's applications for release under categories 8 and 19 of the white paper—"Any person . . . [who] has consistently . . . taken a public and prominent part in opposition to the Nazi system"—were both rejected. In desperation Warschauer hired an eminent London law firm, Stephenson, Harwood and Tatham, to petition the Home Office on his behalf. With his solicitor's help, Warschauer reapplied for release for a third time under category 23, for internees who had previously tried to enlist in the Pioneer Corps but had been rejected on medical grounds or were ineligible due to age restrictions. Applicants for category 23 had to sit before a tribunal, to confirm their anti-Nazi stance.

In August 1941, Warschauer appeared in front of one such tribunal, led by Sir Cecil Hurst, an eminent lawyer who started his career in the Foreign Office, for the final hearing that would decide his fate. Hurst was the former president of the International Court of Justice in The Hague and chairman of a newly created committee tasked to review internees' applications for release under the various criteria of the white paper. A commission of advisers, comprising German and Austrian social democrats and trade unionists, provided additional consultatory support.

The event caused significant consternation at MI5, which was institutionally opposed to anyone who might interfere with its investigations. The Home Office, as one agent put it, had a "deplorable tendency . . . to regard Sir Cecil Hurst's word as law." By now Warschauer's case had come to the attention of high-profile figures in the British security services, many of whom wrote strongly worded letters imploring the Home Office to keep Warschauer behind barbed wire ("A man like he," as one agent implored, "is dangerous and should not be released"), regardless of the tribunal's final judgment.

While the Hurst committee's members had read the extensive

paperwork relating to Warschauer's case, documents that were, as one panel member put it, "uniformly hostile," they did not want to allow the security service's judgments to prejudice their views. The members of the tribunal quizzed Warschauer on every suspicion that had, in secret, been leveled against him to date.

Why did you give the Nazis the copyrights to your patents? Why did you visit the offices of high-ranking figures in the administration? Why did you visit the Fremdenpolizei with your fiancée? Were you ever an intelligence officer? Why were you permitted to enter the Ministry of Information, an office from which all Jews were strictly barred? Why did you set up the Technical School in Hutchinson?

The nature of the questions revealed the extent to which the British security services had investigated Warschauer's life—and offered a clue as to why, to date, all his petitions for release had been turned down. If Warschauer was perturbed by these lines of questioning, he maintained his cool. The tribunal was convinced of his innocence.

"The conclusion reached is that Warschauer is opposed to the Nazi system, that he is actively friendly towards the Allied cause, and that he will remain steadfast towards that cause in all circumstances," Hurst wrote in his final verdict. Hurst concluded that Warschauer was "fervently anti-Nazi," and as such should be released with immediate effect.

THE VERDICT CAUSED A SURGE of anger and frustration at MI5. Theodore Turner, the head of MI5's newly created E Division dedicated to "alien control," was unable to contain his rage. It was, he wrote, "quite intolerable that a committee of unworldly servants should take it upon itself to say that they are satisfied on the strength of a short interview or two and . . . to accept as gospel truth the bare word of the internee in defiance of all other evidence." Turner described the cross-examination by Hurst—a member of the Permanent Court of International Justice—as, simply, "pathetic."

James Craufurd swiftly prepared a thirteen-page document outlining MI5's objections to the committee's verdict. His tone was more diplomatic than Turner's, but equally forceful.

"The genuineness of Warschauer's expressions of anti-Nazi sympathies on which the committee rely," he wrote, "depends on the weight which is to be given to his own uncorroborated statements. In our opinion, no weight whatever should be attached to Warschauer's uncorroborated statements and denials. . . . Warschauer is an undesirable person who would constitute a grave danger to security if he were released."

Craufurd's objections were sufficient to block Hurst's recommendation. MI5 had won the argument, for now. Warschauer would remain at Hutchinson camp, while Craufurd and John Noble worked to uncover the slippery truth.

IF WARSCHAUER HAD ATTRACTED AN uncomfortable amount of attention to his life, Peter Fleischmann felt utterly overlooked as the winter of 1941 approached. He was one of thirty-two men under the age of twenty-one still in Hutchinson. Peter had contemporaries, but he had lost his mentors. And by November, five months after Hinrichsen had left the camp vowing to help Peter, it seemed his friend was just another person who had failed to keep a promise. Extraordinarily, for an orphan whose flight to England had been facilitated by the British state, he was now one of just 388 internees of categories B and C remaining behind barbed wire.

Then Peter received an unexpected letter from Helen Roeder, secretary of the Artists' Refugee Committee. Having facilitated the release of so-called artists of distinction, Helen had not given up the fight for those artist refugees who, like Peter, did not have the necessary reputation to clear the government's bar to freedom. In the letter, Roeder informed Peter that she had, at last, secured him a place at art school. As he was now classified as a student, he could walk free.

There were instructions. Peter was to travel to London and, on arrival, head to an address in Hammersmith, where he would stay with

Helen and her partner, the artist Carel Weight, until a start date could be arranged. On October 7, 1941, one year, two months, and twenty-five days after he arrived in Hutchinson, Peter Fleischmann shook Major Daniel's hand and bade him farewell. While his internment paperwork had reportedly been lost, Peter's Certificate of Registration—the document that listed every address at which he had lived since he disembarked the *Kindertransport* ferry at Harwich—had survived. It was returned to him with a new stamp on the tenth page:

> The holder of this certificate is to be exempted until further order from internment and from the special restrictions applicable to enemy aliens under the aliens order.
>
> —By order of the Secretary of State, "P" Camp

XX

A SPY CORNERED

As THE GATE CLOSED BEHIND him, Peter felt a curious sense of disaffection. The world of Hutchinson and its trivial routines seemed instantly foreign and remote, vulgar in its irrelevance to the now. The roll calls seemed pointless, the camp officials powerless, and the domestic dramas vacuous. Viewed kindly, Hutchinson had been a world of unparalleled opportunity, a time when historic forces had momentarily aligned to gather a unique cross section of men. In no other circumstances before or since have the university don, the local butcher, the celebrated Dadaist, the lawmaker, the baker, and the couture dressmaker been forced to cohabitate and, in doing so, enrich one another's lives.

Outside, looking in, the camp represented only a colossal waste of personnel and resources, a squandering of talent and manpower, the embodiment of a panic measure born of historical ignorance and bedrock xenophobia. By the time Peter Fleischmann boarded the ferry to the mainland, the petty concerns of camp life had gone, replaced by the practical concerns of the wartime commuter. Will a U-boat torpedo strike the ferry? Has a German bomb destroyed the train tracks?

On the mainland Peter headed to Manchester and the house where, sixteen months ago, he had been arrested. There he collected his belongings, bade his former employers a final goodbye, and left for London.

Helen's letter had contained clear instructions: travel to her home in Hammersmith, a house that also doubled as the modest headquarters of the Artists' Refugee Committee. First, however, Peter headed to Hampstead Heath, using the travel money he had been given before leaving the island, to see the only person in Britain he considered to be true family: the woman he knew as Echen Kohsen.

It was a happy but brief reunion; Echen was not only adapting to life as a single mother again—this time without the support of staff or riches—she was also busy writing letters in petition of her husband's release from Hutchinson. Peter kept his misgivings about the Technical School's founder to himself. After promising to keep in contact with Echen, he left for Hammersmith.

Helen Roeder's flat was situated in the shadow of London's Olympia Exhibition Centre, the venue to which the first forty enemy aliens had been brought in the first week of war. Peter knocked on the door of 17 Girdlers Road. Helen greeted him. Although she was just thirty-two, Helen, who often wore billowing, lace Victorian dresses and long patterned headscarves, cut an intimidating figure. The secretary of the Artists' Refugee Committee had heard much about Peter from her clients who had been interned at Hutchinson, with whom she remained in close contact. In the previous war, Helen's father, who was half German, had been drafted into the Pioneer Corps; she understood the complications of being a foreign national in a wartime country. Even so, her artist partner, Carel Weight, had noticed Helen's sympathy and understanding for people deepen and grow during the past year as she had become entangled in the tragic stories of internees. Helen welcomed Peter indoors with kindness and understanding. The smell of bubbling stew, which she always kept on the stove for hungry friends, filled the kitchen.

"We are not wealthy, and we cannot give you money, but you can stay here until we can sort you out," she offered.

The Artists Café in Hutchinson had been a hub of warmth and creative energy, but it had been a temporary, contrived space from which, ultimately, its members hoped to flee as quickly as possible. The house shared by Helen and Carel on Girdlers Road was different: a place of endeavor and excitement that felt both inviting and permanent. The couple had met as art students at Goldsmiths College, and their home in Hammersmith was not only the headquarters of the Artists' Refugee Committee, but also a hive of artistic bustle, with frequent visitors from a world to which Peter yearned to belong.

Helen explained to Peter that her partner had secured him a place at the Beckenham School of Art, where Carel taught for two days a week. Founded in 1902, Beckenham was a hotbed of distinguished artists, craftspersons, and designers; it was responsible for sending more students to the Royal College of Art than any other art school at the time. Not only did the world-class designers Lucienne and Robin Day teach there, Carel had secured Hellmuth Weissenborn a teaching post at the college, at Helen's behest, a few months earlier. It had been straightforward enough to find Peter a place as a student with an endorsement from a man of Weissenborn's repute.

Weight, too, was at the center of London's wartime network of artists. A few months earlier, the Ministry of Information commissioned him to paint a morale-boosting picture of Londoners going about their daily affairs despite the ravages of the Blitz. Weight drew inspiration from the things he saw on his highly perilous commute of twenty miles to and from art college. One day before Peter's arrival, his bus was singled out for attack by a German fighter-bomber. The plane swooped and slowed to make its attack, then, at the final moment, peeled away without firing. The passengers panicked. The bus emptied. Weight remained in his seat at the front of the vehicle, the sole occupant.

The Ministry of Information rejected Weight's depiction of the scene, suggesting that an image of Londoners in a state of panic might not have the desired effect. Weight was a brilliant painter, but a poor propagandist; another painting of his—destroyed when a bomb struck his studio—showed a crowd of frightened-looking Londoners gawking at a poster congratulating them on how well they were coping, a sarcastic or at least satirical questioning of the so-called Blitz spirit. Another four-panel work, based on actual events and eyewitness accounts, charted the escape of a terrified zebra from a flame-engulfed London Zoo.

When Peter arrived at the couple's home, Weight had just been called up to serve in the army. Securing Peter a place at the Beckenham School of Art was one of his last acts before he left for the Royal Armoured Corps. While Peter stayed with the couple, Helen managed to secure him a stipend of half a crown a week to pay for his daily needs, and twenty-five shillings rent, to pay for lodgings at school.

On November 26, 1941, Peter arrived at the Beckenham School of Art in Kent. Just as the Auerbach orphanage had provided a place of sanctuary and enrichment in the swirling depression of postwar Berlin, so Beckenham provided Peter with an oasis of purpose in the encircling desolation of war, with one of his favorite camp tutors, Hellmuth Weissenborn, now formally his teacher.

War cast its long, disruptive shadow over both the students and teachers alike. There were no grants and materials were scarce. A number of Peter's classmates dropped out. Hutchinson, however, had provided useful training for the young Berliner; thanks to the tutelage of Schwitters and the others, Peter could make paint and canvas from whatever materials were available.

"All my years in internment were a great support to me," he said. "I got through this way."

"A WOMAN OF ACTION," AS the *Manchester Guardian* described her, Bertha Bracey "seems to be a member of nearly every committee going." Certainly nobody else had done more to alleviate the suffering of those held in internment camps around the British Isles, despite often firm opposition from men unused to being challenged, especially by a woman.

While Peter was now free, hundreds of refugees from racial and religious oppression remained interned. For Bertha, the fact that refugees to whom Britain granted asylum were still being deprived of that right was a grave injustice. After the hasty arrests, Britain's administrative sloth revealed evidence of similar tendencies in Britain to those in the countries from which the refugees had escaped. Moreover, the lingering mess of internment revealed the danger posed to the civil liberties of British subjects, and how quickly a concatenation of factors could push a government onto an indefensible course of action.

As William Hughes, the Quaker who had moved onto the Isle of Man to better support internees, characterized the situation, Bertha was "oppressed by difficulties with [government] departments" to the extent that even he doubted her ability to overcome the challenges.

With Hughes's help, however, Bertha had improved the lot of those interned on the Isle of Man, making her presence routinely felt both on the island and in Whitehall. As well as producing long lists of recommendations to the government on how to develop and improve both the facilities and organization of the camps, Bertha had ensured that mothers and children were never separated. She had also spearheaded the formation of a married camp to bring together couples such as the archaeologist Gerhard Bersu and his equally eminent archaeologist wife, Maria, who had been interned separately.

Bertha had also spent a significant amount of time considering how she might help promote the work that internees had produced inside the camps. In the spring of 1941, she and her colleague Otto Schiff from the Jewish Refugees Committee began an energetic correspondence with the Home Office in an attempt to set up an inter-camp exhibition of art and design. The idea was for an event that "would enable internees of any denomination to exhibit their productions and offer them for sale," and lay the foundation for "a representative collection which might become a historic record and eventually be placed in some museum or similar institution." To ensure the exhibition was representative, Bertha Bracey wrote to the celebrated Austrian refugee artist Oskar Kokoschka to ask if he would help with the selection and hanging.

The plan came too late, however, stymied by the success of the refugee groups in hastening the artists' releases. As she put it in a letter to Sir Ernest Holderness, a civil servant at the Home Office: "You probably know I have personally been very much impressed by the work done in the camps, though undoubtedly the peak in both quality and quantity has now been passed by the numerous and very welcome releases."

In lieu of a permanent collection, Bracey instead launched a project to enable the sale of articles produced by internees, including artworks. Mr. Angliss, the Home Office representative to the aliens department, secured a showroom where items produced by internees, including mats, model boats, toys, and leather ornaments, were placed on display with prices attached.

FOR BERTHA, THE WORK WAS its own reward. Nevertheless, she was surprised to be selected to receive the Order of the British Empire, which she learned about in December 1941, a few weeks after Peter's release from Hutchinson. The Quaker spent time mulling over the implications of the offer, specifically the message it would send were she, a pacifist, to accept. Might onlookers doubt her convictions? And were there not more deserving candidates from inside the Jewish community?

She wrote to her friend Hubert William Peet, editor of the Quaker's in-house publication, the *Friend*, outlining the results of her deliberations.

> To have selected a member of the Society of Friends in wartime, whose whole energies have gone to helping enemy aliens, is a strange gesture which I felt could not be rebuffed. Especially as, in strictest confidence, I [have been] engaged in a tough tussle with the head of Military Intelligence [Major General Francis Davidson] on a matter which seemed to cut at the very roots of our civil liberties. My pacifist convictions were also understood, [although] I felt it an honour which should have been given to a member of the Jewish community which carries the larger burden.

If Bertha harbored lingering reservations about the award, her friends and colleagues—the only ones who truly understood why this diminutive, staunchly antiwar champion of Britain's supposed enemies had been included—felt uncomplicated delight on her behalf.

"The honour is so RIGHT," wrote one friend on December 18, 1941, shortly after the announcement of the New Year Honours list. "I am so PROUD, PROUD that you are my friend." Many of those who had worked with Bracey on the government's side felt equal delight. "It must be one of the best-earned [honors] in the list," wrote one Home Office civil servant, "and will give great pleasure to all who know you."

To her friends and colleagues the honor represented, in some small way, a gesture of regret regarding the British government's internment policy—or at least a nod to Bertha's role in helping undo the moral and material wrongs of the policy.

"It is a promising sign that in time of war your work should be recognised, and one whose way is far removed from war . . . for work for 'Enemy Aliens,'" wrote one friend. And while the true victims of that policy, the internees themselves, were not recognized, and did not receive any kind of apology or recompense, some of the refugees who Bertha's work had directly benefited, including Oskar Kokoschka, president of the Free German League of Culture (the unofficial club of Hampstead's refugee artists), congratulated her on the award and what it represented.

"Thank you from the bottom of our hearts for all the understanding you have shown towards German refugees," Kokoschka wrote, "and for the splendid and devoted work you have done on their behalf."

Touchingly, Bertha received a letter of congratulations from her friend and fellow campaigner Tess Simpson, secretary of the Society for the Protection of Science and Learning, who had also done so much for Hutchinson's academic internees. "I should have liked the distinction to be a higher one," she wrote. "There is no-one who merits this distinction more than you do; I am very happy indeed about it."

At 10:15 a.m. on February 3, 1942, Bertha Bracey, the former schoolteacher from Birmingham who had opposed the government's internment policies in both word and deed, arrived at Buckingham Palace wearing a nursing services indoor uniform and gloves. There among the towering military men, she received her honor from the King.

The next day, Bertha received a letter from her longtime friend and collaborator Otto Schiff, chairman of the Jewish Refugees Committee. While Bertha had been gallivanting at the palace the previous day, Schiff complained, she had missed out on an important meeting of the various refugee organizations.

"We feel that a protest must be lodged and that it was very wrong of H.M. the King to summon you before him without consulting us," Schiff wrote. "Next time he summons you before him, to receive a higher mark of his esteem still, he must first consult us as to whether it will be convenient for us to release you."

Not to be out-joked by their Jewish friends, Bertha's colleagues at Bloomsbury House posted their own internal list of made-up honors on the wall of the office, one awarded to each member of the team. David Hodgkin, for example, was awarded the R.S.P.C.A., "Regularly Supervising Prisons for Confined Aliens," Maurice Cranston a Ph.D. for "Perusing Hansard Diligently," and Frank Waywell a B.B.C. for being a "Brilliant Book-Cooker." May King received the C.I.D. for "Complete Indifference to Duty."

NOT EVERYONE WAS DELIGHTED AT the news of Bertha Bracey's honor. Ludwig Warschauer had, in October 1940, written her a ten-page letter in which he outlined the Technical School's work in Hutchinson and his plan to replicate and upscale the school outside the camp to provide training to "thousands and thousands" of young refugees, both men and women, across Britain—if she would only assist him in his release.

The plan had come to nothing: another in a pileup of setbacks and rejections. Warschauer had appealed and been rejected for release three times under the government's white paper categories. A further appeal by his employer had failed, and even an appeal from Otto Schiff at the Jewish Refugees Committee in July 1941—which Warschauer had been fortunate to receive, considering his rumored links to the Gestapo—had been refused. Every avenue had been explored, and in turn, every avenue closed.

While he still had some friends in the camp, there were consequences for any man seen fraternizing with Warschauer. MI5 kept a list of his associates in Hutchinson, and nineteen internees were investigated as a result, including Max von Rogister, a lawyer and frequent speaker at the Camp University; the future Olympic skier Hugo Kuranda; and the art collector Paul Wallraf. All but four of the individuals tracked by MI5 were deemed "definitely unsatisfactory from a security point of view." By the time of Peter's release from Hutchinson, friendship with Warschauer could have a serious effect on an internee's prospects. When the engineer's name was discovered written in the diary of Hans Anton Kollinsky, an Austrian who had already been freed from internment, he was arrested and interned for a second time.

By the time of Peter's release, Warschauer had lost the support of the British camp officers upon whose benevolence he had depended. In August 1941, Hutchinson's intelligence officer, Captain Jurgensen, inferred from the constant denials for Warschauer's release that he and Major Daniel may not have had an entirely accurate picture of the internee, whose release they had thus far endorsed. Jurgensen began to interview internees at the camp and quickly realized there was a different side to the man who had charmed the camp authorities into requisitioning an entire house for his purposes.

Only two months earlier, Jurgensen described Warschauer in his report for the Hurst committee as "never wavering in loyalty" and "steadfast to our cause." His assessment now drastically altered: "He is entirely self-centred, cunning and though arrogant-minded, prepared to be obsequious when it suits his purpose," wrote Jurgensen—his anger seemingly accentuated by the fact that he had been taken in—concluding that Warschauer had "abused the confidence placed in him." The MP Herbert Williams, who had initially made eager petitions for Warschauer's release, had also changed his opinion; in a letter to a colleague he wrote of his relationship with Warschauer that "nothing in my life has given me more anxiety."

Major Daniel, however, seemed unwilling to shift his view of an internee who had done so much to improve the standing of Hutchinson camp. In a letter to Echen, he wrote of her husband: "His work for his fellow internees in the camp has been exemplary and I can assure you that the present excellent conditions prevailing are largely due to his untiring hard work and cheerfulness." Some at MI5 even believed that Daniel was willing to overlook suspicions in order to keep the camp's Technical School open, hoping this would count "in his favour should the question arise whether Hutchinson or Onchan will have to close down."

The author and translator Claud W. Sykes, a senior figure at MI5 who concluded that "[Warschauer] would have been a Nazi but for his Jewish blood," wrote a letter recommending that Warschauer be immediately transferred from Hutchinson camp, to separate him both from his cronies and the indulgent commandant.

"It seems to me too dangerous to leave him in a position where he is [Major] Daniel's blue-eyed boy," wrote Sykes.

In March 1942, five months after Peter left the camp and when only about 350 men remained in Hutchinson, Warschauer was transferred from the island to the London Oratory School on Stewart's Grove, in the salubrious London Borough of Chelsea, also known as Internment Camp 001, which was used to house high-security internees.

BY EARLY 1942, THE INVESTIGATOR James Craufurd's suspicion that Warschauer had been sent to England as a Gestapo agent had grown "nearly to a certainty." The evidence collected during MI5's raid on Warschauer's office—in the home he shared with Echen—had provided a mountain of jigsaw pieces. Among the haul there were letters from Dr. Hans Sauer, the man who had ensured Warschauer's smooth exit from Germany, as well as canisters of photographic film rigged to produce a blotted-out image unless developed in a specific way. MI5 spent weeks studying the letter Sauer had sent Warschauer for clues and code words, even employing an expert to analyze Sauer's handwriting ("There is in the writing unusual intelligence, knowledge and mental ability, but a bad man," the expert concluded banally).

Arranging this scattered evidence into a complete picture was proving difficult. Warschauer was an accomplished liar. With each new and more intense interrogation, fact further blended with fiction. Craufurd later learned that when Warschauer was a young man in trouble for financial irregularities, his parents had sent him to an institution that claimed to help patients distinguish between truth and lies. Craufurd wrote drolly that, if true, "the cure was certainly not a permanent success." The interrogator's frustration came to a head when, after a second day of a tortuously long interrogation at the Oratory School on March 31, 1942, he accused the engineer of "telling us a pack of lies." Warschauer produced neither a reaction nor a denial. Instead, he sat with "a kind of glassy look in the eye," and remained absolutely still and silent.

Craufurd and John Noble needed a way to prove that Warschauer was lying. Securing proof of his misdealings in Germany would be impossible. The pair hatched a different plan: to attack Warschauer's most basic assertions about his credentials as an engineer. They had in their files a landing card from when Warschauer had briefly visited Britain in November 1938. On this document Warschauer had listed his occupation as "tailor." Why the discrepancy? The agents called on some experts in engineering to write them some basic questions that could be used to test Warschauer's knowledge, ranging in difficulty from the basic to the sophisticated.

On July 27, 1942, Craufurd put the questions to Warschauer. The supposedly brilliant inventor hedged, blanched, and floundered, claiming that he had "forgotten the answers long ago." Sensing that he had, at last, exposed a crucial crack in the facade, Craufurd asked simpler and simpler questions. As he later wrote in his report, Warschauer, founder of the Technical School, was unable to respond to questions that "a school-boy of thirteen years would answer without difficulty."[*]

Cornered and humiliated, Warschauer finally admitted the truth: he was not an engineer. While he had worked for engineering firms in Germany, he had been responsible for sales and marketing; he had no knowledge of the science. He had relied on the knowledge of engineers like Hermann Rahmer, whom Warschauer had corralled in Hutchinson, to pull together the Technical School and install the camp's wireless system.

The following day, Craufurd and Noble returned to the Oratory School with a new aim: to prove that Warschauer had lied about his service in the First World War. They took a similar approach, asking rudimentary questions about the work of a military officer: how to secure the advance of a party of troops, or when and where to post guards. Again Warschauer failed to provide adequate answers. With the edifice crumbling, he now admitted that he had never been an officer.

On the third day, Craufurd and Noble presented Warschauer with copies of the letters he had written to Dr. Hans Sauer prior to his internment. Craufurd explained that the letters had been analyzed and the experts had discovered a pattern to the correspondence: the number 27 repeatedly appeared, either in the date or in the text.

"Twenty-seven is my lucky number," Warschauer shot back. "I once won thousands of marks betting on it in a game of roulette."

"Enough," said Craufurd. "We know that you are working for the Gestapo. We know that you brought special photographic film and invisible ink into this country. Because of this, and your correspondence with an enemy agent, you will be court-martialled and sentenced as a spy."

Warschauer broke down. Yes, he admitted: I was sent to England by Dr. Hans Sauer to establish here a subsidiary of the Tefi company

---

[*] Two years later, Warschauer claimed in a letter to the Home Office that he was unable to recall the answers to these basic questions due to stress; the MI5 agents, he claimed, had threatened to make "tremendous difficulties" for his wife if he did not cooperate. The accusation was, Craufurd wrote in the margins of the letter, "entirely untrue."

to oversee the installation of bugging devices for the purposes of German espionage. Yes, I received from him invisible ink and the requisite developer, and film to photograph factories and other important buildings. Yes, the number *27* was a signal, so that if I ever received a letter from a stranger in which the number was introduced unobtrusively, I would know the author was, in fact, Dr. Hans Sauer.

Warschauer told Craufurd that he was exhausted. He asked if they could take a break and continue the interview tomorrow.

The following day, in the presence of two alliteratively named witnesses—the Royal Air Force officer Lieutenant Arthur Albert Pearce and the intelligence officer Harold Hammond Hindmarsh—Warschauer gave a statement in which he outlined the circumstances by which he had come to Britain as a German intelligence agent.

LUDWIG WARSCHAUER HAD CAUSED CRAUFURD and Noble considerable difficulties in their prolonged and complex investigation. Still, as the hapless spy began to tell his story, both men felt some sympathy for the circumstances that had shaped his decisions. The Gestapo's methods of coercion had been both ingenious and cruel.

Four years earlier, on Christmas Day 1938, Warschauer was summoned for questioning, having just returned from an overseas trip. Despite his connections in the German government, he felt understandably nervous; one could never be quite sure how a Gestapo summons like this would go. In fact, the questioning was broad and gentle. Afterward, the interrogator told Warschauer to return home. There he would find an old friend waiting for him, a man he had not seen for many years but who was responsible for the lenience that had just been shown.

Warschauer returned home, wondering who this benevolent stranger might be. A man in his mid-forties, clean-shaven with broad shoulders and dark hair—more Slavic-looking than Germanic—was already inside the flat. Warschauer felt the disorientation of being greeted by a stranger in the manner of a close friend.

"Lutz," the man said. "It's me, Hans. We served together in the Garde Kavallerie."

For the next hour the man, Hans Sauer, regaled Warschauer with reminiscences of the time they had spent together.

"He mentioned so many mutual experiences with all the [correct] details . . . that I began to think I must have known him somehow in the past," Warschauer explained to his interrogators.

When Sauer made him an alluring proposal, it was easy for Warschauer to overlook the nagging feeling that he had never before met this man.

"The Gestapo will not let you out of Germany, but I can help you to get a passport," Sauer said. "I will do this out of friendship for you, and a small favour."

It was this promise of escape that, as the weeks progressed, enabled Hans Sauer to entwine himself into Warschauer's life. The pair met on more than thirty occasions, sometimes alone, sometimes with partners and children. As their relationship deepened, Sauer introduced a plan. Warschauer was to travel to England and, having established a base in London, found satellite offices of the Tefi company in Warsaw and Belgrade.

Poland, it seemed, was the key target. Even at this stage Sauer and his superiors did not apparently believe Germany would enter a war with Britain. The focus of Warschauer's espionage mission was, seemingly, countries that Germany planned to invade and to which Britain provided access. In Poland Warschauer's mission was to visit factories, railway stations, electrical and gasworks, and aircraft manufacturers under the guise of a Tefifon salesman. Believing that Warschauer was a representative of an English company, not a German one, the proprietors of these businesses would welcome his pitch. Then, while on the premises, Warschauer would take color photographs, which he would send to Sauer.

Sauer then handed Warschauer four addresses to which he was to send correspondence. The number *27* must feature somehow on both sides of the paper to verify that the letter was both genuine and that it had not been written under duress. (It later transpired that Sauer had wanted to use the code number *17*, most likely because *27* was already being used as a signal by another agent, but Warschauer convinced Sauer to use *27*. Just as he had told MI5, he believed it to be his lucky number, another example of his talent for threading a lie with a truth.)

Warschauer's suspicions that this man was more than a business-man in search of industrial secrets calcified when Sauer introduced Warschauer's elderly mother, his fiancée Echen, and Echen's children into the conversation as leverage.

"If I refused his offer," Warschauer told his interrogators, "[Dr. Sauer said he] could no longer protect me from the Gestapo and the concentration camp . . . my mother's pension would probably be stopped, and she and my wife would be imprisoned."

HAVING EXTRACTED A CONFESSION, CRAUFURD now asked Warschauer to describe how, precisely, he was able to leave Germany, considering the fact his passport was stamped with the *J* to indicate that he was a Jew. Warschauer explained how Sauer had collected him and Echen from his mother's house and accompanied them to the Tempelhof Airport. He described how Sauer met him in a small room by passport control and ensured his bags weren't searched or confiscated. At one o'clock that same afternoon, his plane had descended over Croydon with the vials of invisible ink and its corresponding developer, the camera, and cans of special photographic film stowed in his luggage.

After years of investigation, Craufurd and Noble had their confes-sion. Oblivious or not, Ludwig Warschauer came to Britain as an agent of the German intelligence service, a refugee spy. To Craufurd, who took thorough minutes, Warschauer appeared a broken man, unable to order his thoughts. If Warschauer hoped this might have brought an end to the matter, he was vastly mistaken. Now began a tortuous, monthlong interrogation, during which the officers prized the full backstory from him.

As the days turned to weeks, the fragments were slowly extracted and arranged. Warschauer's confession grew to more than fifty pages. Put together it provided an "appalling picture," as Craufurd described it, of "an adventurer of the sorriest appearance."

The camp stories of extortion were true after all; during the confession Warschauer mentioned that Curt Sluzewski, the Vatican lawyer who first started the rumors about him at Hutchinson, had slept with the German barmaid with whom Warschauer had a blackmail arrangement. By now Sluzewski had immigrated to America, but there seemed to be no reason why Warschauer might fabricate such a personally damaging story.

Craufurd, though, was still not convinced he had the whole truth. Warschauer claimed to have never denounced anyone to the Gestapo, and to have "never betrayed anyone regarding a money transfer." Craufurd believed both statements were false. Warschauer was also resolutely unwilling to take full responsibility for his actions. He blamed his tendency to lie on the fact that, as a boy, "I masturbated a great deal."

There were, in Craufurd's estimation, a few minor redeeming points—or at least extenuating facts. The internee's "ruined character," as the MI5 agent put it, appeared to be a result of his experiences in the First World War—although here, too, there was doubt about what, precisely, Warschauer's role had been. The spy claimed that during that conflict he had been buried alive for six hours under a burning shelter. It had taken eight months of treatment by nerve specialists, he said, to cure him of his fear of fire, which had now, years later, returned to haunt his dreams. As with most of Warschauer's claims, the incident was dubious and impossible to verify. And yet his behavior and compulsive deceitfulness suggested that he had experienced profound trauma at some point in his life.

The fact that, after he arrived in England, Warschauer had disposed of the invisible ink and sold the Leica camera with which he had been ordered to take photographs lent some weight to his claim that he intended to cut ties with his Gestapo handler. He had not, seemingly, conducted any espionage for Germany, a fact that would save him from hanging. And although, in Hutchinson, Warschauer had become "a tyrant," as Craufurd put it, he had nevertheless provided genuine training to hundreds of young men who were now able to contribute to the British war effort. Craufurd concluded that whatever Warschauer's primary motivation in establishing the Technical School, the endeavor was "the only good thing Warschauer ever achieved in his life."

None of this could save him from his predicament, though. Even if Warschauer had never conducted any espionage in Britain, corresponding with a member of the Gestapo was enough to keep him indefinitely interned. This was the result of one of the longest, and therefore most expensive investigations into a suspected refugee spy. Indeed, one of the few successes, such as it was, of the entire internment policy. Yet the revelation that Warschauer had come to Britain as a refugee with an ulterior motive brought little discernible benefit to Britain. It did not justify the panicked mass internment measures that damaged the lives and livelihoods of thousands of refugees, cleaved apart families, and destroyed communities. It did, however, reveal to one woman the true character of the man she had married.

Echen knew nothing of the unfolding drama. Having already lost two husbands, she was willing to do almost anything to keep the third. Her petitions to the Home Office were, as Craufurd put it, constant. This situation could not stand. To bring her petitions to an end, Craufurd told Warschauer that, during her next visit, he must confess to his wife. Echen reported to the Oratory School the following day.

XXI

RETURN TO THE MILL

KURT SCHWITTERS OPENED THE DOOR and welcomed a pretty woman of half his age into the attic room. As she crossed the threshold, Edith Thomas saw a table draped with a white towel, matching blue and white china, a chocolate cake, and a single rose erupting from an eggcup. The walls were covered with brightly colored paintings that produced a symphonic effect of color and dreamlike distraction. To the young switchboard operator from the censorship office, it was an astonishing scene.

Since his release from Hutchinson, Schwitters had transposed both the spirit and aesthetic of his camp studio to the attic of the flat he now shared with his son, Ernst, in a Georgian terraced boardinghouse in Bayswater, just two miles from Helen Roeder's place in Hammersmith. Edith lived in the adjoining flat. Schwitters had accosted her in the hallway and asked if she might help him work the bathroom geyser to fill a bath. At their next meeting, just as Edith was leaving for work, the artist invited her to join him for coffee when she returned.

Schwitters was lonely. His son and daughter-in-law worked all day, and the busyness he had enjoyed in Hutchinson, with an endless supply of commissions and diversions, had left a major void now that he had arrived in a city of endless distractions. Despite moments of despair, the artist's time in Hutchinson had been relatively comfortable.

He'd had enough money to buy a new suit and hire someone in the camp to teach him to play the piano. Friendly internees delivered coal to his attic room so he could keep warm in the evenings. At least three or four times a week he swam in the sea, taking a rubber mattress with him to lie on his back while floating on the waves. He would bring pebbles, shells, seaweed, and even sea creatures back to his room and observe as the animals wriggled and skated in a container of seawater.

In his final months at the camp, Schwitters became friends with Hutchinson's medical officer, Dr. Robert Marshall, the man who had provided the flowers for the camp wedding. Marshall, who lived on the island in a Victorian mansion, was an art enthusiast and owned some Italian copies of great masters. Against protocol, Marshall invited Schwitters to visit his home to produce two paintings: one the view from his house, the other a portrait. Marshall supplied the paint and materials and plied Schwitters with sweets and cake, allowing the internee to wander the grounds, picking roses and marguerite daisies. Despite the despair he'd felt during the Christmas service, the combination of a decent income, space to work, basic comforts, and an eager clientele made Hutchinson, in a strange way, one of the most enriching and productive times in Schwitters's life.

Upon leaving Hutchinson for London on November 24, 1941, he used the haul of eighteen months' worth of detritus he'd kept from the camp to re-create the sanctuary of his Hutchinson attic. Schwitters's wife, Helma, was still stranded in Norway, and until there was an end to hostilities, there was little chance of a reunion. Bored, alone, and starved of female company, Schwitters's intentions were innocent when he invited Edith to coffee. Still, she was startled when, after she sat down at the table, he walked over to his bed and flung back the covers. It was only when the artist produced the jug of coffee, which he had been keeping warm under the sheets, that she could relax.

An oddly sweet relationship soon bloomed between the ailing Dadaist and the former department store model who, having divorced the man she had married in her teens, was not overly concerned about what others might think. Edith knew little about art, but she was bright and interested; despite the age gap, she found both a friend and a confidant in Schwitters, whom she unflatteringly nicknamed "Jumbo" due to his size. Edith soon visited Schwitters each day, poking her head around the door with the cheery greeting, "Want tea?" Schwitters, with his tone poet's ear, squished the question into an affectionate nickname of his own: "Wantee."

For now, the relationship remained platonic, if codependent. Each filled a vacuum for the other: Wantee became the caring, present wife; Schwitters the doting older man able to salve the wounds of Wantee's tumultuous relationship with her bad-tempered father. Schwitters told Wantee that he was married and that he loved his wife. He neglected, however, to mention in his letters to Helma the spritely young woman who had bounded into his life.

DESPITE THE WARMTH AND COMPANY provided by Wantee, Schwitters teetered on the edge of poverty and, when his new companion was out at work during the day, stultifying self-pity. In London, Schwitters discovered his style was too unfashionable for the "*konservativ*" English sensibility, as he described it. Here, the artist complained, "you must not see any brush stroke on the picture." Despite repeated assurances that his pieces would one day be highly valuable, Schwitters struggled to find clients. Desperation led him to apply for unsuitable positions; he received rejections from both the BBC and the department store Selfridges, where he had applied to become a window dresser. When Sir Kenneth Clark, director of the National Gallery who had done so much to help interned artists, refused Schwitters's request to meet, the artist toppled into a depression.

"Life is sad," he wrote on a park bench, using a pencil scrounged from a passerby. "Why did the Director of the National Gallery refuse even to see me? He does not know that I belong to the avant garde? That is my tragedy."

Schwitters, who had enjoyed both wealth and status in Hutchinson's transient society, fell close to destitution. He visited a former camp mate to prize a penny from a collage he had gifted to his friend in Hutchinson. To travel across London without paying, Schwitters developed a ruse. When the bus conductor checked tickets, he would pull from his pocket a mass of crumpled old receipts and pretend to not know which was that day's ticket. Invariably the conductor moved on.

Just before his fifty-sixth birthday, Schwitters off-loaded his misery, as per his habit, in a poem to his absent wife.

"In a world of disappointments, I am alone . . . the world lives on without me, without using my abilities, without giving me the chance to show my talent in my work."

Hutchinson had supplied the artist with an interested audience, space, time, and materials, all of which had revived his energies. Now the camp, the audience, the status—even his attentive student, Peter Fleischmann—were all gone.

ON AUGUST 7, 1942, ECHEN arrived at the gates of the requisitioned London Oratory School. Eight months earlier America had joined the Allies' fight against the Nazis, following the Japanese surprise attack on Pearl Harbor; most German troops were now focused on a grim and costly war of attrition against the Soviet Union on the Eastern Front. The Blitz of London was over and, while war still cast a black shadow across Britain, the city was no longer the focus of Hitler's fight. It was not the first time Echen traveled to the high-security internment camp where her husband had been imprisoned since he'd left the Isle of Man. She had dutifully visited Lutz ever since his transfer to London, often taking her eldest daughter along with her to visit. Today was the first time, however, that she had been ordered to come.

A guard escorted her to one of the classrooms where, surrounded by severe-looking officers, her husband sat. Echen recognized two of the guards as the two mysterious men who had visited and searched her home with Inspector Hoare from Scotland Yard. Lutz looked sick and mournful. The stakes had been made clear. This meeting, Craufurd had explained to his prisoner, was the last and only opportunity to tell the truth.

Warschauer began to explain to his wife how, under threat of reprisals against her and his family, he had agreed to conduct certain tasks for the man the couple knew as Hans Sauer. Warschauer spoke falteringly. Craufurd watched the internee intently, his pencil, as always, poised to take down information that might expose a wrinkle in the timeline. Before he revealed to Echen any specific details about the precise nature of the agreement, however, Warschauer interrupted his confession with a howl of anguish.

"There ensued," as Craufurd wrote in his notes, "a disgusting scene."

Amid cries of distress, Warschauer managed to explain that the previous evening he had swallowed razor blades that he had wrapped in bread. It appeared that the blades had, at this fortuitous moment, begun to take their effect on his digestive tract.

"Take me to the hospital," Warschauer screamed.

As her husband was rushed from the interrogation room wailing in agony, Echen sat facing an empty chair.

AT THE BECKENHAM SCHOOL OF ART, Peter felt that he had finally shaken free of his story, carefully choosing those parts of his life that he wished to keep and discarding the rest. He continued to visit Echen regularly in London and on August 25, 1942, two weeks after her traumatic encounter with her husband, Peter arrived at her home in Hampstead Gardens to celebrate the thirteenth birthday of Monica, her youngest daughter. Through necessity he had learned not to mark the various painful anniversaries in his own life, but his gratitude to Echen and her daughters meant he was sure to not miss theirs.

Just as the new tracks of his life began to lead him into fresh and exciting directions, war, with its thoughtless interruptions, diverted the young artist on an unexpected tour of the craters of his past. On March 23, 1943, sixteen months after he left Hutchinson camp, Peter received his call-up papers, summoning him to the Central Recruit-ment Centre at Euston. There he received a shilling—the symbolic sign of an agreement to serve in the British army—and duly reported to Bradford and the No. 6 Training Centre of the Pioneer Corps. His army document listed his trade on enlistment as "pastry cook." In the section listing Peter's next-of-kin, he struck through the printed name "Doctor Deutsch" and replaced it with "Mrs E. Warschauer." Once again, Peter found himself among a curious crowd, "all sorts of strange people." Army life did not suit Peter, whose artistic spirit strained against the dis-ciplined conformity of military rigmarole. Art again provided a refuge. He started evening classes, and when the staff spied his talent, he was able to bribe the officers into excusing him from exercises in exchange for their portraits.

Despite or perhaps because of his cunning, Peter was selected for officer training and sent to the Royal Army Ordnance Corps at Saltburn-by-the-Sea, in Yorkshire. After graduation, Peter was de-ployed to a munitions camp in York. When he arrived, it became clear that this was a punishment facility for criminals and murderers.

"Again, it was a mistake," he said. "Just one of those things."

Here, among the ne'er-do-wells, Peter found unlikely characters who, like him, had ended up in the wrong place. He became friends with a literary critic called Bates, and the Welsh actor Clifford Evans, equally unsuited to the place. These friendships were flickering lights in a dispiritingly bleak sky. Eventually, Peter reported to his command-ing officer to request a transfer. The request was well-timed. The officer asked Peter if he might be willing to work for the army as an inter-preter, interrogating German prisoners of war. After a short examina-tion, Peter was accepted.

As he was to be interviewing Nazi servicemen, Peter decided it would be prudent to change his surname and obscure his heritage. There were few meaningful options. His grandfather's surname, Deutsch, was about as unhelpful an alias for the role as it was possible to imagine, and he had no wish to adopt his estranged uncle's angliciz-ation, Dale. Since her marriage to Ludwig Warschauer, Echen was no longer a Kempinski nor a Kohsen, and, besides, not one of these names could pass for British. Neither could the names of Peter's friends from Hutchinson: Schwitters, Uhlman, and Hinrichsen all forced a continental accent on the tongue.

There was, however, one name that was both sentimental and practical: that of his closest British friend, Donald Gray Midgley, his former colleague at the Manchester photography studio who had taken pity on him. "Midgley" was sufficiently English-sounding and, when coupled with "Peter," created the pleasing quadri-syllabic effect of a door opening and closing. So that there could be no doubt as to whom his new name paid tribute, Peter chose to also adopt Donald's middle name, Gray. Put together, his new identity would not only honor his friend, but it would also function as an aspirational challenge to embody Donald's gentler virtues of kindness and impulses of generosity.

Newly christened in the waters of British bureaucracy, Peter Midgley was informed of his first posting as an army interpreter. A new name implied new beginnings, but fate dealt Peter a hackneyed plot twist: he was to return to the disused cotton mill that had, three years earlier, been the first stop in his imprisonment. This time, Peter would go to Warth Mills not as a prisoner, but as a guard.

AT THE MILITARY HOSPITAL, THE X-ray confirmed what Craufurd had suspected: there were no razor blades in Warschauer's stomach. Neither, when doctors examined his body, were there any signs of Warschauer having ever attempted a similar act of self-harm. The dramatic exit from the confessional meeting with Echen had been another ruse. Having realized the gravity of his situation—and the fact that a confession could lose him his wife and stepchildren—Warschauer had tried to buy himself some time. Thanks to her husband's dramatic exit, Echen knew only the barest of outlines to the story. Fearing another dramatic display, MI5's agents chose not to bring her back for a second performance.

The next day Warschauer passed a letter addressed to Echen to one of his fellow internees. In it, he claimed that under the stress of interrogation he had confessed to things that he had never done. Despite everything, Warschauer was still unwilling to accept responsibility for his actions. While he had not, it seemed, engaged in any meaningful espionage in Britain, MI5 had proven its agents were right to repeatedly block the government's attempts to release a Gestapo spy into Britain. Now, however, there was the problem of what to do with him.

MI5 did not want the subject of their only truly successful investigation into refugees to be returned to Hutchinson, where the incoming boatloads of internees returning from Canada and Australia, all "unfamiliar with Warschauer's internment record," would provide "a fertile field for his tricks." Besides, the government had been making steady progress in emptying the island's camps; there were now fewer than five thousand internees on the Isle of Man, and the aim was to reduce this number further, not bolster it. Ironically then, the government did not want the man whose internment was justified to be returned to the camp from which he had come.

On November 8, 1942, Warschauer was transferred to Brixton Prison, to join high-risk prisoners such as Oswald Mosley, founder of the British Union of Fascists; the anti-Semitic politician Captain Archibald Ramsay; and Admiral Sir Barry Domvile, a high-ranking naval officer, interned for his ardent support of Hitler. For now, Warschauer would remain interned, not at one of the Isle of Man's breezy camps, but in a London prison cell.

HAVING EXPERIENCED REJECTION AFTER REJECTION from the British art establishment, Schwitters turned to the immigrant community for support. Once a month Fred Uhlman, Klaus Hinrichsen, and other former members of the Artists Café began to meet at Maison Bertaux in Soho, gatherings that, to the delight of the others, Schwitters occasionally attended. Wary of any group that impressed political obligations on its artists, Schwitters turned down an invitation to join the Free

German League of Culture, but he was happy to perform his poems to its members, including the cup-and-saucer-smashing "Silence."

Physical decline, however, soon followed financial ruin. In April 1944, Schwitters staggered down a staircase and collapsed. The stroke left him paralyzed on one side. Unable to write or to paint, rejected by the London art world and menial employers alike, Schwitters's depression blackened. At some point, his strange relationship with Wantee had shifted from companionship to something more, a romance he justified with the belief that she had been sent to him by his wife as support. Wantee moved in to become Schwitters's full-time caregiver.

Then came an unexpected glimmer of opportunity. While recovering from the stroke, Schwitters received word from one of London's most effusive gallery owners, the self-taught German artist Hugo Baruch, who went by the name Jack Bilbo. A former internee of Onchan, one of Hutchinson's sister camps on the Isle of Man, Bilbo had moved to London to establish the Modern Art Gallery, promoting the works of émigré artists in the city. It was a reckless wartime scheme by any measure, and yet Bilbo's institution became a burgeoning success, attracting distinguished patrons including the actors Vivien Leigh and Rex Harrison, and the writers H. G. Wells and J. B. Priestley. Bilbo, who had already shown some of Schwitters's work at the gallery, asked whether the artist might consider a one-man exhibition, staged alongside a separate show titled *Masterpieces*, which was set to include works by Van Gogh, Picasso, Renoir, and, unashamedly, Bilbo himself (whom Schwitters referred to as, tellingly, "a real art gangster").

Schwitters agreed. Bilbo enlisted the art critic Herbert Read to write the catalog essay, in which Read described Schwitters as not only "the supreme master of collage," but also a modernist poet whose work paralleled that of James Joyce. In Schwitters's use of materials, which others might dismiss as litter—"the stones the builders rejected"— Read perceived both philosophical intent and virtue. For Schwitters, who had experienced so many setbacks since his release from Hutchinson, it was a soaring moment of recognition and appreciation.

"I really am very grateful to you," Schwitters wrote in a letter to Read, for whom he then made a collage featuring some of the bus ticket stubs he had used to travel around London.

Bilbo billed Schwitters as no less than the "founder" of Dadaism. This brazenness extended to all areas of Bilbo's life. When Schwitters and Wantee arrived to drop off the last of his paintings for the exhibition, the couple walked into a bitter row. Wantee caught a broom handle as it sailed past. Bilbo, it transpired, had slept with a group of four women the previous night. His wife was currently reacting to her husband's unembarrassed request that she provide the ménage with breakfast.

On December 4, 1944, almost four years after Schwitters cried in despair during the Christmas service at Hutchinson camp, the press arrived at the Modern Art Gallery on Charles II Street for a review of his one-man exhibition. Schwitters gave a recital of his poems to an audience of strangers who had chosen to attend the event out of genuine interest, not because of a lack of other options, as at the camp. The first reviews were full of praise. The public, however, was less enamored and tickets sold poorly. One day in late December, Schwitters sat alone among his pictures in the gallery. The typically upbeat Bilbo entered, grave-faced, and handed the artist a telegram from Switzerland. Schwitters's wife, Helma, was dead.

WARTH MILLS WAS JUST AS massive and drearily portentous as when Peter had first entered its gates as a prisoner. Its population was, however, no longer composed of professors and tinkering sculptors. The days when one might enter a gusty hall and happen upon a Dadaist performing tone poems to an audience of one were gone. Warth Mills was now a well-organized campus for prisoners of war—Camp 177, as it was officially known—and home to no fewer than four thousand captured German servicemen.

Just as in the winter of 1940, when tribunals had divided refugees and enemy aliens according to categories of risk, so German POWs were graded according to their perceived loyalty to Nazism. "Whites" were typically nonprofessional officers and soldiers who had joined up only to serve their country and who were, in some cases, outwardly hostile to the regime that had sent them to war. "Grays" were fair-weather Nazis, waverers whose allyship was based on self-preservation, not ideology. The most dangerous category, "Blacks," were fundamentalists or, as one British report put it, the "incurables."

Warth Mills was filled with Blacks, predominantly members of the Waffen-SS, men whose reputations stemmed from both their prowess in the field and the atrocities they had committed. Every Sunday the entire camp would gather in the open, in front of the building, and sing the "Horst-Wessel-Lied," the strident party anthem, while raising their right arms in a unified Nazi salute. Locals reported hearing the grim dawn chorus from as much as two miles away.

Peter entered the camp wearing the uniform of his former jailors and saw for the first time since he fled the Auerbach orphanage the kind of radicalized young men who had attempted, five years earlier, to burn his home to the ground. The atmosphere was palpably similar, as another visitor put it, to a "hostile tribe confronting an anthropologist with dark looks, impenetrable thoughts and secret customs." While the grease and grime that had characterized Peter's first stay at the mill had been cleaned away, the scent of oil lingered, thick with memories.

THE CHAOTIC, MAKESHIFT CAMP PETER encountered as a prisoner had been transformed by a scaffolding of military rules and routine, a degree of organization without which the British officers would have been unable to maintain order. Fearing for his safety, Peter hid the fact he was German from those he helped to interrogate, doing his best to obscure his accent. His chosen pseudonym became, week by week, not so much a cover as a new identity, one that enabled him to cast off his heritage and the trouble it had brought him.

As Peter had seen during his own internment journey, the tone of a camp was invariably set by the quality and character of its commandant. During his first visit to Warth Mills, the camp had bristled with chaos and abuse, an atmosphere set by Major Alfred Braybrook, the squat officer who addressed his charges from the upturned orange box. Braybrook had been released from his post, arrested, and, on April 17, 1941, charged with stealing from his charges a hundred sovereigns, two typewriters—one of which belonged to Kurt Schwitters's son, Ernst—jewelry, and more than a thousand razor blades. Braybrook was sentenced to eighteen months' imprisonment.

Now the camp was run by a Colonel Selby. During the First World War, Selby had been a POW in Germany and therefore had the experience to manage what was, by any measure, an intimidating prison population. As members of the SS, the prisoners had the most to lose from Nazi defeat and so the greatest incentive to maintain their group identity. The Nazi prisoners at Warth Mills self-moderated, as at many of the German POW camps in Britain, where secret trials were held to judge, for example, whether or not prisoners could be justified in being apprehended rather than dying while resisting capture. The men held secret court-martials, and group-appointed judges delivered brutal actions against defeatists or dissidents, up to and including the death sentence. In another camp in the nearby city of Doncaster, a prisoner who had been subjected to one of these secret trials was discovered strung up in a lavatory, his body daubed with swastikas.

If Peter derived any pleasure from seeing his enemies imprisoned and stripped of their power, this was not an opportunity to gloat—just another frustrating digression from his calling.

"I hated every moment of it," he said.

As the ferry chugged into Douglas harbor, Ludwig Warschauer felt a loosening of bonds. The island held different associations from those formed during the sixteen claustrophobic months he had just spent at Brixton Prison: the restaurant meals, the school, the friendly relationships with officers who, unlike the MI5 agents, never prodded too hard at things that might imperil the status of their camp.

The stress of Warschauer's monthlong interrogation with Craufurd and Noble, followed by an extended period spent in London's miserable prison, had taken its toll. From his cell he had requested an audience with a nerve specialist. The request was denied, and instead Warschauer endured a spell in the hospital, where he had, as one report noted, "wept profusely and made a nuisance of himself expecting all sorts of unwarrantable privileges."

Echen now had a sense of her husband's past dealings, but not enough detail to persuade her to abandon the man who had secured her and her children's passage from Germany. Her faithful petitions on his behalf had brought her husband's case to the MP Eleanor Rathbone. She had argued that, while Warschauer might not be eligible for release, there was no ethical reason to keep him locked up in circumstances that would contribute to his deteriorating health.

Perhaps, the Home Office had reasoned, the solution was to return Warschauer to Hutchinson and allow him to again run the Technical School, or a similar scheme, which would "probably have the desired psychological effect upon him."

Hutchinson's population had drastically altered. Most of the refugees were gone, replaced by more complicated cases. There were men in the camp who posed a clear risk to Britain, such as the former German naval intelligence officer Franz von Rintelen (who, after the First World War, was tried and convicted of spying on America), Japanese POWs, and a clutch of captured merchant seamen. There were men damned by blood, such as Baron Wilhelm von Richthofen, a former Oxford Rhodes scholar and cousin of the infamous German First World War pilot, the Red Baron. And curious cases such as Baron Nicholaus von Nettelbladt, who had married into the position of Lord of Glassenbury Manor, a debilitatingly expensive-to-run stately home in Kent, or Baron Fritz von Tschirschky, a former high-ranking German diplomat who had been interned despite resisting the Nazis.

MI5's Craufurd opposed the plan to send Warschauer to join men like these in the strongest terms. Warschauer was not, the agent wrote, to be returned to the camp, where "sooner or later he [will] again stir up trouble." MI5 and the Home Office reached a compromise: Warschauer could return to the island, but he would stay at Camp MX in Peel, also known as Peveril, a more prison-like compound where category A internees, including members of the British Union of Fascists and the IRA, were held.

None of this was yet known to Warschauer when, for the first time in two years, he stepped onto the Isle of Man. Any excitement that he would shortly return to his comfortable existence in Hutchinson vanished when, instead of a brisk walk to his old camp, Warschauer was taken by car on a twenty-minute drive across the island.

To his undoubted dismay, Peveril camp—dubbed by the locals as "the fascist camp" after some eight hundred British fascist detainees arrived there in May 1941—was quite unlike Hutchinson or the other predominantly refugee camps on the island. It had, since switching from an internment camp to a detainment camp, been the site of fierce riots and at least two escape attempts.

In the autumn of 1941, the MP Osbert Peake visited the island and insisted, against the advice of his guides, that he visit Peveril. When he arrived, the men screamed obscenities and anti-Semitic slurs. Peake, who had the reputation of being a fair-minded humanitarian, was viewed, in the eyes of the fascists, as simultaneously a soft touch toward refugees and an impediment to the far right. The internees screamed, "He's a Jew," and "We want justice," causing such a commotion that a crowd of islanders gathered in the street to watch and listen. If Hutchinson had been a place of art, learning, and muted resentment, Peveril was a place of extremism and fury.

When Major Daniel learned Warschauer had returned to the island, he expressed to the chief intelligence officer on the island, Major S. H. Woolf, "great anxiety to see him again." Woolf agreed and accompanied Daniel on a trip to the camp at Peveril. During the car journey, Warschauer's former commandant pressed Woolf on what he might do to facilitate Warschauer's release. For Major Daniel, the spell was yet to be broken.

If Warschauer felt despondent that his return to the island had not been as favorable as he hoped, the swift arrival of Major Daniel lifted his spirits. The meeting was long, cordial, and had a positive effect on the internee, who felt certain this was a sign his chances of release had suddenly improved. When one of MI5's informants passed this information to his handlers, Noble noted: "It seems most unsuitable that Daniel should see Warschauer, but I suppose it cannot be prevented." The spy's sense of reprieve would be short-lived.

On November 19, 1944, Echen wrote a letter to her husband. During the past four years, she had seen him only in custody, in states of increasingly heightened distress. Yet despite reports of his wrongdoing, Echen loved Ludwig Warschauer, the man to whom she owed her life, the lives of her children, and the lives of her parents. Since the incident at the London Oratory School, however, she knew that her family's freedom had come at significant cost. While Echen might have been able to absorb the impact of each new revelation about her husband's past and even, perhaps, the cruel ruse about the swallowed razor blades, Warschauer's unwillingness to accept blame and to embrace change had, after four years of effort, made her position untenable. "Dear Lutz," she began.

> I admit every man has adversaries, but I cannot believe that there are honest people who have only adversaries and detractors. I have gradually come to the conclusion that you haven't a single friend. Nor can I find anyone who trusts you implicitly, or believes your word, if he really knows you . . . I have done everything humanly possible to help you towards a new and decent life, in spite of the fact that I have the feeling that I do not know all the accusations made against you.
>
> After a long and most difficult struggle and, believe me, many sleepless nights, I have realised that I am facing a problem, which, for me is insoluble. I had hoped that these last years . . . would have given you the courage to be truthful. Instead, you only blame others . . . You begged me in Brixton not to write you any more sharp letters; I will try to resist any feeling of bitterness. Nevertheless, I must simply tell you again today how terribly I've suffered and still suffer because of you . . . Today I see no further possibility of your changing since the last four years should really have done this.

> When we first got to know each other, you promised me that you
> would bring my parents the children and myself out of Germany and
> you kept your promise, and I must say that I have also kept my promise
> and left nothing undone to help you . . .
>
> I beg you not to commit a further injustice and believe that I have
> now suddenly become your adversary or detractor. I would be happy
> if I should hear one day that you have succeeded in leading an upright
> and honest life. I cannot help you anymore. I'm too tired, really, because
> of this bitterest disappointment and experience which I have had to go
> through because of you. Nevertheless—and you should not forget this—I
> will never forget what you have done for the children, for my parents,
> and for me.

Echen's message, written in German, did not reach Warschauer
immediately. When Warschauer's carer, Dr. Barker, read its contents,
he forwarded the letter to Major Woolf along with a note advising that
its message would likely have a significantly negative effect on his patient. The decision to withhold the letter backfired. Having sent her
request for divorce, Echen ceased writing to her husband.* When he
stopped receiving her letters, without explanation, Warschauer experienced "fits of weeping," "loss of memory," "persistent insomnia . . . and
hallucinations of incoming sheets of fire."

Following this reaction, the doctors passed Echen's final letter
to Warschauer. The news of his wife's desertion compounded Warschauer's suffering. In Falcon Cliff Hospital he lost ten pounds in
weight in a week through vomiting. On December 18, 1944, with characteristic melodrama, Warschauer wrote a letter to the aliens department at the Home Office in which he stated that, without his wife,
his life was "valueless." He should be freed and deployed to the most
dangerous parts of London.

"I shall be glad if Fate will allow me to perish in the duty against
the Nazis and so to make my name clean."

---

* It is testament to Echen's character that she continued to write privately to Dr. Barker to inquire
about her husband's health, even after requesting the separation.

Warschauer then wrote a letter to the pope, asking for a priest to visit his cell so that he might convert to Catholicism. He wrote at length of his commitment to Echen, whose love he had lost, he claimed, "under the influence of the cruel outside world." Hoping, perhaps, that the Church would pressure Echen to stay with her husband, he included her home address in his letter.

"Hale or ill," MI5's Noble wrote, "Warschauer runs true to form."

For Echen the relationship was over. It was a decision that, in secret, Craufurd and Noble considered to be "almost certainly the correct one." For Echen, however, it represented an end not only to this particular relationship, but to all matrimony. After the divorce, she would tell her daughters that she had only married Lutz because he had the kind of influence that might enable their escape from Germany. Both girls knew this was not the case and that, in the early stage of the marriage at least, Echen had been much in love. Now, at the age of forty-one, she closed whichever part of her heart had, during the trials of the past decade, remained open to the possibilities of long-term companionship. There would be other flings and ephemeral romances, but she would never again remarry or live with a man.

She did not completely let go. When her husband's itemized belongings from the camp arrived at her house, she hung his portrait by Schwitters in the front room. Only when Warschauer had accepted the marriage was over, and sent word that he wanted the painting back, did she take it down, package it up, and post it to Germany.

XXII

THE FINAL TRIAL

IN MARCH 1944, NINE MONTHS before Echen wrote her letter, the final 172 internees were transferred from Hutchinson to Peveril camp. Then, in November 1944, Hutchinson became a POW camp. It was finally closed in August 1945, after the end of the war. Then, another three months before the camp was officially de-requisitioned. During this time the furniture was repaired and reconditioned, the walls repainted, the blackout film into which so many internees had cut their designs peeled and scraped off the windows. Leftover long-life food, including enough rice to provide every shop on the island a small allocation for rice pudding, was removed and redistributed.

While most of Hutchinson's former internees were desperate to leave the Isle of Man for good, some chose to return. In July 1945, two months after Germany surrendered to the Allied forces, Marjan Rawicz visited the island to deliver a performance—the first of more than a dozen appearances he would make there in the months and years to come—billed as the "first Isle of Man celebrity concert since the war."

This time barbed wire did not separate the pianist from his performing partner, Walter Landauer. One critic described the pair's performance as "the highest peak of perfection." No mention was made in this nor any other of the press reports that both men had once been prisoners on the island, or that Rawicz was a graduate of the Hutchinson Camp University.

After his internment, Professor Gerhard Bersu—the archaeologist who led his fellow internees on a quest to dig on the hills—returned with his wife to continue their work, this time as a free couple. In conjunction with the Manx Museum, Bersu led excavations on various parts of the island, including Ballakaighen and Balladoole, near Castletown. With no internees left on the island to provide supporting muscle, Bersu persuaded airmen stationed at RAF Jurby to help.

On Monday, November 26, 1945, the military handed Hutchinson's houses back to their owners who, five years earlier, had locked their belongings in the attics and moved out. Local reporters accompanied the residents into the former camp. They arrived at a pleasantly tidy scene. The central garden had been well cared for by internee gardeners, and while the speaker system that linked the houses to a microphone in the commandant's building had been removed, residents discovered that their community had been upgraded with wire heaters, shower-bath units, and cubicles.

The paintings, etchings, sculptures, and murals that had adorned the walls of Hutchinson's houses were all gone—at least it appeared so to the journalists who had been allowed to look for the first time. The only item missing from the official inventory was an old piano, inexplicably disappeared.

FOR BERTHA BRACEY, THE END of the war and the closure of the Nazi concentration camps brought with it new and urgent opportunities to support the unjustly imprisoned. Seven years earlier, she had approached the government with a plan to take in ten thousand refugee children following the events of *Kristallnacht*. Now Bertha and her friend and fellow campaigner Otto Schiff proposed a new scheme to bring to Britain any orphan children, up to the age of sixteen, who had survived their ordeal in Nazi concentration camps.*

There were many calls on the government's funds and attention: POWs had to be returned to Britain, troops redistributed, and provisions made for the wives of servicemen. Sir Alexander Maxwell, permanent undersecretary of state to the Home Office, wrote to the home secretary to say he "would have liked to have avoided any scheme for bringing more refugees into Britain." Maxwell, however, was canny enough to recognize that this was a public relations opportunity, too, especially after the internment scandal.

"Obviously this proposal with reference to children will receive [a lot] of public sympathy," he wrote.

The government duly agreed to Bracey and Schiff's plan, on the proviso that no more than one thousand children came, and that none were suffering from tuberculosis. Admission would be temporary—no more than two years—and the children would stay in hostels until they could re-immigrate to Australia, Palestine, or elsewhere. It was a derisory offer considering the scale of the need, but for Bertha here was a second chance to help children who, for whatever reason, had missed the *Kindertransport* and yet survived the war.

At first, it seemed as if they were too late. Either there were no child survivors, or they had already been taken to other countries that had been quicker to commit to accepting survivors. There was also the question of logistics: How to bring such a large group across the continent quickly? As the weeks progressed, Bracey, progressively aware of the horrors of the concentration camps, became ever more concerned that this dillydallying was extending the suffering of the children who had escaped the death camps only to become lost in administrative limbo.

In the summer of 1945, she accompanied Leonard Montefiore, cofounder of the Wiener Holocaust Library, to the War Office. Using her well-practiced skills of gentle but unyielding persuasion, she

---

* Word of this age restriction somehow reached the survivors at Theresienstadt. When the eighteen-year-old Majer Kochen heard this information, he applied to the Czech government for an identity card using a falsified date of birth that made him eligible for rescue.

and Montefiore convinced the department to place at their disposal ten Lancaster bombers for the task of evacuation. The bomb racks would be removed to provide enough space in the hold for passengers. The timing was serendipitous; the War Office needed to return to Czechoslovakia members of the Czech air force currently stranded in England. The planes could take the men to Prague and there collect a group of orphans, survivors of the notorious Theresienstadt concentration camp, and bring them to England on the return journey.

EVEN THOUGH THE CAMP HAD been liberated by Russian forces weeks earlier, by the time the bombers left England, Theresienstadt still presented a hellish scene. Survivors from closer to the front had been transported here, to join the camp's own emaciated survivors, their domed heads exaggerated by malnourishment, their bodies cold, their striped uniforms roomy, with strips of sack bandaged around their feet with rope as makeshift shoes. The rescuers arrived at a camp in the grip of a typhus epidemic.

"People were dying like so many flies," Moniek Goldberg, one of the children chosen for the rescue flight to England, said. "A lot of people had dysentery and were too weak to use the toilets. We could barely distinguish the living from the dead. But the worst of all was the stench. It was unbearable."

While the Red Cross had arrived quickly to provide food and clothing for survivors, the aid came with risks. Many men who had survived years of deprivation died now from abundance; their bodies were unable to absorb the sudden intake of calories.

The Nazis had established the ghetto on November 24, 1941, as a Jewish settlement for German, Austrian, and Czech Jews over the age of sixty-five, First World War veterans, or well-known cultural or political figures. It had doubled as a transit camp, a holding site for Jews on their way to extermination camps in the east. With thirty-five thousand prisoners at any given time, the ghetto was overcrowded and with ruinous sanitation, an ineffectual water system, and inadequate rations. There were, however, a few similarities between Theresienstadt and Hutchinson.

Just as culture had flourished in Hutchinson, so, too, did Theresienstadt's high density of educated internees result in a discordantly rich cultural output. Artists, poets, philosophers, writers, musicians, professors, and scientists all depicted life in the camp via their chosen mediums. Just as Ahrends and Hinrichsen had organized Hutchison's schedule of lectures, Theresienstadt's prisoners also gave and received more than two thousand lectures on a similarly diverse range of topics. As in Hutchinson, the camp housed a lending library, while actors staged plays and musicians performed pieces, including a rendition of Verdi's *Messa da Requiem*.

Unlike Hutchinson, however, whose cultural life had been broadly facilitated by the pride and benevolence of its commandant, Theresienstadt's intellectual and artistic activity was encouraged for propaganda purposes; the intention was to present a model ghetto, false evidence of the Nazi regime's benevolence toward elderly Jews. When three representatives of the Red Cross toured the camp on June 23, 1944, along a preplanned route, their guides highlighted the camp's cultural activities, while prisoners were briefed on what to say when asked questions by the inspectors. After the inspectors left, the prisoners who had met the delegation were killed to obscure the fiction.

On August 11, 1945, the children who had been selected to go to England—most of whom had lost their families in the Holocaust—took the train from Theresienstadt to Prague on the Dresden–Prague railway line, the same track along which the death trains had rolled just a few months earlier. Stormy weather delayed the planes, so the children moved into the Belgická Street Hostel. Three days later, they lined up in the center of Prague for a farewell photograph, then traveled by bus to Ruzyně Airport in the west of the city.

In the morning light of summer, a group of 305 survivors—including forty girls, thirty younger children, between the ages of three and twelve, and one stowaway—walked across the scorching grass toward the plump, stately bombers that would carry them away.

The children sat on the throbbing floor and ate squares of white bread, some craning to see the countryside ticker away beneath them through the plexiglass bubble of the gun turret. After a brief stop to refuel at an airfield in Holland, when the children were given chocolate and oranges, the plane began its descent to Crosby-on-Eden, a wartime airfield just outside Lancaster.

A thrumming group awaited the children as they exited the planes. As well as Bertha's colleague Leonard Montefiore, there were customs officials, representatives of the Ministry of Health, intelligence officers from MI5, and journalists. Despite the crowd, one of the children described their arrival as "like going from hell to paradise."

The survivors made their way to a temporary camp set up on the Calgarth Estate between Troutbeck Bridge and Lake Windermere. The children had suffered extreme and sustained trauma akin to that experienced by frontline soldiers. One, Harry Olmer, who escaped on the plane by assuming the name of another boy who had dropped out, had seen dozens of men executed in front of him, including one who had been shot next to him in a munitions factory. Not knowing how this trauma would manifest, or how best to care for them, the authorities appointed the psychologist Oscar Friedmann to oversee the children's care.

Friedmann worked at Bloomsbury House alongside Bertha Bracey, and like Peter Midgley, had been sent to a Berlin orphanage at the age of ten. He was working as headmaster of a reformatory school when, just before the war's outbreak, he fled from Germany to Britain. Friedmann believed that the key to recovery was to allow the children as much freedom as possible. There were to be, he ordered, no rules that could not be simply explained. He gained a crucial reputation among his charges of being faithful and fair.

"Friedmann always kept his word," one said.

The psychologist's treatments were not only the result of his professional training and experience. He understood something of what it meant to be taken from one's home and forced to live behind barbed wire in a state of confusion and muddle. In Germany he had spent time in the concentration camp Sachsenhausen, where a guard assaulted him, causing permanent partial paralysis in his face. Friedmann had another experience of captivity, too, a story that he did not share so readily: in the summer of 1940, after he had fled to England, he once again lost his freedom when the police arrested and interned him.

Since April 1933, when she cofounded the Germany Emergency Committee, Bertha Bracey had worked to lift thousands of refugees out of danger, to find jobs and homes for the beleaguered, to improve conditions for the interned, and to support those like Friedmann whom she had helped to help others. Reticent and modest, she lived in obscurity until her death in 1989, the only monument to her work being a sculpture in the courtyard of Friends House, made by Naomi Blake, a Holocaust survivor.

WAR WAS OVER, AND FOR the first time since he was sixteen, Peter Midgley stood in a ruined Berlin and surveyed a city unrecognizable from the one he had fled seven years earlier. Buildings had vanished, monuments lay toppled; the soot and dust of the rubbled city mixed with rainwater to create a black porridge that stuck to the shoes.

The previous month, during his onward march to Berlin, the young artist passed corpses on the sides of the road, human debris that extinguished any last vestige of faith in him. If he had hoped for a reprieve from the devastation when he reached Berlin, he was mistaken. British bombs had transformed the silhouette of a city that had already undergone a profound ethnographic change through the expulsion of most of its Jews. Peter had arrived in May—"back to square one," as he put it—just as the Russian army entered the city. His skill as a translator at Warth Mills had been rewarded with this superior, front-seat posting; in the German capital he was to interpret during political meetings, translate newspapers, and help salvage documents as the Allied forces scrabbled to preserve evidence to be used in future war crime trials.

The scale of the administrative work in the deprived surroundings

of a broken city was massive—especially as control of the cleanup operation was being negotiated by Britain, France, Russia, and the United
States. Yet, in what little free time he had, Peter found opportunity to
tour the haunts of his childhood.

He went, first, to the Schönhauser Allee, site of the Auerbach orphanage, which he had not seen since the morning he left to catch the
train out of the city. The gymnasium where the orphans had run at
the vaulting horse; the coach house at the bottom of the garden when,
during the winter, they had chipped the ice from the basins; the little
synagogue with its treacherous gas tap: all were destroyed and gone.
While the site had been turned to rubble during an Allied bombing
raid in the winter of 1943, the systematic destruction of the orphanage
had begun earlier.

On October 19, 1942, the 21st East Transport carried 959 people
away from the German capital to Riga in Latvia. Among them were
almost sixty Auerbach children, aged between two and sixteen, along
with three of their carers. In the nearby Rumbula forest, SS officers
executed each member of the group. The following month, another
train—the 23rd East Transport—left Berlin. Among the 998 passengers, there were seventy-five children, ranging from ten-month-old ba-
bies to sixteen-year-olds, including the remaining Auerbach children.
This train went to Auschwitz. None survived.[*]

WEARING HIS BRITISH ARMY UNIFORM, Peter next made the journey to
the south of the city to the farmhouse where, seven years earlier, he hid
in his grandfather's housekeeper's cellar. Peter arrived unannounced
at Dahlewitz, which was now under Russian control. He knocked on
the housekeeper's front door without knowing if she was alive or dead.
The door opened, and the pair embraced. The situation was desperate.

* In June 2000, students from the Kurt Schwitters High School in Prenzlauer Berg made pottery
toys in memory of Auerbach's murdered children and arranged them on the low wall in the front
garden. The clay figures—and fragments of those subsequently destroyed by vandals—are held
at the Pankow Museum.

The Russians had taken everything—reparations, as they saw it, for the troubles heaped upon their nation by the German people. When Peter arrived, Elizabeth was frying potatoes in shoe polish.

Valuables Peter had buried in Elizabeth's garden had been found and dug up by locals. The depth of his gratitude and affection, the weight of a debt owed, spurred Peter into action. When he returned to his barracks in the city, Peter applied for leave to return briefly to England to collect food for Elizabeth. When he finally returned, the Russians had taken over East Berlin, and Peter was then unable to travel to Dahlewitz in his uniform. He disguised himself as a farmer and took the train without the requisite passes, setting two accomplices on each door of the carriage to check for guards. Peter made it through and paid his debt.

At every stage in his adult life, Peter Midgley's plans had been obliterated by the torrents of history. Soon everything of which he had dreamed since he was a young boy at the Auerbach would become true. He would be accepted into the Royal College of Art. He would graduate with First Class Honours, the top fine art student in his year, rewarded with the RCA's prestigious Rome scholarship. He would become a professional artist, securing commissions to create works for British government departments including the Ministry of Works and the Ministry of Agriculture and Fisheries, as well as prestigious institutions including Oxford, Warwick, and York Universities, and the Royal Naval base in Faslane, on the Gare Loch.

His work would be exhibited around the world, from the Victoria and Albert Museum in London to the Edinburgh Festival in Scotland, culminating, three decades later, in retrospective exhibitions in his home city, Berlin, and at the Barbican in his adopted city of London.

Peter would become a vivid, energetic, and inspirational teacher, always willing to offer a lift to a student in his Renault 4, in exchange for a packet of cigarettes. Through the channel of his lifelong teaching post at the Beckenham School of Art, he would pass on each of the lessons taught to him by his esteemed patrons at Hutchinson camp to the next generation of British artists, teaching his students how to make and mix paint just how he had been taught by Kurt Schwitters.

"I realised early on just how special he was," one of his former students, Nigel Mac-Fall said. "Peter is probably the most underrated artist in the world."

Another of Peter's students, Graham Stewart, would later stay with Peter and his artist wife, Doreen.

"Tiny, mischievous, with long hair and pronounced glasses, always wearing a dirty brown corduroy jacket with a tin of tobacco in the pocket," he would recall. "He was incredibly energetic and would often shout at us: 'Christ, this is *your life*. You must give yourself totally to art'"—a maxim Graham and his friends would parrot around campus, imitating Peter's accent.

The Midgley household would be warm, welcoming, and bohemian, filled with the intermingled smells of oil paints, cigarette smoke, and hot coffee, a pot of which was always bubbling on the stove. Doreen would exert a calming effect on the excitable Peter, sitting at her easel by the kitchen table at the family house. When she became bored, the paintbrush would meander, and Doreen would start to paint trees and flowers trailing up the wall, just as Schwitters had daubed the hallway of the camp office building.

Peter's art would occupy the front bedroom on the first floor, a favela of brushes, pots, canvases, bits of timber, and shredded newspapers. Art was everywhere. One night, Peter's son Gerald, frustrated at not being listened to, would bang too hard on one of the frosted panes of glass on the communal toilet. The next morning Graham would come downstairs to find the gap had been covered with a photograph, cut from a magazine, of Botticelli's *The Birth of Venus*.

Graham would become a distinguished furniture maker, supplying designs to retailers such as Harrods, John Lewis, and Heal's.

"Peter was," Graham would later say, "the biggest influence on my life."

Before all of this could happen, however, Peter Midgley had one final task to complete in his meandering war story.

He bade goodbye to Elizabeth and to the farmhouse that she would later leave to him in her will and left for Nuremberg.

THE WEEK BEFORE HUTCHINSON'S PROPRIETORS returned to their houses, Peter Midgley arrived as an interpreter for the trial at which the most senior surviving Nazi officers were called to account for their actions in front of an incensed world.

Peter was not the only Old Hutchinsonian present for the trial, which began on November 20, 1945. The cartoonist Joseph Otto Flatter, who had been released from Hutchinson shortly before Christmas 1940 to work for the Ministry of Information, had been eager to attend the trials to sketch, in person, the men whom he had lampooned for the past few years.

"I wanted to see them in the flesh," he said. "I went into a huge hall and saw the accused sitting there like little lambs in two rows. I felt pity for them."

Using binoculars, Flatter observed the accused in the dock. He made quick sketches in the courtroom, which he then used to create more elaborate drawings and watercolors in the evenings.

Peter, in his role as an interpreter, was positioned closer to the action. He could clearly see the face of each Nazi as he walked into the courtroom. The accused had been ranked according to their perceived seniority and entered according to their placement. Thick-set and wax-skinned, Hermann Göring, who had the strongest claim as Hitler's second-in-command, entered the room first. Rudolf Hess was next. Hess, appointed Deputy Führer in 1933, had flown solo to Scotland in 1941 in a brazen attempt to single-handedly negotiate for peace with Britain. After crash-landing on a farm south of Glasgow, he was captured and became the sole internee of Camp Z, the fortified mansion of Mytchett Place in Surrey, before being brought to Nuremberg for the trial. The next man was supposed to have been Robert Ley, the brutal head of the German Labor Front. Ley, however, had managed to hang himself in his cell four weeks earlier.

The fourth man in the pecking order, now promoted to third position, entered the courtroom. The figure was gaunt and looked much older than his fifty-two years. It was, however, unmistakably the person with whom, as a young boy, Peter had played hide-and-seek in the wine cellars of the Kempinski restaurant: the wine seller turned German foreign minister, Joachim von Ribbentrop.*

The hearing lasted almost a year. On October 1, 1946, the judge gave his final ruling that Ribbentrop had assisted in conducting criminal policies, particularly those involving the extermination of the Jews. It was Ribbentrop, for example, who in December 1942 ordered the publication in France of *L'Affaire Grynszpan*, a book about Herschel Grynszpan, the young Jewish boy who had stormed the German embassy in Paris and shot the German diplomat Rath, providing the catalyst for *Kristallnacht*, the Holocaust, and, in a way, the internment of more than twenty thousand Jews in Britain. Ribbentrop's book sought to prove "the Jewish wire pulling behind the assassination aimed at the peace of Europe."

At Nuremberg, the judge concluded that Ribbentrop's participation "in the commission of crimes against peace, war crimes and crimes against humanity was whole-hearted."

Sixteen days later the former wine dealer headed a procession of ten surviving prisoners—including Julius Streicher, the former Nuremberg city councillor whom the mild-mannered Bertha Bracey once described as "appalling"—into the prison gymnasium to be executed by hanging.

"My final wish," Ribbentrop said before the hangman pulled a black hood over his head, "is that Germany should recover her unity, and that, for the sake of peace, there should be understanding between East and West." On the rope, he took ten minutes to die.

* * *

---

* Ribbentrop, considered a fool by many of the co-accused, especially Göring, spoke fluent English and believed that his social connections from his times visiting England as a wine seller and foreign minister, might save him. He attempted to call, as witnesses for his defense, King George VI, the Duke of Windsor, Lord Rothermere, and Prime Minister Winston Churchill. All were denied.

ON MAY 3, 1947, PETER MIDGLEY returned to Britain. Two months later he left the army with the rank of staff sergeant, free at last of war and its cratered aftermath, ready to begin a life much delayed. He visited Echen, who had once again reverted her surname to that of her first husband and, in doing so, scrubbed away her association with Ludwig Warschauer. She had lost her husband and, perhaps, her appetite for love, but she decided to remain in the country that had offered her and her children shelter. In December 1948 she became a British citizen.

Despite a pleading letter to the War Office in which Ludwig Warschauer described repatriation as "against any human right," the government deported Echen's ex-husband in December 1945. While his espionage mission had been exposed in Britain, back in Germany internment provided a robust alibi for his wartime activities. Within a year Warschauer had, according to MI5 files, grifted his way to the position of director of an electrical factory in Hamburg, where he oversaw more than fourteen thousand workers.

Even though Echen's eldest daughter, Anita, was angry at her mother for separating her from another father figure, Echen kept the accusations against Warschauer from her children for the remainder of her life. They never understood why she had chosen to leave a man who had made her so happy.

AFTER HE LEARNED OF HIS wife's death, Kurt Schwitters's health had continued to decline. Poor and poorly, he left London with Wantee and retired to Ambleside in the Lake District, a few short miles from the German Prisoner of War Camp Number Two, at Grizedale Hall. A final-hour professional reprieve came in the form of a thousand-dollar grant from the Museum of Modern Art in New York to re-create his *Merzbau*—the room-sized, sculptural collage of found objects that Schwitters had built in Hanover and that had been destroyed in 1943 during an Allied bombing raid. Representatives for MoMA believed the loss should be recouped for history.

An ecstatic Schwitters found a disused barn, formerly used to store gunpowder, and began to fill it with pieces of rope and string, bottles, shells, bits of wood, a child's ball, and a watering can nozzle, much as he had with his attic room in Hutchinson. The artist worked quickly, as if straining to meet a deadline. Then, midway through production, deteriorating health confined Schwitters to bed. He died on January 8, 1948, before the work was finished.

Schwitters received a brief obituary in the local paper, below a story about two dogs that had died during a foxhunt. On the day of his funeral, the village policeman called with the news that his application for naturalization had been successful: Kurt Schwitters was now officially a British citizen. National acceptance was accompanied by a local rejection: the vicar of the church where Schwitters was to be buried denied the artist's final request to mark his grave with one of his sculptures. To do so would be unseemly, the vicar said.

Three years earlier in London, the poet Joyce Parker (who would later marry the dream-haunted Hutchinson artist Erich Kahn) spent a day with Schwitters and Wantee walking along the Thames towpath. At one point, the three of them entered a church, where Schwitters solemnly kissed Wantee.

"His devotion to her was at all times strongly marked, invested with a charming dignity, quite beautiful to see," Joyce later wrote.

As the trio continued along the path, Schwitters recited his poems, just as he had done in the Artists Café and the new hall at Hutchinson.

"When I am dead," he said unexpectedly, "I shall be famous, and my work will fetch great prices."

It was some years before his defiant prophecy came true. When Schwitters's name finally rose in prominence and eminence, a landlady on the island discovered a set of drawings scrawled beneath the wallpaper on the dining room wall. Even though the property was in Peel, on the opposite side of the island to where Schwitters had been interned, the owner claimed that the images had surely been drawn by Hutchinson's most celebrated artist.

"While Waldrick House stands," a local journalist who clearly knew little about Schwitters, his work, or, indeed, basic fact-checking, wrote of the dubious discovery, "an island link remains with the German artist who . . . plagued society with his theories and died unrepentant and unforgiven in isolation."

The building that truly represented a physical link between Hutchinson's artists and the island—the new hall erected in Hutchinson Square in the autumn of 1940, where countless plays and cabarets had been staged, music performed, religious ceremonies held, and, in the case of Schwitters's poetry recitals, saucers broken—did not stand for long.

The permanent residents of Hutchinson Square had little use for the modest-size playhouse that stood among their homes. On April 26, 1946, the building was put up for auction. The "brick-built Concert Hall," as the lot was described, would never again serve its intended purpose: it was listed on the condition the buyer tear the structure down within two months of purchase. So, in the summer of 1946, the bricks toppled, removing the only physical evidence that Hutchinson Square had, for a time, been home to the most unlikely, extraordinary collection of captives ever assembled.

POSTSCRIPT

AT LEAST TWO THOUSAND MEN were imprisoned at Hutchinson between the day of the camp's opening on July 13, 1940, and its closure. Most of the prisoners were classified by the British government as refugees from Nazi oppression who had come to Britain seeking sanctuary, only to be imprisoned as objects of feverish suspicion.

The perversion of the episode was revealed when thousands of these men joined the British army to fight Hitler after, in 1942, the government allowed former internees to transfer to fighting units—among others, the Special Air Service, the Commandos, the Special Operations Executive, the Royal Navy, the Royal Armoured Corps, the Royal Artillery, and the Parachute Regiment. Many Hutchinsonians were among the four thousand internees who joined the Pioneer Corps direct from internment camps and participated in the Normandy landings in June 1944, including Herbert Weil from House 3,[*] and his friend Hans Arenstein, who had come to Britain on a *Kindertransport* and later died while attached to 47 Royal Marine Commando.

Those who were too old or too infirm to fight found other ways to contribute. The Hutchinson optician Horst Archenhold designed the

---

[*] Weil's blazing life trajectory would take him from the beaches of Normandy, into the British security services and, finally, the West German diplomatic corps, where he became a friend of the future US president John F. Kennedy.

periscope that was used to turn the Duplex Drive Sherman tanks into amphibious craft on D-Day. Joseph Otto Flatter produced cartoons for Ministry of Defense propaganda leaflets, more than two billion of which were dropped over Germany as part of a campaign to sow discouragement and dissent among enemy troops ("I saw my cartoons as substitutes for bombs and shells," he said). Former Hutchinsonians focused their energies on reconciliation and peacemaking, too. Dr. Arthur Bratu, who ran Hutchinson's Cercle Française, worked as a public prosecutor in the postwar de-Nazification process. The Ministry of Information enrolled Dr. Walter Zander, the writer who drew musical staves for the depressed conductor Leo Wurmser, to tour Britain and educate servicemen about anti-Semitism.

In the decades that followed, many Hutchinson alumni made substantial contributions to British culture, which was shaped in meaningful ways by those artists and thinkers, architects and musicians who had escaped to Britain. An astonishing number of those whom Britain interned as "enemy aliens" remained in Britain after the war, including Eduardo Paolozzi, a father of British pop art, the Nobel Prize winner Max Perutz, the international judge Sir Michael Kerr, the conductor Peter Gellhorn, and the violinist Norbert Brainin, who was a founding member of the Amadeus Quartet, three of whose four members met while interned on the island.

Former internees helped to cosmopolitanize and professionalize the arts, establishing key commercial art galleries and theaters, or becoming leading members of the graphic design, advertising, publishing, and architectural industries. Their presence exploded the conservatism of visual arts that Schwitters identified in Britain following the First World War—a "torpid period," according to the art historian Edward Lucie-Smith. Exhibitions staged by émigré artists, including many from Hutchinson, influenced Henry Moore, Ben Nicholson, Francis Bacon, and, later, Howard Hodgkin, David Hockney, and Peter Blake.

Artists including Hellmuth Weissenborn and Peter Midgley influenced new generations of British artists via their teaching posts at prominent art schools. And while Bruno Ahrends, modernist architect and instigator and curator of the camp's Cultural Department, died three years after the end of the war, his legacy also endured. Both his son Steffan and grandson Peter followed him into the profession. As cofounder of the celebrated practice Ahrends, Burton and Koralek, Peter designed buildings for Oxford University, Trinity College Dublin, the British embassy in Moscow and, most notoriously, the proposed extension to the National Gallery building on London's South Bank, which Prince Charles famously described as a "monstrous carbuncle." From the Glyndebourne Opera House to the Edinburgh Festival, the contributions of these and hundreds of other former internees, many of whom were asylum seekers, continued to pay dividends beyond the frame of their lifetimes.

TOTALITARIAN RULE HAD, IN ITS accelerating phases, turned the men into outsiders, a status that internment then underscored. Embarrassed by their accents, their names, their history, these men sought to integrate and assimilate as quickly as possible following release, many changing their names to British variants. Otto Patriasz, a printer interned in Hutchinson, adopted the rhythmically pleasing name Oliver Pond; Rudolf Stensch became Ronald Stent; Karl Gebhardt, who, miserably, shared a name with the Nazi doctor who performed surgical experiments on inmates at Ravensbrück and Auschwitz, became the upstanding Charles Sheppard.

The incentive to move on and settle into new lives in Britain had, however, a suppressive effect. In his autobiography, *The Making of an Englishman*—a title that betrays the refugee's pursuit of belonging—Fred Uhlman dedicated only a brief section to internment. On the whole the men left their stories untold. In December 1941, a play based on an island internment camp titled *Eine Reisen nach Castralien*—A Trip to Castralia—was performed in London for the benefit of internees. Set on the fictional island of Castralia, it featured a tribe classified as "homo detained." "The population," as the Austrian refugee paper *Zeitspiegel* described the production, "practices the arts and sciences, especially drawing and poetry." Other than the author Richard Frie-

denthal's 1956 German-language novel *Die Welt in der Nussschale*—
The World in a Nutshell—the play is the only known creative work
based specifically on Hutchinson camp.

To further obscure their past, many internees only mentioned the
events they had experienced while in the company of others who had
also been there. A line from Schwitters's "*Ursonate*" poem became a
shibbolethic phrase, spoken between former internees as a means of
identification.

One greeter said: "*Lanke trr gll . . .*"

The other responded: "*Pe pe pe pe*," "*Zuuka*" or "*Ooka*."

DESPITE THE ADVERSE PHYSICAL AND psychological conditions, many of
those interned at Hutchinson cherished the memories formed during
those strange, emotionally chaotic months behind the wire. The camp
revealed not only the indomitability of the human spirit, but also the
artistic urge for expression in any circumstances. By the end of 1941,
Hutchinson's internees had produced galleries' worth of artworks.

Internment was a leveler. The professor brushed his teeth alongside the student, the archaeologist broke ground beside the farmhand.
Distinctions of class and education were not wholly eradicated, but
their effects were diminished, and, for a moment, worlds collided and,
in that collision, produced unexpected sparks. Even at the moment of a
captive's release, there was an awareness among internees that, regardless of the painful events that brought them into the camp, Hutchinson
might represent a valuable chapter in the life of each man. When the
painter Erich Kahn walked free, the other Hutchinson artists gifted to
him the following lines:

> Now, when you leave the barbed wire
> The slave returns to be a Squire
> You furious entered—don't be impenitent
> For here it was that you grew eminent.

There were certainly some professional benefits to being a Hutchinson alumnus. Enduring professional relationships were formed at the camp; the art dealer Siegfried Oppenheimer would represent Erich Kahn, while writers such as *The Camp*'s first editor Michel Corvin (a.k.a. Leo Freund) and Ronald Stent later wrote books, whose publications were facilitated by men befriended in internment—Hellmuth Weissenborn, who established Acorn Press, and André Deutsch, founder of his eponymous publishing house, respectively.

The tightly woven community that formed in the Artists Café endured, too. Long after the war had ended, former members congregated once or twice a month at the Maison Bertaux café in London's Soho or at Paul Hamann's studio in St. John's Wood, to reminisce. Some kept drawings and paintings by their friends and colleagues on the walls of their homes, an intimate reminder of the unlikely fruits of their time in captivity.

Years later, Klaus Hinrichsen wondered whether internment had inspired artistic work that would not have otherwise existed. He concluded that, without Hutchinson, Uhlman would never have settled upon the powerful image of the child with the balloon had he not been separated from his daughter at her birth. Neither could Kahn have produced "drawing after fearful drawing" foreseeing the Holocaust "had he not daily watched groups of depressed and defeated men huddled together on the camp lawn," nor Ahrends create his utopian plans to reshape the Isle of Man with futuristic glassed high-rise blocks and hotels.

In a letter to friends, Ludwig Meidner wrote that he had "never produced such vivid portraits" as during his internment. For Kurt Schwitters, Hinrichsen concluded that "internment sent him on a new phase in his abstract work."

"And for one nineteen-year-old boy," Hinrichsen added, "his time in Hutchinson determined his later life. His childhood ambition had been to become an artist . . . and Hutchinson gave him that chance." Without internment, Peter Fleischmann would not have learned how to mix and make paints from Schwitters, how to judge perspective from Weissenborn, or how to create sculptures from Paul Hamann.

His time in Hutchinson seeded in him an indefatigable love of art and a belief in its capacity to liberate the human spirit.

"All the good things that have happened to me, happened as a result of my being here," he maintained to the end of his life. It was a judgment shared by his friends and fellow internees. After Peter died in 1991, at the age of sixty-nine, Klaus Hinrichsen delivered the following judgment in his eulogy: "Through his art, Peter overcame the trauma of his youth and rose above his misfortunes." Without Hutchinson, Peter Fleischmann would likely not have become Peter Midgley, Royal Academician.

THE ARTISTIC, LITERARY, AND EDUCATIONAL activities that defined life in Hutchinson were common to most of the British internment camps, although nowhere else matched the heights of quality, output, and organization found on and around "P" camp's square. While anyone was welcome to engage in lectures or artistic pursuits, regardless of class or profession—"It didn't matter if someone was working class or not, as long as he was able to talk about poetry or knew about Shakespeare," as Uhlman put it—not everyone participated.

There were those who would endlessly play cards or poker, or smoke cigars without moving "until the next batch of food parcels arrived." Those who chose to participate were richly rewarded, however. Hellmuth Weissenborn considered it a "miracle of human willpower" how quickly the camp had metamorphosed into a kind of university, one that was, in Uhlman's estimation, "the best . . . I had ever attended."

Hutchinson's cultural life made it easier to bear the loss of liberty, not only for those individuals who were already established in their craft, but also for those who participated and discovered hitherto unknown talents or who developed new interests. There was a utilitarian function to the activities, which helped maintain not only participants' morale, but also their dignity. The cultural program served as a useful diversion, too. Hinrichsen, despite his pride in having witnessed the cultural awakening at Hutchinson, did not lose sight of the primary purpose of "all these frantic activities." They were "a means of distraction from the ever-present anger . . . worry . . . and suffering."

Despite the unexpected advantages that internment gave him, the master engraver Hellmuth Weissenborn described his time in Hutchinson as "a continuous torment." In a letter to his parents, Hellmuth Mirauer—a medical student and member of the Hutchinson theater group—described the government's internment policy as "stupid, dangerous and horrible" and asserted that, through the episode, he had sustained "damage that was not to be repaired."

Few went as far as one former internee, who classed the British policy of internment as a "war crime," but it is indisputable that the hasty measures meted unhappiness and anguish upon thousands of people already navigating the ordeal of fleeing their previous lives in Germany, even, for some, to the point of suicide. By December 1943, when surviving official records appear to end, no fewer than seventy-one internees had died in British camps and a further forty in Canadian and Australian camps, either by their own hand, due to ill-health, or from the physical stress of transport. Fifty-six of these deaths had occurred on the Isle of Man.

As Bertha Bracey's colleague Margaret Collyer, who moved into the women's camp on the island, later put it: "The beautiful weather and . . . the gay face of things . . . hardly suggested what lay behind: keen personal anxiety about relatives, the sense of injury at suddenly being interned, the renewed sense of insecurity, the incompatibility of . . . Jews and Nazis, lack of money, possessions and work."

And while Peter Midgley's life was transformed by the people he met during internment, the episode also triggered feelings of rejection and abandonment that haunted his dreams throughout his life. Once or twice a year he would experience the same recurring nightmare: he was back in the camp; everyone around him was released until, finally, Peter was the last one there, permanently forsaken.

* * *

THERE WAS NO UNIFIED EXPERIENCE of internment, neither generally nor in Hutchinson specifically. Attitudes toward internment
differed between individuals according to their age, temperament, life-
experience, friendships (or lack thereof) in the camp, and the extent of
their investment in outside society.

While Klaus Hinrichsen kept detailed accounts of his time in
Hutchinson, he was only one young man among a large and diverse
population, and his experience was neither universal nor omniscient.
Neither were his views even consistent. During internment, the letters
Hinrichsen wrote to his fiancée, Gretel, bristle with anger and frustration (some of which was directed at the woman who became his wife,
whose "interference" in petitioning the authorities on Hinrichsen's behalf threatened, he feared, his chances of release). In later years, however,
most of what Hinrichsen wrote about his time in Hutchinson glows with
obvious pleasure at having been there, in the camp where it happened.
Hinrichsen was not the only person whose perspective changed.

"In retrospect the proportions shift," wrote the journalist Hans
Jaeger. "The happy ending casts its conciliatory light on everything
which once appeared black . . . [O]ne stops debating the question of
whether it was all necessary."

In a 1945 letter the Oxford academic Paul Jacobsthal described
his time at Hutchinson as "a quiet pleasant episode," a summary that
sharply contrasts with one diary entry written inside the camp that
flatly classed his internment as "a trauma." The drawings Uhlman
produced in Hutchinson offer another unvarnished representation
of an internee's state of mind at the time. Dark skies, ruined buildings, a child hanging from gallows, skeletal figures rowing across a
stormy sea: motifs of the crestfallen. Likewise, Uhlman's diary, written within the camp, is filled with terse accounts of dark days (October 1: "Bad day. Grey Sky. Fear of Winter"; October 11: "Full of
anxiety"; October 19: "Constant depression"; December 17: "Appalling day").

By 1979, however, Uhlman's view had considerably softened.
"Looking back, one shouldn't have been so depressed," he said.

"One should have realised there was a war and that we were in some ways privileged even . . . Compared to the suffering of other people, it was marvellous."

With hindsight, many of Hutchinson's internees recognized that they had been comfortable and safe and, apart from the criminal abuses experienced at Warth Mills, their generally good treatment meant the injustice of the British internment camps could be set in benign contrast to the appalling reality of the Nazi concentration camps—the full details of which only began to emerge after war's end. The internment measures were, after all, motivated by fear, not hatred.

For most of the island's internees, faced with the postwar revelations of the Shoah, their own suffering became relative. It was unbecoming to complain about a brief spell in an internment camp when one's friends and family members had been marched into extinction. Inevitably, there was survivor's guilt. Uhlman later learned that both his parents had died in the lethal chambers of Theresienstadt, while, on the way to Auschwitz, his sister killed herself and her baby.[*] Time plus revelation brought perspective; Uhlman's view of his personal torment was forced to soften.

THE ASSESSMENT OF INTERNMENT SHOULD not only be measured by comparison to the Holocaust, however. Every government must balance its humanitarian obligations with the need to uphold national security. To categorize refugees of Nazi oppression as "enemy aliens," however, was to invite populist scorn and hatred on those in most need of compassion in wartime, and represented a moral failing at a national scale. When, on May 29, 1940, the MP Reginald Sorensen asked what percentage of refugees from Nazi oppression were known to have committed hostile acts, a government spokesman was forced to admit there had not been a single incident by any enemy alien proved by any court of law. To systematically alienate the vulnerable in both law and

---

[*] The trauma of this news was further deepened by the fact that Fred, believing that his mother would ruin married life, had offered to help his parents emigrate to any country except England. It's England or nowhere, Fred's father had replied portentously.

language represents a black mark—a "bespattered page," as Major Cazalet described it at the time—on Britain's war record.

Many internees struggled to find work after their release, employers being reluctant to take a chance on men and women whom the state had seen fit to intern—this despite the government's insistence that there should be no stigma attached to having been interned. And the twin traumas of exile and internment had more lasting negative effects as well. Erich Kahn, once described by the eminent art critic Professor J. P. Hodin as "undoubtedly one of the best artists in the country," was unable to recover his early promise and languished in obscurity, a leading emblem of the so-called lost generation of early twentieth-century European artists. He was certainly not the only interned artist to fail to fully reach his full potential and impact.

For Hutchinson's jailors the years on the island held different kinds of memories and effects. Captain Jurgensen returned to London after the war and joined the post office. He was employed there when, in 1947, he became a British citizen. The following year, on March 19, 1948, a notice appeared in the *London Gazette* to announce that Captain Jurgensen of the Intelligence Corps had been awarded the King Haakon VII Liberty Medal.

There was no such recognition for Hutchinson's commandant, Hubert Daniel, who on September 30, 1947, received a letter from the War Office that stated: "There is no alternative but to relegate you to unemployment." For Daniel, the years spent on the island (where, in 1945 he was appointed second-in-command of all island camps and, the following year, assumed the top position) represented a high point that his life's trajectory would never again match. He died, at sixty-four, on New Year's Eve, 1955. A short obituary in the *West Sussex Gazette* did not mention his time on the Isle of Man, only stating that he was a member of the cricket club, the flower show committee, and "was always ready to help in any way he could."

This tribute, terse and vanilla, would nonetheless have resonated with the artists of Hutchinson camp, who would never forget the kindness shown to them by this smiling, pink-nosed advertising executive.

In 1941, before the last artist left Hutchinson camp, the group presented Daniel with a folder of mounted artworks, each one created
in the camp. It included pieces by Georg Ehrlich, Hermann Fechenbach, Paul Hamann, Erich Kahn, Ernst Müller-Blensdorf, Fred Uhlman, Hellmuth Weissenborn, and others. Kurt Schwitters provided
the front cover, an uncharacteristically sentimental watercolor of the
camp, a tribute to the commandant who had provided space, materials, and encouragement to his artists and who was, as his regrettable
relationship with Warschauer revealed, openhearted to a fault.

Merlin Scott, the young second lieutenant whose eyewitness account of the appalling treatment of internees boarding the HMT
Dunera saved many Italians, Germans, and Austrians from deportation, was killed at Halfaya on May 9, 1941, during the first British
advance into Libya. That day, at least five internees from Hutchinson
walked free, thanks in part to Scott's letter.

THE GENERAL RELUCTANCE OF INTERNEES to pronounce or denounce
their experiences led to a benign whitewashing that has broadly kept
the internment episode obscured from mainstream historiography.
So, too, has the attitude of successive governments, which have never
apologized for the state's treatment of the internees, for the pain and
appalling hardship its policies brought to their families, or for the
events that led to the foreseeable tragedy of the *Arandora Star*, a
shipping disaster with one of the gravest losses of life of the Second
World War.

Only a single sentence spoken by Sir John Anderson in the House
of Commons on August 22, 1940, months before most of Hutchinson's
internees were set free, provided something approaching a mea culpa:
"Regrettable and deplorable things have happened," he said, as if the
cruelties of internment had been the result of natural phenomena, and
not a series of deliberate, misguided choices.

The muddle and cruelty of the internment episode complicates
and upsets the prevailing historical narrative of Britain's role in the

Second World War: a united, courageous nation fighting a just war to defend the persecuted. Perhaps, for this reason, historical research into internment has been handicapped by a culture of secrecy around government documents relating to the episode. While some of the material relating to internment has been released, even today access to some documents is severely restricted, while other papers have supposedly been lost or destroyed—factors that have kept internment separate from the dominant history.

"Injustices have been committed that can never be repaired," claimed one letter, printed in the *Spectator* in August 1940. There has been no attempt to repair the damage by the British authorities. By contrast, in May 2021 the Canadian prime minister, Justin Trudeau, issued a formal apology to the thirty-two thousand Italian Canadians declared "enemy aliens" during the Second World War—six hundred of whom were sent to internment camps.

"Hundreds of Italian-Canadians were interned for the simple reason that they were of Italian heritage," the MP Angelo Iacono told the Canadian Commons. "Parents were taken away from their homes, leaving children without their fathers in many cases and families without a pay-cheque to put food on their tables. Lives and careers, businesses and reputations were interrupted and ruined, and yet no one was held responsible."

No equivalent apology has been made by the British for failing to distinguish between refugees and "enemy aliens" (a dehumanizing term that, in 2021, the US government pledged never again to use): an administrative decision that heaped fresh misery and suffering on individuals and families who had already lost so much.

TO OVERLOOK THE STORY IS to overlook the desolate sense of injustice and loss imposed on tens of thousands of innocent men and women, and to ignore the banal and enduring structures of cruelty and indifference that continue to affect the lives of those seeking refuge and asylum. The British government may no longer use the term "intern-ment," but during the two Gulf Wars and the nebulous "War on Terror," Britain exercised its right to hold individuals without trial merely on suspicion that they might attempt to assist the enemy.

Stateless or undocumented people arriving in Britain are today subject to immigration detention while their cases are considered. Un-like most other European countries, there is no time limit on immi-gration detention in the UK. According to government figures, half of the twenty-four thousand people detained in this way each year come claiming refuge from persecution. A 2019 *Guardian* report found that child refugees were "suffering abuse due to the Home Office and local authorities wrongly classifying them as adults," the same misclassifica-tion that led to the internment of scores of children in adult camps in 1940, a situation that the writer François Lafitte described at the time as "monstrously unjust."

On the US border, former president Donald Trump instituted internment camps for undocumented immigrants. At any given time between May and June 2019, more than two thousand children, sepa-rated from their parents, were being held in the custody of US Border Patrol. The internees were not given enough food or provided with soap or toothbrushes, and often went days in overcrowded conditions without showering.

The battle between a nation's responsibility to help those in need and to maintain national security persists in every age, every genera-tion. The tension between the practical requirement to control borders and the moral imperative to offer sanctuary to those in need still sits at the heart of the political situation in Britain, North America, and elsewhere. The notion of the refugee who is not who he or she claims is an enduring story that can be easily co-opted and used to justify in-stitutional cruelty or overreach. So, while the context and detail shifts, the debate remains the same, as does the potential for history to repeat as each successive generation must answer the same question: How far can we go in the rightful defense of our values, without abandoning them along the way?

"I often ask myself if it could happen again," said Claus Moser, an internee on the island who went on to be the British government's chief statistician.

> The nice answer is: "Good god no." But I think it could. Not exactly in the same circumstances . . . But I was in White-hall for ten years and occasionally [civil servants] are forced into crude, panicked emergency measures that have not been prepared adequately. Politicians get terribly worked up with the crisis of the moment, which they hadn't thought about before . . . it could happen again.

AFTERWORD

ONE SPRING A FEW YEARS ago, I was leafing through a beige folder in
the monastically hushed reading room at the National Archives in south
London, in search of a story. I had recently finished writing a book about
a group of young women who, from a secret bunker in Liverpool, used a
war game to revolutionize British tactics in the fight against the German
U-boats. Their unacknowledged work had contributed to the decisive vic-
tory in the crucial Battle of the Atlantic.

I am a journalist, not a military historian, and my primary interest in that story had to do with the revelatory power of games, not the
harrowing business of conflict. Still, having spent so much time in the
company of these combatants, I had U-boats on the brain.

In March 1941, the Royal Navy captured Otto Kretschmer, the
most famous of the U-boat aces. Kretschmer and his crew were taken
to a prisoner of war camp in the Lake District (a few miles, I would
later discover, from where Kurt Schwitters saw out his final days): a
converted stately home called Grizedale Hall. So many captured German sailors were sent to Grizedale Hall that the house became known
to locals as the U-boat Hotel. It became the site of various escape attempts, and other little-known dramas and shenanigans.

The image of a grand English house overrun with German prisoners of war captured my attention. I imagined the atmosphere to be

like *Downton Abbey*, but with Nazis. It is a compelling juxtaposition, but what was the greater story here? I had come to the National Archives to research British prisoner of war camps, not only Grizedale Hall but also less picturesque venues like Warth Mills, in search of an answer.

The wartime folder was filled with correspondence concerning the administrative difficulties involved in moving POWs between camps in order to ensure the die-hard Nazis were kept separate from ordinary soldiers. Essential, boring war stuff.

I turned a page and straightened. Tucked in the middle of the sheaf, possibly misfiled, was the front page of what looked like a homemade newspaper—the fourth issue, I would later discover, of *The Camp*. Set against the clerical letters and tables elsewhere in the folder, the document was highly arresting. There were hand-drawn illustrations, excitable write-ups of musical concerts and theatrical performances, a long and vivid description of the experience of visiting the camp's post office ("You are treated like a long lost and now happily returned brother, but there is no hurry . . ."), and an advertisement that implored readers to enroll in something called a "Technical School." The text was written in English, and while it appeared to have been produced by wartime prisoners, it included an exhortation from the editor to "tell everybody that you hate the Nazis." *What?*

A cover letter, written by a British army officer named Captain Daniel, accompanied the document. Daniel, it transpired, was the commandant of the men in the camp that had produced the newspaper. Far from being wary of his charges, in his letter Daniel appeared proud of them and their accomplishments. There followed a second letter, written by a woman named Bertha Bracey, calling for an exhibition of artwork produced by the men who were, her letter revealed, prisoners on the Isle of Man.

Like many people, I was only vaguely aware of the fact that Britain had interned German and Austrians during the Second World War. Unlike the wartime internment of Japanese Americans in the United States, which is an episode of ongoing mainstream debate and lament, the British internment of "enemy aliens" (I resist the term, hence the accusatory quotation marks) has been diligently kept separate from the prevailing story Britain tells itself about its wartime character.

The Camp newspaper appeared to offer a window into an unfamiliar, alternate history of the war, where the supposed villains were the victims, and the supposed heroes the perpetrators. The document set me on a new path, not only to learn everything about this hushed world, but also to discover a story, a person, who might compel me through the subject.

PETER MIDGLEY WAS NEITHER THE most famous person interned at Hutchinson camp nor the most obvious candidate for a protagonist. I was, however, drawn to his story: his childhood, his escape from Berlin, the way in which the established artists at the camp took him into their care, trained him, and helped free him. Peter's story appeared to illuminate the wider subject in helpful ways. Orphaned by the Nazis, rescued on the *Kindertransport*, and deemed by one of the most senior judges in Britain to pose no threat to national security, only to be arrested and interned for eighteen months, his story exemplified the inconsistencies of the government's policy making.

His story also presented a number of compelling contradictions: not only did Peter create art that emerged from his suffering, but through the episode he also discovered a calling, a career, arguably a life's work. That internment was, for him, both a blessing and an impediment pulled me away from the gravitational force of a trite conclusion. Peter's personal story is morally complex, much like the broader story of internment.

There is also an alluring unresolvedness here: all those aching, gaping questions about his parents. Take, for example, this exchange, from an interview in 1978 (part of an oral history project to preserve wartime stories): the only surviving record in which Peter speaks about his early life.

Interviewer: Your father was a socialist editor . . .

Peter: Writer. Let's make it general.

Interviewer: What happened to him and your family?

Peter: I don't know. I don't know. I can only go by hearsay, what I was told. The family had a motor crash during a holiday and everyone in the car died. That's his brother, who ran the paper, *Die Freie Meinung*, and himself, and whoever else was in the car. I don't quite know.

Interviewer: What year was this?

Peter: I don't know. I have no records because I was brought up in an orphanage–cum–boarding school. The information I have from my uncle in Manchester, or my aunt, is conflicting . . . So, I don't know.

Such looming question marks can cast a shadow across the entire span of a life. In one sense, the fact that Peter, a Jew living in Nazi Germany, lost his family is unremarkable, almost a cliché. But not knowing when or how they died? Or who they were with? Or whose story, really, to believe? It's one thing to have been made an orphan; it's another to not know how. Peter died with these questions unresolved. Might it still be possible to discover the truth? I wanted to know.

I contacted Peter's son, Gerald, a distinguished academic at the University of Hull. Over a period of several months, Gerald—who speaks with a gentle South London accent, and is ceaselessly patient—answered my deluge of questions and clarifications.

Gerald and his wife, Wendy, both have excellent recall, and, helpfully, a box of documents relating to Peter's life, including the original letter written by Hutchinson's artists seeking a place for him in art school. Still, neither could add anything to Peter's own account of what happened to his parents, Moritz and Alice: they had died in a car accident at Lake Wannsee while traveling with Peter's uncle Hugo, who was editor of an anti-Nazi newspaper. Due to the suspicious circumstances, it was assumed, they told me, that the car had been tampered with.

Road traffic accidents are not necessarily newsworthy, *per se*, but a car that topples into Berlin's most famous lake, resulting in the drowning of all its occupants? Surely such a thing would have been covered by the local, if not national press? Without any clear dates to confine the search, however, the task of sifting through thousands of newspaper editions, especially during such a turbulent period for the German press, posed a major challenge.

I had the title of the Breslau-based newspaper for which Peter's father, Moritz, supposedly wrote and his uncle Hugo supposedly edited, at least. *Die Freie Meinung*—the Free Opinion—which claimed to be the "largest political weekly newspaper of the east." If a suspicious car crash wiped out half of the paper's staff, surely the incident would have been reported in its pages?

Happily, the University of Wrocław holds a copy of every issue in its archives, from the first one, published on January 11, 1919, to the last one published, on December 24, 1931. Might it be possible to sift through the thousands of lines of gothic black German text, twelve years' worth of journalism, in search of a mention of a car crash?

There was an immediate issue, however. Neither Peter's father, Moritz, nor his uncle Hugo were named on the masthead, the place where a print publication lists its staff and their roles. Instead, the editor was a man called Hans Hanteda-Fleischmann. This was a new name, one that did not feature anywhere on the Fleischmann family tree that I had begun to piece together. Was the entire story a fabrication?

I ran a name search for "Hans Hanteda-Fleischmann" in a German newspaper archive. A hit came back in an article from a 1922 edition of a rival paper, *Breslauer Nachtpost*. The article was a hit piece written by Breslau's city councillor, Max Gruschwitz. In it Gruschwitz accused Hans Hanteda-Fleischmann of slandering him via a defamatory article published in *Die Freie Meinung*.

"Hans Hanteda," Gruschwitz noted in the piece, "was a pseudonym. The editor's real name? Hugo Fleischmann.

Having confirmed that Peter's uncle did edit Breslau's most salacious newspaper, I began to search the masthead of each weekly edition. If the story about the crash at the lake was true, then Hans Hanteda's name must have disappeared as editor of the paper at the same time.

It took a few hours to locate the moment when the newspaper's editorship changed: October 18, 1930. I didn't have to look far for the reason. The story had made the front page:

HANS HANTEDA-FLEISCHMANN KILLED IN AN ACCIDENT

Hanteda-Fleischmann is no more: on Wednesday 15th of this month, he died on his way to the Riesengebirge [the Giant Mountains], where he had intended to relax for a few days with a friend. The driver of the car lost control of the vehicle at a dangerous bend near the village of Nimmersatt . . . The car rolled over twice. Hans Hanteda-Fleischmann was so severely injured that he lost his life at 11pm that night.

If this was the accident that Peter had been told about from a young age, all of the details were different. The crash had occurred not in Germany, but in Poland. Hugo had been with a friend, not his wife. Crucially, Peter's parents were not present at all.

I checked the following week's edition of the paper for a follow-up story, with some more details. There, on the front page, was a full obituary, complete with a photograph of Hans and a note from his widow, Marie.

Peter had been lied to. His parents had not died in a car crash—or, at least, not alongside his uncle, who definitely *did* die in a car crash.

I ordered copies of any documents the German government held on Moritz and Alice Fleischmann. Set within the context of all this intrigue, any basic information about the couple's births, marriage, and deaths could help dredge the true story of what had happened.

When copies of the documents arrived, the information therein only compounded the tragedy. Moritz and Alice had been married on

February 25, 1920. The following year, Alice gave birth to their only child, Peter. Within six weeks the couple were divorced. Alice suffered from mental illness and died, probably from suicide, shortly thereafter. Moritz, either unwilling or unable to care for Peter alone, left his son with his ex-father-in-law, Alfred, who became Peter's primary carer. For Alfred it must have been kinder and easier to tell a young boy that his parents had died in an accident.

When Peter Fleischmann fled Berlin on December 1, 1939, not only was his father alive, he was also living in Berlin. City records show that, at that time, Moritz resided on Strassburger Strasse, a five-minute drive from the Auerbach orphanage. When Peter arrived in England he was not, as he had been led to believe throughout his life, an orphan. But when he returned to Berlin as a soldier in 1945, things had again changed. On March 2, 1943, Moritz was taken to the Auschwitz concentration camp and murdered. Peter died knowing an incorrect version of the truth, but the truth nonetheless: his father had been killed by the Nazis.

Would it have been better to know the truth, or worse? Perhaps it would have made no difference at all. These were, after all, stories about ghosts, people who had never been there for Peter. Those who were—his grandfather, his grandfather's housekeeper, the Auerbach's directors, Donald Midgley, Kurt Schwitters, Helen Roeder—had each stepped into the parental void and played their role. Changing the story about his parents wouldn't have changed any of the things that had enabled Peter to survive his ordeal or to thrive regardless.

PETER WAS JUST ONE INDIVIDUAL in a camp that, at its most populous, numbered more than twelve hundred captives, each with his own history and legacy. And Hutchinson was just one of dozens of camps around Britain, Canada, and Australia; the combined total of internees stretched into the tens of thousands (Peter Fleischmann was not even the only Peter Fleischmann interned on the Isle of Man). As much as I had come to adore Peter, it seemed unfair that so many men might go unacknowledged in a book about the camp.

As I read the various accounts of life in Hutchinson, pored over issues of *The Camp* and the cultural schedules, and tracked down letters, I began to compile a list of the names of men who had been there. At first, I was mainly interested in finding the eminent individuals who had been at the camp, men whose achievements made a mockery of their internment. Every new and verified discovery of a noted professor, a celebrated musician, an influential lawmaker, or a feted artist bolstered my central argument against the government's policy and validated the book's title.

In time, however, I found the names of, to borrow a politician's term, "ordinary men"—people neither famous nor feted, but no less deserving of justice. The project evolved into something else, something that felt mission-like, and that began to border on an obsession.

In my mind I saw Hutchinson's population facing me as a vast crowd. Most of the men's faces were blanked out. My task, as I now saw it, was to reveal those faces, or at least pull from obscurity their names, their dates of birth, and occupations. Each night, after my writing was done, I'd start to work through the Home Office database of internee cards, hunting for evidence of alumni. The database allowed me to call up five hundred records in a twenty-four-hour period, up to a limit of five thousand records per month. The research became a strenuous ritual, energized by the sporadic discovery of a card marked "Hutchinson," when another man in the spectral crowd gained a name, a face, the bones of a story.

Something curious happened. With each new discovery, Hutchinson camp's population felt a little less extraordinary, at least in the sense that Fred Uhlman had meant when he wrote: "Never before or since have I met such an extraordinary collection of people in such a small place." *Of course*, most of the internees were not professors at world-famous universities, or musicians oft-summoned to play for royalty, or artists who had exhibited across European galleries. Hutchinson's population was much like any other random cross section of society:

a glorious mixture of factory workers and artisans, teachers and intellectuals, doctors and mechanics, builders and chefs. To claim otherwise began to feel like an unhelpful romanticizing.

And yet, there was also something comforting about the normality of the emerging picture. Placed in these unusual circumstances, this ordinary cross section of society had achieved the extraordinary. Together, they had turned a prison into a university, a camp into a cultural center, a boardinghouse into an art gallery, a jumble of wires into a broadcasting station, a field into a fitness club, a lawn into a concert amphitheater. Hutchinson became a microcosm of civilization, and the extraordinariness lay not in the accolades of each individual captive, but in how, as a collective, they embodied humanity's better urges, even while besieged by its baser ones.

To remember their names is to celebrate that achievement, while holding the hope that, for all its marvel, never again will there be a camp like Hutchinson.

VISIT **WWW.HUTCHINSONCAMP.COM** *FOR A FULL* *list of men verified to have been interned at Hutchinson camp.*

BIBLIOGRAPHY

A NOTE ON SOURCES

SPECIAL MENTION MUST BE MADE of two sources. Interned at the camp for its opening on July 13, 1940, the art historian Klaus Hinrichsen remained behind the wire for a little less than a year, until his release on June 18, 1941. A chronicler by training, Hinrichsen wrote and spoke about his experiences in the camp at various points during his lifetime and—considering the vigor with which he sought to correct mistakes and misrememberings—viewed himself as the primary keeper of Hutchinson's history and promoter of its legacy.

Without Hinrichsen's detailed notes, writings, and papers, many taken with him from the camp and later distributed among various London archives, including the Tate, the Imperial War Museum, and the Wiener Holocaust Library, much of the information contained in this account would have been lost. At the time of Hinrichsen's death in 2004, however, his most substantial recollection, a novelistic journal, remained unpublished. This account, which Hinrichsen describes as a "collage of people and events suddenly remembered," defies straightforward categorization, mixing historical fact with both real and fictional characters to create a quasi-memoir. To complicate matters further, mindful of the risk of legal action, Hinrichsen anonymized the names of some real individuals in his account (Ludwig Warschauer, for example, became "Ludwig Lemberger").

Hinrichsen once joked that his friend and fellow internee Fred Uhlman's anecdotes about life in Hutchinson changed with time and retelling. Uhlman was, Hinrichsen claimed, more of a raconteur than a documentarian. The same might be said of Hinrichsen, however, whose various recorded accounts often differ from one another, albeit in minor ways. Unless otherwise noted, only events and individuals mentioned in Hinrichsen's writings that are backed by secondary and tertiary sources have been included in this book.

Hinrichsen's professional interests coupled with his dominant contribution to the history of the camp has led to, arguably, a disproportionate focus on his social circle, namely the artists. That Hutchinson has become known as the "Artists' Camp" is predominantly thanks to Hinrichsen. Hutchinson might just as accurately be referred to as the "Writers' Camp" (there were more than two dozen writers and journalists held there), or the "Lawyers' Camp" (of which there were at least thirty), or the "Professors' Camp," as the number of academics interned comfortably outstripped the professional artists.

A new source, the letters of Kurt Treitel (which were stored for eighty years by his family) have helped somewhat, in this book, to redress the balance in favor of the less eminent internee. Treitel, who was interned at Hutchinson for five months from its opening until his release on November 22, 1940, wrote regularly to his friends and family, sometimes more than once a day, and painstakingly copied each letter he wrote into a diary for his own record. Youthful energies led Treitel to record details of life in the camp that the older men did not, in most cases, consider worth jotting down.

A resident of House 2, directly next door to Peter Midgley, Treitel considered his home to have the most vibrant and friendly community in all of Hutchinson. Yet, even its best-known residents—the pianist Hans Fürth, the flautist Rudolf "Rolf" G. Meyer (identified, during the writing of this book, as the subject of one of Schwitters's portraits), and the camp father's second-in-command, Friederich Wittelshöfer—have barely been written about before.

Treitel is a useful source, too, as he had the rare and possibly unique distinction of working in just about every job going in Hutchinson camp. With the expansive curiosity of adolescence, Treitel worked at the camp library alongside the Oxford professor Dr. Paul Maas, studied at Ludwig Warschauer's Technical School, assisted at the camp newspaper alongside Michael Corvin, and, finally, toiled in the camp office, where he administered internees' desperate applications for release. His letters are keenly useful, not only because they were written at the time (by contrast, most of Hinrichsen's recollections were penned at a remove of several decades), but also because they were not recorded with an editor's eye on publication or posterity, unlike the writings of those such as Paul Jacobsthal, who later distributed edited copies of his internment diary among his Oxford friends, or Fred Uhlman, who altered his diaries at various stages throughout his life.

Hinrichsen, by contrast, opted for the obscure literary form of the quasi-memoir partly because he did not have access to the official records of internees' names and dates against which to check his recollections. In a 1989 letter to Peter Midgley, for example, he asks his old friend if he can help identify which artist lived in which house and who "Lehmann," an internee writer mentioned in Schwitters's letters, might be. (The individual in question was almost certainly Otto Lehmann-Russbüldt, a German activist-writer who, like Schwitters, came to wartime Britain via Norway.)

By the time of the writing of this book, following a Freedom of Information Act request, the full index of Enemy Alien Registration Cards held by the Home Office is now available to the public. These documents, which number tens of thousands, list the name of each internee, his or her date and place of birth, occupation at the time of arrest, and, in many cases, include a handwritten annotation to identify the individual's date of release and even, occasionally, the specific camp or camps in which they were held. This database has been invaluable in corroborating information regarding many of Hutchinson's internees whose names or details appear in the diaries and memoirs of their fellow prisoners either half-remembered or misspelled.

Before he died, Hinrichsen deposited thirty-five of the forty-five weekly Camp University lecture schedules that ran between week one (July 22, 1940) and week forty-five (June 11, 1941) in the Imperial War Museum archive, along with all but one issue of *The Camp*, from its debut issue in September 1940, to its final edition in January

1942. These documents provide a vast list of camp speakers' surnames, which can now be checked against released official records to construct a roll call of Hutchinson's internees. The most comprehensive list of Hutchinson's internees yet compiled, triangulated from this and dozens of other sources, and checked against the Home Office records, features in this book.

Finally, the majority of the information about Ludwig Warschauer is drawn from a long series of wartime security files recently opened to the public—TNA KV-2-1139 to 1142—and the British government's security files relating to Echen Kohsen—TNA HO 382/760—opened following a Freedom of Information request made by the author. Unusually, the names of MI5's principal investigators on the case were not redacted, which led to an interesting conversation with J. G. Craufurd's son and daughter-in-law, who were unaware of this chapter in his life.

ARCHIVAL SOURCES

AA: Arolsen Archives

AP: Associated Press

AUA: Australian Archives

BBC: *Berlin 1945* documentary film, BBC, 2020

BEF: *His Majesty's Most Loyal Aliens*, documentary film, Bewick Films, 1991

BL: British Library

BLO: Bodleian Library, Oxford

BP: British Pathé

BUL: Birmingham University Library

CJH: Center for Jewish History

DLW: Digital Library of University of Wrocław (complete set of *Die Freie Meinung*)

DNB: Deutsche Nationalbibliotech

FWR: Hitler's Black Book, Forces War Records

HLS: Schonfeld, Rabbi Solomon, Hartley Library, University of Southampton

IFZ: Instituts für Zeitgeschichte, Munich

IWM: Imperial War Museum

JBB: *Jailed by the British*, Channel 4 documentary film, 1982

JMB: Jewish Museum Berlin

LBC: Leo Baeck Institute Library Periodical Collection

LBI: Leo Baeck Institute

LMA: London Metropolitan Archives

LPL: Lambeth Palace Library

LSF: Library of the Society of Friends

MJM: Oral History Collection, Manchester Jewish Museum

ORT: Obchestvo Remeslenogo Truda, www.ort.org

RCM: Royal College of Music website

RVM: Letters of Ralph Vaughn Williams

SAH: Schwitters Archive, Hanover

TATE: Tate Archive

THE: The Holocaust Explained.org

TIA: The Internet Archive

TKS: The Keep Archive (University of Sussex branch)

TMM: The Manx Museum

TNA: The National Archives, Kew, Surrey

USHMM: United States Holocaust Memorial Museum

UW: University of Warwick

WJR: World Jewish Relief (Online resource)

WHL: Wiener Holocaust Library (Online)

WLC: Wiener Library Collections

UNPUBLISHED SOURCES

Daniel, Major H. O. Family papers. Courtesy of William Daniel.

Darton, Lawrence. *An Account of the Work of the Friends Committee for Refugees and Aliens 1933–50.* Unpublished manuscript. Courtesy of the Library of the Society of Friends.

Hinrichsen, Klaus. *A German for Ten Weeks.* Unpublished memoir. Courtesy of the Hinrichsen family.

———. Unpublished internment letters, July 1940–May 1941. Courtesy of the Hinrichsen family.

Jacobsthal, Dr. Paul Ferdinand. Original Diary Manuscript. Special Collections, Bodleian Library. Courtesy of the Council for At-Risk Academics (CARA).

Marx, Professor Ludwig. Internment diary and letters. The Keep Archive, University of Sussex.

Midgley, Doreen. *An Artist's Career and Contemporary Events*. Unpublished dissertation. Courtesy of Gerald Midgley and Wendy Gregory.

Mirauer, Helmuth. Unpublished memoir addressed to parents, January 1946. Courtesy of Carl Mirauer.

Moratz, Ralph. *Escape from the Holocaust*. Online memoir. https://ralphm1935.wordpress.com

Paolini, Stefano. *Missing Presumed Drowned*. self-published memoir.

Private Papers of Mr and Mrs O. Pond. Held at Imperial War Museum.

Schubert, Monica. *Where Am I at Home?: The Memoirs of Monica Schubert*. Courtesy of the author.

The Camp (issues September 1940 to January 1942). Imperial War Museum, LBI E. 16588.

Treitel, Kurt. Unpublished letters dated July–October 1940. Courtesy of the Treitel family.

Turney, Alexander. *Auerbach Memoirs*. Unpublished collection, 1920–2011. TIA.

Warschauer, Ludwig (unattributed). *History of 'P' camp*. Imperial War Museum, IWM 6355.

PUBLISHED SOURCES

Ahrends, Peter. *A3: Threads and Connections*. London: Right Angle Publishing, 2015.

Ambrose, Tom. *Hitler's Loss: What Britain and America Gained from Europe's Cultural Exiles*. London: Peter Owen, 2001.

Anonymous. *Displaced German Scholars: A Guide to Academics in Peril in Nazi Germany During the 1930s*. San Bernardino: Borgo Press, 1993.

Arendt, Hannah. *Eichmann in Jerusalem*. London: Penguin, 1994.

Bailey, Brenda. *A Quaker Couple in Nazi Germany*. York: William Sessions Ltd., 1994.

Balfour, Michael (ed.). *Theatre and War 1933–1945: Performance in Extremis*. Oxford: Berghahn Books, 2001.

Bartrop, Paul R., with Gabrielle Eisen. *The Dunera Affair: A Documentary Resource Book*. Victoria: Jewish Museum of Australia, 1990.

Baumel-Schwartz, Judith. *Never Look Back: The Jewish Refugee Children in Great Britain, 1938–1945*. London: Purdue University Press, 2012.

Belinfante Herzberg, Lillian. *The Past is Always Present*. Bloomington: Archway Publishing, 2015.

Bloch, Martin. *Ribbentrop*. London: Little, Brown, 2003.

Bohm-Duchen, Monica. *Art in Exile in Great Britain, 1933–45* (exhibition catalog). London: Belmont Press, 1986.

Bohm-Duchen, Monica, ed. *Insiders Outsiders: Refugees from Nazi Europe and Their Contribution to British Visual Culture*. London: Lund Humphries, 2019.

Borchard, Ruth. *The Service Exchange in an Internment Camp*. London: Friends' Book Centre, 1943.

Bosetzky, Horst. *Kempinski erobert Berlin: Roman*. Berlin: Jaron Verlag, 2010.

Bowra, C. M. *Memories, 1898–1939*. London: Weidenfeld & Nicolson, 1966.

Brinson, Charmian and Richard Dove. *A Matter of Intelligence*. Manchester: Manchester University Press, 2014.

Brinson, Charmian, Anna Müller-Härlin, and Julia Winckler. *His Majesty's Loyal Internee: Fred Uhlman in Captivity*. London: Vallentine Mitchell, 2009.

Busch, Tristan (a.k.a. Andreas Schütz). *Major Kwaplitschka: Entlavter Geheimdienst*. Vienna: Danubia Verlag, 1950.

Caestecker, Frank, and Bob Moore, eds. *Refugees from Nazi Germany and the Liberal European States*. New York: Berghahn Books, 2010.

Carlebach, Julius, et al. *Second Chance: Two Centuries of German-Speaking Jews in the United Kingdom*. Heidelberg: Mohr Siebeck, 1991.

Carter, Miranda. *Anthony Blunt, His Lives*. London: Macmillan, 2001.

Cesarani, David, and Tony Kushner. *The Internment of Aliens in Twentieth Century Britain*. London: Frank Cass, 1993.

Chambers, Emma, and Karin Orchard, eds. *Schwitters in Britain*. London: Tate, 2013.

Chappel, Connery. *Island of Barbed Wire*. London: Robert Hale, 1984.

Clifford, Rebecca. *Survivors*. London: Yale University Press, 2020.

Cooper, R. M., ed. *Refugee Scholars: Conversations with Tess Simpson*. Leeds: Moorland Books, 1922.

Corvin, Michael. *The Magic Kite*. London: Acorn Press, 1946.

Crawford, Sally, Jaś Elsner, and Katharina Uhlmschneider, eds. *Ark of Civilization: Scholars and Oxford University, 1930–1945*. Oxford: Oxford University Press, 2017.

Cresswell, Yvonne, ed. *Living with the Wire: Civilian Internment in the Isle of Man During the Two World Wars*. Douglas, UK: Manx National Heritage, 1994.

Cronin, Gloria L., and Ben Siegel, eds. *Conversations with Saul Bellow*. Jackson: University Press of Mississippi, 1995.

Crossley, Barbara. *The Triumph of Kurt Schwitters*, Ambleside, UK: The Armitt Trust, 2005.

Dove, Richard, ed. *"Totally Un-English"?: Britain's Internment of "Enemy Aliens" in Two World Wars*. Yearbook of the Research Centre for German and Austrian Exile Studies, vol. 7, Amsterdam: Editions Rodopi B.V., 2005.

Erlhoff, Michael. *Kurt Schwitters Almanach*. Hanover, Germany: Postskriptum Verlag, 1983.

Fast, Vera K. *Children's Exodus: A History of the Kindertransport*. London: I. B. Tauris, 2011.

Feather, Jessica. *Art Behind Barbed Wire*. Liverpool: National Museums Liverpool, 2004.

———. *Help Us Germans to Beat the Nazis*. London: Victor Gollancz, 1941.

Friedländer, Saul. *Nazi Germany and the Jews: The Years of Persecution, 1933–1939*. New York: HarperPerennial, 1997.

Fröhlich, Elke, ed. *Die Tagebücher von Joseph Goebbels*. Munich: K. G. Saur Verlag, 1996.

Fry, Helen. *The King's Most Loyal Enemy Aliens: Germans Who Fought for Britain in the Second World War*. Chalford, UK: Sutton Publishing, 2007.

Gauye, Oscar, Gabriel Imboden, and Daniel Bourgeois, eds. *Documents Diplomatiques Suisses*, vol. 12. Bern, Switzerland: Benteli, 1994.

Gerhardt, Uta, and Thomas Karlauf. *The Night of Broken Glass*. Cambridge, UK: Polity Press, 2012.

Gershon, Karen, ed. *We Came as Children*. London: Victor Gollancz, 1966.

Gilbert, Sir Martin. *The Boys: Triumph over Adversity*. London: Weidenfeld & Nicolson, 1996.

Gillman, Leni, and Peter Gillman. *"Collar the Lot!": How Britain Expelled and Interned Its Wartime Refugees*. London: Quartet, 1980.

Goldenberg, Myrna, and Amy Shapiro, eds. *Different Horrors, Same Hell: Gender and the Holocaust*. Seattle: University of Washington Press, 2013.

Greene, Graham. *The Ministry of Fear*. London: William Heinemann, 1943.

Harris, Mark, and Deborah Oppenheimer. *Into the Arms of Strangers*. London: Bloomsbury, 2001.

Hirschfeld, Gerhard. *Exile in Great Britain*. Berg, Switzerland: Leamington Spa, 1984.

Hutton, Robert. *Agent Jack: The True Story of MI5's Secret Nazi Hunter*. London: Orion, 2018.

Isherwood, Christopher. *Mr. Norris Changes Trains*. London: Hogarth Press, 1935.

Judex. *Anderson's Prisoners*. London: Victor Gollancz, 1940.

Kaiser, Fritz. *Degenerate Art: The Exhibition Guide in German and English*. Iowa: Ostara, 2012, translation of German original, 1937.

Kapp, Yvonne, and Margaret Mynatt. *British Policy and the Refugees, 1933–1941*. London: Frank Cass, 1997.

Kirsch, Jonathan. *The Short, Strange Life of Heschel Grynszpan*. New York: Liveright, 2013.

Kochan, Miriam. *Britain's Internees in the Second World War*. London: Macmillan, 1980.

Kremer, Roberta S., ed. *Broken Threads: The Destruction of the Jewish Fashion Industry in Germany and Austria*. Vancouver: Berg, 2006.

Lach, Friedhelm, ed. *Kurt Schwitters: Das literarische Werk*. Cologne: DuMont Buchverlag, 2004.

Lafitte, François. *The Internment of Aliens*. London: Penguin, 1940.

Levitt, Ruth, ed. *Pogrom November 1938: Testimonies from Kristallnacht*. London: Souvenir Press, 2015.

Lichti, James Irvin. *Houses on the Sand?: Pacifist Denominations in Nazi Germany*. Oxford: Peter Lang, 2008.

London, Louise. *Whitehall and the Jews, 1933–1948*. Cambridge, UK: Cambridge University Press, 2000.

Longerich, Peter. *Himmler*. Oxford: Oxford University Press, 2012.

MacDougall, Sarah, and Rachel Dickson, eds. *Forced Journeys: Artists in Exile in Britain c. 1933–45*. London: Ben Uri Gallery, 2009.

Moggridge, Donald, ed. *The Collected Writings of John Maynard Keynes*. Cambridge: Cambridge University Press, 1978.

Nebel, Otto. *Text und Kritik* 3536. Munich: Verlag Text und Kritik, 1972.

Neurath, Eva. *Recollections*. London: Thames & Hudson, 2016.

Nündel, Ernst. *Wir spielen, bis uns der Tod abholt: Briefe aus fünf Jahrzehnten*. Berlin: Ullstein Verlag, 1990.

Nyburg, Anna. *Émigrés*. London: Phaidon, 2014.

——. *From Leipzig to London: The Life and Work of the Émigré Hellmuth Weissenborn*. New Castle, DE: Oak Knoll Press, 2012.

Office of United States Chief of Counsel for Prosecution of Axis Criminality, *Nazi Conspiracy and Aggression*. Washington, DC: US Government Printing Office, 1947.

Olden, Rudolf. *The History of Liberty in Germany*. London: Victor Gollancz, 1946.

Parkin, Simon. *A Game of Birds and Wolves*. London: Sceptre, 2019.

Penrose Antony. *Roland Penrose: The Friendly Surrealist*. London: Prestel, 2001.

Pistol, Rachel. *Internment during the Second World War*. London: Bloomsbury Academic, 2019.

Powell, Jennifer, and Jutta Vinzent. *Art and Migration: Art Works by Refugee Artists from Nazi Germany in Britain*. Birmingham, UK: George Bell Institute, 2005.

Presler, Gerd, and Erik Riedel. *Ludwig Meidner: Catalogue Raisonné of His Sketchbooks*. Munich: Prestel, 2013.

Read, Anthony, and David Fisher. *Kristallnacht: The Unleashing of the Holocaust*. New York: Peter Bedrick, 1989.

Robertson, Terence. *The Golden Horseshoe*. London: Evans Brothers, 1955.

Roeder, Helen. *Helen's Sketchbook*. London: Camberwell Press, 1985.

Sansom, William. *Westminster in War*. London: Faber & Faber, 1947.

Schwab, Gerald. *The Day the Holocaust Began: The Odyssey of Herschel Grynszpan*. New York: Praeger, 1990.

Sebba, Anne. *Battling for the News*. London: Hodder & Stoughton, 1994.

Shatzkes, Pamela. *Holocaust and Rescue*. London: Vallentine Mitchell, 2004.

Shepherd, Naomi. *A Refuge from Darkness: Wilfrid Israel and the Rescue of the Jews*. New York: Pantheon, 1984.

Sherman, A. J. *Island Refuge: Britain and Refugees from the Third Reich, 1933–39*. London: Routledge, 1994.

Shirer, William L. *The Rise and Fall of the Third Reich*. New York: Simon & Schuster, 1960.

Sinclair, Iain, ed. *London: City of Disappearances*. London: Hamish Hamilton, 2006.

Southeby's Catalogue. *Works of Art and Furniture from the Collection of the late Paul Wallraf*. London: Sotheby's, 1983.

Stent, Ronald. *A Bespattered Page?: The Internment of His Majesty's "Most Loyal Enemy Aliens."* London: André Deutsch, 1980.

Stephan, Alexander. *"Communazis": FBI Surveillance of German Émigré Writers*. New Haven, CT: Yale University Press, 2000.

Sullivan, Matthew Barry. *Thresholds of Peace*. London: Hamish Hamilton, 1979.

Tausig, Otto. *Kasperl, Kummerl, Jud.* Vienna: Mandelbaum Verlag, 2005.

Thalman, Rita, and Emmanuel Feinermann. *Crystal Night.* London: Thames & Hudson, 1974.

Turner, Barry. *. . . And the Policeman Smiled.* London: Bloomsbury, 1990.

———. *Waiting for War: Britain 1939–1940.* London: Icon Books, 2020.

Uhlman, Fred. *The Making of an Englishman.* London: Victor Gollancz, 1960.

Vinzent, Jutta. *Identity and Image: Refugee Artists from Nazi Germany in Britain.* Alfter, Germany: VDG Weimar, 2005.

Webb, Simon. *British Concentration Camps: A Brief History from 1900–1975.* Barnsley, UK: Pen & Sword, 2016.

Webster, Gwendolen. *Kurt Merz Schwitters: A Biographical Study.* Cardiff: University of Wales Press, 1997.

Weight, R. V. *Carel Weight: A Haunted Imagination.* Newton Abbot, UK: David & Charles, 1994.

Weissenborn, Hellmuth. *Hellmuth Weissenborn, Engraver: With an Autobiographical Introduction by the Artist.* Andoversford, UK: Whittington Press, 1983.

West, Nigel, ed. *The Guy Liddell Diaries, Volume I: 1939–1942.* London: Routledge, 2005.

Wheeler-Bennett, John. *John Anderson: Viscount Waverley.* London: Macmillan, 1962.

Williams, Bill. *Jews and Other Foreigners: Manchester and the Rescue of the Victims of European Fascism, 1933–40.* Manchester: Manchester University Press, 2011.

Wilson, Sarah. *Essay: Kurt Schwitters in England,* Tate Gallery Library and Archives (web).

ACKNOWLEDGMENTS

THANK YOU TO THE FAMILIES of Hutchinson camp's internees and guards who shared their memories, documents, photographs, and paintings for the research of this book, and without whom this story could not have been told in this way.

Thank you to Peter Ahrends, grandson of Hutchinson's cultural director, Bruno Ahrends; Alison Archenhold, daughter of Horst Archenhold; David Wertheim, cousin of Ernest Bello; Robert Bianchi, son of Cesari Bianchi; Michael Corvin, grandson of *The Camp*'s first editor, Leo Freund-Corvin; Clare Fraenkel, granddaughter of the author Heinrich Fraenkel; Glen David Gold, grandson of George Gercke; Dana Gillespie, daughter of Hans Gillespie; Leonie Mellinger, daughter of Renee Goddard; Judy Shrewsbury, granddaughter of Walter Goldschmidt; Sylvia Gohr, granddaughter of Simon Guttmann, who, having survived two world crossings by ship as an internee, died at Hutchinson camp; Peter Hallgarten, son of Fritz Hallgarten; Karen Hopper, granddaughter of the artist Paul Hamann; Natasha Hillary, daughter of Karl Hirschfield; Elaine and Paul Honigmann, grandchildren of Hans Honigmann; Josh Reynolds, great-grandson of Hans Kollinsky; H. Shani, relative of Rudolf Melitz; Judith Elam, granddaughter of Peisech Mendzigursky; Robert Moser, son of Claus Moser; Stephan Feuchtwang, son of Wilhelm Feuchtwang and stepson of the publisher Walter Neurath; John Ötvös, son of Josef Ötvös; Carl Mirauer, son of Hellmuth Mirauer; Clemence Schultze and Martin Rush, daughter and son-in-law of Dr. Rolf Schultze; Francis Uhlman and Caroline Compton, son and daughter of Fred and Diana Uhlman; John West, son of Dr. Paul Wegner; Carola, Nikolaus, and Alexandra Weil, the children of Herbert Weil; Benjamin and Michael Zander, sons of Dr. Walter Zander.

Thank you to William Daniel, Sarah Peacock, and Wendy Bentall, grandson and granddaughters of Major Hubert Daniel. And special thanks to Henry Wuga, who kindly shared his memories of being plied with drink on the Isle of Man by an MI5 informant. Thank you to Antony Penrose, son of Roland Penrose, cofounder of the Artists' Refugee Committee.

Thank you to Sir Robert and Lady (Georgina) Craufurd, son and daughter-in-law of Sir James Gregan Craufurd, MI5's primary investigator into the case of Ludwig Warschauer.

Very special thanks to Gretel Hinrichsen, Jacquie Richardson, and Nic Hinrichsen, wife, daughter, and son of Dr. Klaus Hinrichsen, for providing access to those documents belonging to their father that are not held in public archives; to David Treitel and Jonathan Tel, sons of Kurt Treitel, for providing access to the many letters their father sent from Hutchinson; to Patricia Webb, for sharing her memories of her great-aunt, Bertha Bracey.

Very special thanks to Gerald Midgely and Wendy Gregory, son and daughter-in-law of Peter Midgley, and to Monica Schubert and Catherine and Hilary Gregory, daughter and granddaughters of Echen Kohsen.

Thank you to Uwe Westphal, for sharing transcripts and personal documents relating to the internment of Puck Dachinger and Fritz Rosen, and to Tim Rubidge, student and scholar of Sigurd Leeder, for sharing his memories of his teacher. Thank you to Professor Tony Kushner for providing scans of Fritz Engel's unpublished memoir. Thank you to Dr. Richard Hawkins for information related to the internment of Dr. Hans Honigmann, and to Dr. Joachim Rott for information relating to the internment of Dr. Bernhard Weiss.

Thank you to Nigel Mac-Fall and Graham Stewart for sharing their memories of Peter Midgley, their former art tutor at Ravensbourne College of Art and, in Graham's case, his former landlord.

Thank you to the architect Wayne Gander for his reproduction of Bruno Ahrends's camp schematic.

Thank you to the art historian Monica Bohm-Duchen; Richard Shaw, director of Unity House and the Warth Mills Project; Becky Wright, librarian at the Library of the Society of Friends; Tor Scott, collections and research assistant at the Scottish Gallery of Modern Art; Fran Lloyd, professor of art history at Kingston University. Thank you to Dr. Sally Crawford and Dr. Katharina Ulmschneider, senior research fellows at the Institute of Archaeology, Oxford University.

Thank you to Yvonne Cresswell, curator of social history, Kirsty Neate, head of collections, and Kim Holden, library and archives assistant at the Manx Museum. Thank you to Anthony Grenville and Professor Charmian Brinson, cofounders of the Centre for Exile and Refugee Studies, Institute for Modern Languages Research, University of London. Thank you to Dr Rachel Pistol, King's College London, for her kind support and feedback. Thank you to Valeria Carullo, curator of the Robert Elwall Photographs Collection, RIBA British Architectural Library. Thank you to Mike Levy, for his feedback on information relating to the *Kindertransport* initiative. Special thanks to Dr. Isabel Schulz, curator of the Kurt Schwitters Archive, Sprengel Museum, Hanover; and to Dr. Anna Nyburg, Imperial College, London, for her generous support and encouragement throughout the writing of this book.

Special thanks also to Laura Berry and Dr. Cornelia Pohlmann for their research support mapping the genealogies of various internees and guards, and in locating living relatives, both in the UK and Germany. Thanks to Samuel Hills for research support.

Thank you to Liz Lazarus and Leslie Kay BEM, from the Federation of Jewish Services, for information regarding boardinghouses used by Jewish refugees in Manchester during 1939–40. Thank you to the historian Daniel Snowman and Norbert Meyn, principal investigator at the Royal College of Music, for their assistance in identifying musicians in the camp.

Thank you to Kathryn Hallam-Howard, who, with Jacquie Richardson, transcribed Dr. Klaus Hinrichsen's unpublished letters written during his internment from 1940 to 1941. Thanks to Ian Latham for supplying the photograph of Kurt Schwitters's portrait of Bruno Ahrends.

Thank you to Rachel Ward for her assistance in translating articles from *Die Freie Meinung* and other newspapers of the era. Special thanks to Jeremy Bines for his wide-ranging translation work, including that of Kurt Treitel's original German-language diary entries, Otto Tausig's German-language memoir, and various newspaper articles relating to Peter's uncle, Hans Hanteda-Fleischmann.

Thank you to my editors, Juliet Brooke, Colin Harrison, and Emily Polson, and to Jane Finigan at Lutyens & Rubinstein, and David Forrer at Inkwell. Thank you to Paul Parkin and Tony Cantale for their careful reading of early drafts of the manuscript, and to my family and friends for their support.

NOTES

EPIGRAPH

ix **"in a pool":** Kurt Schwitters, "Short Hills," Jean Brown papers, 1916–95, Getty Archive, Santa Monica, California.

CHAPTER 1: BARBED-WIRE MATINEE

1 **Clear warm air:** Sansom, *Westminster in War*, 27. **2 Each window was covered:** Peter Midgley: Oral History, MJM, 1988.45. **2 after a German U-boat:** Bertha Bracey, "Chairman's Report on the Isle of Man Camps, 28th October–2nd November 1940," LSF, YM/MfS/FCRA. **2 From the open windows:** The Viennese music professor Stefan Pollmann, writing under the pseudonym "Perlmann," in his "Music Review," published in the camp's *Almanac 1940–1941*, mentions some men's habits of viewing an open-air performance from the top floors of their houses. **2 Outside the wire fence:** Ibid. **2 Eight weeks earlier:** Klaus Hinrichsen, "Cultural Flashlights," Hutchinson *Almanac 1940–41*; Hinrichsen, unpublished account, 11. **2 Captain Hubert Daniel:** Hubert Owen Daniel (DOB March 31, 1892), GRO, vol. 1d, 1057. **3 remove the spark plugs:** Chappell, *Island of Barbed Wire*, 154. **3 a beekeeper:** Dr. Fred Uhlman, "Diary of an Internee," private papers, IWM, 6781. **3 Morse code:** Klaus Hinrichsen: Oral History, June 1978, IWM, 3789. **4 grounds of Eton:** Uhlman, "Diary of an Internee." **4 At Cambridge University:** Walter Wallich: Oral History, June 1979, IWM, 4431. **4 The police came:** Peter Midgley: Oral History. **5 hounded by depression:** Uhlman, *The Making of an Englishman*, 232. **5 May 23** Listing in the *Times*, May 22, 1940. **6 "Can't you use one of them?":** Hinrichsen, unpublished account, 62. **6 "My friend, I am a pianist, not a gynecologist":** As quoted in ibid., 62–63. **6 one piano collapsed:** Klaus Hinrichsen, "Art in Hutchinson Camp—A Personal View," c. September 1986, TATE, TGA 20052/1/7/12. **6 A date was set:** Hinrichsen, *His Majesty's Most Loyal Aliens*, BEF. **7 "unforgettable":** Hinrichsen, "Art in Hutchinson Camp—A Personal View."

CHAPTER II: FIVE SHOTS

12 **from American films:** Read and Fisher, *Kristallnacht*, 3–4. 13 *"Juden raus!"*— Jews out!: As quoted in Arendt, *Eichmann in Jerusalem*, 228. 13 **"I've already done":** Kirsch, *The Short, Strange Life of Herschel Grynszpan*, 89. 14 **Herschel explained his plan:** Schwab, *The Day the Holocaust Began*, 74. 15 **"What is the purpose":** Kirsch, *The Short, Strange Life of Herschel Grynszpan*, 105. 15 **Concentrating to keep his voice:** Read and Fisher, *Kristallnacht*, 6. 16 **"I need to see a gentleman":** As quoted in Kirsch, *The Short, Strange Life of Herschel Grynszpan*, 107. 16 **a hotbed of espionage-themed intrigue:** *L'Intransigeant*, November 8, 1939. 16 **"a confidential . . . document":** As quoted in Schwab, *The Day the Holocaust Began*, 6. 17 **The gun:** Ibid., 5. 19 **At around nine o'clock:** Friedländer, *Nazi Germany and the Jews*, 271. 19 **One reveler reported:** Read and Fisher, *Kristallnacht*, 62. 19 **"Shall I tell you what happened to him?":** Ibid. 20 **spontaneously erupt:** Friedländer, *Nazi Germany and the Jews*, 271. 20 **"The Führer decides":** *Die Tagebücher von Joseph Goebbels*, November 10, 1938.

CHAPTER III: FIRE AND CRYSTAL

21 **He may lose the fight:** Gerald Midgley to author, May 2020. 22 **From their offices in Breslau:** As reported in *"Die Abrechnung mit der 'Freien Meinung',"* *Breslauer Nachtpost*, June 21, 1922. 22 **In one 1922 article:** Ibid. 22 **palatial apartment:** Midgley, *An Artist's Career and Contemporary Events*, 12. 23 **collecting . . . horse manure:** Gerald Midgley to author, May 2020. 23 **full-time resident:** Date of arrival: October 17, 1933, as per Peter Fleischmann orphanage registration document, AA. 23 **Joachim von Ribbentrop:** Gerald Midgley to author, May 2020. 24 **She donated money:** Monica Schubert to author, April 2021. 24 **she invited him to call her "aunt":** Ibid. 24 **Before dinner:** Ibid. 24 **tree-lined:** See various photographs taken inside Auerbach orphanage c. 1936, JMB. 25 **what they could afford:** Turney, *Auerbach Memoirs*, 4. 25 **Toys were plentiful:** See various photographs taken inside Auerbach orphanage c. 1936, JMB. 25 **chip the ice:** Gerald Midgley to author, May 2020. 25 **Every Hanukkah:** Turney, *Auerbach Memoirs*, 4. 25 **One of the governesses:** "Fairness Was Written Very Large," Oral History, Jewish Histories in Prenzlauer Berg, Museum Pankow. 25 **prone to a favoritism:** Walter Frankenstein: Oral History, Der AK Historisch-politische Bildung, Museum Pankow. 26 **classic plays:** Photographs of performances by Auerbach children of Molière's *Les Femmes savantes*, and Gotthold Lessing's *Minna von Barnhelm*, survive in the Jewish Museum Berlin. 26 **One night each week:** Ibid. 26 **"To fulfil its true purpose":** As quoted in an entry for "Baruch Auerbach" in the *1906 Jewish Encyclopaedia*, 299. 26 **There was dis-**

cipline: "Fairness Was Written Very Large," Oral History. **26 sixteen children:** Turney, *Auerbach Memoirs*, 4. **26 162 Schönhauser Allee:** The orphanage was founded in 1832 on Berlin's Rosenstrasse. Sixty-five years later the orphans moved onto the new, especially built neo-Gothic campus on Schönhauser Allee. **26 a depression-gripped Berlin:** Turney, *Auerbach Memoirs*, 2. **26 "another workless, empty day":** Isherwood, *Mr. Norris Changes Trains*, 90. **26 a whispered reputation:** Moratz, *Escape from the Holocaust*. **27 "Don't be afraid":** Hugo Moses, Manuscript 39, Houghton Library, Harvard University, as quoted in Gerhardt and Karlauf, *The Night of Broken Glass*, 22. **27 "Do you know why we've come here?":** Ibid. **28 "Following the attempt":** "Copy of Most Urgent Telegram from Munich, of November 10, 1938, 1:20 a.m.," Nuremberg Documents PS-3051. **28 "Wipe your asses":** Ibid. **28 In Germany's capital:** Thalmann and Feinermann, *Crystal Night*, 43. **28 Goebbels specifically ordered:** Joseph Goebbels, "*Tagebucheinträge vom 10. und vom 11. November 1938*," diary entry as reproduced in Fröhlich, *Die Tagebücher von Joseph Goebbels*. **29 "My dear Reverend":** Ibid., 42. **29 At the Auerbach orphanage:** "List of Synagogues Burned Down in Berlin, Cologne and Halberstadt," November 22, 1938, WL, 1375/40. **29 racial epithets:** Johnny Eichwald, as quoted in Turner, . . . *And the Policeman Smiled*, 11. **30 Königstädtische Oberrealschule:** Now the Käthe-Kollwitz-Gymnasium. **30 Rather than direct:** Peter Midgley curriculum vitae, Midgley Family Papers. **30 "There and then I decided":** Peter Midgley: Oral History, MJM, 1988.45. **30 Older children like Peter:** Herzberg, *The Past Is Always Present*, 50. **31 "Stay together":** Ibid. **31 Soon, harassment:** Heinz Stephan Lewy, as quoted in ibid., 50. **31 routinely attacked:** Moratz, "Berlin Goodbye," *Escape from the Holocaust*, ch. 1. **31 "The Gestapo":** Peter Midgley: Oral History, here rendered as dialogue. **31 The secret police:** In 2018, Walter Frankenstein, another Auerbach resident who was three years Peter's junior, told a reporter from the *Juedische Allgemeine* ("I Was Never Afraid," May 11, 2018) that he also received the warning from the benevolent officer that the Gestapo was coming to arrest him. **32 creaked open the gate:** "Witness Recalls the Horrors of Kristallnacht 80 Years Ago," November 6, 2018, AP, 4181108. **32 He had known the mob:** "Holocaust Survivor Recalls 'Night of Broken Glass' Horrors," AP, November 8, 2018. **32 But where to hide:** "I Was Never Afraid." **32 known as the North Synagogue:** JMB. **32 sometimes attend ceremonies:** Herzberg, *The Past Is Always Present*, 73. **32 the night's targets:** Shirer, *The Rise and Fall of the Third Reich*, 525–29. **32 "You need to leave now":** As quoted in "I Was Never Afraid." **33 barely older than some of the children:** Ibid. **33 "*Beeilt euch*":** Herzberg, *The Past Is Always Present*, 81. **33 There was an abrupt crash:** In another account, the older boys cranked opened the windows. While destruction was avoided, the damage to the orphanage's synagogue was sufficient enough that, each week thereafter, the Friday evening service was held in the dining room.

CHAPTER IV: THE RESCUERS

34 mostly lapsed Jews: These "non-Aryans" were typically people with Jewish ancestry who no longer identified with the Jewish community but who, according to the Nuremberg laws of genealogy, were still classified as Jews. At this time, individuals who were not born of a Jewish mother were not given help from the official Jewish organizations. **34 Germany Emergency Committee:** Later renamed the Friends Committee for Refugees and Aliens. **34 including Reinhard Heydrich:** At first Bertha and her staff couldn't make out the signature; when they deduced the author, she "nearly fainted"; Bertha Bracey: Oral History, 1980, IWM, 4646. **34 Joachim von Ribbentrop:** Letter to Ribbentrop, December 21, 1936, LSF, YM/MfS/FCRA, 125/2. **35 even Hitler himself:** Bertha worried that her correspondence with leading Nazis might lead the British authorities to question her loyalties, so she visited the Home Office to explain that her letters both to and from these "disreputable" sources could all be reasonably explained, if necessary. **35 Documentation spilled:** Brenda Bailey, "Bertha Bracey's Work with Jewish Refugees," LSF, YM/MfS/FCRA, 125/2, Box L. **35 There was need everywhere:** According to minutes of a meeting of the Germany Emergency Committee held on January 6, 1936, Bertha was forced to take the preceding year off due to illness. Throughout 1935 Marjorie Bayes worked as acting secretary in her stead. **35 Eleanor Rathbone, likened the work:** Eleanor Rathbone, *New Statesman and Nation*, April 15, 1939. **35 "encourage other nations to unload their Jews on us":** Ibid. **35 a person's best hope:** The Quakers did not work alone. Bertha collaborated closely with the German Jewish Aid Committee, at the time situated in Woburn House, a three-minute walk from her office. Ostensibly, the work was divided along religious lines: Woburn House dealt with cases relating to practicing Jews; Drayton House dealt with non-Aryan cases, people of no religious affiliation, and political refugees. In reality the groups often shared and collaborated on cases. **36 her father worked as a carpenter:** Henry and Annie Bracey, 1911 Census. **36 She spent her first summer holiday:** Bertha Bracey: Oral History. **37 "The poison, however, was spreading":** Ibid. **37 "What we see now":** "International Schools for Refugees," *Western Morning News*, April 23, 1934, 5. **37 Their comments:** Anti-Semitism: Minutes and Reports, TNA, HO 262/9. **38 "Although I loathe anti-Semitism":** As quoted in Shatzkes, *Holocaust and Rescue*, 31. **38 Ogilvie-Forbes wrote:** Telegram from Sir G. Ogilvie-Forbes, November 10, 1938, TNA, FO 371/21636. **38 "chased through the streets":** "Eye for an Eye, Tooth for a Tooth," *News Chronicle*, November 11, 1938. **38 losses of 1.7 million marks:** Thalmann and Feinermann, *Crystal Night*, 64. **38 "The natural and fully justified outrage":** Ibid. **39 "The only thing that could finally slow":** "Looting Mobs Defy Goebbels," *Daily Express*, November 11, 1938. **39 "We killed Secretary vom Rath":** Friedlander, *The Years of Persecution*, 276. **39**

"**some prominent**": Strang to G. Ogilvie-Forbes, November 9, 1938, TNA, FO 371/21636, C13660/1667/62, f. 234. **39 to meddle in "a wasp's nest":** Olgilvie-Forbes to Strang, no. 662, AGM Cadogan, minute, November 10, 1938, TNA, FO 371/21636, C13661/1667/62, f. 236. **40 "like a sort of electric current":** Margareta Burkill as quoted in Fast, *Children's Exodus*, 14. **40 "Never in my life":** Letter from Albert Einstein to Wilfrid Israel's mother, reprinted in Martin Buber, *Wilfrid Israel: July 11th, 1899-June 1st, 1943* (London: Marsland, 1944). **41 "sacrificially cared":** Lichti, *Houses on the Sand?*, 96. **41 In the days:** Letter from Bertha Bracey, as quoted in Bailey, *A Quaker Couple in Nazi Germany*, 95. **41 When she arrived:** Ibid. **41 a masterpiece of collaboration:** For a detailed account of the events and individuals involved in formulating the specifics of what became the *Kindertransport* operation, see Baumel-Schwartz, *Never Look Back*, ch. 3. **42 "any possible way by which":** Neville Chamberlain, *Hansard*, House of Commons, vol. 341, col. 505, November 14, 1938. **42 Even prominent Jewish representatives:** Cabinet minutes, November 16, 1938, TNA, CAB 23/96. **42 might be earmarked for:** Conclusions, Cabinet Committee on Foreign Policy, November 14, 1938, TNA, CAB 27/624. **42 Churchill had written an open letter:** Ibid. **42 Movement for the Care of Children from Germany:** Later, the Refugee Children's Movement (RCM). **43 Better to assume the risks:** As quoted by Hoare in a speech to the House of Commons, *Hansard*, November 21, 1938, vol. 341, cc1428–83. **43 Visas and alien cards would be waived:** "Jewish Children from Germany," London *Times*, December 3, 1938. **43 "put no obstacle"** *Hansard*, November 21, 1938, vol. 341, cc1428–83. **43 blond girls were favored:** Caestecker and Moore, *Refugees from Nazi Germany and the Liberal European States*, 171–84. **44 more than six hundred applications:** Goldenberg and Shapiro, *Different Horrors, Same Hell*, 201. **44 The proposal was dubbed:** Fast, *Children's Exodus*, 21. **44 expected to have left Britain:** Letter to Bertha Bracey from Norman Nicholson, Friends Committee for Refugees and Aliens, LSF, YM/MfS/FCRA. **44 three other Berlin institutions:** Baumel-Schwartz, *Never Look Back*, 113. **45 "free of vermin":** As per Gisela Spanglet's medical certificate, https://harwichhavenhistory.co.uk/escape/. **45 return to the orphanage:** Peter Midgley: Oral History, MJM, 1988.45. **45 Accompanied by Rafael and Max:** Letter from the Foreign Office to the Netherlands Legation, November 29, 1938, TNA. **45 boarded a bus:** Peter Midgley: Oral History. **45 Anhalter Bahnhof:** "*Wie die Kindertransport tausende Leben retteten*," *Tagesspiegel*, November 30, 2017.

CHAPTER V: SUNSET TRAIN

46 hauled his daughter: Harris and Oppenheimer, *Into the Arms of Strangers*, 108. **47 "My mother insisted":** Gershon, *We Came as Children*, 19. **47 Some re-**

garded it: Hana Eardley: Oral History, IWM, 16975/2/1–2. **47 carried no photographs:** "The Kindertransport Children 80 Years On: 'We Thought We Were Going on an Adventure,'" *Guardian*, November 6, 2018. **47 contain their grief:** Ernest Pollack, "Departure to Freedom Curtailed," unpublished memoir, WLC. **47 "strangely quiet":** Gisella Eisner, "Cottage Pie on Tuesdays," unpublished memoir, WLC. **47 "full orphans":** Other Auerbach orphans followed on later transports. For example, a group of twenty children from the orphanage took a *Kindertransport* on July 7, 1939 (see Herzberg, *The Past Is Always Present*, 89). **48 depending on the child:** Hilary Gregory—whose grandmother, Echen Kohsen, took taxis between the Berlin stations to wave to her two daughters, much to their consternation—to author, May 2020. **48 were joined by the other evacuees:** This included orphans from other German cities, such as, on this day, a group from the Herren of the Paulinenstift—Pauline Foundation Girls' Orphanage—in Hamburg. As reported by "Frau H. G. from Lübeck," "Eyewitness Reports Regarding the November Pogrom," WHIL, 1375. **48 One kreuzer black:** Gerald Midgley to author, May 2020. **49 "another collection":** Turner, . . . *And the Policeman Smiled*, 45. **49 "I'll have that":** Gerald Midgley to author, April 2020. **49 he would become an artist:** Peter Midgley: Oral History, MJM, 1988.45. **50 A crowd:** As reported by "Herr H. A. from Bremen," "Eyewitness Reports Regarding the November Pogrom," TWL, 1375. **50 set up tables:** As reported by "Frau E. R. from Hamburg," ibid. **50 move their watches back:** Ibid. **50 sparkling water and lemonade:** As reported by "Herr A. R. from Bünde," ibid. **50 As they boarded:** Turner, . . . *And the Policeman Smiled*, 51. **50 not enough rooms:** "Burning Orphanage Ordeal," *Shields Daily News*, December 2, 1938; Gershon, *We Came as Children*, 30. **51 The sea was rough:** "Sad Jewish Refugees Arrive in England," *Gloucester Citizen*, December 2, 1938. **51 "over our shoulders":** Gershon, *We Came as Children*, 31. **51 At 5:30:** Ibid. **51 Langdon called out each child's name:** "Burning Orphanage Ordeal" **51 media fascination:** "Jewish Child Refugees Arrive from Germany," BP, 93583. **52 "sad-eyed":** Ibid. **52 "There was laid out":** "Burning Orphanage Ordeal." **53 summer dresses in December:** Peter Midgley: Oral History. **53 "What have I come to?":** As quoted in Turner, *Waiting for War*, 149. **53 During the summer months:** "Report on a Visit to Dovercourt Refugee Camp," Women's Voluntary Services, January 12, 1939, TNA, MH 55/689. **53 There was no heating:** "In Camp with the Refugee Children," *Jewish Chronicle*, December 9, 1938. **53 They ate porridge:** "Burning Orphanage Ordeal." **54 Anna Essinger:** Fast, *Children's Exodus*, 36. **54 "None of us will ever forget":** As quoted in Sybil Oldfield, "'It Is Usually She': The Role of British Women in the Rescue and Care of the Kindertransport Kinder," *Shofar: An Interdisciplinary Journal of Jewish Studies* 23, no. 1 (January 2004): 57–70. **55 "three little girls":** "In Camp with the Refugee Children." **55 One man drove:** Ibid. **55 learned songs:** Gershon, *We Came as Children*, 31.

CHAPTER VI: THE BASEMENT AND THE JUDGE

56 gruffly shown: Peter Midgley: Oral History, MJM, 1988.45. **56 As a university lecturer:** Williams, *Jews and Other Foreigners*, 49. **56 first to lose his job:** Arye Carmon, "The Impact of the Nazi Racial Decrees on the University of Heidelberg," Shoah Resource Center, International School for Holocaust Studies, 4. **57 the so-called *Säuberung*:** Initially, Jewish officials could be exempted if they had assumed their position before August 1, 1914, had fought in the First World War, or had lost a father or son in the conflict. **57 "absolute blasphemy":** Bertha Bracey: Oral History, 1980, IWM, 4646. **57 Within six weeks:** "Displaced German Professors," London *Times*, May 24, 1933, 10. **57 press release appeared:** Ibid. **57 Academic Assistance Council:** Known, from 1936, as the Society for the Protection of Science and Learning. **57 10 percent:** London, *Whitehall and the Jews*, 48. **58 split his time:** Williams, *Jews and Other Foreigners*, 56; Peter Midgley: Oral History. **58 "He did not want to know me":** Peter Midgley: Oral History. **58 back was turned** Ibid. **59 "a hiding place from the winds":** Prime Minister Stanley Baldwin, "The National and Empire Program," CBC, December 8, 1938, http://www.cbc.ca/archives/entry/jewish-refugees-already-fleeing-germany. **59 "rather a nice progression":** Bertha Bracey: Oral History. **59 The lease allowed:** Lafitte, *The Internment of Aliens*, 48. **59 "rich, clever and un-loveable":** Chamberlain to Hilda, July 30, 1939, BUL 18/1/1110. **60 the arrests of at least twenty spies:** Research by the scholar Nicholas Hiley contests this, the official account of the 1914 arrests, arguing that it is a founding myth that greatly exaggerates both the scale and impact of the action by the agency. **60 "broken up the spy organisation":** As quoted in Gillman and Gillman, *"Collar the Lot!,"* 9. **61 twenty-seven internment camps:** Ibid., 28. **61 "A proper Nazi":** George W. Gercke, "Behind This Nazi Regime," *Independent*, May 19, 1933. **61 "one huge enemy prison camp":** Margery West as quoted in Dove, *"Totally Un-English"?*, 13. **62 immediately killed:** Webb, *British Concentration Camps*, 51. **62 "war emergency":** Gillman and Gillman, *"Collar the Lot!,"* 26. **62 most "can be presumed":** Committee of Imperial Defense, Sub-Committee on the Control of Aliens in War, Proceedings, February 20, 1939, TNA, CAB 16/211. **62 just thirty-six officers:** Hutton, *Agent Jack*, 59. **62 "In the meantime":** Diaries of Guy Maynard Liddell, intelligence officer, TNA, KV 4/185. **63 "From an MI5 point of view":** Entry for August 30, 1939, West, *The Guy Liddell Diaries*, 12. **63 just as eager:** Gerald Midgley to author, May 2020. **63 "Leave to land":** Peter Fleischmann Certificate of Registration. This twenty-four-page document recorded every address where Peter stayed in the UK. Changes had to be logged within forty-eight hours at the local police station and verified with an "Aliens Registration Office" stamp. **63 As Peter later put it:** Peter Midgley: Oral History. **63 a shelter for young Jewish refugees:** The unattractively named Home for

Aged, Needy and Incurable Jews; Leslie Kay BEM, former trustee, the Federation of Jewish Services, to author, July 2020. **64 "I saw sights":** Peter Midgley: Oral History. **64 "British poverty . . . stank":** Bertha Bracey: Oral History, 1980. **64 Austrian homes clean:** It was, perhaps, unfair to compare British families who had endured the cumulative violence of generational poverty with the Viennese families, some of whom had been wealthy and middle-class just a few years earlier, plunged only into privation by war and its aftermath. **64 Peter learned:** Peter Fleischmann Certificate of Registration. **65 On September 1, 1939:** Gillman and Gillman, *"Collar the Lot!,"* 32. **66 "A number of aliens":** "Aliens," HC Deb, September 4, 1939, *Hansard*, vol. 351, cc366–70. **67 "It was felt":** Letter from Sir John Anderson to Lord Halifax, November 7, 1939, TNA, FO 371/22941. **67 "unnecessary suffering"** As quoted in Gillman and Gillman, *"Collar the Lot!,"* 64–65. **67 remote and mitigated:** Wheeler-Bennett, *John Anderson*, 239; Gillman and Gillman, *"Collar the Lot!,"* 45. **67 "Farce":** Diaries of Guy Maynard Liddell. **68 become so aroused:** Marcel Berlins, "A Chief Justice Got Away with Murder," *Independent*, August 2, 1998. **68 two and a half guineas:** US National Archives Diplomatic Branch records (740.0015 European War 1939/895) as quoted in Gillman and Gillman, *"Collar the Lot!,"* 42. **68 He would be aided:** "Conditions in Camps: Report by Ex-Internee; Correspondence with George Lathan MP," TNA, HO 215/27. **68 They were free:** Klaus Hinrichsen: Oral History, June 1978, IWM, 3789. **69 woefully ill-equipped:** Louis Gutmann-Polangen, "Arandora Star Victim: A Supplement to the White Paper," March 21, 1941, TNA, HO 213/1431, 13. **69 lacked the experience:** Ibid. **70 Birch watched:** Ibid., 15. **70 "not running around":** Klaus Hinrichsen: Oral History. **70 "[The magistrates] were out of their depth":** Neurath, *Recollections*, 55. **70 "Refugee from Nazi Oppression":** Peter Fleischmann Certificate of Registration. **70 64,243 enemy aliens:** London, *Whitehall and the Jews*, 170. **70 "It is very easy in wartime to start a scare":** As quoted in Wheeler-Bennett, *John Anderson*, 239.

CHAPTER VII: SPY FEVER

71 **to an English father and German mother:** Sebba, *Battling for the News*, 158. **71 chew gum to steady her nerves:** Ibid., 163. **71 Later, her eyewitness reports:** Ibid. **72 one of the best-paid journalists:** Ibid., 160. **72 "bombed as they left Holland":** "Germans Dropped Women Parachutist as Decoys," *Daily Express*, May 13, 1940, 3. **73 inflated to mythic proportions:** The 4,500 parachutists who partook in the invasion represented a tiny fraction of the total invasionary force of some 360,000 men. **73 Bland titled his account:** Nevile Bland, "Fifth Column Activities," TNA, FO 371/25189/7941, code 49, file 7941. **74 "damned good stuff":** Gillman and Gillman, *"Collar the Lot!,"* 104. **74 "im-**

mediate action": Wheeler-Bennett, *John Anderson*, 244, here rendered as dialogue. 74 **Before May 1940:** Judex, *Anderson's Prisoners*, 109. 74 **"far better to intern all the lot":** *Hansard*, vol. 360, April 23, 1940. 74 **"We ought to have interned the lot":** As quoted in Lafitte, *The Internment of Aliens*, 171. 75 "Now the enemy in our midst": As quoted in Judex, *Anderson's Prisoners*, 110. 75 The figure was, in fact, just 73,500: Ibid., 102. 75 "You can't say which is good and which bad": Ibid., 111. 76 "It is lamentable how quickly": Ibid., 13–14. 76 "tremendous public demand": *Hansard*, vol. 362, July 10, 1940. 76 Peter broke the silence: Hinrichsen, unpublished memoir, 54. 76 provisional kindness: Baumel-Schwartz, *Never Look Back*, ch. 1. 77 desire to belong: Turner, . . . *And the Policeman Smiled*, 33. 77 **On December 23, 1939:** Peter Fleischmann Certificate of Registration. 77 **"I'd rather paint shop signs":** Peter Midgley: Oral History, MJM, 1988.45. 77 **When Donald was called up to serve:** Ibid. 78 **sixteen and sixty:** Initially the cabinet suggested the upper age limit should be seventy; Anderson successfully petitioned for the policy to apply only to those up to the age of sixty. 78 **"made so suddenly":** As quoted in Judex, *Anderson's Prisoners*, 5. 78 **"Fifth Column elements":** The Bland Report, TNA FO 371/25189. 79 Through the tribunals: Anderson, *Hansard*, vol. 357, March 1, 1940. 79 "No half measures will do": *Manchester Guardian*, May 13, 1940. 79 "large round-up of aliens": War Cabinet minutes, May 15, 1940, TNA, CAB 65/7. 79 "I felt compelled": *"Münchner Neueste Nachrichten,"* March 13, 1933, quoted in Longerich, *Himmler*, 150. 80 "some sort of neurosis had taken grip": Klaus Hinrichsen: Oral History, June 1978, IWM, 3789. 80 "refrain from speaking German in the streets": "While You Are in England: Helpful Information and Guidance for Every Refugee," German Jewish Aid Committee, WLC, 00527. 80 a crescendo of measures: Wheeler-Bennett, *John Anderson*, 244. 80 On May 15: Minutes of Germany Emergency Committee, June 18, 1940, LSF, YM/MfS/FCRA. 81 fourteen further recommendations: War Cabinet minutes, May 27, 1940, TNA, CAB 65/7. 81 the Home Defense (security) Executive: Little is known about this group, colloquially known as the Swinton Committee. All related files remain, at the time of this writing, either locked away, or have, according to the Foreign Office, been destroyed. 82 "There is . . . another class": House of Commons, *Hansard*, vol. 361, cc.787–98, June 4, 1940. 82 "collar the lot": It is not clear whether this phrase, long associated with the introduction of general internment, was said by Churchill, or merely attributed to him as a paraphrase. 82 **Rene Levy:** The Frenchman Levy, born on October 20, 1896, wrote under the pen name René Elvin. 82 **"the biggest haul":** René Elvin, "Isle of Forgotten Man," *Spectator*, March 28, 1941. 83 **"much-vaunted democratic liberties":** As quoted in Judex, *Anderson's Prisoners*, 9. 83 early hours: "More Aliens Are to Be Interned," *Manchester Evening News*, July 5, 1940. 83 "Get your clothes": Peter Midgley: Oral History. 83 an hour or two: Judex, *Anderson's Prisoners*, 10.

CHAPTER VIII: NIGHTMARE MILL

84 **It was as if, the teenager thought:** Peter Midgley: Oral History, MJM, 1988.45. **84 Its proprietors had been forced:** William R. Hughes, "Report on Visit to Warth Mills Internment Camp," July 10, 1940, LSF, YM/MfS/FCRA. **84 viscid and slippery:** Kochan, *Britain's Internees in the Second World War*, 97. **85 Corinthian capitals:** Ibid., 4. **85 From Bury station:** Professor P. Jacobstahl, unpublished memoir, IWM. **85 "To be marched":** Kochan, *Britain's Internees in the Second World War*, 97. **85 men loitering:** Anonymous survivor testimony as appears in "Reports on Camps III," Council of Austrians in Great Britain, August 20, 1940, LSF, YM/MfS/FCRA. **85 Lancashire Regiment:** Stent, *A Bespattered Page?*, 153. **85 "a nightmare":** Peter Midgley: Oral History. **85 150-by-120-foot:** Jacobstahl, unpublished memoir. **85 groups of twenty-five:** Anonymous survivor testimony as appears in "Reports on Camps III," Council of Austrians in Great Britain. **85 An interpreter translated:** Jacobstahl, unpublished memoir. **86 German U-boat crew:** It is more likely this man was one of the German merchant seamen, known via William Hughes's official report, to have been interned in Warth Mills. **86 "We will soon win the war":** Peter Midgley: Oral History; Gerald Midgley to author, June 2020. **86 behind a row of tables:** Jacobstahl, unpublished memoir. **86 At Kempton Park:** Jonathan Treitel to author, June 20, 2020. **86 pocketed their stethoscopes:** Anonymous survivor testimony as appears in "Reports on Camps III." **87 Academics argued:** By showing the officer a certificate bearing Oxford University's seal, the Paul Jacobsthal convinced the soldier searching his belongings to allow him to keep his copy of Homer's *The Odyssey*. **87 "increase one's loquacity":** U. Hirsch, "Freedom," *The Camp*, no. 15, August 11, 1941. **87 disguised as a greengrocer:** Private papers of Professor P. Jacobstahl, IWM, 4693: 6. **87 "panicky and cruel":** Sir Claus Moser speaking in *Jailed by the British*, JBB. **87 a horsehair blanket:** Tausig, *Kasperl, Kummerl, Jud*, 45ff. **87 chewed by vermin:** Anonymous survivor testimony as appears in "Reports on Camps III," 3. **87 requested newspapers:** Leo Kahn: Oral History, February 1979, IWM, 4300. **87 "You will not treat us as criminals":** Anonymous survivor testimony as appears in "Reports on Camps III." **88 bayonets:** Ibid. **88 Peter squeezed:** Peter Midgley: Oral History; Klaus Hinrichsen, unpublished memoir, 79. **88 interned in South Africa:** AJR Refugee Voices Testimony interview (RV125). Klaus Hinrichsen was interviewed by Anthony Grenville on November 20, 2003. **88 massive hands:** Hinrichsen, unpublished memoir, 62. **89 felt the need to be ready:** Private papers of Professor P. Jacobstahl, 10–11. **89 "Put that light out!":** Tausig, *Kasperl, Kummerl, Jud*, 46. **89 more than fifty men:** Uhlman, *The Making of an Englishman*, 230. **89 Olden, had collapsed:** Tausig, *Kasperl, Kummerl, Jud*, 47. **90 "really significant" men:** Crawford, Elsner, and Ulmschneider, *Ark of Civilization*, 208. **90 recruited by British Intel-**

ligence: Ambrose, *Hitler's Loss*, 82. **90 "most depressing sight"**: Jacobstahl, unpublished memoir. **90 a single bathtub:** Anonymous survivor testimony as appears in 'Reports on Camps III,' 3. **90 as early as four o'clock:** Hughes, "Report on Visit to Warth Mills Internment Camp." **90 sixty buckets:** Kochan, *Britain's Internees in the Second World War*, 99. **90 toward the end of the day:** Joe Pieri, as quoted in Paolini, *Missing Presumed Drowned*, 62. **90 "performed in public":** Jacobstahl, unpublished memoir. **90 volunteered in exchange:** Kochan, *Britain's Internees in the Second World War*, 99. **91 Dr. Simon Isaac:** "Dr. Simon Isaac: Ex-Professor at University of Frankfort Dies in London," *New York Times*, January 28, 1942. **91 It was a week:** Anonymous survivor testimony as appears in "Reports on Camps III," 3. **91 "hellish labyrinth":** Jacobstahl, unpublished memoir. **91 "Many [have] ceased to believe":** "Report by Ex-Internee," TNA, HO 215/27. **92 an irritable internee:** Hinrichsen, AJR Refugee Voices Testimony interview. **92 "permanently slighted":** Hinrichsen, unpublished account, 79. **92 "rid of the taste":** Tausig, *Kasperl, Kummerl, Jud*, 46. **93 focus switched:** Lawrence Darton, "An Account of the Work of the Friends Committee for Refugees and Aliens 1933–1950," unpublished manuscript, LSF, YM/MfS/FCRA. **93 on June 13:** "Diary of Recent Events Affecting the Work of the Germany Emergency Committee," LSF, YM/MfS/FCRA. **94 "I saw you in Sachsenburg":** Hughes, "Report on Visit to Warth Mills Internment Camp." **94 "not yet decided":** Anonymous survivor testimony as appears in "Reports on Camps III," 3. **95 "anything was alright":** Kochan, *Britain's Internees in the Second World War*, 78.

CHAPTER IX: THE MISTED ISLE

99 Whenever an unfamiliar boat: This version of the Isle of Man's foundational myth appears in *The Magic Kite* by Hutchinson's newspaper editor, Michael Corvin, 58–59. **99 white-maned, champing waves:** This is taken from James Joyce, *Ulysses*. **99 tonight take four:** Hinrichsen, unpublished account, 11. **99 smuggled a guitar:** Ibid. **100 "Any other Germans living here?":** Klaus Hinrichsen: Oral History, June 1978, IWM, 3789. **100 As Hinrichsen explored the ship:** Hinrichsen, unpublished account, 80. **100 a young prodigy:** MacDougall and Dickson, *Forced Journeys*, 21. **101 "Be kind to us when the others arrive":** Renee Goddard, eyewitness testimony in *Jailed by the British*, JBB. **101 "I never knew so many Jews were Nazis":** Various sources, e.g., M. F. Perutz, "That Was the War," *New Yorker*, August 12, 1985, 35. **101 "They plead persecution":** "Internment of Aliens Demanded," *Isle of Man Examiner*, June 14, 1940, 5. **102 Earlier that day:** "Closing of Roads: Hutchinson Square District, Douglas," *Isle of Man Examiner*, July 12, 1940, 2. **102 double-barbed-wire fencing:** Private papers of Professor P. Jacobsthal, IWM, 4693: 18. **102 Under spotlights:** AJR

Refugee Voices Testimony interview (RV125). Klaus Hinrichsen was interviewed by Anthony Grenville on November 20, 2003. **102 a former police constable:** "Register of leavers from the Metropolitan Police: Ambrose Harry Potterton, warrant number 126538. Joined on 6 December 1937, and left on 4 December 1938. Last posted to E Division as a PC," TNA, MEPO 4/350/114. **102 one-time head porter:** Hinrichsen, unpublished account, 11. **102 a gift, he claimed, from Indian natives:** Private papers of Professor P. Jacobsthal, 20. **102 three of the houses:** Klaus Hinrichsen: Oral History. **102 thirty-five men per building:** Kurt Treitel, unpublished letter to his parents, dated July 25, 1940. **102 stood close to Eric Kahn:** Hinrichsen, AJR Refugee Voices Testimony interview. **102 foreign correspondent:** Hinrichsen, unpublished account, 11. **102 roll call would take place at 0730:** Kurt Treitel, unpublished letter to his parents, dated July 24, 1940. **103 no curtains:** Klaus Hinrichsen: Oral History. **103 lightbulbs had been removed:** Private papers of Professor P. Jacobsthal, 13. **103 "billeted in a brothel":** Hinrichsen, unpublished account, 12. **103 common room:** Private papers of Professor P. Jacobsthal, 12. **103 a kitchen, bathroom, and toilet:** Ibid. **103 over the age of fifty-five:** Ibid., 13. **104 entangled in the barbs:** *His Majesty's Most Loyal Aliens*, BEF. **104 watched the stars:** Hinrichsen, unpublished account, 13. **104 The mellow, insistent call of a bugle:** Ibid., 12. **105 "Start by counting yourself":** Ibid. **105 The bordering pavement:** Klaus Hinrichsen: Oral History. **105 "built for the else forlorn":** William Wordsworth, "On Entering Douglas Bay, Isle of Man," *Itinerary Poems of 1833*. **105 prepared as the camp hospital:** Numbers 34 and 35. According to Hinrichsen, Dr. Alexander McPherson, a surgeon who had recently been appointed medical officer for the town of Douglas, ran the camp hospital at the time of the camp's opening. By early September 1940, according to other sources, the military physician Dr. Robert Marshall had become Hutchinson's doctor, with the support of eminent medical internees. **106 Hydrangeas bloomed:** Private papers of Professor P. Jacobsthal, 18. **106 "large-scale internments of the 1914–18 war":** "The Alien Camp," *Mona's Herald*, May 14, 1940, 4. **107 415 men:** Chappel, *Island of Barbed Wire*, 53. **109 He was nursed:** Wendy Bentall to author, March 2019. **107 first at the paper importer Westwall:** H. O. Daniel, family papers, courtesy of William Daniel. **108 Captain Daniel began:** As quoted in Hinrichsen, unpublished account, 11. **108 "To avoid becoming demoralized":** Hinrichsen reconstructed the text of this inaugural address more than forty years after the event. While it cannot offer a reliable record of the precise words spoken, the art historian maintained that his account represents the gist of these speeches and exchanges. **108 "humane and sincere":** Private papers of Professor P. Jacobsthal, 20. **109 Casper George Jurgensen:** DOB January 21, 1898, GRO, vol. 23, 114. **109 a forty-two-year-old Norwegian:** Jurgensen only became a British citizen after the war, on January 11, 1947. **109 "I hope you have recovered":** As quoted in Hinrichsen, unpublished account, 15. **109 "He seemed to be a human being":** Various sources confirm that Second Lieutenant C. G. Jurgensen was Hutchinson's intelligence officer from the camp's first day. According to a notice published in the *London Gazette* on January 3, 1941, however, he only formally joined the Intelligence Corps six months after the camp's opening. Likewise, Jurgensen only became captain on August 29, 1941. **109 each of the three streets:** This trio of representatives was known as the Council of Three. **109 *Lagerväter*:** The term "Führer" was self-evidently taboo. **109 the camp's emergent hierarchy:** Initially the British referred to these positions of responsibility in the military terms "house captain" and "camp captain," but, after the turbo-militarism of the Nazi regime, most internees preferred the title of "housefather," with its softer, quasi-pastoral implications. **110 empowering internees:** Private papers of Professor P. Jacobsthal, 19. **110 Radios were forbidden:** Various sources, e.g., Herbert Lindemeyer: Oral History, December 6, 1983, USHMM. **111 The Berlin lawyer Curt Sluzewski:** Hinrichsen, unpublished account, 16, 60. **112 "starve anyway":** As quoted in ibid., 17. **112 Artists' Refugee Committee:** Penrose, *Roland Penrose*, 92. **113 MP Sir Henry Page Croft:** Unfortunately for Fred, his well-connected father-in-law disliked Germans, Jews, and artists and did nothing to prevent or overturn Fred's subsequent internment in Hutchinson camp, aside from writing a single letter to the Home Office. **113 the group's first secretary:** In the months between the Artists' Refugee Committee's foundation and the start of the war, the committee raised around £4,000 and helped between twenty and thirty people, predominantly artists, immigrate to Britain. Some settled around Hampstead Heath in a close-knit, outsider community. **113 at least three hundred painters, sculptors, and graphic artists:** Powell and Vinzent, *Art and Migration*, 7. **113 There was Paul Hamann:** Bohm-Duchen, *Art in Exile in Great Britain*, unpaginated. **114 whose clientele . . . included:** Information courtesy of Royal Albert Memorial Museum. **114 "the most exquisite written":** Fraenkel, *Help Us Germans to Beat the Nazis*, 116. **115 "Whenever we have set in motion":** *Hansard*, vol. 362, July 10, 1940. **115 "pull a camel through the eye of a needle":** Ibid.

CHAPTER X: THE UNIVERSITY OF BARBED WIRE

117 twenty thousand men: "World War I History," Prees Heath Common Reserve. www.preesheathcommonreserve.co.uk. **117 "like slices of cake":** Tausig, *Kasperl, Kummerl, Jud,* 47. **117 "still appreciate the romance":** As quoted in Judex, *Anderson's Prisoners,* 71. **117 Captured merchant seamen:** Peter Midgley: Oral History, MJM, 1988.45. **117 internal fences divided:** Ibid. **117 mostly emptied of older men:** Zander, "Adventures in Reconciliation," 1. **117 never have been interned:** Rabbi Schonfeld estimated that as many as two thousand internees—around 7 percent of all those interned—suffered from tuberculosis, diabetes, heart disease, or other serious infirmities. **117 had been transferred:** Report on Rabbi Dr. S. Schonfeld's Visits to Internment Camps for Aliens, on July 16–23, 1940, LSF, YM/MfS/FCRA, 1. **118 desperately needed warm clothes:** Letter to Chief Rabbi Dr. Schonfeld from Walter Nussbaum, supervisor of Prees Heath camp, July 20, 1940, HLS, MS 183/228/1/465. **118 little to do:** AJR Refugee Voices Testimony interview (RV79). Walter Brunner was interviewed by Rosalyn Livshin on October 28, 2004. **118 pounding the material:** Tausig, *Kasperl, Kummerl, Jud*, 47. **118 "My soul is sad":** Letter to Regina Marx from Professor Ludwig Marx, July 5, 1940, TKS, SxMs91/1/2. **118 "life seems so senseless":** Letter to Regina Marx from Professor Ludwig Marx, July 14, 1940, TKS, SxMs91/1/2. **118 sing the harmonies:** Zander, "Adventures in Reconciliation," 2. **118 employed by the BBC:** Leo Wurmser, "Singing a Song in a Foreign Land," RCM. **119 Wurmser spent the next week:** Benjamin Zander to author, June 2020. **119 "He recovered visibly":** Zander, "Adventures in Reconciliation," 2. **119 A professor in medicine:** Peter Midgley: Oral History. **119 without electricity:** Zander, "Adventures in Reconciliation," 2. **119 use as a canvas:** Peter Midgley: Oral History. **120 eaten only gray porridge:** Kurt Treitel, unpublished letter to parents, dated July 24, 1940. **120 Hinrichsen saw:** Klaus Hinrichsen, unpublished account, 24. **120 On the table:** Ibid. **120 "What the hell is going on here?":** Hinrichsen's unpublished account (p. 4ff) is the source of the dialogue in this scene, which should be taken as impressionistic rather than journalistic. The pertinent details—that Warschauer arrived in Hutchinson on the day of its opening, was briefly a resident in Hinrichsen's house, kept "attendants," boasted of powerful contacts who would soon facilitate his release, and flaunted his wealth in the camp—are all facts verified in official MI5 documents. **120 Dressed only in a tracksuit:** A letter of endorsement written by Hutchinson's intelligence officer, Captain Jurgensen, contained in Warschauer's security files, confirms that Warschauer "has been interned in this camp since the opening on 13th July 1940," TNA, KV2–1139b; the description of the tracksuit comes from Hinrichsen, unpublished account, 23. **120 arrested on July 12:** "Ludwig Max Warschauer" document dated October 28, 1941, TNA, KV 2/1139: 7. **121 After lunch each house:** Private papers of Professor P. Jacobstahl, 13. **121 Soon after his arrival:** Walter Wallich: Oral History, IWM, 4431. **121 Count von Lingen:** Nor "George Mansfield," another pseudonym "Lingen" used. **122 no man was permitted to withdraw:** Some internees chose to swear an oath of allegiance to Germany to receive pocket money from the Swiss Legation. Doing so automatically placed the internee in category A and rendered them ineligible for release without special authority. No Hutchinson internees were found, during the research for this book, to have taken the "deal." **122 "In this camp the Oxford professor":** Private papers of Professor P. Jacobstahl, 14. **122 "I can't help laughing":** Hinrichsen, unpublished account, 23. **123 prom-**

ised to invest: Ibid., 24. **123 "[Warschauer's] complete sincerity":** Letter to
S. L. Edwards, War Office, from Sir Herbert Williams MP, May 28, 1940, TNA,
KV 2/1139_2. **123 visited the engineer's home office:** Monica Schubert to author, April 2021. **123 most of the internees:** Fritz Hallgarten: Oral History,
IWM, 3976. **123 should be allowed to vote:** Hinrichsen, unpublished account,
18. **124 former private secretary:** Stephan, *"Communazis,"* 55. **124 The don
appeared:** Ibid., 19. **124 Burschell allocated departments:** The organization of
these various departments was not settled for several weeks. In the fifth issue of
The Camp newspaper, dated October 20, 1940, Burschell laid out his full and
final proposal for Hutchinson's internal organization, which included a press
department, a careers adviser, and a sanitary department. **124 which distributed:** Peter Midgley: Oral History. **124 Each official was paid:** Klaus Hinrichsen: Oral History, June 1978, IWM, 3789. **124 wore a white plastic rosette:**
Hinrichsen, unpublished account, 51. **124 vaguely resent:** Ibid. **124 "He overestimated his friends' reliability":** Michael Corvin, "Farewell, Fredric Burschell," *The Camp*, no. 7, November 3, 1940. **124 "Even a god would not be able
to":** Frederic Burschell, "Camp-Father's Task," *The Camp*, no. 5, October 20,
1940, TNA, HO 215/437. **125 selected a location:** Hinrichsen, unpublished account, 20. **125 "the chance to DO something":** As quoted in Judex, *Anderson's
Prisoners*, 88. **125 "disillusion and despair":** Ibid. **125 Ahrends was an architect:** Ahrends, *A3*, 79. **126 On July 15:** Kurt Treitel, unpublished letter to his
parents, dated July 17, 1940. **126 "nasty cackle of laughter":** Hinrichsen, unpublished account, 20. **126 Might not some of these men:** Klaus Hinrichsen:
Oral History. **126 prepare them for the school exams:** Hutchinson's intelligence officer, Captain Jurgensen, telephoned headmasters at various schools to
request schedules of the curriculum, while some of the university professors
offered to tutor small groups. **126 officially founded on July 17, 1940:** Klaus
Hinrichsen, "Cultural Flashlights," Hutchinson *Almanac 1940–41*. **127 My
Hutchinson University:** Hinrichsen, unpublished account, 21. **127 oversee the
schedule of academic lectures:** "Hutchinson Camp University Organising
Committee," July 31, 1940; "Hutchinson Internment Camp, Cultural Events Programmes and Schedules, 1940–41," IWM, 5382. **127 Heinfried "Heinz" Beran,
taught English:** Beran, whose English mother came from Norwich, had taught
the subject in Berlin at the Berlitz School of Languages. Since immigrating to
Britain in 1935, he had taught German, now at the London branch of the same
school. He worked, for a time, for the Austrian section at the BBC. He was arrested at Dartington Hall in Devon, alongside another Hutchinson internee, Sigurd Leeder, the head of the School of Dancing. **127 musical performances:** Due
to the high concentration of artists in the camp, Hutchinson gained a reputation
for being impoverished of musicians. ("We were rich in professors and painters,
but poor in musicians," Fred Uhlman later wrote.) This is plainly untrue. As well
as Marjan Rawicz, a raft of skilled musicians performed in the camp, including

Hans Fürth, a Royal Academy of Music graduate; the musicologist Professor Richard Glas; the singer Professor Stefan Pollmann; and the pianist Egon Reisz. Alfred Blumen, the Austrian-born pianist who later performed with Richard Strauss on record, was interned at the camp. The Oxford academic and composer Egon Wellesz and the director of the Dartington Hall Music Group and conductor of the English Opera, Hans Oppenheim, were both interned at Hutchinson. So, too, were Peter Ebert, future director of Glyndebourne Opera, and a young Wolfgang Lesser, later president of the Association of Composers and Musicologists. In addition to the classical composers and performers, the inaugural issue of *The Camp* newspaper mentions "a new mouthorgan band" that "will no doubt achieve great success in the future." **127 chess, bridge, and boxing tournaments:** "Hutchinson Camp University Organising Committee," July 31, 1940; "Hutchinson Internment Camp, Cultural Events Programmes and Schedules, 1940–41." **127 ninety copies:** Schonfeld Folder 240, HLS. **127 orange boxes:** H.F., "The Camp Library," *The Camp*, no. 13, January 14, 1941. **127 sympathetic ear:** On the evidence of some letters published in early editions of *The Camp* newspaper, despite a world-class lineup of speakers, some internees felt there was room for improvement. **128 The committee worked quickly:** Private papers of Professor P. Jacobsthal, 21. **128 Dr. Simchowitz:** A radiologist at the Royal Berkshire Hospital, Reading. **128 "a subject in the world that wasn't discussed":** Fritz Hallgarten: Oral History. **128 "a miracle of the human will":** Weissenborn, *Hellmuth Weissenborn, Engraver*, xiv. **128 "beautiful fairy-dreams":** Hirsch Uri (writing as "Ulli Hirsch"), "Freedom," *The Camp*, no. 10, November 24, 1940. **128 arrived in Hutchinson on July 17:** Private papers of Professor P. Jacobsthal, 12. **128 "ghostlike professors":** Ibid., 30. **129 "boring," "stupid," and "inadequate":** Ibid., 23. **129 "dwindling audience":** Both Kästner's and Heinemann's names were decorously redacted in most versions of Jacobsthal's original typed manuscript. **129 putting golf balls:** In a letter to his parents Kurt Trietel recorded that a miniature golf course "opened" on the lawn on August 1, 1940, two weeks after the camp's founding. **129 There would be a group of chattering walkers:** Scene as described by Hirsch Uri (writing as "Ulli Hirsch"), "Freedom," *The Camp*, no. 10, November 24, 1940. **129 "thirst for knowledge"** Hinrichsen, unpublished account, 20. **129 Each had attracted audiences:** "Hutchinson Camp University Organising Committee," July 31, 1940; "Hutchinson Internment Camp, Cultural Events Programmes and Schedules," 1940–41. **130 "eagerly discussed the finer points":** Richard Friedenthal: Oral History, November 1978, IWM, 3963. **130 Every evening a scurry:** Uhlman, *The Making of an Englishman*, 233. **130 twice-weekly sojourns to the beach:** Kurt Treitel, unpublished letter to "O.E.," dated August 17, 1940. **130 Captain Alexander, commandant of Mooragh camp:** Report on Rabbi Dr. S. Schonfeld's Visits to Internment Camps for Aliens, on July 16–23, 1940, LSF, YM/MfS/FCRA, 2. **130 "a model community":** Ibid. **131 "let me assure you":** Klaus

Hinrichsen, "Peter Midgley and Internment," speech delivered at Woodlands Art Gallery, Blackheath, July 17, 1992, TGA, 20052/2/20.

CHAPTER XI: THE VIGIL

132 Michael Corvin: Né Leo Freund, the name the writer used both prior to internment and in his postwar life in California. **132 "Michael Corvin reading from own writings":** As Corvin delivered a series of weekly lectures under this title, it is unclear which specific lecture contained his account of the disaster. **133 huddle in the front garden:** Private papers of Professor P. Jacobsthal, IWM, 4693: 26. **133 Ibiza to England in 1936:** Michael Corvin to author, June 2021. **134 June 30, 1940:** Lord Snell, "*Arandora Star* Inquiry," TNA, PREM 3/49; Louis Gutmann-Polangen, "*Arandora Star* Victim: A Supplement to the White Paper," March 21, 1941, TNA, HO 213/1431: 36. **134 from Huyton camp:** Klaus Hinrichsen, unpublished memoir, 45. **134 Menacing coils of barbed wire:** Paolini, *Missing Presumed Drowned*, 89. **134 twelve-pound antiaircraft gun:** Ibid. **134 On June 14:** Hirschfeld, *Exile in Great Britain*, 174. **135 473 German:** Snell, "*Arandora Star* Inquiry." **135 War Office had selected a group:** War Office, "Memorandum on Aliens," July 27, 1940, TNA, PREM 3/49. **135 six days to decide:** Snell, "*Arandora Star* Inquiry." **135 There was Willi Blumens:** Gutmann-Polangen, "*Arandora Star* Victim," 44. **136 as a chaperone:** John Ötvös to author, May 2021. **136 one of the royal princesses:** Gutmann-Polangen, "*Arandora Star* Victim," 41. **136 "mismanagement, lack of foresight, forethought and consideration":** "Internment of Aliens," House of Lords Debate, August 6, 1940, *Hansard*, vol. 117, cc107–39. **136 Canada's offer had been gladly received:** London, *Whitehall and the Jews*, 169. **137 at best spurious:** Italians, who had not yet been officially categorized according to their suspected risk by tribunals, were particularly vulnerable to misclassification and selection for deportation by MI5. **137 "Even to my tired eyes":** *Jailed by the British*, JBB. **137 recently returned:** Diary of Gerhard Miedzwinski, as quoted in Gillman and Gillman, "*Collar the Lot!*," 190. **137 The ship departed:** "Account Compiled from the Reports of Chief Officer and Chief Engineer of SS *Arandora Star*," July 4, 1940, TNA, PREM 3/49. **137 a zigzag course:** Diary of Uwe Radok, as quoted in Gillman and Gillman, "*Collar the Lot!*," 190. **138 no Royal Naval escort:** "Account Compiled from the Reports of Chief Officer and Chief Engineer of SS *Arandora Star*." **138 pro-Nazi songs:** Gutmann-Polangen, "*Arandora Star* Victim," 27. **138 "subversive liars":** Lt-Col. W. P. Scott, Commanding Officer, "Q" Troops, Dunera, to Colonel Robertson, War Office, London, AUA, MP 729/6, File 63/401/141. **139 The ship did not stop:** Gutmann-Polangen, "*Arandora Star* Victim," 44. **139 pink gin and beer:** Diary of Gerhard Miedzwinski, as quoted in Gillman and Gillman, *"Collar the Lot!,"* 191. **139 "zig-zag number ten":** "Account Compiled from the Reports of Chief Officer and Chief Engineer of SS *Arandora Star."* **140 Both the main and standby generators:** Ibid. **140 within two minutes:** Ibid. **140 none of the military personnel:** Lieutenant J. F. Constable as quoted in Paolini, *Missing Presumed Drowned,* 96. **140 There were twelve working lifeboats:** "Account Compiled from the Reports of Chief Officer and Chief Engineer of SS *Arandora Star."* **140 the ironwork came loose:** Harold Finney eyewitness testimony, as quoted in Paolini, *Missing Presumed Drowned,* 101. **141 "greatly hampered":** "Account Compiled from the Reports of Chief Officer and Chief Engineer of SS *Arandora Star."* **141 The troops attempted to prize:** Paolini, *Missing Presumed Drowned,* 100. **141 none volunteered:** "Account Compiled from the Reports of Chief Officer and Chief Engineer of SS *Arandora Star."* **141 Captain Moulton coolly asked for a glass of water:** "Arandora Star's Last Hours," London *Times,* July 5, 1940, 6. **141 refused to jump:** Paolini, *Missing Presumed Drowned,* 102. **141 "the finest thing I have ever seen":** "A Hero of the *Arandora Star,"* Hartlepool *Northern Daily Mail,* August 2, 1940, 4. **142 A geyser of steam:** "Arandora Star's Last Hours," 6. **142 Then, swirling silence:** Interview with Rando Bertoia, as quoted in Paolini, *Missing Presumed Drowned,* 107. **142 third officer:** Interview with Rupert Limentani, as quoted in Paolini, *Missing Presumed Drowned,* 107. **142 cut abruptly short:** Victor Tolaini, as appears in *Jailed by the British,* JBB. **142 "leaf of a book":** Lou Beschizza, as appears in ibid. **142 A Royal Air Force Sunderland flying boat:** "Account Compiled from the Reports of Chief Officer and Chief Engineer of SS *Arandora Star."* **143 three-mile area to the west:** "Enemy Submarine Attacks on Merchant Shipping: Reports," TNA, ADM 199/141. **143 "painfully slow":** "Account from Commanding Officers HMCS *St. Laurent,"* July 4, 1940, TNA, PREM 3/49. **143 an Austrian and evangelical Christian:** John Ötvös to author, May 2021. **143 worked throughout the night:** "HMCS *St. Laurent's* Race to Rescue the Enemy," *Maclean's,* November 19, 1960. **143 driven to Mearnskirk Hospital:** Gutmann-Polangen, "Arandora Star Victim," 41. **144 "Germans and Italians fight for lifeboats":** "Arandora Star Sunk by U-boat," London *Times,* July 4, 1940, 4. **144 "There is absolutely no truth in the statement":** "Account Compiled from the Reports of Chief Officer and Chief Engineer of SS *Arandora Star."* **145 Other survivors of the disaster:** Other survivors of the *Arandora Star* interned in Hutchinson included the film director Fred Weiss, the chemist Heinz Künstlinger, the inventor Franz Madler, the wine merchant Hans Mankiewicz, the company director Otto Scholz, and Josef Ötvös, the doctor who had provided aid to his fellow internees on the rescue ship.

CHAPTER XII: THE SUICIDE CONSULTANCY

146 **The War Office planned to produce:** Minutes of the Germany Emergency Council (meeting with Major Coates), July 9, 1940, LSF, YM/MfS/FCRA. 146 **"ghastly rumours and gnawing anxiety":** René Elvin, "Isle of Forgotten Man," *Spectator*, March 28, 1941. 146 **"the ensuing disstress":** Ibid. 146 **Within three weeks:** Kurt Treitel, unpublished letter to his parents, dated August 9, 1940. 146 **the most popular texts:** H.F., "The Camp Library," *The Camp*, no. 13, January 14, 1941. 147 **found Nazi propaganda:** Jonathan Trietel to author, June 2020. 147 **All but the most optimistic:** Uhlman, *The Making of an Englishman*, 231. 147 **fully expected to wake up:** Herbert Lindemeyer: Oral History, December 6, 1983, USHMM. 147 **put on show trials: Klaus** Hinrichsen, unpublished account, 94. 148 **"rats in a cage":** Fritz Hallgarten: Oral History, IWM, 3967. 148 **turned off the gas supply:** Shepherd, *A Refuge from Darkness*, 148. 148 **six men had hung themselves:** Report on Rabbi Dr. S. Schonfeld's Visits to Internment Camps for Aliens, on July 16–23, 1940, LSF, YM/MfS/FCRA, 1; letter from Helmuth Mirauer, January 6, 1946. 148 **following the example of a Mr. Schiff:** Probably Arthur Schiff (DOB December 6, 1881), although not listed in the Home Office records of internee deaths. 148 **on July 3:** Anonymous diary entry from a Huyton internee, as quoted in Judex, *Anderson's Prisoners*, 89. 148 **Arthur Just:** "Missing believed drowned on way to I.O.M.," written on Arthur Just Alien Card (DOB August 15, 1894), TNA, HO 396–260. 148 **"If those swine":** Fraenkel, *Help Us Germans to Beat the Nazis*, 118. 149 **hidden from Camp Father Burschell:** Hinrichsen, unpublished account, 94. 149 **The pair offered demonstrations:** Ibid., 95. 149 **how to make a reliable hanging noose:** Officials recorded cases of suicide at almost all the main internment camps, including Hutchinson, where Kurt Schier died by suicide on July 11, 1943. According to official documents, there was at least one case of murder, in Camp F, where Nestor Huppunen was stabbed to death on April 20, 1943. 149 **"unpleasant incident":** Winston Churchill letter to Lord Snell, November 10, 1940, TNA, PREM 3/49. 149 **"Nazi sympathisers":** *Hansard*, vol. 362, July 9, 1940. 150 **only 27 percent:** Judex, *Anderson's Prisoners*, 111. 151 **"He [has been] first combed out":** *Hansard*, vol. 362, July 10, 1940. 151 **"That feeling changed":** Ibid. 151 **A hobbyist lepidopterist:** "Who We Are," Merlin Trust, http://merlin-trust.org.uk/about-us/. 152 **the men returned to Liverpool via train:** Diary of Alfred Lewinsky, as quoted in Bartrop, *The Dunera Affair*, 161. 152 **shoved with a rifle butt:** Albert Karolyi eyewitness testimony, as quoted in Bartrop, *The Dunera Affair*, 150. 152 **appeared to be drunk:** Diary of Alfred Lewinsky, as quoted in Bartrop, *The Dunera Affair*, 162. 152 **Scott watched:** Merlin Scott, letter to father, TNA, FO 371/25192, folio 241. 152 **one of his nails torn off:** Harry Jay eyewitness testimony, as quoted in Bartrop, *The Dunera Affair*, 152. 152 **"a thor-**

oughly bad show": Merlin Scott, letter to father. **153 quickly curdled to out-rage:** Lou Beschizza, as featured in *Jailed by the British*, JBB. **153 gross mistreatment of prisoners:** Eventually, the commanding officer and two of his subordinates were brought before a court martial. **153 "not met a single soul":** John Maynard Keynes to Francis C. Scott, July 23, 1940, in Elizabeth Johnson and Donald Moggridge, *The Collected Writings of John Maynard Keynes*, vol. 22 (Cambridge, UK: Cambridge University Press, 1978), 190–91. **154 The house-mates finally ruled:** "1st Judgement of Privy Court of House Arbitration 2, House 2 Douglas," August 9, 1940, Kurt Treitel papers. **154 "any fish into salmon":** Like every other house cook, Weissenborn received sixpence a week for his work, payment he initially tried to refuse, until he was told it was a camp rule. **154 the artist bowed:** Nyburg, *From Leipzig to London*, 86. **154 carrying blackout material:** Bertha Bracey, "Chairman's Report on the Isle of Man Camps, 28th October–2nd November 1940," LSF, YM/MfS/FCRA. **154 Hutchinson's windows:** Different internees remember the window material differently. The sharp lines that can be seen in surviving photographs of the window etching sug-gest, as per Peter Midgley's recollection, that polymer film was used, not paint. **155 "intensely depressing":** Bracey deemed it "inexcusable" that blackout cur-tains still had not been fitted by the end of the summer, "in anticipation of the long winter nights." The murk caused by this military oversight surely contrib-uted to internees' experiences of depression, but it also gifted the camp a canvas for something approaching a new art form. **155 Weissenborn began to cut more:** Cesarani and Kushner, *The Internment of Aliens in Twentieth Century Brit-ain*, 191. **155 In House 19:** "Nail, Knife and Razorblade," *The Camp*, no. 7, No-vember 3, 1940. **155 canteen of profiteering:** In fact, according to a report for the Central Department of Interned Refugees, the canteen's profits were fed back into the camp. Around three-quarters of the profits were paid into a fund to sup-port destitute cases, and the remainder put toward the cost of cultural activities for the internees. **156 He had a soft, loose mouth:** Transcript of "Interned with Kurt Schwitters," May 1988, TATE, TGA 20052/1/5/19. **156 socks pocked:** Uhl-man, *The Making of an Englishman*, 234. **156 chaotic manner:** Kaiser, *Degener-ate Art*, 2. **157 *Merz Picture 32A*:** Merz was Schwitters's label (coined after he cut the syllable from an advertisement for *Kommerzbank*) for his own idiosyncratic form of collage, an ambiguous blend of contemporary, abstract styles that was, broadly, poorly received by contemporary art critics. If pressed, it is likely that he would have described his artistic mode as *Merz*, not Dadaist or *Sturm*, which were, strictly, influences on his work, not defining traditions. Nevertheless, the Berlin Dadaist and satirist Walter Mehring described Schwitters as "a steadfast Dadaist . . . the most kind-hearted and considerate of them all." **157 Group 9 of the exhibition:** Kaiser, *Degenerate Art*, 26, 60. **157 shave and neglect:** Undated letter from Edith Thomas, as quoted in Webster, *Kurt Merz Schwitters*, 335. **157 "Do you have any leftovers?":** Erlhoff, *Kurt Schwitters Almanach*, 111, here rendered as dialogue. **157 adding bromide to the oats:** Fritz Hallgarten: Oral History. **157 When one housefather asked why:** Hinrichsen, unpublished account, 75. **157 the first to recognize Schwitters:** Webster, *Kurt Merz Schwitters*, 309. **158 "a surprisingly limp handshake":** Transcript of "Interned with Kurt Schwitters." **158 "As soon as I can lay my hands on some paint":** Ibid. **158 the deep pocket of his loden jacket:** Peter Midgley: Oral History, MJM, 1988.45. **158 The call-and-response continued:** The details in this anecdote vary between tellings; in Hinrichsen's version, the banker lived in a house on the opposite side of the square (perhaps number 43, which faced number 19), and he and Schwitters would bark at each other not between floors, but across the lawn. **158 investigate the noise:** Hinrichsen, unpublished account, 46. **159 "elevated to a sort of illuminated scroll":** Cesarani and Kushner, *The Internment of Aliens in Twentieth Century Britain*, 193. **159 mixing crushed graphite from lead pencils with margarine:** Ibid. **159 unofficial spokesman for the group:** It is obvious why an art dealer would ingratiate himself with the artists among whom he now, fortuitously, lived, and why he might help facilitate their work. Indeed, after the war, Oppenheimer represented Erich Kahn. Oppenheimer was not the only art collector at Hutchinson. **159 Oppenheimer was an overpowering character:** Klaus Hinrichsen, "Art in Hutchinson Camp—A Personal View," talk delivered at Camden Arts Centre, September 17, 1986, TATE, TGA 20052/1/7/12. **160 "We have a number of very well-known artists here":** As quoted by Hinrichsen in *His Majesty's Most Loyal Aliens*, BEF. **160 forbidden from accepting a place in art college:** Wendy Bentall to author, March 2019. **160 set aside studio space on the top floor:** Hinrichsen, unpublished account, 20. **160 recently beaten Hutchinson's team at soccer:** Hinrichsen, "Art in Hutchinson Camp—A Personal View." **160 The pastry cook was an Austrian refugee:** The café owner's name is, alas, seemingly lost to history. If Hinrichsen or Uhlman recalled the name, neither recorded it; the curator of the Manx Museum on the Isle of Man says that she has never come across the name in the archives. **161 "What about a Hutchinson Café?":** Hinrichsen, unpublished account, 59. **161 provided some existing member had recommended them:** Ibid. **161 There was to be no talk:** Hinrichsen, "Art in Hutchinson Camp—A Personal View." **161 Bruno Ahrends, as head of the Cultural Department:** "Artists Café, Hutchinson Camp," December 1940, TATE, TGA 20052/2/7/28. **162 Ludwig Meidner:** In his lifetime Hinrichsen expressed continued amazement that he hadn't been aware that an artist of Meidner's stature was also interned at Hutchinson camp, and confusion as to why Meidner shunned the Artists Café. The reason is simple: Hinrichsen had left the camp by the time Meidner arrived. **162 many other musicians, composers and actors were never, seemingly, invited:** For example, the film directors Fred Weiss and Peter Margitai (later "Maxwell," whose oeuvre includes the TV series *The Adventures of Robin Hood*), the German composer Wolfgang Lesser, the playwright Franz Bönsch, and the cartoonist Joseph Otto Flatter all lived in Hutchinson at the time, yet were apparently not associated with the café. **162 "the most revolting piece of writing in our time":** As quoted in Webster, *Kurt Merz Schwitters*, 65. **162 games of poker:** E.g., entry for November 22, 1940, "Diary of an Internee," private papers of Dr. F. Uhlman, IWM, 6781. **162 Richard Friedenthal recited . . . from memory:** Hinrichsen, "Art in Hutchinson Camp—A Personal View."

CHAPTER XIII: INTO THE CRUCIBLE

163 **It was the night before the Luftwaffe:** "Air Raids in Cheshire During World War Two," Cheshire Roll of Honor, https://www.cheshireroll.co.uk/cheshire-air-raids. **163 The journey to Liverpool caught:** Peter Midgley: Oral History, MJM, 1988.45. **164 On Monday August 26, 1940:** While Peter had no recollection of these dates, in a letter to his parents Kurt Treitel recorded the arrival date of Prees Heath's internees. **164 "a return to civilization":** Tausig, *Kasperl, Kummerl, Jud*, 50. **164 dawn exercises held on the lawn square:** Kurt H. Böhm, "Sport," *The Camp*, no. 4, October 15, 1940, LBI. **164 Breakfast: 8:15. Lunch: 12:30. Supper: 7:00:** Kurt Treitel, unpublished letter to his parents, dated July 24, 1940. **165 escaping to Britain on a fishing boat:** Bratu, who had worked alongside resistance groups in Belgium, reportedly later worked as a British intelligence officer. **165 proto-aerobics session on the lawn:** "Physical education with music," 16:45, August 21, 1940, Cultural Department Programme, no. 5, "Hutchinson Internment Camp, Cultural Events Programmes and Schedules," 1940–41, IWM, 5382. **165 In the six weeks since its opening:** William W. Simpson, "Report on a Visit to the Isle of Man, November 2nd–6th, 1940," LSF. **165 fixed watches:** Darton, *An Account of the Work of the Friends Committee for Refugees and Aliens, 1933–50*, LSF, YM/MfS/FCRA, 83, 87. **166 apply to chop wood:** Peter Midgley: Oral History. **166 island's airport:** Herbert Lindemeyer: Oral History, December 6, 1983, USHMM. **166 purchase items on credit:** Hellmuth Weissenborn: Oral History, MJM, 1988.48. **166 generic notes:** *Deutsches Exilarchiv 1933–1945*, EB autograph 681, DNB. **166 Otto Haas-Heye:** The fashion designer Harald Mahrenholtz, who opened his fashion house on Curzon Street in 1936, was also interned at Hutchinson, as was his former teacher, the artist Ludwig Meidner. **166 everyone recognized his work:** Frustratingly little has been written about the highly influential Haas-Heye, who taught at the famous Reimann School in London. His daughter, the Nazi party member turned resistance fighter Libertas Schulze-Boysen, was executed by the Nazis on December 22, 1942, at Plötzensee Prison in Berlin. **166 "amazingly vivid":** Michael Corvin, "Artifical Flowers," *The Camp*, no. 6, April 6, 1941, IWM. **166 A shop was opened:** William R. Hughes, "Report on a Visit to the Isle of Man," September 10, 1940. **166**

no income or funds: The lawyer and wine dealer Fritz Hallgarten, Hutchinson's so-called minister of welfare, looked after this group, disbursing one shilling per week to each man with which to buy items from the camp shop, and arranging for army boots to be given to those who had none. **167 offering to sketch their portrait:** Peter Midgley: Oral History. **167 £3 for a head and shoulders:** Schwitters adjusted his prices after the writer Heinrich Fraenkel suggested he opt for the more reassuringly expensive five guineas. **167 straightforwardness of the portraits:** Peter Midgley: Oral History. **167 "I had always wanted to paint":** Ibid. **167 "here was a natural talent":** Karl Hinrichsen eulogy for Peter Midgley, TATE, TGA 20052/2/20. **168 the unique companionship:** Greene, *The Ministry of Fear*, ch. 6. **168 bushy-eyebrowed internees:** Hinrichsen, unpublished account, 77. **168 The older men showed Peter:** Peter Midgley: Oral History. **168 "Everything thereafter . . . was just a recap":** Ibid. **168 "remarkable aptitude":** A. Z., "Art Exhibition," *The Camp*, no. 2, September 29, 1940, LBI. **168 plainly representational:** Peter Midgley: Oral History. **169 "arrogant and opinionated brat":** Hinrichsen, unpublished account, 77. **169 "ghastly son":** Brinson, *His Majesty's Loyal Internee*, 91. **169 collapsed piano:** Fred Uhlman: Oral History, TNA 4441. **169 studded with found objects:** Erlhoff, *Kurt Schwitters Almanach*, 111. **170 an unenviable arrangement:** Webster, *Kurt Merz Schwitters*, 313. **170 the novelist Saul Bellow:** Later a neighbor to Hellmuth Weissenborn. **170 the same stillness:** As quoted in Cronin, *Conversations with Saul Bellow*. **171 "We have been Hitler's enemies":** As quoted in "His Majesty's Most Loyal Internees," *Quadrant* 53 (May-June 1968). **171 "Some of us believed":** "Report by Ex-Internee," TNA, HO 215/27. **171 "settle down miraculously":** Uhlman, *The Making of an Englishman*, 227. **171 "special torture":** *Jailed by the British*, JBB. **172 Peter watched the poet:** Fraenkel, *Help Us Germans to Beat the Nazis*, 115. **172 given birth:** Uhlman, *The Making of an Englishman*, 239. **172 Uhlman was not alone:** Ibid., 232. **172 "it causes a trauma":** Private papers of Professor P. Jacobsthal, IWM, 4693. **172 "continuous torment":** Weissenborn, *Hellmuth Weissenborn, Engraver*, xiv. **173 the letters would have to stop:** Peter Midgley: Oral History. **173 "singularly unconcerned":** Hinrichsen eulogy for Peter Midgley. **173 "hottest crater":** As quoted in Presler and Riedel, *Ludwig Meidner*, 6. **174 "The camp here is quite wonderful":** As quoted in Kochan, *Britain's Internees in the Second World War*, 125. **174 "I could never have afforded":** AJR Refugee Voices Testimony interview (RV202). Francis Steiner was interviewed by Jana Buresova on March 10, 2017. **174 a successful career:** Known today and hereafter in the text as the *New Statesman*. **174 Victor Gollancz:** In 1940 the ebullient Gollancz, famous for publishing Daphne du Maurier and John le Carré's bestsellers, released the first book about internment during the Second World War. Titled *Anderson's Prisoners*, it was written by the Labour Party politician Herbert Delauney Hughes under the pseudonym Judex. **174 provided the author with a typewriter:** Fraenkel, *Farewell to Germany*, 26. **174 excused the**

writer: Ibid. **174 Routine and absorption:** Curiously, Fraenkel was not the only internee at Hutchinson whom Victor Gollancz had commissioned. Gollancz had also paid Dr. Harald Schmidt-Landry a £100 advance to author a book about Jews in Germany. Unlike Fraenkel, Landry never delivered his manuscript. **174 endlessly sweeping the roads:** Jonathan Treitel to author, June 2020. **175 first offered Peter membership:** Hinrichsen implies that this age limit was official "club" policy, but it's equally probable that, until Peter's arrival, no teenager much felt like hanging out with a group of rather idiosyncratic men who were, Hinrichsen aside, at least twice his age. **175 "emotional and romantic":** Hinrichsen, unpublished account, 58. **175 lured . . . by the promise of cake:** Ibid. **175 committing snippets to memory:** Peter Midgley: Oral History. **175 "would be obliged":** Hinrichsen, unpublished account, 25. **176 "did not like the scheme at all":** Sir Cecil Hurst, "Ludwig Max Warschauer: Notes of Interview on 12th August 1941," TNA, KV 2/1139. **177 "I loosen my revolver belt":** Hinrichsen, unpublished account, 37. **177 "he was a fascist":** Ibid., 25. **177 narrow-minded and humorless:** Dr. F. Uhlman, "Diary of an Internee," private papers, September 18, 1940, IWM, 6781.

CHAPTER XIV: THE FIRST GOODBYES

178 "Fifty-three . . . refugees": *Hansard*, vol. 363, July 30, 1940. **179 the blind pensioner:** *Hansard*, debate, vol. 117, August 6, 1940. **179 "right to interfere":** *Jewish Chronicle*, May 10, 1940, and May 24, 1940. **179 "disgraceful hounding":** *Jewish Chronicle*, July 26, 1940, and August 2, 1940. **179 "less rigid attitude":** War Cabinet minutes, August 1, 1940, TNA, CAB 65/8. **179 around 150 per day:** Kochan, *Britain's Internees in the Second World War*, 124. **179 "I always thought":** *Hansard*, vol. 364, August 15, 1940. **180 "Most regrettable and deplorable":** Ibid. **180 "humanity and justice prevail":** V. Ogilvie, "Public Opinion about Aliens Ignored," Letter to the Editor, *Spectator*, August 23, 1940, 3. **180 "Injustices have been committed":** Sebastian Stafford, "The Aliens Question," Letter to the Editor, *Spectator*, August 16, 1940, 12. **181 drawers strung from laundry lines:** One of Uhlman's drawings of the café shows that the room in House 15 continued to be used to dry laundry during meetings. **181 "Is this not the same principle?":** Letter to George Bell from G. Leibholz, August 20, 1940, LPL. **182 "profoundly disappointing":** "The Internment Scandal," *Spectator*, July 26, 1940, 5. **182 "The Cabinet is apparently convinced":** Judex, *Anderson's Prisoners*, 100–101. **182 "incapable of sober justification":** London *Times*, August 22, 1940. **182 "To fructify the life of the country":** Letter to Sir Granville Bantock from Ralph Vaughan Williams, August 21, 1940, RVM, VWL1430. **183 "seen the military folly":** *New Statesman*, August 10, 1940. **183 "Art cannot live behind barbed wire": *New Statesman and Nation*, August 28, 1940. **183 When Fraenkel finished:** Hinrichsen, unpublished account, 59. **184 "That newspapers are a nuisance":** "Debating Society," November 1, 1940, Cultural Department Programme, no. 15; "Hutchinson Internment Camp, Cultural Events Programmes and Schedules," 1940–41, IWM, 5382. **184 "That saving money is unwise":** "Debating Society," October 13, 1940, Cultural Department Programme, no. 13; "Hutchinson Internment Camp, Cultural Events Programmes and Schedules," 1940–41, IWM, 5382. **184 "That beauty in women is of greater importance than intelligence":** "Debating Society," January 3, 1941, Cultural Department Programme, no. 24; "Hutchinson Internment Camp, Cultural Events Programmes and Schedules," 1940–41, IWM, 5382. **184 "That slavery should be reintroduced":** "Debating Society," January 31, 1941, Cultural Department Programme, no. 28; "Hutchinson Internment Camp, Cultural Events Programmes and Schedules," 1940–41, IWM, 5382. **184 signed the letter:** One of the letter's signatories, the society portraitist Carl Felkel, was released shortly before its publication. **184 "It was the beginning of my life":** Peter Midgley: Oral History, MJM, 1988.45. **184 "the prevailing feature of camp-life":** William R. Hughes, "Skeleton Report and Recommendations," undated, LSF, YM/MfS/FCRA. **185 "O' Isle of bearded Man":** Untitled poem by Walter Heydecker, inscribed in a drawing book owned by Paul Henning, TGA, 20052/2/8/7. **185 extended only to married men:** Kurt Treitel, unpublished letter to his parents, dated July 28, 1940. **185 Couples were offered:** Judex, *Anderson's Prisoners*, 86. **185 "heart-breaking scenes":** As quoted in Kochan, *Britain's Internees in the Second World War*, 157. **185 left the camp:** Kurt Trietel, unpublished letter to his parents, dated August 2, 1940. **185 await the next outbound ship:** There appears to be no official record of whether this group of couples was successfully deported and, if so, whether their ship fared better against the U-boat menace than did the passengers of the *Arandora Star*. **185 "bewildered and unhappy":** Judex, *Anderson's Prisoners*, 87. **186 notorious black book:** Dr. Hans Honigmann, "Hitler's Black Book," FWR. **186 Fifty men:** "Life in Aliens' Camps Told by Men Who Have Been Released," *News Chronicle*, August 6, 1940, 1. **187 at least a thousand of whom were classed as infirm:** Judex, *Anderson's Prisoners*, 78. **187 a letter of endorsement from the pope:** Benjamin Zander to author, June 2020. **187 "His great misfortune is to be unknown":** "Report by Ex-Internee," HO, 215/27. **188 "somebody who has been everywhere":** Klaus Hinrichsen: Oral History, June 1978, IWM, 3789. **188 he began to pray:** Tausig, *Kasperl, Kummerl, Jud*, 47. **188 "so devoted himself":** Murray to vice-chancellor of Oxford University, July 6, 1940, Gilbert Murray papers, BLO, 88/41. **188 "It was a miracle":** Tausig, *Kasperl, Kummerl, Jud*, 47. **188 forced to promise:** Judex, *Anderson's Prisoners*, 100. **189 During the visit she left £15 in cash:** Minutes of the German Emergency Committee general committee meeting, August 27, 1940, LSF, YM/MfS/FCRA, 4. **190 "basic theoretical knowledge":** Ludwig Warschauer, "Memorandum with Scheme of Training," October 19, 1940, LSF, YM/MfS/FCRA, 4. **190 a fleeting setback:** Many internees, both at Hutchinson and elsewhere, proposed inventions to the War or Home Office that they claimed would revolutionize the war effort. In October 1940, for example, Eric Brust, of Hutchinson's House 4, proposed a scheme to rejuvenate old car batteries. Theodore Zerkowitz, of House 38, proposed a textile-based waterproof tire. The Nobel Prize–winning physicist Leo Neumann, who was interned at York Racecourse, proposed an infrared light that could, he claimed, be used to track German planes in the Blitz. These and other proposals can be read in the National Archives file HO 214/415. **190 The eighteen-year-old Kurt Treitel:** Kurt Treitel, unpublished letter to his parents, dated August 24, 1940. **191 illegal fascist German-British friendship organization:** Hinrichsen, unpublished account, 23. **191 driving a Mercedes:** "Ludwig Max Warschauer," document dated October, 28, 1941, TNA, KV 2/1139: 4. **191 used by the Nazis to secretly record:** Ibid., 2. **191 "I don't want anything to do with him":** "Ludwig Max Warschauer," TNA.

CHAPTER XV: LOVE AND PARANOIA

192 **no powers to reverse the policy:** Brinson and Dove, *A Matter of Intelligence*, 103ff. **192 the unit responsible, in part, for investigating internees:** Ibid., 14. **193 in desperate need** In July 1939, MI5 had a complement of 36 officers. By January 1940 this figure had grown to 102. **193 A graduate of University College, Oxford:** Biographical information courtesy of Sir Robert and Lady Georgina Craufurd; intelligence service information from TNA, KV 2/1139, and others. **193 he had already been engaged in "War Trade":** J. G. Craufurd later inherited the title of 8th Baronet of Kilbirnie. He upheld the Official Secrets Act until his death in 1970 and told his family nothing of his work during this period, which they learned of only during the research for this book. **193 Informants D, E, and X:** E.g., W. C. Edwards, "Report for Sir Cecil Hurst's Committee," MI5, September 23, 1941, TNA, KV-2–1139_2. **193 There was neither financial compensation:** Brinson and Dove, *A Matter of Intelligence*, 157. **193 Henry Wuga was a sixteen-year-old internee:** Henry Wuga to author, March 2019. **194 One day a man arrived:** Ibid. **194 The cuff links on his shirt:** J. G. Craufurd, "Report on Ludwig Max Warschauer," October 24, 1941, TNA, KV 2/1139: 4. **194 "It is not desirable":** J. G. Craufurd, "Report on Ludwig Max Warschauer," July 16, 1940, TNA, KV 2/1139: 2. **195 provided by one of the camp doctors:** "Internee's Wedding Ceremony in Orderly Room," *Ramsey Courier*, September 6, 1940, 4. **195 a brilliant white dress and veil:** Hinrichsen, unpublished account, 97. **195 the couple had secured visas to Cuba:** The inscription "Emigrated to Cuba" is crossed out on Bodenheimer's aliens card, suggesting that the journey was, at the very least, delayed. **195 sound of breaking glass:** Ibid. **196 "as if pos-**

sessed": Klaus Hinrichsen, unpublished account, 97. **196 "a little celebration"**: Invitation dated September 4, 1940, private papers of Dr. F. Uhlman, IWM, 6781. **196 "trivial facts"**: "Diary," Jacobsthal Archive, BL, Special Collections file 1935–57, MS. S.P.S.L. 182/2 Diary: 14–15. **196 The set designer Ernst "Este" Stern:** Hinrichsen, unpublished account, 79. **196 her teeth would fall out:** Peter Midgley: Oral History, MJM, 1988.45. **196 developed a fascination:** Midgley, *His Majesty's Most Loyal Internees*, documentary, 1991. **197 "a hopeless situation"**: Peter Midgley: Oral History. **197 share his weekly letter allocation:** Hinrichsen, unpublished account, 78. **197 "blaming me, threatening me"**: Nyburg, *From Leipzig to London*, 100. **198 presented her with an orange:** Stephan Feuchtwang to author, March 2020. **198 invited her out to dinner:** Neurath, *Recollections*, 58. **199 "Dear boy"**: Hinrichsen, unpublished account, 59–60. **199 Matuschka held one shoe:** Ibid., 73. **199 "liked very much"**: Klaus Hinrichsen: Oral History, June 1978, IWM, 3789. **199 considerable number of women:** Chappell, *Island of Barbed Wire*, 53. **199 three hundred of whom were pregnant:** Bertha Bracey, "Isle of Man Internment Camps: The Great Improvements Made in Six Months," *Manchester Guardian*, February 21, 1941. **199 apply for a permit:** Bertha Bracey, "Chairman's Report on the Isle of Man Camps, 28th October 1940–2nd November 1940," LSF, YM/MfS/FCRA. **200 messages were long out-of-date:** According to a report by William Hughes, this policy changed in late November, when letters were allowed to pass directly between camps on the island. **200 wife of a Lutheran pastor:** Brinson, *"Totally Un-English"?*, 101–2. **200 forced to share beds:** In the House of Lords on August 6, 1940, Lord Farringdon raised the case of a sixteen-year-old Jewish girl, forced to share a bed with a Nazi woman. **200 and forced to remain in their bedrooms:** Letter to the Editor, *Rushen Outlook*, no. 1 (December 1940): 9. **200 "Oh there is a bad smell"**: Erna Simion: Oral History, December 1978, IWM, 4. **200 discussing which of the local houses they would take:** Eileen Mylchreest speaking in *Jailed by the British*, JBB. **201 "You are all enemy aliens"**: Hinrichsen, unpublished account, 59–60. **201 picked out from the selection:** Kochan, *Britain's Internees in the Second World War*, 158. **201 came to £270:** Bracey, "Chairman's Report on the Isle of Man Camps, 28th October 1940–2nd November 1940." **202 viewed with special vigilance:** Fritz Hallgarten: Oral History, IWM, 3967. **203 A duplicating machine:** A Roneo or Gestetner, according to Hinrichsen. **203 appointed as publisher:** Stephen Feuchtwang to author, May 2020. **203 the prosaic title *The Camp*:** Internees in other camps on the island and the mainland produced similar newspapers, including the *Sefton Review*, the *Mooragh Times*, the *Central Promenade Paper*, the *Onchan Pioneer*, the *Rushen Outlook*, *Unity* (the camp at York racecourse) and the drolly titled *Awful Times*. **204 "the pretty green of the dividing canvas"**: Michael Corvin, "The Shower Bath," *The Camp*, no. 1, September 21, 1940, 2. **204 "[a] most promising start"**: Due to a lack of space, Hutchinson's sculptors could show only photographs of the work they had, to date, produced inside the camp. **204 held the information back:** Fred Uhlman, for example, notes in his diary that he learned of Olden's death on September 24, three days after the first issue of *The Camp* was published. **204 "His loss is irreparable":** Frederic Burschell, "Rudolf Olden," *The Camp*, no. 1, September 21, 1940, 9. **205 fifty-three speakers:** H. M. Rahmer, "2,700 Yards," *The Camp*, no. 13, January 14, 1941, LBI. **205 "it made a great impression on us":** Kurt Treitel, unpublished letter to his parents, dated October 29, 1940. **205 Soon internees used the radio system:** Rabbi Dr. S. Schonfeld, "Report on Visit to Internment Camps," November 5–7, 1940, LSF, YM/MfS/FCRA, 2. **205 vinyl records:** For example, at 7:45 p.m. on Sunday, May 18, 1941. **205 "Truly it is wonderful, this invention":** Following his release, Cargher formalized his camp pseudonym and immigrated to Australia, where he became one of the country's best-regarded radio broadcasters, specializing in classical music. Cargher was later made a member of the Order of Australia, but there is no record of his having spoken about his internment. **206 The system also enabled the commandant:** Klaus Hinrichsen: Oral History, June 1978, IWM, 3789. **208 tipsy from afternoon drinks:** Ibid. **206 "Everything else: yes. That: no":** Captain Jurgensen, "Report on Ludwig Max Warschauer," August 5, 1941, TNA, KV 2/1139: 1–2. **206 two and three pounds a week just from playing cards:** "Ludwig Max Warschauer," document dated October 28, 1941, TNA, KV 2/1139: 9. **206 "in effect, the camp leader":** Jurgensen, "Report on Ludwig Max Warschauer," 1. **207 "The only millionairess in Berlin":** Peter Midgley: Oral History, here rendered as dialogue. **207 "You are a liar":** Ibid. **207 a towel stitched with the initials *E.K.*:** "List of Articles in Kit Bag Belonging to Warschauer, Ludwig," TNA, KV 2/1142_2.

CHAPTER XVI: THE HEIRESS

211 Boggum: Monica Schubert to author, April 2021. **211 her elder was galled:** Catherine and Hilary Gregory to author, May 2020. **211 left during the Berlin Olympics:** Bosetzky, *Kempinski erobert Berlin*, 265. **211 A family of diamond merchants:** Catherine and Hilary Gregory to author, May 2020. **212 her husband of seven years:** Julius Kohsen, "Memories of My Life," unpublished memoir, LBI, ME 1610: 83. **212 He was practiced at dissuading his daughter:** Catherine and Hilary Gregory to author, May 2020. **213 footage of a thunderstorm:** Schubert, *Where Am I at Home?*, 10. **214 Echen did not feel she had the luxury:** J. G. Craufurd, "Notes on Interview with Mrs. Echen Warschauer," MI5, May 18, 1942, TNA, KV 2/1139. **214 At her father's urging:** Ibid. **214 in the spring of 1938:** "Ludwig Max Warschauer Curriculum Vitae," TNA, KV 2/1140. **214 Dr. Lisse visited Echen's house:** Craufurd, "Notes on interview with Mrs. Echen Warschauer." **214 concealed debts:** Ludwig Max Warschauer security files, TNA, KV 2/1139: 1. **215 miraculously reissued:** "Ludwig Max Warschauer

Curriculum Vitae." **215 As he passed through the barrier:** Ibid., 8. **215 would be declared void:** Shatzkes, *Holocaust and Rescue*, 83. **215 at the St. Marylebone registration office:** "Ludwig Max Warschauer," October 28, 1941. **215 the happiest they ever saw her:** Catherine and Hilary Gregory to author, May 2020. **216 There was no chance:** Peter did not record whether he spoke to Echen during this visit to the camp, although it is highly improbable. Visitors did not enter the camp's central perimeter, but instead met their loved ones or business partners in the Intelligence Office, situated at the north end of the lawned square behind a line of barbed wire. **216 "there will be . . . many [internees]":** *Hansard*, Lords Chamber, vol. 117, September 5, 1940. **216 Only a hundred:** Estimated figure recorded in Kurt Treitel, unpublished letter to his parents, dated August 30, 1940. **216 half-nibbled by a mouse** Kurt Treitel, various unpublished letters to his parents, dated July-October 1940. **217 hung the provocative biscuits:** Klaus Hinrichsen: Oral History, June 1978, IWM, 3789. **217 "pining for me":** Peter Midgley: Oral History, MJM, 1988.45. **217 Uhlman regularly sat with Peter:** Ibid. **217 "own beginnings":** Hinrichsen, unpublished account, 59–60. **217 to orchestrate the rescue of artists:** The committee's main prewar achievement was to facilitate the escape to Britain of the so-called Kokoschka Bund, which included the sculptor Margaret Klopfleisch. This group of Czech artists had been forced into hiding following the Nazi occupation of Prague. The painter from whom the group took its name, Oskar Kokoschka, had already arrived in Britain independently. Apart from asking Kokoschka's permission to use his name, these artists had no special connection with him. **218 "a man's innocence":** Helen Roeder, "Release of Interned Artists," Artists' Refuge Committee, August 21, 1940, TATE, 8812.1.4.182.4: 1. **218 "If this method fails":** Ibid., 3. **218 "The list of those who have applied":** Letter to Kenneth Clark from Helen Roeder, Artists' Refuge Committee, undated (likely late August 1940), TATE, 8812.1.4.182.5. **218 "a mountain of feathers for a star":** Letter to Kenneth Clark from Helen Roeder, September 5, 1940, TATE, 8812.1.4.182.4. **219 In May 1940:** Cooper, *Refugee Scholars*, 134–35. **219 532 academics:** Ibid., 150–51. **220 "[the] department moves three and a half times faster than a tortoise":** Ibid., 157. **220 all new tribunals:** Letter to Helen Roeder from Kenneth Clark, Artists' Refuge Committee, September 3, 1940, TATE, 8812.1.4.182.17. **220 "too old for internment anyway":** Letter to Kenneth Clark from Helen Roeder, September 6, 1940, TATE, 8812.1.4.182.19. **221 warning of the scam:** A surviving poster can be found in the London Metropolitan Archives, ACC/2793/03/05/02. **221 have their cases examined:** *Hansard*, House of Commons, vol. 365, October 8, 1940. **222 "too busy being hunted to achieve distinction":** Letter to Sir Kenneth Clarke from Helen Roeder, September 6, 1940. **222 Eighty-five percent:** At least five thousand were also interned in Canada, Australia, and other dominions. **222 Siegmund Stiegel:** "Lists of Deaths Reported," TNA, HO 215/420. **222 "the advanced age of many":** "Correspondence, Minutes," HLS, MS183/228/1. **222 used as a Jewish** chapel: "War Office Correspondence; Internment Camp Lists of Names," HLS, MS183/240/1. **222 At least forty-five men died:** "Lists of Deaths Reported." *Note*: Records of internee deaths survive only up until December 1943. **223 returned from Sydney:** Bartrop and Eisen, *The Dunera Affair*, 401. **223 occasionally teaching the other internees French:** E.g., Cultural Department Week 36, "Cercle Française," March 31, 1941. **223 Men like Gugen:** Following his release from Hutchinson, Gugen cofounded E. T. Skinner & Co., which become one of the world's largest sellers of diving masks, rubber swim fins, and wet suits. In 1953, Gugen cofounded the British Sub-Aqua Club, the national governing body for recreational diving in the UK, which, at the height of its popularity, had more than fifty thousand members. The journalist Peter Small once wrote of Gugen's contribution to the sport: "It is impossible to over-estimate what Oscar Gugen has accomplished." **223 "Mr. von D":** Probably Emil Drews (DOB April 6, 1897), the only victim of unknown nationality whose surname begins with a *D*. **224 He died on the *Arandora Star*:** Darton, "An Account of the Work of the Friends Committee for Refugees and Aliens 1933–50," unpublished manuscript, LSF, YM/MfS/FCRA, 72.

CHAPTER XVII: ART AND JUSTICE

225 Situated next to the camp laundry: Klaus Hinrichsen, "Cultural Flashlights," *The Camp: Almanac 1940–41.* **225 to a ping-pong table:** Michael Corvin, "Sports and Entertainment," *The Camp*, no. 13, January 14, 1941. **225 fashion an altar from an upturned orange box:** Ibid. **226 "How long will its erection take?":** Anon, "Entertainment in the Camp," *The Camp*, no. 6, October 27, 1940, LBI. **226 "It was too early":** Klaus Hinrichsen, "Art in Hutchinson Camp: A Personal View," talk delivered at Camden Arts Centre, September 17, 1986, TGA 20052–1–7–12. **226 the visit of Lord Lytton:** "On the Occasion of Lord Lytton's Visit," illustration by Aodlf "Dol" Mirecki, *The Camp*, no. 7, November 3, 1940. **227 "a nightmare":** Ibid. **227 not enough to sate the carver's appetite:** Müller-Blensdorf was the most eager of all the artists interned in Hutchinson to display and commemorate his camp work. Two months later, on January 14, 1941, Hutchinson camp's third and final art exhibition opened, this time in House 37. It was an event entirely dedicated to the sculptor's life and work. **227 too cumbersome for anyone to later evict:** Klaus Hinrichsen: Oral History, June 1978, IWM, 3789. **227 cut the collars:** Gerald Midgley to author, May 2020. **228 thirty-six showers:** William R. Hughes, "Report on Isle of Man Internment Camps," September 10, 1940, LSF, YM/MfS/FCRA. **228 once per week** Kurt Treitel, unpublished letter to his parents, dated September 21, 1940. **228 stock beer on October 5:** Kurt Treitel, unpublished letter to his parents, dated October 5, 1940. **228 one pint per day:** Captain Daniel, "Commander's Announcements," *The Camp*, no. 3, October 6,

1940. **228 "extremely secure surroundings":** Klaus Hinrichsen: Oral History. **228 "on the wrong tack":** "It's Difficult to Keep the Balance," *The Camp*, no. 5, October 20, 1940, HO 215/437. **228 preposterous they could order a bottle of French Sauternes:** Kurt Treitel, unpublished letter to his parents, dated October 25, 1940. **229 organized the provision of tools:** Darton, *Friends Committee for Refugees and Aliens*, LSF, YM/MfS/FCRA, 85. **229 "nomos":** "Routine," from the Greek. **229 becoming as zoo animals:** Private papers of Professor P. Jacobsthal, IWM, 4693: 31. **230 wearing a crown of silver foil:** AJR Refugee Voices Testimony interview (RV125). Klaus Hinrichsen was interviewed by Anthony Grenville on November 20, 2003. **230 "our future . . . forever and all eternity":** Quoted in Crossley, *The Triumph of Kurt Schwitters*, 40. **230 "I paint since 1909":** Webster, *Kurt Merz Schwitters*, 312. **230 ink studies of local flowers:** One of these floral drawings is owned by the family of Schwitters's fellow internee Walter Goldschmidt. **230 to cut him a suit:** AJR Refugee Voices Testimony interview (RV125). Klaus Hinrichsen was interviewed by Anthony Grenville on November 20, 2003. **230 "I hear lectures on philosophy":** Letter to Henriette Schwitters from Kurt Schwitters, dated August 18, 1940, as quoted in the essay, Wilson, "Kurt Schwitters in England," TATE. **231 implied he was flameproof:** Klaus Hinrichsen: Oral History (with thanks to Anna Nyburg, who assisted with the identification of "Schaltenbrand"). **231 Robert Marshall:** This portrait was sold at auction in May 1993 with the title *A Portrait of Douglas Marshall*. The "Douglas," surely, refers to the town where the portrait was painted (and where Robert Marshall lived), and not the sitter's name. **231 Hans Terner and Rudolf Meyer:** Schwitters painted Meyer, who played flute in camp productions, holding the instrument. **231 "an amateurish painter":** Private papers of Professor P. Jacobsthal, IWM, 4693. **232 "intellectual imposter":** Ibid. **232 The pugilist's chest fills the frame:** The portrait of Warschauer sat in Echen's home until after the war, at which point it was sent to Germany. During the writing of this book, Echen's daughter, Monica Schubert, identified the portrait as that which depicts her stepfather, and the same that once hung in her mother's London home. **232 Schwitters chose to enter a selection of the portraits:** The whereabouts of the Eisler portrait, which can be seen in photographs of the second exhibition taken by Captain Daniel, is currently unknown. **232 "Place your order for a portrait":** Hinrichsen, "Art in Hutchinson Camp: A Personal View." **233 "it will help you not only to keep your chin up":** Michael Corvin, "Life, Art and Future," *The Camp*, no. 8, November 13, 1940. **233 Ralph Vaughan Williams made a petition:** Letter from Ralph Vaughan Williams to Adrian Boult, October 4, 1940, RVW, VWL1458. **233 a Player's Navy Cut cigarette packet:** Hinrichsen in conversation, July 18, 1994, as quoted in Wilson, "Kurt Schwitters in England." **233 to make a leaving cake:** Fritz Hallgarten: Oral History, IWM, 3967. **234 Tuesday, November 19:** Cultural Department Schedule No. 18, November 18–24, 1940; "Hutchinson Internment Camp, Cultural Events Programmes and Schedules,"

1940–41, IWM, 5382. **234 "For many of us it is exactly twenty weeks today":** "The Campfather's Address to the Commander on Occasion of the Opening of the Second Art Exhibition," *The Camp*, no. 10, November 24, 1940. **235 he selected pieces . . . he enjoyed far less:** AJR Refugee Voices Testimony interview (RV125). Klaus Hinrichsen was interviewed by Anthony Grenville on November 20, 2003. **235 widened the scope of the exhibition:** "Punch and Judy," *The Camp*, no. 9, November 17, 1940, 4. **235 The businessman Hans Gussefeld:** Hinrichsen, "Art in Hutchinson Camp: A Personal View." **235 "very pleased":** Dr. F. Uhlman, "Diary of an Internee," private papers, IWM, 6781. **237 "They do not want your £375":** *Hansard*, vol. 365, November 7, 1940. **237 "I venture to suggest":** Letter to Sir John Moylan from Sir Frank Newsam, November 19, 1940, TNA, HO 215/437. **238 Pollmann returned to the stage:** Concert program, November 19, 1940; "Hutchinson Internment Camp, Cultural Events Programmes and Schedules," 1940–41, IWM, 5382. **238 "The mystery at last got lifted":** K.E.H., "Epilogue," *The Camp*, no. 11, December 2, 1940, 13.

CHAPTER XVIII: HOME FOR CHRISTMAS?

239 a hundred applications: Kurt Treitel, unpublished letter to his parents, dated October 25, 1940. **239 Nobody was surprised:** Hinrichsen, unpublished account, 52. **239 Captain Daniel's "pet" internees:** Letter to R. K. D. Renton, dated February 14, 1941, TNA, KV 2/1139_2. **240 "There can be no doubt":** Letter from War Office security liaison officer to R. K. D. Renton, March 1, 1941, TNA, KV 2/1139_2. **240 "mysterious visitors":** Stent, *A Bespattered Page?*, 176. **240 out of bounds:** Hinrichsen, unpublished account, 51. **240 Friedrich Burschell had collected proof:** Ibid., 52. **241 who made it clear:** Ibid. **241 As well as the scheduled walks:** Some internees refused to partake in these excursions. Both the graphic artist Hellmuth Weissenborn and the wine dealer Fritz Hallgarten refused to be seen in public under armed escort. "I will only leave [the camp] as a free man," Hallgarten declared. **241 "up and down the beach":** Millicent Faragher speaking on *Jailed by the British*, JBB. **242 their first trip to the local cinema:** Dr. F. Uhlman, "Diary of an Internee," private papers, September 18, 1940, IWM, 6781. **242 "appear human":** Hinrichsen, unpublished account, 96. **242 "storms of applaud [*sic*] and cheers":** K.E.H., "Cinema and Variety," *The Camp*, no. 10, November 24, 1940, 9. **243 searched the premises:** Hinrichsen, unpublished account, 96. **243 If they were fortunate:** "Emper," "Our Farmers," *The Camp*, no. 9, November 17, 1940, 6. **243 "You bring home the conviction":** Ibid. **244 The commandant canceled the opportunity:** Private papers of Professor P. Jacobsthal, IWM, 4693, 14. This was, evidently, a temporary cancellation. By November, when one internee wrote about his experiences volunteering on local farms for *The Camp*, the scheme had been reinstated. **244 The chicken:** Hellmuth Weissenborn: Oral History, IWM, 3771. **244 one of his former students:** Nyburg, *From Leipzig to London*, 85. **244 scheduled for October 27:** Uhlman, "Diary of an Internee." **244 "You can't go there":** Hinrichsen, unpublished account, 86. **245 "I took ten men and I brought back ten men":** Stent recounts a near identical incident in his book *A Bespattered Page?*, except in his version the missing internee fell asleep in the cinema. This man, too, then took a taxi back to the camp. Stent's version seems unlikely, however, as those guarding the cinemagoers would certainly have checked the seats thoroughly after each performance to avoid this exact situation. Both the Douglas cinema and the Manx museum are a mere ten-minute walk from Hutchinson camp, a fact that throws additional doubt onto the precise details of both versions. **245 "burrows and manganese":** Uhlman, "Diary of an Internee." **245 a dozen helpers:** Hinrichsen, unpublished account, 65. **245 Captain Jurgenson vetted all applicants:** Ibid. **246 a fossil-collecting banker:** Ibid. **246 "What is going on here?":** As quoted in ibid., 66. **247 "Who is Hutchinson?":** Hinrichsen's unpublished account is the sole source for this anecdote about the officer (who was no lesser rank than a general in his vivid telling). The dialogue is certainly secondhand, as Hinrichsen does not claim to have been a member of Bersu's archaeological party and cannot be identified in any of the photographs of the group's members. **247 In early December:** Bersu's archaeological work continued to develop after he left Hutchinson and moved into the married camp with his wife. By the end of 1941, according to minutes of the Central Department for Interned Refugees, Bersu had six full-time assistants. **247 listened to an update from Bersu's assistant, Ernst Nassau:** Michael Corvin, "Camp Officials' Outing," *The Camp*, no. 11, December 2, 1940, 7. **247 "smoothly":** Fraenkel, *Farewell to Germany*, 27. **247 Fraenkel obtained:** Ibid., 30. **248 The commandant took the manuscript:** Ibid., 28. **249 Fraenkel received a telegram;** Ibid., 29. **249 Following his release:** An excerpt—another tribute to the beloved Rudolf Olden —was published in *The Camp Almanac*, shortly before the book's official publication. **249 Peter . . . did not exist:** Peter Midgley: Oral History, MJM, 1988.45; Hinrichsen, unpublished account, 99. **250 "It's quite a good loophole":** Letter to Sir Kenneth Clarke from Helen Roeder, September 6, 1940, TATE, 8812.1.4.182–19. **250 "My friends, I come here in order to discuss":** As recalled by Fritz Hallgarten: Oral History, IWM, 3967. **250 Davidson's speech became firmer:** Hinrichsen, unpublished account, 68. **251 "[E]nlistment in the Pioneer Corps would be quite illogical":** Bertha Bracey, "Chairman's Report on the Isle of Man Camps, 28th October–2nd November 1940," LSF, YM/MfS/FCRA. **251 "two basic options":** Kochan, *Britain's Internees in the Second World War*, 165. **251 "invalid and infirm":** Ibid. **251 sent to train in Ilfracombe, Devon:** Fry, *The King's Most Loyal Enemy Aliens*, 1–12. **251 just outside the camp wire:** Hinrichsen, unpublished account, 69. **252 "The carriage is firm, but elastic":** Michael Corvin, "Left—Right—Left," *The Camp*, no. 6, April 6, 1941. **252 a trickle had become a stream:** Kurt Treitel, unpublished letter to his parents, dated October 15, 1940. **252 "I cannot agree to your offer":** Peter Midgley: Oral History. **253 "made the acquaintance of a young student of art":** Letter to Mrs. Maria Petrie, Abbotsholme School, from members of the Hutchinson Artists Café, December 8, 1940, courtesy of Gerald Midgley and Wendy Gregory. **254 "endless gloom":** Uhlman, *The Making of an Englishman*, 243. **254 "Haven't I lost enough?":** Lach, *Kurt Schwitters*, vol. 1, 135. **254 "always the same people":** Ibid., 134. **254 Bertha Bracey arranged a donation:** Minutes of the meeting of the Central Department for Interned Refugees, December 5, 1940, TNA, HO 294/224. **254 a national candle shortage:** Letter to "P" Camp Commandant from Secretary to Chief Rabbi, November 20, 1941, HLS, MS.240, vol. 2. **254 a notoriously decadent Christmas party:** As recalled by Leonard Körting, quoted in Webster, *Kurt Merz Schwitters*, 102. **255 "to believe in love":** "Letter to Helma Schwitters," December 24, 1940, in Nündel, *Wir spielen, bis uns der Tod abholt*, 162. **255 triggered epileptic fits:** Webster, *Kurt Merz Schwitters*, 306. **255 As the men around him sang:** "Letter to Helma Schwitters," in Nündel, *Wir spielen, bis uns der Tod abholt*, 162.

CHAPTER XIX: THE ISLE OF FORGOTTEN MEN

256 "Good day, Mrs. Warschauer": J. G. Craufurd, "Notes on Interview with Mrs. Elizabeth Warschauer," May 18, 1942, TNA, KV 2_1140. **256 Sir John Anderson:** Monica Schubert to author, February 2021. **256 carried off boxes:** Memorandum by John Noble, October 31, 1941, TNA, KV2–1139: 1. **258 extort the target for money:** Letter to Douglas Lowe from W. C. Edwards, August 14, 1941, TNA, KV2/1139 with the full story of the scheme revealed in "Interrogation of Ludwig Max Warschauer," July 27, 1942, TNA, KV2/1141_2: 1. **258 he had been hospitalized:** Captain Jurgensen, "Secret Intelligence Report: Hermann Moritz Rahmer," January 20, 1941, TNA, KV2–1139. **258 blackmailed by Warschauer:** Ibid. **258 "His eyes, I think, are dark":** Craufurd, "Notes on Interview with Mrs Elizabeth Warschauer." **259 "truthful and sincere":** Ibid. **259 "swept away many of the artists in this camp":** Michael Corvin, "Sports and Entertainment," *The Camp*, no. 13, January 14, 1941. **259 archived at the London School of Economics:** Letter to Professor R. S. T. Chorley, Home Office, from Dr. Dickenson, LSE, December 12, 1940, TNA, HO 215/437. **260 12,500 internees had walked free:** Kochan, *Britain's Internees in the Second World War*, 175. **260 "A man who is neither scientist":** As quoted in Kochan, *Britain's Internees in the Second World War*, 165. **261 "People were leaving the camp left, right and center":** Peter Midgley: Oral History, MJM, 1988.45. **261 "Other people cared very little about me":** Ibid. **261 the Cultural Department suspended its program:** As noted in Cultural Department Programme, no. 28 (January 28-February 4, 1941), IWM. **261 The first serious actors:** Anon, "Entertainment in the Camp," *The*

Camp, no. 6, October 27, 1940, LBI. **262 The early theatrical performances:** Philo Hauser, "Camp Youth," *The Camp*, no. 3, October 6, 1940, LBI. **262 George Bernard Shaw's one-act play:** Cultural Department Programme, no. 15 (October 28–November 3, 1940), IWM; Anon, "Entertainment in the Camp." **262** *Of Mice and Men*: Cultural Department Programme, no. 16 (November 4–11, 1940), IWM. **262 both male and female:** In Hasek's *The Good Soldier Švejk*, Tausig portrayed both male and female characters; he played Dr. Bull in an adaptation of G. K. Chesterton's *The Man Who Was Thursday*, Daja in Gotthold Lessing's *Nathan the Wise*, Franz in Friedrich Schiller's *The Robbers*, and Mrs. Barthwick in John Galsworthy's *The Silver Box*. **262 man in a high-necked green shirt:** Tausig, *Kasperl, Kummerl, Jud*, 46. **263 Tausig dusted his hair:** Ibid., 50–52. **263 Schwitters offered:** According to Tausig, the portrait was lost in the camp. He also claimed that Schwitters had a wart on his left cheek that he would transpose onto the portraits of many of his sitters—a kind of artistic signature for cognoscenti. "I have a wart on my chin," Tausig wrote. "That was a big psychological problem for him: should he paint this one, that one, or both?" **263 "The story of the difficulties":** Anon, "Entertainment in the Camp." **263 The brightness of the stage lights:** Ibid. **264 "four pianos going off at the same time":** Gerry Wolff, "To Produce a Play," in Camp Hutchinson Youth, as quoted in Balfour, *Theatre and War 1933–1945*, 98. **264 a frisson of glamour:** Weiss, who studied for stage at Vienna Burgtheater, started his career as a film actor, making his first appearance in 1925. He starred in silent films before making his directorial debut at Sascha-Film in Vienna. Weiss fled to England in 1935, working predominantly on documentaries before his eventual arrest, despite having directed an anti-Nazi film, *The Vagabond*. **265 identifiable by the POW jackets:** One of the Canadian returnees gave Peter his jacket, which, despite the fact it had a red target circle on the rear, Peter continued to wear for many years. **265 "From Story to Film":** Cultural Department Programme, no. 29 (February 3–9, 1941); "Hutchinson Internment Camp, Cultural Events Programmes and Schedules," 1940–41, IWM, 5382. **265 "Film Art":** Cultural Department Programme, no. 34 (March 17–23, 1941); "Hutchinson Internment Camp, Cultural Events Programmes and Schedules," 1940–41. **265 "On the Making of a Film":** As well as delivering lectures on the finer points of chess playing, Heinrich Fraenkel also spoke on the film industry in Hutchinson, delivering one lecture titled, simply and alluringly, "Hollywood." **265 "the bank, the censor and the moving picture industry":** Review of "Everything About the Production of Films," by "Walter," *The Camp*, no. 15, August 11, 1941. **266 "The audience was stunned":** Ibid. **266 for a weekly subscription of sixpence:** "H. Hn.," "Reading Room," *The Camp*, no. 10, November 24, 1940, LBI. **266 "[C]onditions . . . have improved enormously":** Minutes of the Germany Emergency Committee general committee, February 4, 1941, LSF, YM/MfS/FCRA, 2. **266 special requirements:** See the papers of Rabbi Dr. Solomon Schonfeld, held in the Hartley Library Special Collections archive at the University of Southampton, which record the names of hundreds of Jewish cases within Hutchinson. **266 unleavened bread:** "War Office Correspondence," papers of Rabbi Dr. Solomon Schonfeld, executive director of the Chief Rabbi's Religious Emergency Council, Item 240, folder 01, HLS. **267** "We are glad to have you here": H.G. Dittmar, "Welcome Onchanians!," *The Camp*, no. 14, July 28, 1941, LBI. **267 pierced by the horn of a rhino:** Fred Uhlman papers, IWM, 27. **267 pick the heads from flowers using a small lasso:** Freddy Godshaw (née Adolf Gottschalk), "Internment Camp 1940–1," *WW2 People's War*, BBC. **267 "better acquainted with English Life":** *Collegio Dante* Cultural Department Programme, no. 42 (May 12–19, 1941); "Hutchinson Internment Camp, Cultural Events Programmes and Schedules," 1940–41. **267 a first-aid course:** "Results of the First Aid Examination held on 23rd June 1941," *The Camp*, no. 14, July 28, 1941, LBI. **267 A chess tournament:** Heinrich Fraenkel and Harald Landry, both of whom were writing books for Victor Gollancz at the time, drew first place in the chess tournament, with an equal number of wins and losses. **267 His application to the Auxiliary Military Pioneer Corps:** Interned Enemy Aliens Tribunal: Category 23, Report 845, TNA, KV 21139_1. **268 "I am afraid that there is nothing more that we can do":** Letter to L. Warschauer from Esther Simpson, January 30, 1941, TNA, KV2–1139–2. **268 eminent London law firm:** Letter to the Home Office (Aliens Department) from Stephenson, Harwood and Tatham, September 17, 1941, TNA, HO 382/760. **268 category 23:** Rachael Pistol, "Routes Out of Internment—a Handy Reference Guide to White Paper Categories." rachelpistol.com. **268 In August 1941, Warschauer appeared:** Notes on this interview, held August 12, 1941, can be read in TNA, KV2–1139. **268 "A man like he":** "Re: Mr. L. Warschauer, Hutchinson camp, I.O.M.," letter from "H.E." to M/S, Section B8c, June 27, 1941, TNA, KV2–1139. **269 "fervently anti-Nazi":** "Interned Enemy Aliens Tribunal Report," October 7, 1941, TNA, KV2–1139. **269 "quite intolerable that a committee of unworldly servants":** T. F. Turner, "Note on Ludwig Warschauer File," TNA, KV2–1139. **270 "an undesirable person":** J. G. Craufurd, "Ludwig Max Warschauer," October 26, 1941, TNA, KV2–1139. **270 one of thirty-two men:** Minutes of the Central Department for Interned Refugees, October 2, 1941, LMA, ACC/2793/03/05/02: 2. **270 one of just 388 internees:** Minutes of the GEC, November 25, 1941, LSF, YM/MfS/FCRA, 3.

CHAPTER XX: A SPY CORNERED

272 The roll calls seemed pointless: In Hinrichsen's unpublished account, p. 99, he describes these specific feelings of alienation as experienced by a young orphan when leaving Hutchinson. Here, either Hinrichsen is recounting Peter's testimony, as shared to him, or he is ascribing his own feelings upon leaving the camp to the orphan. They are recounted here as representative of the internee experience. **273 the modest headquarters of the Artists' Refugee Committee:** "Bloomsbury House: Directory of Welfare Organisations," LSF, YM/MfS/ FCRA, 11. **273 First, however, Peter headed:** Proof of this detour is recorded in Peter Fleischmann's Certificate of Registration. **273 17 Girdlers Road:** In a 1978 interview, Peter identified the location of the flat as Blythe Road, a neighboring street. His original Certificate of Registration lists the address where he stayed as Girdlers Road, however. The 1939 Census confirms that Helen Roeder was registered as living at 17 Girdlers Road. **273 billowing, lace Victorian dresses:** See Carel Weight's 1938 portrait *Helen*, confirmed by the artist in a 1991 interview—"National Life Story Collection: Artists' Lives," BL, C466/07— to be of Helen Roeder. **273 Carel Weight, had noticed:** Introduction by Carel Weight, *Helen's Sketchbook*, unpaginated. **273 she always kept on the stove:** Roeder, *Helen's Sketchbook* (see chapter titled "Leo Pavia"), unpaginated. **273 "We are not wealthy":** Peter Midgley: Oral History, MJM, 1988.45. **274 for two days a week:** "National Life Story Collection: Artists' Lives." **274 Founded in 1902, Beckenham:** Later known as Ravensbourne College. **274 more students to the Royal College of Art:** Nyburg, *From Leipzig to London*, 118. **274 Carel had secured Hellmuth:** Ibid., 119. **274 the Ministry of Information:** Weight, *Carel Weight*, 29. **274 might not have the desired effect:** Ibid. **275 secure him a stipend:** Peter Midgley: Oral History. **275 "All my years in internment":** Ibid. **275 "A woman of action":** "Pacifist in the Honours List," *Manchester Guardian*, January 3, 1942. **276 "oppressed by difficulties":** Letter to Bertha Bracey from William Hughes, January 4, 1942, Bertha Bracey Papers, LSF, MSS 930. **276 "internees of any denomination":** Letter to Otto Schiff from Sir Ernest Holderness, March 13, 1941, TNA, WO 208/3527. **276 Bertha Bracey wrote to . . . Oskar Kokoschka:** Minutes of the meeting of the Central Department for Interned Refugees, July 10, 1941, TNA, HO 294/224. **276 The plan came too late:** In June 1941, Bracey wrote that the Ministry of Information was interested in supporting such an exhibition, perhaps to help undo the public relations damage done by the internment measures. This is, however, the last piece of surviving correspondence relating to the project, which appears to have fizzled out. **277 "very much impressed":** Letter to Sir Ernest Holderness from Bertha Bracey, April 2, 1941, TNA, WO 208/3527. **277 secured a showroom:** Minutes of the meeting of the Central Department for Interned Refugees. **277 "To have selected a member of the Society of Friends in wartime":** Letter quoted in "Bertha's Work for German Jewish Refugees," a lecture delivered at Warwickshire General Meeting by Brenda Bailey, August 8, 1993, Bertha Bracey Papers, LSF, MSS 930. **278 "It is a promising sign":** Letter to Bertha Bracey from "Gerhard," January 1, 1942, Bertha Bracey Papers, LSF, MSS 930. **278 "Thank you from the bottom of our hearts":** Oskar Kokoschka, January 9, 1942, Bertha Bracey Papers, LSF, MSS 930. **278 who had also done so much:** Tess also eventually received an OBE, in 1956.

278 **"I should have liked the distinction to be a higher one":** Letter to Bertha Bracey from Esther Simpson, January 5, 1942, Bertha Bracey Papers, LSF, MSS 930. 279 **"We feel that a protest must be lodged":** Letter to Bertha Bracey from Otto Schiff, February 3, 1942, Bertha Bracey Papers, LSF, MSS 930. 279 **written her a ten-page letter:** Letter from Ludwig Warschauer, October 19, 1940, Camp Reports, LSF, MSS 930. 279 **A further appeal:** J. D. Denniston, "Extract from Home Office file W.11758," October 19, 1941, TNA, KV2/1139_1. 280 **MI5 kept a list of his associates:** Ludwig Max Warschauer security files, TNA, KV2/1139_1. 280 **arrested and interned for a second time:** Josh Reynolds (great-grandson of Hans Kollinsky), to author, December 2020, corroborated in a letter to Douglas Lowe from W. C. Edwards, August 30, 1941, TNA, KV2/1139. 280 **"never wavering in loyalty":** Captain Jurgensen, "Report on Ludwig Max Warschauer," June 4, 1941, TNA, KV2/1139_2. 280 **The MP Herbert Williams:** Letter to Herbert Morrison, M.P. from Herbert Williams, M.P., November 6, 1942, TNA HO 382/760. 280 **"He is entirely self-centred":** Captain Jurgensen, "Report on Ludwig Max Warschauer," August 5, 1941, TNA, KV2/1139_2. 281 **"hard work and cheerfulness":** Letter to Echen Warschauer from Major Daniel, January 29, 1941, TNA, HO 382/760. 281 **"should the question arise":** Unlabelled report, B.8.c, July 5, 1941, TNA, KV2/1139_2. 281 **"It seems to me too dangerous":** Letter to "Ronald Kenneth Duncan Renton" from Claude W. Sykes, July 5, 1941, TNA, KV2/1139. 281 **only about 350 men remained:** Minutes of the Central Department for Interned Refugees, May 28, 1942, LMA, ACC/2793/03/05/02: 1. 281 **Internment Camp 001:** Organization of Internment Camp 001 (Oratory Schools), TNA, KV 4/324. 281 **canisters of photographic film rigged:** "Report on the Films Sent to the Photographic Department," TNA, KV2 1140_1. 282 **"There is in the writing":** "Handwriting Expert's Opinion About Sauer's Writing," Scientific Section, Appendix C, TNA, KV2 1141_2. 282 **Arranging this scattered evidence:** Letter to S.L.B. from J. G. Craufurd, April 22, 1942, TNA, KV2/1139_2. 282 **"a kind of glassy look in the eye":** "Notes on Interrogation of Ludwig Max Warschauer," March 31, 1942, TNA, KV2/1139_2: 37. 282 **They had in their files:** Security files relating to Elisabeth Warschauer a.k.a. Kohsen. TNA, HO 382/760. 283 **he had no knowledge of the science:** "Interrogation of Ludwig Max Warschauer," July 27, 1942, TNA, KV2/1141_2: 1. 283 **"Twenty-seven is my lucky number":** Ibid., 2. 283 **"Enough":** Ibid. 283 **Dr. Hans Sauer:** Sauer was confirmed to have used the aliases "Harald Kinberg," "Lowenstejnherz," and "Holm." 284 **He asked if they could take a break:** Undated letter to "D.D.G." from John Noble, TNA, KV2/1141_3. 284 **A man in his mid-forties:** "Statement Taken from Ludwig Max Warschauer," July 29, 1942, TNA, KV2/1141_2: 2. 285 **"Lutz," the man said:** Ibid., here rendered as dialogue. 285 **"I can help you to get a passport":** "Statement Taken from Ludwig Max Warschauer," August 11, 1942, TNA, KV2/1141_2: 2. 285 **Warschauer was to travel to England:** Ibid., 4. 285 **The number 27 must feature somehow:** Ibid. 286 **"If I refused his offer":**

"Statement Taken from Ludwig Max Warschauer," July 29, 1942, 2. **287 "an adventurer of the sorriest appearance":** John Noble, "Summary of Interrogation of Ludwig Max Warschauer," TNA, KV2/1141_3: 2. **287 The camp stories of extortion were true:** J. G. Craufurd, "Summary of Interrogation of Ludwig Max Warschauer," TNA, KV2/1141_2: 15. **287 "I masturbated a great deal":** Ibid., 5. **287 "ruined character":** Noble, "Summary of Interrogation of Ludwig Max Warschauer," 2. **287 Warschauer had disposed of the invisible ink:** "Statement Taken from Ludwig Max Warschauer," July 29, 1942, 10. **288 "the only good thing Warschauer ever achieved in his life":** Craufurd, "Summary of Interrogation of Ludwig Max Warschauer," 14–15

CHAPTER XXI: RETURN TO THE MILL

290 the animals wriggled and skated: Letter to Helma Schwitters from Kurt Schwitters, December 1940, quoted in Crossley, *The Triumph of Kurt Schwitters*, 40. **290 in a Victorian mansion:** When he visited the house, Schwitters, whose eyesight was by now failing, initially mistook these copies for the priceless originals. Marshall had also been a camp doctor during the First World War and some of these pictures had been restored by internees for a modest sum. Marshall, who was president of the Manx Language Society, died on November 6, 1943, before Hutchinson's closure. **290 plied Schwitters with sweets and cake:** Letter to Helma Schwitters from Kurt Schwitters, June 23, 1941, SAH. **290 eighteen months' worth of detritus:** Packing up his belongings before he left Hutchinson was, as Schwitters wrote to his wife, "a frightful business." Even discounting the mountains of knickknacks, the crates he constructed to transport his paintings were unable to accommodate all of the work he had produced, which Schwitters estimated to number between two hundred and three hundred pieces. **291 "you must not see any brush stroke":** Unpublished manuscript, as quoted in Webster, *Kurt Mertz Schwitters*, 331. **291 applied to become a window dresser:** Ibid., 337. **291 "Life is sad"** Friedhelm, *Kurt Schwitters*, vol. 3, 298. **292 Invariably the conductor moved on:** Webster, *Kurt Mertz Schwitters*, 340. **292 "I am alone":** "*An Helma*," Friedhelm, *Kurt Schwitters*, vol. 1, 139. **292 dutifully visited Lutz:** "Copy of Permit for Miss Anita Kehsen [sic] to Visit Ludwig Warschauer," March 26, 1942, TNA, KV2 1140_1. **292 A guard escorted her:** J. G. Craufurd, "Summary of Interrogation of Ludwig Max Warschauer," TNA, KV2/1141_2: 15. **293 the last and only opportunity:** Undated letter to "D.D.G." from John Noble, TNA, KV2/1141_3. **293 "a disgusting scene":** Craufurd, "Summary of Interrogation of Ludwig Max Warschauer," 15. **293 on August 25, 1942:** Monica Schubert to author, April 2021. **294 No. 6 Training Centre:** Peter Fleischmann Certificate of Registration. **294 He started evening classes:** Peter Midgley: Oral History, MJM, 1988.45. **294 "one of those things":** Ibid. **294 a literary critic**

called Bates: Possibly H. E. Bates. **295 when doctors examined his body:** "Minute Sheet: Note to Major Edwards from J. G. Craufurd," December 3, 1944, TNA, KV2/1142_1. **296 confessed to things that he had never done:** Craufurd, "Summary of Interrogation of Ludwig Max Warschauer," 15. **296 incoming boatloads of internees:** According to the minutes of the Central Department for Interned Refugees, dated August 7, the first transport of internees had just returned from Australia. Thirteen men were released on landing, one sent to Falcon Cliff hospital on the island, and the remaining 125 went to Hutchinson. A second batch was due "very shortly." **296 "a fertile field for his tricks":** Letter from G. R. Mitchell, October 20, 1942, TNA, KV2 1141_3. **296 fewer than five thousand:** Of these, no more than four hundred of this number were now classified as refugees from Nazi oppression. **296 the aim was to reduce this number further:** Gillman and Gillman, *"Collar the Lot!,"* 286. **296 turned down an invitation:** Letter to the Free German League from Kurt Schwitters, September 1, 1945, SAH. **298 made a collage featuring some of the bus ticket stubs:** See Bohm-Duchen, *Insiders Outsiders*, 180. **298 provide the ménage with breakfast:** Letter to Gwendolen Webster from Edith Thomas, October 10, 1990, as printed in Webster, *Kurt Mertz Schwitters*, 344. **299 the "incurables":** "Report on Visit of Camp No. 1 at Grizedale Hall," TNA, FO 939/82, 2. **299 a unified Nazi salute:** At the time, Germans were required by law to make the salute during the singing of the anthem. **299 the grim dawn chorus:** Sullivan, *Thresholds of Peace*, 97. **299 "hostile tribe confronting an anthropologist":** Ibid. **299 doing his best to obscure his accent:** Peter Midgley: Oral History. **300 As members of the SS:** Sullivan, *Thresholds of Peace*, 285. **300 justified in being apprehended:** See Terence Robertson's *The Golden Horseshoe* for an extended description of one such trial, presided over in secret by the U-boat captain Otto Kretschmer. **300 secret court-martials:** Peter Midgley: Oral History. **300 "I hated every moment":** Ibid. **301 "the desired psychological effect":** Note from Home Office filed A.R.P. I/P 5058 re: Ludwig Max Warschauer by D. Mayhew, June 17, 1944, TNA, KV2 1142_2. **301 "sooner or later he [will] again stir up trouble":** Letter to Home Office from J. G. Craufurd, dated July 3, 1944, TNA, KV2 1142_2. **302 members of the British Union of Fascists and the IRA:** Chappell, *Island of Barbed Wire*, 125ff; "Ludwig Max Warschauer Minute Sheet," TNA, KV2 1142_1. **302 eight hundred British fascist detainees:** Chappell, *Island of Barbed Wire*, 151. **302 The internees screamed:** Ibid., 156. **302 Warschauer's former commandant:** Note to J. G. Craufurd from E. Colledge, ref. PF.49327, vol. 8, TNA, KV2 1142_1. **303 "It seems most unsuitable":** Note to E. Colledge from John Noble, September 25, 1944, ref. PF.49327, vol. 8, TNA, KV2 1142_1. **303 "I admit every man has adversaries":** Letter to Ludwig Warschauer from Echen Warschauer, November 19, 1944, TNA, KV2 1142_2. The translation reproduced here is MI5's own. **304 along with a note** Letter to Mr. Paterson from J. G. Craufurd dated January 12, 1945, TNA, KV2 1142_2. **304 "I shall be glad if Fate will allow me to**

perish": Petition to Aliens Department from Ludwig Warschauer, December 8, 1944, TNA, KV2 1142_2. **305 "Warschauer runs true to form":** Minute Sheet, Ludwig Max Warschauer, ref. PF.49327, vol. 8, TNA, KV2 1142_1. **305 There would be other flings:** Monica Schubert to author, April 2021. **305 she would never again remarry:** Warschauer did not accept Echen's request to dissolve the marriage. Even after the war, while restarting his life in Hamburg, he claimed to acquaintances that his wife and children were waiting for him in England. **305 package it up, and post it to Germany:** The portrait in question disappeared for decades until, in March 2007, the Horster Auktionshaus in Germany listed it for auction. At the time, the painting was attributed to an "anonymous artist," only to be withdrawn from sale when the auction house learned that it was by Schwitters. Echen's daughter Monica Schubert identified Warschauer as the sitter during the writing of this book; she recognized both the subject and the painting from her childhood.

CHAPTER XXII: THE FINAL TRIAL

306 furniture was repaired: "Ramsey," *Isle of Man Examiner*, October 26, 1945. **306 enough rice to provide every shop:** "Rice Pudding Again!," *Ramsey Courier*, October 26, 1945. **307 "the highest peak of perfection":** "Magnificent Concert at Villa Marina," *Mona's Herald*, July 3, 1945. **307 Bersu convinced airmen:** "A Manx Viking Burial" *Isle of Man Times*, November 24, 1945. **307 Monday, November 26, 1945:** "Boarding Houses De-Requisitioned," *Ramsey Courier*, November 23, 1945. **308 Australia, Palestine, or elsewhere:** London, *Whitehall and the Jews, 1933–1948*, 267. **308 Either there were no child survivors:** Leonard G. Montefiore, address given to the Cambridge University Jewish Society on October 18, 1946. **308 In the summer of 1945:** Bertha Bracey, "Work of the Society of Friends for Refugees from the Hitler Regime in Central Europe," undated, file G15, WLC. **308 she and Montefiore:** Montefiore had been in Paris in May 1945 and saw firsthand the arrival of the first survivors of the camps, "like corpses that walked." **309 ten Lancaster bombers:** Gilbert, *The Boys*, 369. **309 The timing was serendipitous:** Michael Honey (Misa Honigwachs), *"Bilong Notbilong," Journal of the '45 Aid Society*, no. 18 (December 1994). **309 "It was unbearable":** "The Windermere Children," *BBC History* magazine, April 2020. **309 died now from abundance:** Gilbert, *The Boys*, 334. **310 more than two thousand lectures:** "Theresienstadt Ghetto," WHL, https://www.theholocaustexplained.org/the-camps/theresienstadt-a-case-study/. **310 three representatives of the Red Cross:** The previous month the Nazis deported 7,503 prisoners from Theresienstadt to Auschwitz to lessen crowding in the camp-ghetto in preparation for the Red Cross visit. **310 On August 11, 1945:** The children were identified and chosen by the United Nations Relief and Rehabilitation Administration. **310**

from Theresienstadt to Prague: Gilbert, *The Boys*, 369. **310 305 survivors:** "The Boys," WJR. **311 chocolate and oranges:** Joan Stiebel, "Children from the Camps," *Journal of the '45 Aid Society*, no. 19 (December 1995). **311 "like going from hell to paradise":** Robert Philpot, "How Holocaust Survivors Went from Hell to Heaven," *Times of Israel*, January 27, 2020. **311 dozens of men executed in front of him:** "The Boys," WJR. **311 "Friedmann always kept his word":** Lola Hahn-Warburg, "In Memoriam: Oscar Friedmann," *AJR Journal* (March 1959). **312 a guard assaulted him:** Gilbert, *The Boys*, 290. **312 a black porridge:** Testimony as quoted in *Berlin 1945*, episode one, 2020, BBC. **312 "back to square one":** Peter Midgley: Oral History, MJM, 1988.45. **313 almost sixty Auerbach children:** "A Place of Memory: Baruch Auerbach's Orphanage," Senate Chancellery Cultural Affairs flyer, "Art in Public Spaces," 2014. **314 frying potatoes in shoe polish:** Peter Midgley: Oral History. **315 "how special he was":** Nigel Mac-Fall to author, November 2020. **315 "incredibly energetic":** Graham Stewart to author, November 2020. **315 "the biggest influence":** Ibid. **316 "I wanted to see them in the flesh":** Joseph Otto Flatter: Oral History, 1980, IWM, 4765. **317 much older than his fifty-two years:** Bloch, *Ribbentrop*, ch. 24. **317 "the Jewish wire pulling":** As quoted in Schwab, *The Day the Holocaust Began*, 183. **317 "whole-hearted":** *Nazi Conspiracy and Aggression*, Opinion and Judgment, 113–16. **318 reverted her surname:** "Change of Name," *London Gazette*, May 14, 1946. **318 Two months later:** Midgley, P.G. Army Number 13041735. Courtesy of Army Personnel Centre. **318 "against any human right":** Ludwig Max Warschauer security files, TNA, KV2/1142. **318 oversaw more than fourteen thousand workers:** "Leo Warschauer—Source: Victoria," March 11, 1947, TNA, B.4.A. KV2/1142. **319 a story about two dogs:** Webster, *Kurt Merz Schwitters*, 394. **319 "When I am dead":** Joyce Kahn, "Schwitters in Barnes," *Oasis*, no. 6 (1972): 52–3. **320 "plagued society with his theories":** "War Prisoner's Art Preserved on Peel Boarding House Walls," *Isle of Man Examiner*, May 28, 1954. **320 put up for auction:** "Important Sale by Public Auction: Boarding Houses and Land," *Isle of Man Examiner*, April 12, 1946.

POSTSCRIPT

321 Hans Arenstein: A.k.a. Harry Andrews, service number 6436352. **321 died while attached to 47 Royal Marine Commando:** Carola Weil to author, November 2020. **321 Horst Archenhold designed the periscope:** Alison Archenhold to author, October 2020. **322 "I saw my cartoons as substitutes":** Vinzent, *Identity and Image*, 152. **322 educate servicemen about anti-Semitism:** Benjamin Zander to author, June 2020. **322 "a torpid period":** As quoted in Nyburg, *From Leipzig to London*, 77. **323 changing their names to British variants:** This practice, of course, long predated internment. Esther Simpson was born

Esther Sinovitch; she changed her name to sound more British shortly after she began helping academics flee Europe in 1933. Many internees who joined the Pioneer Corps were told to choose new surnames to protect relations still living in Germany and Austria were they to be captured. **323 the Austrian refugee paper *Zeitspiegel*:** *Zeitspiegel* 40, December 6, 1941, as quoted in Hirschfeld, *Exile in Great Britain*, 179. **324 a shibbolethic phrase:** Hinrichsen, unpublished account, 48. **324 "Now, when you leave the barbed wire":** Unattributed poem for Erich Kahn, Hinrichsen papers, TATE, TGA 20052/2/20. **325 at the Maison Bertaux café in London's Soho:** Klaus Hinrichsen, "Art in Hutchinson Camp: A Personal View," talk delivered at Camden Arts Centre, September 17, 1986, TGA 20052–1–7–12. **325 high-rise blocks and hotels: Ibid. 325 "never produced such vivid portraits":** Presler and Riedel, *Ludwig Meidner*, 23. **325 "internment sent him on a new phase in his abstract work":** Hinrichsen, "Art in Hutchinson Camp: A Personal View." **326 "working class or not":** Fred Uhlman: Oral History, IWM, 4441. **326 "miracle of human willpower":** Weissenborn, *"Mein Leben in London,"* in *Illustration 63, die Zeitschrift für Buchillustration*, no. 2 (1980): 44. **327 "distraction from the ever-present anger":** Klaus Hinrichsen, "Peter Midgley and Internment," speech delivered at Woodlands Art Gallery, Blackheath, July 17, 1992, TGA, 20052/2/20. **327 "a continuous torment":** Weissenborn, *Hellmuth Weissenborn, Engraver*, xiv. **327 "stupid, dangerous and horrible":** Letter from Helmuth Mirauer, January 6, 1946. **327 "war crime":** Busch, *Major Kwaplitschka*, 256. **327 seventy-one internees had died in British camps:** This figure does not include the victims of the *Arandora Star* tragedy. **327 Fifty-six of these deaths had occurred on the Isle of Man:** "Lists of Deaths Reported," TNA, HO 215/420. **327 "The beautiful weather and . . . the gay face of things":** Darton, *Friends Committee for Refugees and Aliens*, LSF, 80. **327 permanently forsaken:** Peter Midgley: Oral History, MJM, 1988.45. **328 "In retrospect the proportions shift":** Hans Jaeger, "Rückblick auf's Imnternment," unpublished manuscript dated July 17, 1941, IFZ. **328 "a quiet pleasant episode":** Paul Jacobstahl letter to Dr. J. C. Skemp, November 16, 1945, BLO file 1935–57, MS. S.P.S.L., 182/2. **328 "a trauma":** Paul Jacobstahl diary, IWM, 28. **328 "Appalling day":** Brinson, *His Majesty's Loyal Internee*, various. **328 "one shouldn't have been so depressed":** Fred Uhlman: Oral History. **329 forced to admit:** *Hansard*, House of Commons Debate, May 29, 1940, vol. 361, cc521–3. **330 Many internees struggled to find work:** Minutes of the meeting of the Central Department for Interned Refugees, January 2, 1941, LMA, ACC/2793/03/05/02, 1. **330 he became a British citizen:** *London Gazette*, February 21, 1947. **330 awarded the King Haakon VII Liberty Medal:** *London Gazette*, March 19, 1948. **330 "relegate you to unemployment":** H. O. Daniel, family papers, courtesy of William Daniel. **330 appointed second-in-command of all island camps:** Ibid. **330 "always ready to help in any way he could":** *West Sussex Gazette*, January 12, 1956. **331 a folder of mounted artworks:** Photograph of artist contributor list from folder, courtesy of William Daniel. **331 killed at Halfaya on May 9, 1941:** Second Lieutenant Merlin Montagu-Douglas-Scott Rifle Brigade, service number 113658, Christ Church College, Oxford online obituary. **332 "no one was held responsible":** "Italian-Canadians to Get Formal Apology for Treatment During Second World War," *Canadian Press*, April 14, 2021. **332 a dehumanizing term:** "'Aliens' No More: Biden Administration Directs Immigration Officials to Use 'Inclusive Language,' " *Forbes*, February 16, 2021. **333 "wrongly classifying them as adults":** Diane Taylor, "Home Office Labelling Child Asylum Seekers as Adults Leads to Abuse," *Guardian*, May 29, 2019. **334 "it could happen again":** Sir Claus Moser speaking in *Jailed by the British*, JBB.

PHOTO CREDITS

THROUGHOUT

ii–iii   Photo overlooking Hutchinson Internment Camp and Douglas Bay. © The estate of Hubert Daniel/Tate Images.

vi   Recreation of original map by Bruno Ahrends, courtesy of Wayne Gander.

8–9   Photo of Peter Fleischmann shortly after disembarking the *Kindertransport* ferry in England, December 2, 1938. © AP/ Shutterstock.

96–97   Photo of guards and internees during roll call outside the buildings at Hutchinson Internment Camp. © The estate of Hubert Daniel/Tate Images.

208–9   Photo of artist working on a small carved figure. © The estate of Hubert Daniel/Tate Images.

INSERT ONE

1. Photo of Herschel Grynszpan, November 1938. © ullstein bild/ullstein bild via Getty Images.

2. Photo of teenaged Peter Fleischmann, 1930s. Courtesy of the Midgley family.

3. Synagogue on fire during *Kristallnacht*, November 9, 1938. © Jewish Museum Berlin.

4. The destruction on the morning of November 10, 1938. Bettmann/CORBIS/ Bettmann Archive/Getty Images.

5. Peter Fleischmann shortly after disembarking the *Kindertransport* ferry in England, December 2, 1938. © AP/Shutterstock.

6. Arrest of an "enemy alien" in the summer of 1940. Unknown source.

7. Cartoon by Sir David Low, *Evening Standard*, July 19, 1940. © Associated Newspapers Ltd.

8. *Hunger Strike 1*, by Hermann Fechenbach, 1943. Courtesy of the Fechenbach estate.

9. *The Square*, Paul Henning, 1940. Courtesy of the Daniel family.

10. Hutchinson internees behind barbed wire. © The estate of Hubert Daniel/Tate Images.

11.   Photo of Captain Daniel at his desk at Hutchison camp. © The estate of Hubert Daniel/Tate Images.

12.   Photo of Margery Daniel. Courtesy of the Daniel family.

13.   Regimental Sergeant Major Ambrose Harry Potterton conducting morning roll call at Hutchinson camp, 1940. © The estate of Hubert Daniel/Tate Images.

14.   Cartoon by Adolf "Dol" Miriecki, *The Camp*, Issue 3, 6 October 1940. © Leo Baeck Institute Library.

15.   Hutchinson internees waiting to collect their food rations, 1940. © The estate of Hubert Daniel/Tate Images.

16.   Sketch by Ludwig Meidner. © Ludwig Meidner-Archiv, Frankfurt.

17.   Woodblock print by Hellmuth Weissenborn. Courtesy of the Weissenborn estate.

INSERT TWO

1.   Portrait of Klaus Hinrichsen by Kurt Schwitters, 1941. Courtesy of the Hinrichsen family.

2.   Portrait of Bruno Ahrends by Kurt Schwitters, 1941. Courtesy of Peter Ahrends. Photograph: Ian Latham.

3.   Portrait of Marjan Rawicz by Kurt Schwitters, 1940. Courtesy of the Sprengel Museum, Hanover.

4.   Portrait of Rudolph Olden by Kurt Schwitters, 1940. Courtesy of the Sprengel Museum, Hanover.

5.   Photo of Hitler at the *Entartete Kunst* exhibition © bpk.

6.   *Aerated V* by Kurt Schwitters, 1941. © akg-images.

7.   Ernst Schwitters photographs of his father, Kurt, reading *Ursonate* in London in 1944. Bpk/ Sprengel Museum, Hanover.

8.   Photo of Ludwig Warschauer. Courtesy of the Kohsen family.

9.   Portrait of Ludwig Warschauer by Kurt Schwitters, 1940/1. Photograph © Horster Auktionhaus.

10.   Photo of James G. Craufurd. Courtesy of the Craufurd family.

11.   Photo of Hutchinson camp's Technical School. © The estate of Hubert Daniel/ Tate Images.

12.   Photo of the lion tamer Johann "Brick" Neunzer. © The estate of Hubert Daniel/ Tate Images.

13.   Illustration by Fred Uhlman depicting Hutchinson camp's Artists Café. © The estate of Fred Uhlman/Image file © The estate of IWM.

14. The second art exhibition in Hutchinson camp, November 1940. © The estate of Hubert Daniel/Tate Images.

15. Portrait of Helen Roeder. © The estate of Carel Weight. All rights reserved 2021/Bridgeman Images.

16. Portrait of Eleanor Rathbone. © The estate of Sir Herbert James Gunn. All rights reserved 2021. Bridgeman Images, image file: © National Portrait Gallery, London.

17. Photo of Bertha Bracey. Courtesy of the Bracey family.

18. Group photo with Echen Kohsen. Courtesy of the Kohsen family.

19. Photo of Echen Kohsen at the opening of a Kempinski restaurant. Courtesy of the Kohsen family.

20. Cross-stitch square by Ludwig Warschauer. Courtesy of the Kohsen family.

21. Photo of a young Peter Fleischmann on a horse. Courtesy of the Midgley family.

22. Peter Midgley in the army. Courtesy of the Midgley family.

23. The Nuremberg trials. © Bettmann Archive/Getty Images.

24. Peter Fleischmann's first self-portrait, 1940. Courtesy of the Midgley family.

25. Peter Midgley's last self-portrait, 1978. Courtesy of the Midgley family.

INDEX

Logan, David, 151
London School of Economics, 57, 259
London *Times*, 40, 57, 125, 143–44, 182, 218, 266
Low, David, 185

Maas, Paul, 127
Mac-Fall, Nigel, 315
Magnus, Georg, 17–18
Mahrenholz, Harald, 114, 264
Man. *See* Isle of Man
Marchant, Hilde, 71–73
Mark, Robert, 137
Marshall, Robert, 195, 231, 232, 290
Martin, Kingsley, 183
Marx, Ludwig, 117
mass internment policy
    Churchill's approach to, 3, 78–79, 82
    criticism of policy of, 183, 191
    ending of mass internment in, 179
    fifth column rumors and, 3, 72–75, 78, 79, 82, 179–80
    later denial and rationalization of, 179–80
Matuschka, Count Franz Josef von, 114, 172, 199
Maxwell, Sir Alexander, 308
Megaw, Basil, 245
Meidner, Ludwig, 162, 173, 325
MI5
    arrest of individuals sent to internment camps by, 65–66, 74
    camp informants used by, 193, 303
    list of names used by, 60–61, 63
    mass internment policy and, 67
    suspicious refugees reported to, 3
    tribunals for enemy aliens and, 62
    Warschauer's application for release and, 268, 269–70
    Warschauer's investigation by, 176n, 192, 207, 239–40, 341n, 257–58, 280, 281–82, 283n, 287, 318
    Warschauer's return to camp opposed by, 296, 301–2

Midgley, Donald, 77
    Fleischmann's letters to while at Hutchinson, 172–73
    Fleischmann's name change and, 295
Midgley, Peter. *See* Fleischmann (later Midgley), Peter
Mirauer, Hellmuth, 265, 327
Mirecki, Adolf "Dol," 159, 260
Montefiore, Leonard, 308–9, 311
Mooragh camp, Isle of Man, 3n, 130, 173n, 247n
Morrison, Herbert, 221–22
Moser, Claus, 87, 334
Moses, Hugo, 26–27
Moulton, Edgar, 137, 141
Movement for the Care of Children from Germany, 42–43
Muirhead, Captain, 117
Müller-Blensdorf, Ernst
    artwork of, 6, 88, 331
    camp art exhibitions and, 225, 227–28, 237n
    camp artists and, 113, 161, 169n, 175
    Fleischmann's learnings from, 95, 119, 155, 168
Munster, Rudolf, 123, 202

Nagorka, Wilhelm, 16, 17
Nathan, Alex, 66
Nazi officials
    barriers for Jews leaving Germany from, 35
    Bracey's letters to, for release of a social worker, 34–35
    destruction of synagogues ordered by, 28–29
    Kindertransport inspection by, 48
    Nuremberg trial of, 316–17
Nazi regime
    Bracey's witnessing of rise of, 36–37
    Britain's reaction to violence of, 38, 39–43
    control of schools by, 29–31
    degenerate art and, 5, 88, 156–57, 173n, 229